Among its many strengths, this book masterfully crafts a true customer journey, establishing connections between direct and indirect business that capture the essence of the modern luxury experience.
Cristiana Cinotti, Global Wholesale Director, Moncler

Gabriella has perfectly captured the essence of Italian hospitality within an international group, as well as the importance of authenticity in people and services.
Luca Finardi, Area Vice President Operations, General Manager, Mandarin Oriental Hotel Group

In *The Future of Luxury Customer Experience*, Professor Gabriella Lojacono offers a forward-looking analysis of the evolution of luxury brands in a tech-driven era. This book combines in-depth research, including interviews and extensive field analysis, with practical insights on enhancing customer engagement through technology and emotional connectivity. Essential for students and executives alike, it serves as a crucial guide to navigating the complexities of modern luxury markets with innovative strategies and a customer-centric approach.
Guia Ricci, Managing Director and Partner, Fashion & Luxury, Boston Consulting Group

The Future of Luxury Customer Experience

How to create high-value, personalized omnichannel experiences

Gabriella Lojacono

KoganPage

Publisher's note

Every possible effort has been made to ensure that the information contained in this book is accurate at the time of going to press, and the publishers and authors cannot accept responsibility for any errors or omissions, however caused. No responsibility for loss or damage occasioned to any person acting, or refraining from action, as a result of the material in this publication can be accepted by the editor, the publisher or the author.

First published in Great Britain and the United States in 2024 by Kogan Page Limited

2nd Floor, 45 Gee Street   8 W 38th Street, Suite 902
London   New York, NY 10018
EC1V 3RS   USA
United Kingdom

www.koganpage.com

Kogan Page books are printed on paper from sustainable forests.

ISBNs

Hardback   978 1 3986 1547 2
Paperback   978 1 3986 1545 8
Ebook   978 1 3986 1546 5

British Library Cataloguing-in-Publication Data

A CIP record for this book is available from the British Library.

Library of Congress Cataloging-in-Publication Data
Names: Lojacono, Gabriella, author.
Title: The future of luxury customer experience : how to create high-value, personalized omnichannel experiences / Gabriella Lojacono.
Description: London ; New York, NY : Kogan Page, 2024. | Includes bibliographical references and index.
Identifiers: LCCN 2024023112 | ISBN 9781398615458 (paperback) | ISBN 9781398615472 (hardback) | ISBN 9781398615465 (ebook)
Subjects: LCSH: Customer relations. | Electronic commerce.
Classification: LCC HF5415.5 .L65 2024 | DDC 658.8/12–dc23/eng/20240613
LC record available at https://lccn.loc.gov/2024023112

Typeset by Integra Software Services, Pondicherry
Print production managed by Jellyfish
Printed and bound by CPI Group (UK) Ltd, Croydon CR0 4YY

CONTENTS

Takeaways 77
References and further reading 78

4   Luxury, arts and culture: How luxury Maisons have become prominent cultural actors
    Cyrille Vigneron 80

    Luxury Maisons as cultural actors 81
    The cultural world has evolved in its appreciation of savoir-faire 82
    The continuous interplay between culture and luxury 84
    Takeaways 87

5   Experience-led luxury strategies: How brands are reshaping customer activation and engagement
    Gabriella Lojacono 89

    Differentiation through experiences along the customer journey 94
    Brand experience: Touchpoints, determinants and impact 110
    From storytelling to story-living 113
    Crafting experiences at different levels 116
    Crafting experiences by building communities 118
    The evolution of brand collaborations: From commercial hype to experiential depth 124
    One size does not fit all: Localized experiences 127
    Takeaways 134
    References and further reading 135

6   Seamless retail: Bridging the digital and physical divide
    Gabriella Lojacono 138

    From point of sale to point of experiences 141
    Freedom within a framework: Retail rituals and golden rules 151
    The renaissance of retail: The rise of pop-up stores 154
    Experience-enhancing technologies 160
    The seamless brand retail landscape for a unified experience 161
    Assessing the experience-led and seamless retail strategies: A roadmap 172
    Takeaways 179
    References and further reading 179

FOREWORD

Luxury is a nomadic concept. It is shaped by changes in society, by the evolution of our values, our tastes and our geopolitical scenarios. While it may appear evanescent, luxury is underpinned by very solid fundamentals: a global value exceeding €1,500 billion euros, and a consistent growth rate of 6 per cent for personal luxury goods over the past three decades. At the present moment there are around 400 million high-net-worth individuals, and this figure is expected to rise to 550 million by 2030. This diverse audience varies in terms of needs and cultural differences: by 2030, 40 per cent of luxury customers are expected to be Chinese, a significant shift from the traditionally American consumer base.[1]

It is therefore clear that the concept of luxury requires more in-depth exploration: it is a complex, ever-changing world that is increasingly innovative and willing to step out of its comfort zone, while maintaining its aura and timeless appeal.

The Future of Luxury Customer Experience offers a contemporary and authoritative analysis of the world of luxury and its unique characteristics. It highlights key challenges that must be addressed by professionals in the luxury sector and serves as a valuable contribution to the ongoing monitoring of luxury, a 'nomadic' element that necessitates consistent evaluation over time. For instance, dramatic changes have occurred in the past decade with the advent of new technologies and e-commerce opportunities that were once considered inappropriate for luxury goods and services. Sustainability, nowadays a strategic cornerstone, has become central to all luxury brands, transforming the business models of many companies. Furthermore, the rise of emerging economies has redefined the key luxury markets: Europe was the leading market until 2020, but Asia is expected to take the lead by 2030. This perfect storm constitutes a revolutionary shift, promising both enormous potential and significant disruption for the sector.

Altagamma, the Italian foundation established in 1992, serves as the ambassador of Italian luxury, its member companies representing the pinnacle of Italian creativity across various sectors: fashion, design, food and beverages, hospitality, automotive, yachting and jewellery. Each year we monitor the global luxury landscape and trends with our surveys, among which is the 22nd edition of the Altagamma-Bain Worldwide Luxury Market Monitor. Altagamma members are described as cultural and creative entities: a combination of the 'cultural' element, linked to Italian heritage, the brands' DNA and the unique characteristics of the Italian landscape; and the 'creative' element, which encompasses the ability to constantly innovate, reshape the brand paradigm, and lead in every aspect, from production to communication. Past and future, tradition and innovation, timeless elements and new solutions coexist in our luxury experiences, all aimed at engaging and involving our customers in the most impeccable and fascinating manner possible.

Italian luxury, with its perfect blend of culture and creativity, can be traced back to the Renaissance, a pivotal period in Italian history when art, culture and individual freedom were at the forefront. The Renaissance marked the beginning of a quest for uniqueness and personal expression. Leonardo da Vinci created the symbol of the Renaissance in 1490: Vitruvian Man, the individual who becomes the measure of the universe. For Vitruvian Man, there is no rule other than personal vision, choice and the ability to decide. Luxury, with all its iconic expressions in fashion or design, is the most powerful way to express an individual's vision. It is an intrinsic expression of vitality, dynamism and freedom.

Italy has always been a country deeply rooted in art, aesthetics and beauty. It is no surprise that it has become the country capable of manufacturing 80 per cent of the world's luxury fashion and design products, and is the global leader in the construction of superyachts. We Italians also have a deep-rooted passion for fine food, matched by our ability to design iconic supercars. Craftsmanship is a crucial and distinctive element of luxury, as each product must possess a unique personality and unparalleled excellence, which transform it into an exquisite work of art. From the Tuscan hills to the sun-drenched Amalfi Coast, from the Venetian lagoons to the monumental sunsets of Rome, Italy's rich cultural heritage is woven into every stitch, every brushstroke and every design. Every product tells a story of tradition, innovation and unparalleled sophistication.

Il bello, il buono e il ben fatto – 'the beautiful, the good and the well-made' – encapsulates Italian luxury, highlighting the fact that aesthetics are increasingly linked to ethics. This concept is reminiscent of the Ancient Greek ideal of *Kalos kai agathos*: the good and the beautiful. Italian brands have always embraced this imperative, even before the advent of ESG and sustainability targets. Each Italian luxury brand is deeply intertwined with its territory and the craftsmanship of its local people, making respect for the environment and its inhabitants a natural and innate value.

However, each luxury brand – Italian or otherwise – has a global dimension, with key markets to address including China, India, Japan, Korea, the USA, the United Arab Emirates, Brazil and, very soon, Africa. Their audience extends far beyond their customers, with their impressive social media profiles reaching millions of people. Over time, luxury brands have changed from passionate manufacturers to international retailers, and then from media companies to socio-cultural agents discussing global topics such as diversity, art, inclusion, Black Lives Matter and more. The aforementioned delicate balance between tradition and innovation is matched today by the challenge of respecting individual and local DNA – the Made in Italy touch, for instance – while remaining relevant for a global, very diverse and younger audience.

As we travel through the world of global luxury, let us take the time to appreciate the nomadic nature of this elusive concept, the creativity that drives its evolution, and the distinctive characteristics of Made in Italy luxury that continue to captivate us. In a world where change is the only constant, luxury stands as an emblem of timelessness, innovation and a profound passion for excellence, reminding us that it is not merely about positioning and status but, above all, about individual expression, respect, and artistic passion.

Stefania Lazzaroni
Managing Director, Fondazione Altagamma

1 Altagamma-Bain Worldwide Luxury Market Monitor, 2023

ABOUT THE AUTHOR

Gabriella Lojacono is Associate Professor of International Management and Luxury Management at Università Bocconi and SDA Bocconi School of Management. She is Strategic Adviser for B4I, a catalyst for the most innovative and high potential ideas and startups of Bocconi University, and Director of the Executive Master in Luxury Management – EMiLUX.

She was a senior researcher of the Gucci Lab, Università Bocconi from 2018 to 2020. From January 2017 to December 2020, she was Faculty Deputy of the Strategy and Entrepreneurship Knowledge Group at SDA Bocconi. She teaches International Strategy at the MBA full time and has run several executive education open programmes and custom initiatives at SDA Bocconi with some of the leading companies in apparel and leather goods, design, jewellery, hospitality, F&B, automotive, eyewear and cosmetics. Her research projects have focused on the international growth of the Made in Italy industries and companies as well as on luxury strategy and business models.

She is the author of numerous books and articles on her topics of interest, including, in 2021, *Resilience of Luxury Companies in Times of Change* with co-author Laura Ru Yun Pan, published by De Gruyter. Her works have been published in *Economia & Management*, *MIT Sloan Management Review*, *Long Range Planning*, *Strategic Change* and *International Business Review*, among others. She has authored numerous case studies, filed in international databases, about multinational enterprises such as Nespresso, Bottega Veneta, Davines, Inditex, Ferrari, Illy, Valentino, Nike and Gucci.

Gabriella earned a degree in Business Administration with a specialization in Finance, a PhD in Economics and Management from Università Bocconi, and an ITP (International Teachers Programme) organized by ISBM at HEC in Paris. During her PhD she was a Visiting Scholar at Copenhagen Business School and researcher in Design Continuum in Boston on Design Thinking projects.

ACKNOWLEDGEMENTS

I'm grateful to Giulia Angoscini for her invaluable contributions to my work. A brilliant thinker and kind soul, she was always ready to engage in meaningful discussions about my ideas, often providing perfect examples to illustrate complex concepts. Her guidance during my New York trip was instrumental, especially in uncovering hidden gems that significantly broadened my perspective. The discovery of Eleven Madison Park, a destination for memorable experiences, was a direct result of her insightful recommendations.

My heartfelt thanks go out to Anna Dato, my beacon of beauty expertise. Her vibrant spirit, infectious optimism and sharp insight into Asian culture have been a guiding light. The Asian and Indian influences that permeate this book are a testament to our daily conversations, where even a simple idea blossoms into something grand under her touch. Her astuteness and cultural acumen have been invaluable in enriching the content of this book.

Thanks to Hugo Ribeiro Da Silva, XRS Holding, CEO/Shareholder Porsche Center Oporto, Porsche Center Braga, Porsche Center Baleares and Bentley Oporto. My friend Hugo has been precious in offering insights into the luxury car dealership experience. He possesses a unique talent for creating engaging in-store animations and experiences, enhancing client interactions post-purchase. His approach not only illustrates the art of captivating luxury clients, but also sheds light on the subtleties of maintaining lasting relationships in the automotive sector.

The book's insights and interpretations, though my own, greatly benefited from the extensive network of companies and executives who provided invaluable inputs. My deepest gratitude goes to all contributors, with a special acknowledgment to those most involved, whose perspectives and experiences have significantly enriched the content and understanding of the luxury industry presented in this book. Their collective wisdom and expertise have been instrumental in shaping the narrative and analyses within these pages.

At Audemars Piguet: Marco Viganò, Chief Client Officer; Jérémie Comel, Head of Client Relations.

At Boffi SpA: Roberto Gavazzi, CEO; Nicolo Gavazzi, Vice President and Founder of Up To You Anthology.

At Bottega Veneta: Bartolomeo Rongone, CEO, Marta Bevilacqua, WW Ecommerce and Omnichannel manager; Stéphanie de Bodinat, WW Retail Experience Director; Francesca Ricci Bitti, WW Ecommerce director; Ioana Andreea Zeres, Head of Global Talent Acquisition, People Engagement, Employer Branding and Inclusion & Diversity Committee Leader.

At Bulgari Hotels & Resorts: Attilio Marro, Senior Director; Goffredo Dell'Appennino, General Manager Milano.

At Cartier: Cyrille Vigneron, WW CEO and President; Angela Au-Yeung, International Innovation Director; Arnaud Carrez, Senior Vice President, Chief Marketing Officer; Viviana Caslini, Art & Culture Director; Annabelle Diez Strategic Projects Director; Vianney Duault, Commercial Director – Southeast Europe; Lucio Forgione, Deputy Boutique Manager Montenapoleone; Roberto Grandis, Director Cartier Milano Montenapoleone; Pierre Rainero Direction Image, Style et Patrimoine; Rodolphe Ratzel, Managing Director – South East Europe (Italy and Greece); Elisabetta Rondelli, CMO, Marketing, Communication & Client Director, South East Europe.

Heartfelt thanks especially to CEO Cyrille Vigneron, whose early insights significantly shaped the outline and flow of the book's concepts. His intelligent guidance on convergences and divergences has been invaluable, providing a clear vision of trends in luxury. Cyrille's generous contribution of a chapter on the role of luxury brands in cultural settings and the inspirational power of arts and culture for brands has been an essential addition to this work.

At Damiani Group: Giorgio Damiani, Vice President; Matteo Blandi.

At Dorchester Collection: Beth Aarons, Global Executive Director, Dorchester Collection Academy at Dorchester Collection – FCIPD, FIH; Paola Iemallo, Human Resources Director at Principe di Savoia, Hotel Eden (Dorchester Collection); Andrea Greggio, Creative Director of Operation, Principe di Savoia, Hotel Eden (Dorchester Collection); Eugenio Pirri, CEO Dorchester Collection.

At Ferrari: Salvatore Ancoretti, Head of Customer Experience, Dennis de Munck, Head of Employer Branding and University partnerships, Reno de Paoli, Global Marketing Director, Maria Carla Liuni, Chief Brand Officer.

At Mandarin Oriental: Francesco Cefalù, Chief Development Officer, MOHG, Luca Finardi, Area Vice President Operations & General Manager Milan, Emma Sticca, Executive Office Manager Milan.

At Meta: Evita Barra, Automotive, Mobility and Luxury Industry Director; Diana Emmert, Head of Luxury.

At Moncler: Cristiana Cinotti, Global Wholesale Director, Matteo Gallo, Omnichannel Excellence and Operations Senior Manager, Elena Mariani, Strategic Planning and Investor, Alberto Tripodi, Global Director of Omnichannel Client & Performance, Relations Director.

At Prada Group: Lorenzo Bertelli, Executive Director; Marta Monaco, Director, Financial and Corporate Communication; Benedetta Petruzzo, CEO at Miu Miu.

At Valentino: Jacopo Venturini, CEO; Federica Braga Talent & Performance Manager | Internal Communication, EB, HRBP; Federico Ferrari, Global CRM Director; Giulia Ghiselli, Head of Client Engagement; Salvatore Golotta, Corporate & Internal Communication; Violante Valdettaro, Heritage & Archive Coordinator .

The book has been enriched not only by contributions from brands with multiple representatives, but also by the generous support of individual managers. These managers have shared their unique perspectives and experiences, adding depth and diversity to the content. Their insights have been invaluable in shaping the narrative and understanding of luxury management dynamics. This collective input from various industry professionals underscores the collaborative nature of the work and the wide-ranging expertise that has informed its creation: Serena De Marte, Vice President Global Retail Excellence at Tiffany; Francesco Viana, Managing Director Europe, Russia and Middle East at Loro Piana; Soizic Paff, Archive Curator at Dior; Jean-Marc Pontroue, CEO at Panerai; Catherine Alix-Renier, Chief Executive Officer at Jaeger-LeCoultre, Moreno Faina, Director at Università del caffè at illycaffè S.p.A., Alberto Tha, Senior Sales Manager Southern Europe – Oracle Retail, Federica Parisi, Senior Account Executive presso Salesforce, Nicola Coropulis, Chief Executive Officer at Poltrona Frau; Diego Roggero, General Manager Portrait Milano – Lungarno Collection; Filippo Cavalli, Partner at Style Capital SGR, General Manager and Board member at forte forte Srl, Board member at Zimmermann, board member at LuisaViaRoma, Board member at MSGM, Board Member at SOEUR; Ambra Martone Vice President ICR, President Accademia del Profumo, Co-Founder Marvin LabSolue,

Creative Director Magna Pars l'Hotel à Parfum; Benedetto Lavino, Managing Director & Owner Bottega Verde / Presidente Cosmetica Italia; Sara Betteghella, Chief Sustainability Officer at OTB Group; Mélanie Brinbaum, Chief Brand Officer at Nestlé Nespresso SA.

A heartfelt appreciation goes to Altagamma Foundation, especially Managing Director Stefania Lazzaroni, for the invitations to crucial industry events and discussions on market data and trends with leaders in the field. Additionally, a special thanks to Guia Ricci, Managing Director and Partner at Boston Consulting Group (BCG) in Fashion & Luxury, for her invaluable support in Bocconi's educational activities. Her team's insights, particularly in the Luxury Consumer Insight with Altagamma, have been crucial in highlighting consumer frustrations, especially online, and the urgent need for genuine customer-centric approaches in luxury management.

ABOUT THE CONTRIBUTORS

Cyrille Vigneron has been the President and Chief Executive Officer of Cartier SA since January 1, 2016. Prior to this role, Cyrille was President of LVMH Japan and worked for Richemont from 1988 to 2013, rising to become Managing Director of Cartier Japan, President of Richemont Japan and, finally, Managing Director of Cartier Europe. Cyrille started his career at Companie Générale des Eaux before joining Pechiney. He is a graduate of ESCP Europe business school. Born in 1961, a French national and a father of four children. Cyrille is a music lover and a devotee of Japanese culture, as shown by the writing and publication of his book, *De geishas en mangas: Chroniques du Japon d'aujourd'hui* (Editions Albin Michel, 2009).

Stefania Carraro is Senior Lecturer of Sustainability at SDA Bocconi School of Management, where she teaches in custom executive programmes, and is currently a member of the SDA Bocconi School of Management Sustainability Lab. Stefania has been at SDA Bocconi since November 2019. Since 2022, she has been Programme Coordinator of the Executive Master in Luxury Management (EMiLUX). At SDA Bocconi Stefania has conducted numerous research and education projects with Atlantia, Enel, Unicredit and Diesel. Currently she is Coordinator of the Furniture Pact, a Monitor of the Wood and Furniture Supply Chain. Her research activities focus on corporate sustainability, environmental management, ESG and technology and innovation management. Stefania achieved a double degree in Civil Engineering and Architecture from University of Trento with a final dissertation on sustainable models from Columbia University and an Executive Masters in Business Administration from SDA Bocconi School of Management.

Laura Ru Yun Pan is a lecturer at SDA Bocconi School of Management. She specializes in luxury strategy, international management and digital transformation. She co-authored a book titled *Resilience of Luxury Companies in Times of Change* with Gabriella Lojacono in 2021, and has published works in the areas of Web 3.0, metaverses and blockchain technologies. Laura has a background in Chemical Engineering and Food Manufacturing and graduated with a MBA from SDA Bocconi School of Management in 2018. She joined LVMH subsequently, before moving into academia in late 2019.

Guido Tirone is an accomplished executive who specializes in digital and luxury, with a strong background in advanced analytics gained through extensive work experience, academic research and teaching. He currently holds the position of VP Data & Analytics at Canyon Ranch. Prior to this Guido was the Senior Director of OmniChannel Analytics at Neiman Marcus, where he led all aspects of analytics and experimentation for the company's stores and digital ecosystem, including data mining and machine learning. He managed a high-performing analytics team responsible for providing valuable insights and recommendations across the organization, and improving the omnichannel customer experience to drive incremental revenue growth. In addition, Guido is a senior lecturer for the University of Texas at Dallas, where he develops and teaches graduate courses on Marketing Analytics and Insights, and acts as a liaison and leading expert between the faculty and the corporate world. He is also Fellow at SDA Bocconi School of Management where he teaches Advanced Analytics in the Executive Master in Luxury Management (EMiLUX).

Introduction

GABRIELLA LOJACONO

This book ventures beyond current trends to explore the future of luxury experiences. It acknowledges that, while specific brand and product preferences of future generations remain unpredictable, the enduring appeal of being delighted, surprised, inspired by arts and culture and personally (and emotionally) connected is undeniable.

The luxury retail landscape has experienced a significant transformation, defying earlier predictions. Online presence has stabilized, while brick-and-mortar stores continue to dominate, taking on more robust and multifaceted roles that extend beyond mere transactional functions. Retail teams are now strategic curators of the customer experience. Communication strategies have diversified, utilizing various channels, including high-impact ones like TikTok, for broader reach. Client data collection has evolved beyond basic forms, emphasizing the necessity to go beyond detailed demographic and transactional information for more effective client profiling and segmentation. The pervasive role of technology in enhancing customer engagement and experience in the luxury sector is underscored by the fact that all major brands are engaged in long-term, technology-related and data science projects. This trend highlights a universal recognition within the industry of the critical importance of integrating advanced technological solutions to maintain relevance and elevate the customer experience in today's digitally-driven market landscape.

This revolutionary shift in the luxury world calls for an open-minded approach, equipped with new competencies and surrounded by talented individuals who can navigate and thrive in this new luxury world.

Contrasting the standardized and frustrating experiences, as depicted in Audrey's journey in Chapter 5, the book offers a collection of best practices and innovative ideas for enhancing luxury experiences. Emphasizing the crucial role of inclusivity, it underscores welcoming everyone as potential enthusiasts, ambassadors or VIPs, integral to the evolving narrative of luxury consumer story-living. The book emphasizes the importance of blending human touch with technology to create seamless retail experiences, bridging digital and physical realms.

Originating from the author's previous work on the resilience of luxury companies, it delves into the evolving landscape of luxury, enriched by technology and Experience-Led Strategy (ELS). The book is a culmination of extensive interaction with luxury companies, insights from the Executive Master in Luxury Management (EMiLUX) at SDA Bocconi School of Management, a flagship international programme travelling to different cities worldwide. Additionally, inquisitive talented young students in various luxury-focused courses and initiatives, from MSc to summer school, provide a daily stimulus to embark on new conversations and raise new research questions.

The book's empirical foundation is also drawn from 48 in-depth interviews across Europe, the US and Asia, and a tested and refined ELS assessment. This extensive research, conducted over 10 years, includes 560 field analyses, each assessing at least three brands. The longitudinal approach provides a deep dive into the evolving dynamics of luxury brand experience, showcasing a rich expertise in the luxury world.

The book is designed for a diverse audience deeply interested in the world of luxury. It caters to master's students in luxury management, enhancing their academic and practical understanding of the luxury sector. Passionate enthusiasts of luxury will find this book a rich source of information and inspiration. For executives of luxury companies who seek to deepen their grasp of luxury allure and those from multinational corporations in premium markets looking to elevate their business strategies, this book offers valuable insights drawn from luxury logics to aid in trading up.

The book spans 12 chapters, journeying through the multifaceted world of luxury. It delves into various aspects of luxury management, brand experiences and market strategies. Each chapter offers unique insights and case studies, reflecting on the evolution and nuances of the luxury industry. The chapters collectively provide a comprehensive overview, capturing the essence of luxury brands, their interaction with evolving consumer expectations and the critical role of innovative retail experiences in shaping brand identity and customer loyalty. This exploration is grounded in extensive research and real-world examples, making it a valuable resource for understanding luxury's dynamic landscape.

All chapters in the book are authored by Gabriella Lojacono, except for Chapters 4 and 8 to 12, which are curated by technical experts specializing in their respective fields. These chapters offer an in-depth exploration of topics such as arts and culture, digital transformation, artificial intelligence (AI) and sustainability.

Chapter 1 sets the foundation of the book, discussing the dynamic nature of the concept of luxury and its inspirational value in current times. It challenges conventional views of luxury, advocating for a new, multi-dimensional approach to understanding luxury brands. The chapter transitions into a discussion about the players in the luxury market and their growth strategies. It delves into the key elements of brand identity, focusing on iconic signs, supply chain, country of origin and organizational culture, highlighting their critical roles in shaping and maintaining the unique character of luxury brands.

Chapter 2 delves into the dynamic world of luxury, acknowledging its resilience and adaptability in the face of economic and socio-political challenges. It explores how the luxury sector is not static but rapidly evolving, necessitating a re-evaluation of traditional perceptions. The chapter dissects the concept of 'blurred lines' in luxury, examining the seamless integration of physical goods and experiential content, and how luxury brands now navigate new market territories and societal shifts. It references seminal works in management studies that discuss innovation strategies and the redefinition of industry boundaries.

Chapter 3 delves into how authenticity is perceived when there's alignment between a brand's announced values and its actions as well as alignment between heritage, present, future and continuous commitment to quality and stylistic coherence. It emphasizes the importance of a strong, differentiated company culture in contributing to a genuine and honest brand identity.

Chapter 4 by Cyrille Vigneron explores the evolving relationship between luxury, art and culture. Initially, luxury and art were distinct, with culture being a public affair. Cartier's Fondation pour l'art contemporain in 1984 marked a shift, demonstrating private sector contributions to art. Now, luxury groups are recognized as significant cultural actors. The chapter discusses how applied arts gained recognition, luxury brands' involvement in art exhibitions and their role in art history. It analyses the changing perceptions of art and luxury's integration, how luxury enhances country images and its impact on urbanism and architecture. The interplay between luxury brands, art and cinema is also examined, highlighting collaborations with artists and celebrities and the influence of luxury on cityscapes and culture.

Chapter 5 delves into the multifaceted nature of brand experiences in the luxury sector, underscoring the importance of creating deep emotional connections and lasting memories beyond mere transactions. It emphasizes the significance of operational excellence, personalization and cultural sensitivity in crafting distinctive experiences. Luxury brands are encouraged to engage customers as active participants in their brand story, fostering community and loyalty. The chapter cautions against aggressive sales tactics, advocating for genuine, respectful customer interactions that honour individual preferences and emphasize the value of unique, personalized experiences. The chapter opens the boundaries to discover the power of strategic collaborations with players in other industries with the aim of supporting ELS.

Chapter 6 explores the evolving role of retail stores in luxury brands, emphasizing their multifaceted functions beyond mere sales points. It examines how stores like the Cartier boutique transform into spaces for diverse experiences, including product showcases, events, exhibitions, pop-ups and interactive animations. These stores serve as platforms for customer engagement and brand storytelling (or story-living), blending commercial moments with cultural enrichment. The chapter also delves into the integration of online and offline realms, highlighting the challenge of replicating in-store richness in the digital space and the importance of seamless retail strategies. It stresses the significance of a unified, cohesive shopping journey, where physical and virtual touchpoints are harmoniously integrated to offer a consistent brand experience. The chapter concludes by emphasizing the need for continuous strategy refinement and the role of stores in crafting enduring connections with customers.

Chapter 7 delves into the necessity of integration of operational systems (ERP) and client-facing activities in luxury retail. It highlights the role of technology in creating seamless experiences, focusing on 'onestock' capabilities to offer limitless purchase options. The chapter emphasizes the importance of omnichannel strategies and advanced clienteling, powered by data analysis that looks beyond annual metrics to consider a client's lifetime value. Advanced CRM systems and AI-based strategies are key to personalizing client interactions, improving stock management and enhancing the overall customer experience. Sales associates, equipped with data-driven insights, are pivotal in elevating client relationships and boosting the tier of VICs and VVICs in the CRM pyramid.

Chapter 8 by Guido Tirone looks at the significance of CRM, its historical evolution and emerging trends. The chapter analyses in detail the emerging trend from the collection of customer data and creation of customer profiles to leveraging data through analytics and AI to create omnichannel engagement via customer-centric marketing, all while taking advantage of new cloud-based solutions. In today's highly competitive business landscape, CRM plays a crucial role in enhancing customer loyalty, improving customer retention and increasing sales and marketing efficiencies. CRM allows companies to build stronger relationships with their customers. By understanding customer preferences and behaviours, companies can tailor their products, services and marketing efforts to meet individual needs, and ultimately increase customer loyalty.

Chapter 9, also by Guido Tirone, is about optimization. Optimization plays a crucial role in the luxury industry, contributing to various aspects of business operations and customer experiences. This chapter analyses the significance of optimization in the luxury industry, from understanding the luxury customer to allocating budget across different channels and initiatives to leveraging analytics and machine learning for evaluating success and implementing real-time adjustments. Optimization in the luxury industry is a multipronged strategy that goes beyond operational efficiency, ranging from maintaining brand reputation to ensuring operational efficiency, all while delighting the customer. The strategy encompasses preserving the essence of luxury and adapting to changing market dynamics while ensuring that the brand remains synonymous with exclusivity and exceptional quality. Achieving this balance contributes to long-term brand loyalty and sustained success in a highly competitive market.

Chapter 10 by Laura Ru Yun Pan explores the various technological transformations that are being applied to the luxury industry – from Digital Product Passports to NFC 'Crypto Tags' that serve to prevent counterfeiting and the revolutionary application of non-fungible tokens (NFTs) as a means of CRM management. Here we look at several case studies of luxury brands utilizing new technologies as a means of enhancing customer experience both in the pre- and post-purchasing journeys. Some notable themes discussed include gamification, traceability and provenance and customer loyalty.

Chapter 11 by Stefania Carraro examines the shift toward ethical and sustainable luxury supply chains. It starts by addressing the need for greater transparency, improved animal welfare and human rights protection. The author urges the adoption of circularity principles to reduce waste and recycle materials, emphasizing how transparency is crucial for consumer trust and brand reputation, and calls for better practices in animal welfare and human rights. The chapter offers practical solutions, highlighting technological innovation and the influence of consumer activism in advocating for change. Further, the chapter explores supply chain transparency and its benefits, delves into ethical concerns like fair labour practices and showcases examples of brands that have successfully implemented ethical supply chains.

The text navigates the balance between cost, quality and ethics within the complexities of global supply chains and regulatory environments. In conclusion, the chapter synthesizes the discussions and insights, projecting a vision for the future of luxury supply chains that prioritize ethical practices.

Chapter 12, also by Stefania Carraro, focuses on sustainability in the context of luxury brands, with particular attention to the role of CSR, circularity principles and authentication in the second-hand luxury market. The chapter begins by charting the evolution of CSR initiatives, showing how luxury brands are increasingly incorporating sustainable practices as a core component of their corporate identity, particularly through efforts to support the burgeoning market for pre-owned luxury goods. It explores the integration of circular economy principles, highlighting how luxury brands are redefining product lifecycles to minimize waste and promote recycling.

The chapter also addresses the rise of authenticated second-hand luxury markets and the importance of maintaining brand integrity. It delves into how luxury brands are meeting global CSR initiatives, circular economy integration and the challenges of ensuring authenticity in pre-owned luxury goods. The narrative underscores the industry's proactive stance in aligning with changing consumer expectations and environmental accountability, reflecting on the broader implications for luxury consumption and brand legacy.

1

The alchemy of luxury: Brand identity and value creation

GABRIELLA LOJACONO

Luxury has been analysed from different points of view, not least in terms of significant market values and growth rates achieved even in recent times, which are certainly not happy from an economic and socio-political point of view.

If it remains true that luxury knows how to deal with crises well, it is also true that it is not static and quickly finds new structures, explores new opportunities and evolves its DNA by wisely exploiting its strategic assets. The result of this evolution and acceleration of phenomena is a world different from the one we have known for years and which has been characterized by stability. Many of the things that have been said about luxury now need to be questioned, and it's necessary to find new ways to describe it.

In short, we cannot put luxury brands on a two-dimensional map and think this image will remain valid for a long time, and have value from a managerial standpoint.

This chapter represents an effort to, first of all, present some characteristics without which it is not possible to talk about luxury goods; then it moves on to present the main players, with a brand-level perspective. The chapter closes with the elements that determine the architecture of these brands and, if well formulated, generate high brand equity.

The chapter's content captures the transformative and multifaceted nature of luxury, offering a deep dive into understanding its core elements and the 'magic' behind successful luxury branding.

What makes a brand part of the world of luxury?

Talking about luxury requires great subjectivity and cultural sensitivity. Luxury is in fact a complex and multifaceted concept that can vary significantly from one geography to another. What is considered luxury in one culture may differ in another. Dubois, Laurent and Czellar (2001) explored consumer attitudes toward luxury products across different cultures. Their research revealed that attitudes toward luxury are complex and vary significantly among consumers from diverse cultural backgrounds. By understanding these segments, brands can better tailor their expansion strategies to cater to the specific preferences of consumers in different cultural contexts. Their research emphasized the importance of considering cultural nuances when developing localization strategies to appeal to a global audience.

However, there are some requisites that clearly mark the territory of luxury. How can we understand what is luxury and what is not?

Pursuit of perfection, craftsmanship, desirability

First and foremost, the high-quality, exquisite craftsmanship and obsession with detail is something that cannot be missed. 'Obsession with detail' can be understood as a relentless pursuit of perfection in every aspect of a product or service. This manifests in a meticulous attention to the minutiae that might be imperceptible to most but are paramount to the luxury experience. It is the fine stitching, the precise alignment of patterns and the exceptional customer service that together create an aura of exclusivity and excellence synonymous with luxury.

Luxury is about desirability, and the strategy for fostering desire and avoiding people's frustration is a fine art. Francesco Viana, Managing Director Europe, Russia, Middle East at Loro Piana, articulates this delicate equilibrium with insight (personal correspondence). He observes that as certain products gain heat within the market, the imperative isn't merely to satisfy immediate demand but to strategically manage it. Viana emphasizes the sophistication involved in planning and forecasting, underscoring that it's not about creating scarcity for its own sake or excluding any particular clients. Instead, it's about ensuring that the brand's offerings are meted out in a way that preserves their allure and specialness without oversaturating the market or diminishing the products' perceived value.

In his words, the intent is to avoid a situation where, after a surge in sales, products vanish from visibility, leaving none for the subsequent months. It's a careful choreography of supply, anticipation and sustained interest which, at Loro Piana, requires a six-month rolling forecast condensed into the immediacy of one month's meticulous planning. Then, the waiting list is also a tool to modulate supply and demand thoughtfully.

Exclusivity

An essential characteristic is exclusivity. The concept of exclusivity in the context of luxury has been a significant topic of research in management studies. Scholars have explored how exclusivity influences consumer perceptions, brand equity and purchase intentions in the luxury market (Vigneron and Johnson, 2004; Kim and Kim, 2015). Exclusivity can be investigated along the following dimensions:

- Exclusivity of the target. Luxury is not for everyone, it is for those who understand it, value it, love it, desire it.
- Exclusivity of the offer. Luxury tends to focus on the value created (and captured) over the logic of volume. The psychology of consumption teaches that the lower the availability on the market, the greater the customer's desirability. This is even so if the price increases twice a year.
- Exclusivity of information. Luxury is a muffled world that does not like large-scale communication. Some relevant information (for example, relating to services offered or events) is conveyed through selected channels and only to the relevant audience.
- Exclusivity of distribution. The access points to the offer are limited and mostly directly operated by the brand.

Timelessness

Another important characteristic is timelessness: luxury items are designed to resist trends and time. They possess a timeless appeal that transcends passing fads. However, it is not certain that the brand portfolio is made up only of iconic and timeless objects, although these represent a fundamental element of the brand's identity. They undergo a reinterpretation over time, to adapt to new social and aesthetic canons, just as they can coexist with newly introduced objects and/or with greater 'seasonal' content.

In their 2009 article, Kapferer and Bastien delve into the distinctive nature of luxury management, emphasizing the importance of preserving the exclusivity and desirability of luxury products while also managing the balance between tradition and innovation. This leads to addressing one of the most common paradoxes in the world of luxury, namely how to preserve and nurture iconic, historical products while still giving space to the new (Lojacono, 2021). When the centre of gravity of a luxury brand is too much on the 'fashion' side (that is, it adheres to current trends and adopts a logic based on seasonality), it can be perceived negatively in times of crisis (decadent or indecent). Luxury is often criticized for what it represents, and judged on moral grounds. In such periods, luxury must be more discrete and reserved, more reassuring than playful. On the other extreme, and in periods of euphoria, too 'serious' brands that do not propose something new become boring or dusty, not appealing anymore (Vigneron, 2021). As an example of a brand closely linked to iconic products, consider Hermès, 56 per cent of whose leather goods turnover, according to Bernstein estimates, is accounted for by their Kelly (launched in 1930) and Birkin (1983) bags alone (Williams, 2023).

A visit to Tiffany's landmark store on Fifth Avenue in New York, internally renovated by Peter Marino (but still keeping the same façade) and reopened in April 2023, represents first and foremost a historical journey. The customer is 'educated' on the distinctive characteristics of the brand (the supply of diamonds and their cut, the choice and purchase as a moment of joy, etc); the iconic pieces are displayed in a scenic and memorable way (from the yellow diamond to the creations of Jean Schlumberger and Elsa Perretti). These pieces are expertly mixed with the most recent collections or items, like the new jewellery in the Lock or Knot collection.

Personalization

Luxury is not just owning a product (and above all not a product to show off to others); it's also about the experience associated with it. Then, the keyword for luxury brands is personalization, at all points of interaction, including tailored offerings and services (Aiello et al, 2008). Personalized approaches to individual preferences contribute to enhancing customer engagement within the luxury market and building stronger connections between luxury brands and their customers.

Personalization unfolds in multiple directions, starting from promotions, to individualized services and experience, to recommendations based on customer's preferences, up to made to order (MTO). By allowing customers to actively participate in the creation of their items, MTO not only meets individual preferences but also strengthens customer-brand relationships. It is a production approach whereby products are manufactured only after an order is placed by a customer. Items are not produced in advance or kept in stock; instead, they are crafted based on the specific requirements and preferences of individual customers. MTO allows customers to customize certain aspects of the product, such as size, colour, material or other features, according to their preferences. This approach is seen in various industries, including clothing, furniture and automotive.

MTO offers a highly personalized shopping experience. Customers feel a sense of involvement as they participate in the design process, selecting the features they desire. At the same time, MTO allows companies to produce items that are specifically crafted for particular customers, reducing the risk of excess inventory. This tailored production approach ensures that resources are allocated efficiently, contributing to a more personalized product lifecycle. Gucci and Ferragamo have made MTO one of their main competitive weapons for very important customers (VICs), offering a wide selection of fabrics, applications and embroidery with which to make jackets, shirts, ties, etc.

Aspirational and inspirational value

Lastly, luxury is purchased out of necessity; it has a strong aspirational and inspirational value. Even in difficult times, moving the centre of gravity towards functionality and value for money is a fatal mistake because brands lose their appeal and aspiration. By its nature, luxury is desired, but not useful. Luxury starts where necessity stops (Vigneron, 2021).

These are experiences, products or services that are sought not to explain a function of use (that is taken for granted), but to signal a lifestyle or identity that people aspire to achieve and that represent a person's desires. Aspirational consumption, while often seen as materialistic in the past, can be viewed in modern times as a means of personal growth and self-improvement. It reflects human desires for progress, achievement and a better quality of life. It's a concept deeply rooted in social psychology and consumer behaviour. Aspirational products also carry symbolic meanings associated with wellbeing and self-esteem, and no longer with mere social recognition, or cultural affiliation. Owning or using these products serves as a symbol of achieving personal life goals. Aspirational consumption is tied to one's self-identity. People use products and brands for their happiness and to construct and communicate their identity to others. Above all, at the time of purchase, connoisseurs do not want to conform to other people who may have recently arrived in the world of luxury and therefore want to show off at all costs. Experts who have been navigating luxury for years want to experience and buy products as much as possible to feel different and unique.

In their article, Ostrovsky and Ryan (2018) investigate the emotional and psychological drivers behind the aspiration for certain products and brands, highlighting the role of self-expression as a powerful motivator. The authors argue that consumers aspire to own products and engage with brands that align with their self-identity and personal narratives. The study emphasizes the importance of brand engagement, where consumers actively participate in the brand's story and values, fostering a sense of belonging and self-expression. That's the reason personalization becomes more and more important.

Consumers bring their aspirations and emotions into their interactions with the brand, affecting their perceptions of value and satisfaction. The understanding of consumer expectations and emotions can offer valuable insights to create meaningful and impactful experiences and customer relationship strategies (Patrício, Fisk and Cunha, 2008).

The concept of inspirational value has an even more subtle meaning. The consumers, especially the new generations, share the values of a brand, they are inspired by them and want to inspire other people at same time. Research findings shed light on the unique emotional connections and inspirations that brands can evoke, providing insights into the psychological dimensions of consumer behaviour in the realm of luxury (Pontes, Rebelo and Loureiro, 2020). In this context, the 'inspirational consumer' represents an individual who is deeply moved and motivated by luxury crafted experiences, leading to brand loyalty and positive word-of-mouth.

How to identify key players in a world of blurring lines

Chapter 2 will describe in depth the concept of blurring lines that also means that the association between luxury and specific industries or countries is now anachronistic. The great Maisons expand all over the world, have international creatives, incorporate added value created outside national borders and explore new territories: art, design, hospitality. And they do it organically, through acquisitions or collaborations with brands and institutions. The convergence of social interests in these companies means that corporate social responsibility is placed first in the strategic agenda of the CEOs who have also decided to join forces to establish the Fashion Pact. Fashion, sports, lifestyle and luxury brands, together with suppliers and retailers, have thus committed to achieving a series of ambitious goals focused on three main areas: climate, biodiversity and oceans (Kering, nd).

These brands become important players in the global scenario of art, culture, environment and social responsibility because they represent something important also for the image of the country.

These brands have left their territory of legitimacy by offering, in the same assortment and even in the same stores, items at higher prices (for example, high-end jewellery for clothing and leather goods companies) or at lower prices, even if more expensive than comparable ones in mass or premium markets. When a brand goes beyond its territory of legitimacy it does so in its own way, so quality and price should be above the average for the same category. However, time spent in a new category can allow brands to become more expert, gain recognition and increase perceived value. This was the case for Hermès, which started quietly in the world of watches, with models no less inferior to those of the specialists, then gradually increased the value created and the perceived value and grew significantly with much more expensive watches (and larger volumes). In the same way, Bulgari, which is also strong in the watch sector, sells many leather goods at high prices.

This possibility of successfully ranging across different territories, without diluting one's image, is only permitted to the 'big' luxury brands (the Powerhouses) that have a heritage based on centuries-old roots (a brand like Bulgari boasts an origin that dates back to 1884) and a turnover exceeding €5 billion. In this case, the brand becomes even more important than the country of origin.

These Powerhouses are also 'market makers': they set the price and the others must adjust accordingly. Rolex is the point of reference in the world of watches, just as Hermès is for bags, Chanel for jackets or Cartier for bangles. If the price is higher, the customer wonders if it's really worth it.

Immediately after the Powerhouses we have the 'Minor League', brands with turnovers of €2–5 billion, often linked to the core business (and also to some iconic products), from which it is difficult to escape, and without worldwide notoriety. They are perhaps strong brands in Japan, but irrelevant for example in Europe.

Another way of identifying strategic groups is to look at how they position themselves with respect to the continuum between tradition (and therefore the weight of iconic and timeless products) and innovation. We can thus talk about 'Heritage Icons' like Chanel, Hermès and Rolex with a rich history, timeless designs, often family-owned. In this case, customers are looking not so much for the latest fashion products but for legacy, authenticity, investment goods and tradition. Then we have 'Innovators and Trendsetters' like Gucci, Louis Vuitton and Prada who place greater emphasis on experimental designs or collaborations with artists and designers. Consumers are fashion-forward individuals, trendsetters and creative minds.

Then, there is the world that bases its business model on exclusivity taken to the extreme with 'limited editions', limited production runs, exclusive events or personalized experiences like Rolls-Royce, Bentley and Ferrari. The target is usually made up of high-net-worth individuals, collectors, status-conscious consumers.

These segments are not rigid; brands can evolve and move between segments based on market trends and consumer preferences.

Readers should explore further in the book to gain deeper insights into specific brands, their strategies and their influence on the luxury market.

The physiognomy of the brand: What impacts consumer perceptions

How do luxury brands create value and communicate it externally? There are some important ingredients for the generation and communication of value, elements that must be consistent with each other:

1 values and corporate culture

2 emblematic signs

3 key people

4 supply chain and territory

5 touchpoints along the consumer journey

Culture is a key ingredient in brand identity, and values are a significant component of this culture. A positive, customer-centric culture often results in superior customer experiences, strengthening your customer-centric brand identity.

A culture that encourages innovation and agility can lead to the brand being seen as forward-thinking and responsive to market needs. Engaged employees who believe in the organization's values are more likely to represent the brand positively. Their enthusiasm and dedication contribute significantly to the brand's identity, especially in interactions with customers.

Values are the guiding principles of an organization. They define what the organization stands for and believes in. When these values are ingrained in culture, they shape how employees behave and make decisions, directly influencing brand identity. When a brand's values align with those of its customers, a strong emotional connection is created. For example, if a brand values environmental sustainability and its customers do the same, this shared value strengthens the brand's identity in the eyes of these customers. Just as a brand that has a culture oriented towards innovation, risk-taking and respect for diversity stimulates internal button-up entrepreneurship: everyone in the organization knows that they can actively contribute to the company's success and that their ideas are valued.

Consistent demonstration of values builds trust. When a brand acts in line with its stated values, it establishes credibility. Trust and credibility are fundamental elements of brand identity, especially in the eyes of consumers. Values can be a significant differentiator in a competitive market. If a brand's values resonate with a specific target audience, this distinguishes the brand and attracts customers who identify with those values, thus shaping the brand's unique identity.

> A genuine luxury brand transcends time with its distinctive heritage, deep-rooted values and enduring principles. In my role at Bottega Veneta, I have had the unique privilege of piecing together the story of our beautiful brand over six decades of existence, thanks to meaningful conversations with our inspiring founders. Today, more than ever, we remain committed to the exquisite design and unmatched craft we proudly uphold. Our bags take days, not just hours, to be created and continue to complement our clients' silhouettes. We continue to celebrate the individual and proudly remain no logo. Our philosophy continues to embrace our motto 'When Your Own Initials Are Enough'. We aspire, just as our founders, to spark inspiration and dreams around an inclusive brand with an exclusive product.
>
> Bartolomeo Rongone, CEO, Bottega Veneta (personal correspondence)

The organizational culture, deeply rooted in shared values, is a cornerstone of brand identity. It influences how employees represent the brand, how customers perceive the brand and how the brand is positioned in the market.

These values are often also communicated outside the organization to emphasize the peculiarities of the brand in the competitive arena and the founding elements of the business model. Racing and performance are part of Ferrari culture just as horse riding is part of Hermès' DNA and the world of sailing is part of Rolex's culture. Let's see how some brands define their values.

> Panerai stands for an Exclusive Technical Sports Watch Maison, made of Unmistakable Italian Design as well as Mechanical Content and Creative Innovations closely associated to the Sea World.

The official value statement for Panerai conveys a distinctive positioning and identity for the brand: an exclusive and technically advanced watch-maker with a strong emphasis on Italian design, mechanical excellence and a creative spirit closely linked to the maritime world. This statement not only communicates the brand's core values, but also provides potential customers with a clear understanding of what makes Panerai watches unique and desirable.

Let's break down the key elements. Panerai positions itself as a brand specializing in crafting high-quality, exclusive technical sports watches. This suggests a focus on precision, craftsmanship and functionality suitable for sports activities. Then, Panerai emphasizes its Italian heritage in design. The use of 'unmistakable' implies a unique and recognizable aesthetic that reflects the brand's Italian identity, possibly drawing on elements from Italian art, culture or craftsmanship. The mention of 'Mechanical Content' signifies a commitment to excellence in watchmaking. It suggests that Panerai watches are not just stylish accessories but also intricate pieces of engineering, with a focus on traditional mechanical movements. Panerai commits to being at the forefront of creative innovations. This implies a dedication to pushing the boundaries of watchmaking through inventive design and technological advancements.

The last part suggests a thematic connection to the world of the sea. Panerai has historical ties to the naval industry, and this statement reinforces the brand's commitment to creating watches inspired by and suitable for marine environments.

Tiffany has a brand ethos centred on optimism, love, inclusivity and creativity. As a brand, Tiffany radiates positivity, embracing a spirit of hope and enthusiasm. Love is a foundational principle, symbolizing the deep connections and emotional resonance Tiffany strives to create; its objects are intended to celebrate and elevate love. Inclusivity is at the heart of

Tiffany's philosophy, fostering a sense of belonging and celebration of diverse stories. Creativity is the driving force, inspiring innovative expressions that elevate the Tiffany experience. Together, these values form the essence of Tiffany, shaping a brand that exudes joy, connection, openness and artistic innovation.

Acqua di Parma is about 'Mastering Simplicity, Perfect Imperfection, Sunny Sophistication'.

'Mastering Simplicity' signifies the brand's commitment to embrace elegance through the power of understatement. 'Perfect Imperfection' acknowledges the beauty found in imperfections, celebrating uniqueness and authenticity in every creation. 'Sunny Sophistication' encapsulates Acqua di Parma's distinctive blend of a warm, optimistic spirit with sophisticated craftsmanship, capturing the essence of a bright lifestyle. Together, these values form the cultural foundation of Acqua di Parma, shaping a brand that cherishes simplicity, authenticity and a sophisticated warmth that resonates with those who appreciate the beauty in life's imperfections.

The Cartier website mentions the following core values:

> Cartier, whose name is synonymous with open-mindedness and curiosity, sees beauty in everything. Creativity, freedom, sharing and excellence are all central to its value. This vision enables a creative territory that is shaped around unique style. From jewellery to fine jewellery to watchmaking and perfumes, Cartier's creations symbolize the fusion of exceptional savoir-faire and timelessness.

Creativity is at the heart of Cartier's identity, inspiring innovative designs that transcend trends and captivate the imagination. Beauty, as a core value, goes beyond aesthetics – it's a standard upheld in every creation, reflecting a dedication to crafting objects of enduring allure. Excellence is the hallmark of Cartier's craftsmanship, promising unparalleled quality and attention to detail. Cartier's creations are imbued with a fusion of exceptional savoir-faire and timelessness. What makes Cartier's values particularly noteworthy is their ability to serve as a unifying thread, creating a consistent attitude across diverse business endeavours. Whether in crafting exquisite jewellery, watches, or engaging in other product lines, Cartier's commitment to creativity and beauty becomes a guiding principle, ensuring a harmonious and recognizable brand identity.

A strong, positive culture, aligned with brand values, creates a powerful brand identity that resonates with customers and fosters long-term loyalty. Authenticity in the context of organizational values and culture is a powerful and transformative concept that goes beyond mere slogans or outward appearances. It's about aligning those core values and cultural identity of an organization in a way that reflects its true essence. This topic will be delved into in a dedicated chapter of this book.

The second important element has to do with the emblematic signs of the brand. You don't need to see the logo to recognize a Bottega Veneta bag made with the famous Intrecciato technique, a Gucci bamboo bag, a Porsche car, a Royal Oak by Audemars Piguet, a Tiffany box, a bronze Panerai watch or a Loro Piana Summer Walk.

The processing techniques, certain distinctive services, the materials used, all contribute to delineating this dimension. The iconic elements of Acqua di Parma are, together, the cylindric box in yellow, a colour which historians say has been used on the facades of Parma's buildings since 1700; the Art Deco bottle with the black Bakelite cap designed in 1930; the minimal logo with the ducal crest of Parma and Piacenza, testifying to the noble roots of the founder and the magnificence of the city of origin. Created in 1916, Colonia is the olfactory signature of Acqua di Parma, with notes of lemon, bergamot, orange, lavender, rose and rosemary enhanced by vetiver, sandalwood and patchouli.

A third important element is how the brand is associated with some key figures of the company who embody its values and represent it, from the creative directors and CEO to the brand's ambassadors (it could also be very important customers). In line with Panerai's values oriented towards 'extreme' adventure and passion for sport, the brand of Italian origin, part of the Richemont group, has had Mike Horn and Sylvester Stallone as its testimonial and reference archetypes. What better representative of Audrey Hepburn's sense of optimism and joy than *Breakfast at Tiffany's*? And Dolce & Gabbana couldn't choose a better protagonist of the Sicilian character of Monica Bellucci's brand – just as Aston Martin finds itself perfectly at ease in Sean Connery's British elegance.

The winning duo Francesca Bellettini and Anthony Vaccarello marked the recent success of Saint Laurent as well as in the period 2015–21. Marco Bizzarri and Alessandro Michele were considered the architects of Gucci's transformation both from a creative and market point of view, becoming a more appealing brand for the new generations.

Fourth, the supply chain helps to define the brand's identity when suppliers contribute to the innovation processes and the quality of the output and territoriality creates essential positive externalities (the so-called 'Country of Origin Effect').

Panerai was founded in Florence in 1860 by Giovanni Panerai. Initially, the company focused on designing and producing precision instruments, including compasses and depth gauges, for the Italian Navy. It wasn't until several decades later, in the early 20th century, that Panerai expanded its offerings to include wristwatches. The brand gained recognition for its association with the Italian Navy and the development of durable, luminescent watches designed for military use. The acquisition by Compagnie Financière Richemont SA, the Swiss luxury goods group, in 1997 marked a significant step in the development of Panerai as a prominent luxury watch brand. Richemont's ownership has played a crucial role in the global expansion and success of Panerai in the luxury watch market. Even though the headquarters have officially become Geneva, where almost all company functions are located, the brand features a combination of design aesthetics made in Italy and Swiss watchmaking precision – production is entirely in Switzerland, like all other luxury brands.

Finally, there are all the touchpoints in the consumer journey through which the brand communicates and reaches the final consumer. This includes point of sales, client experiences, events and animations, elements that are extensively covered in the remaining chapters of this book.

Takeaways

This chapter encompasses the essence of luxury, its terminology, and the elements that define the identity and value of luxury brands.

The chapter opens with an exploration of the multifaceted concept of luxury, examining its subjective nature and cultural variance. It emphasizes luxury's pursuit of perfection, craftsmanship and desirability, underlining the strategic balance of supply and demand. Key elements like exclusivity, timelessness and personalization are discussed, highlighting luxury's aspirational and inspirational values. The chapter reflects on luxury's ability to transcend mere necessity, representing lifestyles and identities, and how brands like Loro Piana, Hermès and Tiffany embody these principles. Luxury's emotional and psychological impact is also examined, showcasing its influence on consumer behaviour and brand loyalty.

It closes with a focus on brand identity. Luxury brands create and communicate value, focusing on five key elements: values and corporate culture, emblematic signs, key people, supply chain and territory, and consumer journey touchpoints. It highlights the significance of a brand's culture and values in shaping identity, the role of unique symbols and key figures in brand representation, the impact of supply chain and geographical roots and the importance of consumer interactions. These components collectively define a luxury brand's essence, setting it apart in the competitive market and forging a distinctive identity.

References and further reading

Aiello, G, Donvito, R, Godey, B, Pederzoli, D and Wiedmann, K P (2008) Using E-customer relationship management to understand the role of the web-site for luxury brands, *Journal of Retailing and Consumer Services*, **15** (5), pp. 332–39

Dubois, B and Duquesne, P (1993) The market for luxury goods: Income versus culture, *European Journal of Marketing*, **27** (1), pp. 35–44

Dubois, B, Laurent, G and Czellar, S (2001) Consumer segments based on attitudes toward luxury: Empirical evidence from twenty countries, *Marketing Letters*, **12** (2), pp. 163–75

Kapferer, J-N and Bastien, V (2009) The specificity of luxury management: Turning marketing upside down, *Journal of Brand Management*, **16** (5–6), pp. 311–22

Kering (nd) Il Fashion Pact: i promi passi verso la trasformazione del settore, www. kering.com/it/news/il-fashion-pact-i-promi-passi-verso-la-trasformazione-del-settore/ (archived at https://perma.cc/3J4E-42CG)

Kim, H J and Kim, W G (2015) The effects of brand prestige, perceived prestige, and brand affection on brand loyalty: A mediation model, *European Journal of Marketing*, **49** (5/6), pp. 939–61

Lojacono, G (2021) Key strategic paradoxes in the world of luxury, Chapter 2, in G Lojacono and L Ru Yun Pan (2021) *Resilience of Luxury Companies in Times of Change*, De Gruyter

Lojacono, G (2023) Prioritizing Value Over Volume: Bottega Veneta, Case Study, SDA Bocconi

Ostrovsky, Y and Ryan, J (2018) Aspirational products and brands: The role of brand engagement and self-expression, *Journal of Consumer Research*, **45** (5), pp. 1034–53

Patrício, L, Fisk, R P and Cunha, J F (2008) The role of consumer aspirations, desires, and emotions in value co-creation, *Journal of Service Research*, **11** (1), pp. 49–64

Pontes, A I, Rebelo, T and Loureiro, S M C (2020) Emotional and inspirational values in curated fashion, *Journal of Retailing and Consumer Services*, **54**, p. 102,034

Vigneron, C, (2021) Foreword, in G Lojacono and L Ru Yun Pan (2021) *Resilience of Luxury Companies in Times of Change*, De Gruyter

Vigneron, F and Johnson, L W (2004) Measuring perceptions of brand luxury, *Journal of Brand Management*, **11** (6), pp. 484–506

William, R, (2023) Inside Hermès' Best-in-Class Leather Goods Strategy | Case Study, *Business of Fashion*, www.businessoffashion.com/case-studies/luxury/hermes-leather-goods-strategy-handbags-birkin-kelly/ (archived at https://perma.cc/CJT8-KP3D)

2

(Un)setting the boundaries: The world of luxury and its protagonists

GABRIELLA LOJACONO

The concept of 'blurred lines' is important because it emphasizes the fact that it is now useless to distinguish between physical goods and experiences. Product is valueless unless enriched by experiential content. Strolling through the streets of New York, you'll encounter sought-after destinations where the boundaries between interior design, architecture, entertainment, music and international cuisine seamlessly blend. Have you encountered La Mercerie? Nestled within the Roman & Williams Guild space in Soho, it opened its doors in December 2017. Is La Mercerie a restaurant? A furniture store? A bookstore? Does it truly matter?

You enter a realm where R&W showcases their own designs of furniture, lighting and home accessories alongside a meticulously curated selection of goods from around the globe. Simultaneously, you can savour flawless French cuisine crafted by Chef Marie-Aude Rose.

You're drawn to the experience itself. Perhaps it's the desire to escape the city's grime and noise, or perhaps it's the allure of shopping, knowing that nearly everything you interact with can be purchased within this space. Whatever the reason, it's your own unique and personal experience.

Have you heard of ABC Home&Carpet in New York? Is it a carpet and accessories store? A venue to enjoy exceptional music? An academy offering cooking courses? A destination where you can indulge in brunch following a Saturday yoga session?

It's all of that and more: a design store that doubles as a special destination, where you can pick American, vegetarian and Mexican cuisines at the same time. It is, as *New York Style Magazine* (Nadelson, 2020) aptly put it, 'the New York store where furniture is theatre'.

It's an immersive experience. The restaurant spaces, while somewhat segmented, allow for effortless movement between them. They are in a way divided, but you can effortlessly move through them. A common thread binds them, yet each possesses its own distinct character. The entire experience is masterfully orchestrated by the starred Chef Jean-Georges Vongerichten. Do you need a specific intention to get there? Perhaps, but that intention can evolve and transform from the moment you step into this space to the moment you leave it. Let it be 'blurred'.

Just prior to the pandemic, the Fotografiska photography museum announced its merger with NeueHouse, a New York-based co-working and social membership space. The merger, operated by CultureWorks, united these two artistic powerhouses and introduced New York City to a realm of new and undefined artistic possibilities. Are you wondering what the Fotografiska space is? It's certainly not a traditional museum, and Veronica, the restaurant within its walls, not a place where you go just to eat. Is it a museum or a social club? Does it truly matter? Let's leave behind preconceived notions of products, spaces and experiences and embrace the trendy experience economy model, which emphasizes its restaurant, entertainment and architectural offerings. No labels needed.

Anyone who visits Milan has Fondazione Prada as an obligatory stop on their itinerary – a destination also loved by the citizens of Milan themselves. What is Fondazione Prada? A hub that wants to promote research and discussion on important topics such as neurodegenerative diseases or longevity? A cultural institution promoting art, cinematography and photography exhibitions? A cinema with a programme of movies, documentaries, public meetings and special projects conceived by international personalities such as Pedro Almodóvar, Roman Polanski, Damien Hirst and John Baldessari? A well-curated restaurant? It is all this and more.

This chapter will showcase numerous examples of these 'contaminations', providing empirical evidence that luxury is increasingly permeating diverse spheres while simultaneously being influenced by various economic and social phenomena.

Blurring lines: Converging and diverging phenomena

Luxury cannot be associated only with specific price ranges, nor at least with well-identified sectors. In recent years, multiple exogenous factors (the pandemic, trade wars, geo-political instability, generational change, the rapid advancement of new technologies, etc) have led to questioning well-established definitions and classifications. A keyword of this new system is 'blurring lines', a multifaceted concept. In fact, it can indeed imply both convergence and divergence at the same time, depending on the context in which it is used. It means that is hard to make distinctions between things less clear or definite.

This ambiguity is originated from the fact that convergence and divergence (C&D) can be simultaneously present; they often interact to create innovative and hybrid classifications. When two distinct categories or concepts converge, they blend together, creating something new and diverging from the existing clusters.

First, blurring the lines can indicate the merging or convergence of previously distinct or separate concepts, categories or ideas. On the other hand, blurring the lines can also imply differentiation or divergence, especially when boundaries between categories become less defined. Traditional classifications are challenged or redefined. This process of C&D that happens concurrently is common in dynamic and evolving fields like technology, fashion and luxury goods.

Here are just a few examples where convergence (and divergence) in luxury goods is evident. Do you think that the Baby Boomers would ever have included a pair of sneakers, although of good aesthetic and technical quality, among luxury goods? Now, luxury brands have created luxury sneakers, blending high fashion aesthetics with the comfort and style of athletic footwear. This product line can even represent an important percentage of sales relating to the shoe category as well as contributing to a 'fresh' image of the brand. This convergence appeals to fashion-conscious consumers seeking both luxury and comfort.

In the context of retail and technology, blurring the lines between online and offline means that these 'environments' are becoming more similar in communication, assortment, clienteling, etc, leading to a convergence of messages and functionalities. Luxury brands create seamless experiences between online and offline channels. Customers can browse products online and make purchases in-store, or vice versa, converging digital and physical retail spaces. Just as today wholesale and retail have convergent functions and support each other. Even the companies that have pushed the accelerator on retail have selected their wholesale partners with agreements made in the image and likeness of retail stores.

There is no better (and more extreme) case than Rolex to explain this concept. It is the only watchmaking company to have almost 100 per cent of its turnover coming from the wholesale channel. This is strictly controlled through exclusive dealership agreements. This business model is not affected by Rolex's decision to acquire Swiss retailer Bucherer (100 stores worldwide) in 2023 from Jorg Bucherer. The 86-year-old grandson of founder Carl Bucherer was in fact left without direct descendants and wanted to preserve the continuity of the company. In official communications, Rolex stated that their move indicates the brand's desire to sustain the success of Bucherer and preserve their partnership initiated in 1924.

Bucherer has retained its retail brand and its management team remained unchanged (Smith, 2023). Rolex watches also continue to be sold in independent mono-brand and multibrand stores (ie via the wholesale channel).

What was said above is evidence of divergence, and means overcoming the concept of omnichannel (ie integration between channels) and thinking about a new 'experience-based' space, given that from the consumer's point of view the access door to the brand is perceived as unique, wherever it is.

Apple is successfully navigating the market of smartwatches, created by the convergence of traditional watches with smart technology. This new category diverges from the existing classifications of traditional watches or digital gadgets.

Therefore, the meaning of 'blurring the lines' depends on the specific situation or context in which it is used, and it can convey both convergence and divergence, often indicating a situation where the boundaries between concepts or categories are becoming more fluid or ambiguous.

Where convergence and divergence happen: Key areas of analysis

The blurring lines referred to in the luxury world are a result of brands venturing into new trajectories (exploring new territories, collaborations, materials and experiences) and the influence of external factors such as multiple social pressures, demographic change and technological advancements. This C&D, spurred by innovative brand strategies and external forces, is reshaping traditional boundaries and creating new paradigms within luxury.

This concept is not new in management studies. In 1994, the seminal book *Competing for the Future* by Hamel & Prahalad discussed strategies for competing in rapidly changing industries and markets. It explored how companies can blur industry lines and create new market spaces through innovation. In 2005, Kim and Mauborgne introduced the concept of 'blue ocean strategy' in which companies create new market spaces by blurring industry boundaries, thus making competition irrelevant. Their book provided practical frameworks for companies aiming to innovate across industries. The classic paper by Tushman and Anderson (1986) explored how technological changes can disrupt industries and blur traditional boundaries. It provides insights into how firms respond to discontinuities in their environments.

In this section, we present specific aspects of this complex phenomenon in luxury and highlight some key areas of analysis of C&D (see Figure 2.1).

These areas also represent analytical lenses offering unique perspectives on the evolving luxury landscape. These lenses serve as tools or frameworks through which researchers and managers can focus their analysis on particular aspects of the broader scenario, leading to a deeper understanding of the C&D elements within each area.

FIGURE 2.1 Convergence and divergence: Key areas of analysis

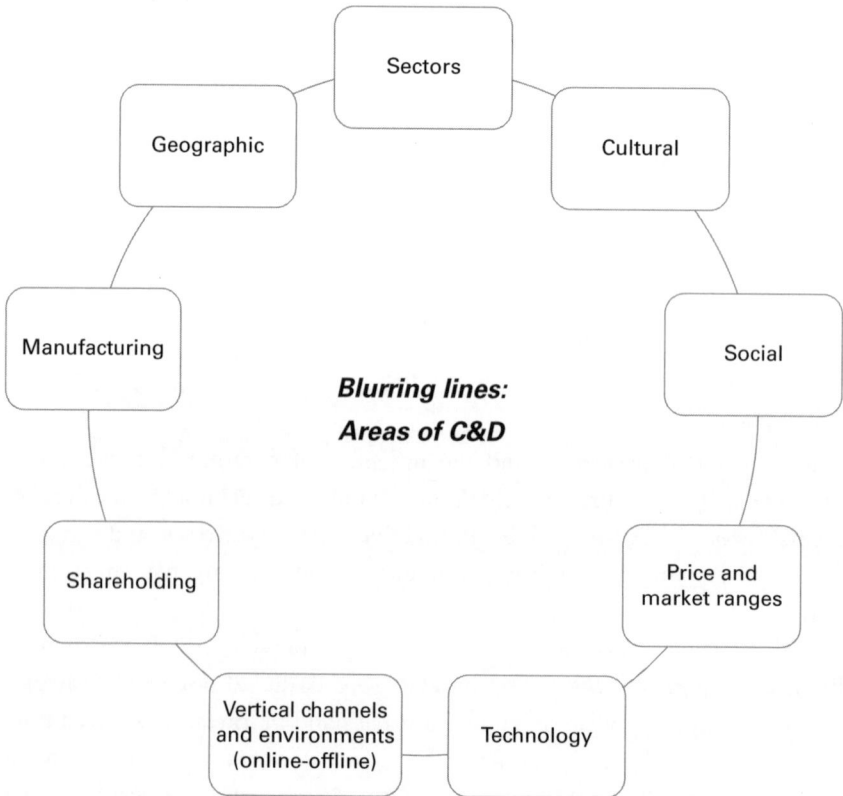

Geographic C&Ds

The first phenomenon that stands out is that of a converging world: a global luxury market is created that shares the same points of reference, regardless of people's country of origin. Now people can live in London, New York, Hong Kong and Shanghai and have something that is very convergent: they could listen to Taylor Swift the same way as BlackPink or other K-pop groups, and watch the same *Barbie* movie. Luxury consumers represent an international audience which, regardless of where their country of origin is, want to buy Hermès and stay at the Four Seasons, Hyatt or Aman; they are happy if they find some references everywhere, although with different nuances, like Niko Romito at Bulgari, or Arva and Nama at Aman, or Zuma and Nobu. The same concept might also transfer to arts and culture with Basel Art Fair, which moves to Dubai, Paris and Miami and becomes a 'brand name' itself.

Hence, blurred lines also signify a converging international perception of luxury, including hospitality, products, experiences, events, etc. Luxury connoisseurs travel across countries not only to buy, which can be done in their home country, but to enjoy major events such as fashion shows or exhibitions of different brands in different cities. They also know that sometimes they need to do a sort of 'bundle deal' in shopping: I buy to be invited, and/or I buy something to have access to other items I want. No matter where I come from, I know the process I need to pass through to get access to the luxury world. Customers know that they can more easily obtain an iconic bag or pair of shoes if they first and repeatedly create a purchasing basket diversified by type, which represents a gatekeeper to the much-coveted object.

Despite this convergence, it is necessary to recognize significant local specificities (eg services requested) that brands are often not aware of. The topic of 'localization' of luxury brands will be discussed in Chapter 5 in this book.

A converging world also means cross-fertilization of different cultures and new players becoming more and more relevant on the international scene. In the luxury market, there are not only Western brands operating today, but also successful brands and retail operators originating from Australia, Asia, Africa and the Middle East. Reports from reputable sources like Deloitte, Bain & Company, BCG and McKinsey highlight the rise of Asian luxury markets and brands. The same studies often report the impact of Asian luxury consumers on the global luxury market.

In India, the retail market is developing within powerful hubs resulting from the foresight and investments of operators such as Reliance Industries, and many international brands are piling in.

There is also increasing presence of African, Asian and Middle Eastern designers and brands at major Fashion Weeks. As well as Shanghai Fashion Week, Tokyo Fashion Week, Dubai Fashion Week and the Indian Fashion Week in London testify to the vitality of new markets and the commitment to wanting to be in the spotlight of global luxury. These events serve as platforms for local luxury brands to showcase their collections to a global audience. Shanghai Tang (China), Zhang Huimei (China), Zuhair Murad (Lebanon), Elie Saab (Lebanon), Sabyasachi Mukherjee (India), Thebe Magugu (South Africa), Don Morphy (Cameroon) and Lisa Folawiyo (Nigeria) are a few case studies of successful Asian and Middle Eastern luxury brands with global recognition and market penetration. Many of these designers and brands have received international awards showcasing their excellence in the luxury market.

In the vibrant landscape of design, the fusion of diverse creative minds often results in groundbreaking aesthetics. One noteworthy trend reshaping the contours of Western design is the infusion of Asian creativity, bringing forth a harmonious blend of styles, sensibilities and cultural narratives. This contamination is not separated from criticisms that have repeatedly raised the issue of cultural appropriation (Lojacono, 2022).

In the furniture industry, many Italian luxury brands have collaborated with Asian and American architects and designers, indicating the industry's recognition of their talent and market influence. They are very active in product design, interior design and architecture, making an important contribution both to the product portfolio of companies and to the implementation of turnkey projects in different market segments (hotels, offices, theatres, private residences, etc). Being able to incorporate the creativity of foreign designers into the conception and development processes also allows companies to create projects with a strong international flavour which can therefore better satisfy preferences, habits, lifestyles and cultures in other countries.

Two remarkable designers, Kensaku Oshiro and Shi-Chieh Lu, epitomize this cross-cultural collaboration, showcasing the exquisite confluence of Italian sophistication and Asian design. Kensaku Oshiro, a renowned designer born in Okinawa, has seamlessly integrated his cultural heritage with Italian design principles, infusing spaces and objects with an exquisite blend of minimalism and functionality. His collaboration with Italian design houses has resulted in furniture collections that celebrate the perfect marriage between Japanese precision and Italian elegance for B&B Italia, Poltrona Frau and De Padova.

Taiwanese-designer Shi-Chieh Lu brought a unique perspective to the realm of Italian design through his collaborations with Poltrona Frau. With the Ming's Heart Armchair, Lu has pioneered a design language that resonates with global audiences. Lu regards architecture and design as social events not simply as a creation of art. Lu has won many international awards, including China Annual Top 10 Influential People of Interior Design in 2015 and his activity has covered both retail (eg the Douchanglee Concept Store in Tiger City, Taichung, the JCD Design Award in 2005, the Aesop Store in Breeze Center, JCD Design Award 2006 and the IFI 2007 Gold Award) and hospitality.

Poltrona Frau's collaborations have recently opened up to the world of fashion and in particular to one of the protagonists of made to order (MTO) in the area favoured by luxury connoisseurs in London, Savile Row. In fact, it was Ozwald Boateng, of Ghanaian origin, who contributed to Poltrona Frau's Culture and Craft line in 2023 by creating wool rugs, tribal pillows, wallpapers adorned with the Kente motif, African-inspired scented candles, etc (Bertoli, 2023).

Sector C&Ds

To multiply the points of possible contact with customers and enrich their experience, luxury companies are bringing together different sectors, increasing the degree of horizontal expansion. The luxury industry has witnessed a notable blurring of lines between sectors, exemplified by unexpected expansions in product offerings. Traditionally specialized brands are now venturing into diverse areas, such as Hermès offering fine table sets and Chanel and Dior delving into high jewellery. This trend demonstrates a significant shift in the industry, where brands are no longer confined to their original domains but are exploring and integrating new categories into their portfolios, reflecting a dynamic evolution in the luxury market.

The most common direction of growth (from automotive, to leather goods, to watchmaking and jewellery, etc) into is the 'unrelated exploration' (Lojacono, 2021), to approach the world of hospitality in different ways, and as a way of learning sophisticated customer engagement and experience techniques.

The Palazzo Versace hotel, located on the Gold Coast in Queensland, Australia, officially opened its doors in September 2000. It was the world's first fashion-branded hotel, a collaboration between the Versace fashion house and the Australian property developer Sunland Group. The hotel's design reflects the distinctive style and luxury associated with the Versace brand, featuring opulent Italian furnishings, marble floors and bespoke Versace fabrics and designs throughout the property. This first destination has been then followed by the opening of Palazzo Versace Dubai in Jaddaf Waterfront in 2021, 'a Neoclassical masterpiece with subtle traces of Arabian architecture' (Palazzo Versace, nd).

Bulgari Hotels and Resorts, in collaboration with Marriott, currently boasts nine properties, in Milan, London, Bali, Beijing, Dubai, Shanghai, Paris, Rome and Tokyo. Founded in 2001, it boasts important records as it is both the only collection of Italian hotels present internationally and the largest hotel group belonging to a luxury brand. Next openings are planned in Ranfushi (2025), Miami Beach and Los Angeles (2026).

Many moves showcase luxury groups' expansion into the hospitality sector. Le Cheval Blanc is the hotel chain that belongs to LVMH (Louis Vuitton Moet Hennessy) which since 2006 has managed five hotels in St. Tropez, Courchevel, as well as in the Maldives, the Caribbean and Paris. By 2026, Louis Vuitton will open its first branded hotel on the Champs-Elysées in Paris, adjacent to its largest store on the avenue. The hotel, previously a site for HSBC Bank and originally a hotel in 1898, will cover an area of 6,000 square meters. It will feature an architectural transformation that echoes the brand's iconic trunks, with a grand Monogram trunk to adorn its Haussmann-style façade.

The Lungarno Collection, a venture by the renowned Italian fashion house Salvatore Ferragamo, exemplifies the seamless blend of luxury lifestyle and hospitality. Founded by Leonardo Ferragamo, the Lungarno Collection has become synonymous with exquisite design, impeccable service, and a unique fusion of fashion and architecture. Founded in 1999 with the first Lungarno Hotel and Apartments in Florence on the Arno River, it added three hotels in Rome, Florence and Milan under the Portrait brand.

In 2010, Armani Hotel Dubai was inaugurated inside the Burj Khalifa in Dubai, the first hotel born from the collaboration between Giorgio Armani S.p.A and Emaar Properties PJSC. In 2011, Armani Hotel also opened in Milan in the building originally designed by Enrico A Griffini in 1937, in the heart of the Fashion District.

These examples have not remained isolated, even if other brands have opted, so far, not to create a multi-location chain. The Hôtel des Horlogers by Audemars Piguet was inaugurated in June 2022 in Le Brassus where the Hôtel de France stood, founded in 1857 to welcome visitors from all over the world to the Vallée de Joux. The hotel was an important stop on the Chemin des Horlogers, the route that connected the watchmaking workshops of the Vallée de Joux to Geneva, where the watches were then sold. In 2003, Audemars Piguet purchased and renovated this historic hotel, which opened its doors in 2005 under the name Hôtel des Horlogers. Later, wanting to embark on a more ambitious and sustainable project, Audemars Piguet closed the hotel in 2016 and began the renovation which was entrusted to Bjarke Ingels Group and the Swiss architecture firm CCHE, the same two partners who also designed the Musée Atelier Audemars Piguet located within walking distance. The architecture of the building follows the topography of the Vallée de Joux thanks to a zigzag structure that gradually integrates into the surrounding meadows.

These examples have been followed by other brands where the hotel seems more aimed at following a creative and personal passion rather than having concrete business objectives. For example, the Vermelho (which means 'red' in Portuguese) is the hotel opened in 2023 by Christian Louboutin in Melides, a rustic village an hour and a half south of Lisbon.

Explorations in the world of hospitality continue as well with exclusive restaurants that are:

- 'On the street', such as Polo Bar, Ralph's Bar or Bar at Ralph Lauren, different formats by Ralph Lauren in Milano, Chicago, Parigi, New York and Chengdu. Added to these is Ralph's Coffee, a chain of 24 coffee shops around the world founded in 2014 in New York.

- Inside brands' boutiques, such as the Monsieur Dior Restaurant in the historic location of Avenue Montaigne in Paris.

- In department stores such as Prada Caffè or Tiffany's Blue Box Bar at Harrods in London or in Dubai Mall, which follow the one by Daniel Boulud within the Landmark on Fifth Avenue in New York.

Growth in the world of hotels, restaurants and bars has also occurred through acquisitions. For instance, luxury brands have been seen to acquire historical landmarks in the *pasticceria* world in Milan, such as Cova (purchased by LVMH) and Marchesi (by Prada).

In December 2018, the LVMH group announced the acquisition of the Belmond group. Founded in London in 1976 under the name Orient-Express Hotels Ltd, Belmond was born with the acquisition of the historic Hotel Cipriani in Venice and owes its original name to the legendary train which, starting in 1883, began connecting Paris to Istanbul. It is precisely thanks to this company, in fact, that its carriages returned to travel between London and Venice in 1982, after having been abandoned due to competition from air transport.

Over time, Belmond has expanded its destinations, across all continents. It is also currently responsible for the Belmond Royal Scotsman rail service and PeruRail. The offer also includes boat trips, safaris and the 21 Club restaurant in New York. Even today, the Hotel Cipriani in Venice on the island of Giudecca remains open to the public. The Venice Simplon-Orient-Express is the iconic train that connects Venice to Geneva and Paris. In Italy, Belmond manages also properties in Portofino (the Splendido and the Splendido Mare), Tuscany (Casole Castle and Villa San Michele), the Amalfi coast (Villa Margherita and Caruso, both in Ravello) and Sicily (Villa Sant'Andrea and Grand Hotel Timeo in Taormina). Belmond is the protagonist of a major expansion around the world in France, Portugal, Russia and Spain.

The highest concentration of hotels is in the United Kingdom, where the company is headquartered, including the Cadogan Hotel in London, built on Sloane Street in 1887. Belmond also appears in the most fascinating locations in North and South America: La Samanna in the French Antilles, the Maroma Resort & Spa in Mexico's Riviera Maya, the Copacabana Palace in Rio de Janeiro and the Sanctuary Lodge in Machu Picchu. In Asia, the brand is present in Cambodia, Laos, Indonesia and Myanmar.

Those illustrated above are examples of personal luxury goods brand extensions in the world of hospitality. However, there are also examples of the widening of the scope of brands originating in hospitality that expanded into private residences and vacation homes, offering high-end living experiences. This convergence combines luxury travel with the comfort and privacy of a home, catering to a discerning clientele. Some luxury properties offer concierge services, housekeeping, private chefs and chauffeur-driven cars, providing residents with a luxurious lifestyle. This can include exclusive travel packages, gourmet dining experiences, personalized spa treatments and cultural events. Aman offers branded residences around the world, including in destinations such as Bali, Tokyo, New York City and Miami.

Aman Residences provide guests with the opportunity to own a piece of the Aman lifestyle, often in secluded and exclusive locations.

The Four Seasons, Ritz-Carlton, St Regis, One&Only, Rosewood, Six Senses, etc operate private residences in various locations, offering luxurious villas, condos or apartments with access to the hotel's amenities and personalized services including butler service, fine dining and spa facilities.

Another interesting interplay is that between hospitality, health and wellness. In fact, players in the world of hospitality had been paying increasing attention to the wellbeing of their customers by creating spas and offering body and facial treatments. This has also led to investing in formats dedicated to wellbeing such as Asaya, a Rosewood's signature concept offering a variety of wellness programmes led by experts and tailored around ever-changing needs and desires. The Asaya brand was originally launched at Rosewood Phuket and it is founded on five pillars – emotional balance, fitness and nutrition, physical therapies, skin health and community (Rosewood Hotels, nd). A second Asaya wellness spa opened in 2024 at the luxury hotel and spa operator's hotel Rosewood Schloss Fuschl, with eight treatment rooms, indoor and outdoor swimming pools and a fitness centre.

However, this crossover between the worlds of wellbeing, health and hospitality, due to divergence, has given rise to a new category of players, the 'longevity clinics' which are neither a hotel in the strict sense, nor a hospital, nor a medical clinic, nor a spa. The Longevity clinics are specialized resorts that promote physical and mental wellbeing, by offering health-focused retreats and wellness-oriented products and services, advanced diagnostics, cutting-edge treatments and personalized therapies to address aspects of aspects holistically.

Luxury destinations, like Clinique La Prairie (CLP) in Montreux, offer wellness retreats that include personalized fitness programmes, spa treatments and healthy cuisine. Founded in 1931, Clinique La Prairie is a 34-suite health resort, a mix between a full-fledged medical facility – with 50 doctors with over 30 in-house medical specialties – a multi-award-winning spa and luxury hotel with bespoke services. The longevity mission of CLP is around four pillars: preventive health care, nutrition, movement and wellbeing. It receives about 2,000 guests across 80 countries every year with a repeat clientele rate of 60 per cent. CLP's ultimate expertise in the science of longevity and high customization is represented in the Revitalization Platinum package, 7 days/6 nights priced at 119,000 CFH.

Clinique La Prairie expanded globally to launch up to ten health resorts, similar to the retreat concept found at the Montreaux institute. The company is also aiming to launch up to 40 longevity hubs – think of these as medi-spas that offer day retreats – in key cities around the world. There are currently four hubs in Bangkok, Doha, Madrid and Taipei.

Combining this expansion of the hospitality world with the brands' retail strategies, aimed at seeking the best locations for their flagships, brings out an interesting luxury real estate market. 'Luxury real estate' refers to a category of high-end properties characterized by exceptional features. These properties often surpass standard market offerings in terms of design, location, amenities and lifestyle experience. Luxury real estate embodies a blend of architectural brilliance and superior interior and exterior features, creating a sophisticated environment. This market has been even more challenged by the innovation of retail strategies by luxury brands aimed at augmenting the customer experience by locating pop-up stores in travel destinations.

The illustrated examples involved the expansion of personal luxury goods (PLG) brands into distant worlds, such as hospitality, often in partnership with specialized operators in the sector. In the past, some PLG brands have also entered the automotive and motorcycle sectors, through collaborations with companies in these sectors. An example of this is the Vespa 946 Christian Dior. The opposite is also true, ie luxury automotive brands that have created new business lines in personal luxury goods. An example for everyone is that of Ferrari.

In 2022, the brand's brief to the new Chief Brand Officer (CBO), Maria Carla Liuni, was clear: Ferrari should continue to affirm itself as a fully-fledged luxury player by simultaneously (a) elevating brand, products and experiences for customers; (b) expanding Ferrari's unique value proposition, beyond its core (sports cars and racing); and (c) preserving the brand DNA.

The creation of the Lifestyle division was the path that would allow Ferrari to seize further growth opportunities due to the following rationales:

1 Business opportunity. Luxury market de facto is a single arena competing for the same customers' discretionary spending: over a trillion of target spending, of which Ferrari covered only a small share (around 1 per cent). Ferrari could leverage the aspirational capacity of its brand to concretely evaluate opportunities especially in the PLG segment which – after cars – was the most relevant in terms of size, growth, visibility and role in the society (Bain & Co, 2023).

2   Brand platform. Arguably, no other (car) brands has built such a strong
    legacy of Italian excellence: 'Ferrari sells so much more than cars, it sells
    a way of life. The brand conveys unrivalled status, desirability and
    creative excellence' (Maria Carla Liuni, personal correspondence).

Ferrari needed to understand the appropriate way to do it. The new CBO
found herself having to bring order to the policies of the past in the old
'Diversification Unit' (later renamed 'Lifestyle') and to clearly identify what
fell within this business line and what did not.

From a preliminary analysis it became immediately clear that the
Diversification Unit was at the time a container for everything that wasn't a
car, from credit cards to fragrances to desk objects to scooters, with multiple
licensing agreements that risked brand dilution and were not of real
economic value. The top ten licensees created 80 per cent of the revenue of
the division. There was therefore a queue of around 40 licensees and related
objects which caused fragmentation, management costs and no significant
impact in terms of turnover.

This situation was also generated by a rather physiological mechanism.
To cover the costs related to F1, Ferrari was looking for sponsors that, in
order to see a partial return on their investments, required a licensing agreement for some items. It was therefore decided to substantially reduce the
number of licensors and establish a strong partnership with licensors that
could develop the brand in categories where Ferrari didn't have expertise
and/or the right distribution channels (ie watches or sunglasses). The choices
of professional partners would allow Ferrari to provide a better product,
service or experience.

Carla Maria and her team simultaneously tried to identify the 'higher'
values of a brand that is by its nature connected to the world of cars. A
'Brand Bible' was born based on a series of interviews carried out within the
company and semi-qualitative market research with owners and fans. The
Ferrari brand is undoubtedly much bigger than the business it generates; it
is among the most aspirational brands, with universal values influenced by
the thoughts of the founder, Enzo Ferrari. It was necessary to understand
how to 'translate' these values to other categories and how to create a brand
culture within the organization.

For Ferrari to be consistent along all touchpoints, it was critical that all
business units were informed by the same set of values, the same storytelling:

- a story of uncompromising ambition, vision and drive
- a shared passion with a visceral and insatiable desire to win
- a culture of innovation and craftmanship

- a pioneering spirit driven by a relentless search for excellence
- a unique 'Italian-ness' – Italy is and always will be part of the Ferrari's soul, just as Ferrari will always be part of Italy's
- the design, the beauty, the lust for life – everything Ferrari does is inspired by the beauty of landscape, architecture and thousands of years of history, art and design

Ferrari is a symbol of uniqueness and exclusivity. Increasing the brand coverage to enter other categories was a way to push beyond the boundaries of what's established and strive for innovation.

Today, the Lifestyle division's audience includes 'Ferraristi' (owners of cars, collectors, future Ferraristi), 'tifosi' (fans) and the so-called 'Brand Admirers' who love the brand even if they don't own a car or are not F1-addicted. With the above in mind, a gradual approach in the offering and a targeted market segmentation was a must. The clothing collection – signed by Rocco Iannone with his first show in Maranello in June 2021 – has the following structure:

1 The Atelier line which takes up the Ferrari philosophy of customization and MTO. Here, Ferrari benefits from events (eg Pebble Beach) aimed at car customers, during which trunk shows are organized.

2 Ferrari Collection – ie the world of ready-to-wear and leather goods inspired by racing spirit, yet elegantly rooted in Italian heritage, offering pieces that are both 'high' and 'hype' for a life in motion of a female target. These lines have the single and elegant little prancing horse as their logo.

3 Merchandising for Ferrari's fans, which features the classic yellow shield with SF (Scuderia Ferrari) logo. It is distributed at races and via third-party channels for the fans. This merchandising must meet the high-quality Ferrari standards, thanks to the guidance and supervision of the licensees which is included in Rocco's responsibility.

The philosophy behind all of it is simple: 'Every product must become an object of desire; every experience must become a memorable one for our customers' (Maria Carla Liuni, personal correspondence).

Manufacturing C&Ds

A luxury product is intended as a platform where various important specializations converge. First, brands place the production of specific products or particular processing phases in countries, from Switzerland to India, where unparalleled skills are valued. Second, luxury brands try to control more and more activities upstream, increasing the degree of vertical integration, beyond traditional specializations.

RELOCATING PRODUCTION FOR RESOURCE AND ASSET SEEKING
'Swiss-made' is essential for the production of luxury watches. That's why Chanel, Cartier and Bulgari have watch factories in Switzerland. The American Tiffany produces more and more products in Europe, and this is justified by the know-how present in France, Italy and Switzerland.

The majority of luxury brands, especially in haute couture, do all their embroidery in India due to its top-notch craftsmanship. A craftsman can take more than 200 days to embroider and embellish an entire dress to perfection with stones, pearls and sequins. To celebrate this excellence in workmanship, Dior held its fashion show in India in 2023 with the indispensable contribution of the embroiderers of the Chanakya School of Craft in Mumbai. The school was founded in 1986 to pass on this know-how from generation to generation – a passion for India that united all of Mariagrazia Chiuri's predecessors, from John Galliano to Gianfranco Ferrè (who had spent part of his life in the country) to Marco Bohan. The COO of the brand therefore remains an essential element, but is enriched with stimuli and contributions from different countries.

Historically, India was the largest producer and exporter of beads. It was the first country to invent the diamond drill and later on the technique of mining the diamonds with the help of this drill was taught to the Romans. India continues to be the second largest consumer of gold and the gems and the jewellery industry dates back at least 5,000 years. There is a lot of craft and know-how spread across different regions and the domestic market continues to have a plethora of techniques and product categories.

India is a leader in the gem and jewellery industry, which contributes over 7 per cent to its GDP with total merchandise exports totalling US$39.77 billion in 2022 (around 5 per cent of global exports), making it the world's fifth largest exporter. The industry employs over 5 million people, both directly and indirectly, and is one of the most important sectors of the Indian economy (Gem & Jewellery Export Promotion Council, nd).

India's expertise in the gem and jewellery industry is extensive, covering the entire supply chain from mining and cutting to polishing and manufacture of jewellery. The following are some of India's key areas of expertise:

- Diamond cutting and polishing: India is the world's largest centre for diamond cutting and polishing, accounting for over 90 per cent of the world's total diamond polishing. The country has a highly skilled work-force and state-of-the-art facilities.

- Coloured gemstone mining and cutting: The country has a rich history of coloured gemstone mining and cutting to the highest standards.

- Jewellery manufacturing: India is a major manufacturer of gold, silver and diamond jewellery. The country has a large number of jewellery manufacturing units. Historically the manufacturing was primarily for internal consumption, however, since the late 1980s India has also exported jewellery to the rest of the world.

- India specializes in all kinds of hand-made jewellery, particularly focusing on stone-intensive products. Over the years, factories in India have developed a unique mix of craftmanship along with the latest technology and automation, thereby making it a destination of choice for brands.

India has also set up several special economic zones to promote trade, and most businesses in this zone adopt world-class best practices in operations and follow international standards for doing business. There is an increased focus on sustainability and traceability, and factories are making extensive investment in these areas to cater to a growing need for transparency.

EXPANDING VERTICALLY

All the main luxury brands have long directed their financial resources by investing in suppliers, often small and family-run out of their country of origin. These policies usually lead to shared management and leave original entrepreneurs in charge of managing the companies (Seares, 2023). The strategic aim is to have full control over the supply chain, acquire unique techniques, get access to rare inputs, foster innovation and even increase production capacity.

That's the reason why Cucinelli bought 43 per cent of the equity of the knitwear manufacturer Lanificio Cariaggi Lanificio, Chanel acquired a majority stake in Italian knitwear company Paima, and Fendi took a majority stake in Italian knitwear company Maglificio Matisse. Together, Prada and Ermenegildo Zegna Group announced they were jointly taking a majority shareholding in Filati Biagioli Modesto, a producer of cashmere and noble fibres. Zegna has made several acquisitions over time, such as weaving mill Tessitura Ubertino (in 2021), jersey fabric manufacturer Gruppo Dondi (2019), milliners Cappellificio Cervo (2018) and textile manufacturer Bonotto (2016), all coordinated and subsequently managed by a specially created entity, the 'Luxury Textile Laboratory Platform', which primarily supports owned brands Zegna and Thom Browne.

In 1985, Chanel established Paraffection, a subsidiary aimed at preserving traditional craftsmanship by investing in small, specialized artisanal workshops. This initiative allowed these ateliers to upgrade equipment and train new artisans, ensuring the survival of unique métiers d'art. By 2019, ten of these acquired entities, including renowned names like Lesage and Maison Michel, were relocated to a bespoke facility in Paris named 19M, symbolizing Maison, mode (fashion) and métier (craftsmanship), situated in the 19th arrondissement, further cementing Chanel's commitment to artisanal heritage.

LVMH Group is a serial acquirer of suppliers and has made multiple investments to strengthen its production sourcing through its owned brands and LVMH Métiers d'art, the entity that since 2015 has been grouping artisanal manufacturing laboratories in the world specializing in exceptional materials. The most recent is the acquisition of the majority of the capital of Leo shoes (234 million in revenues in 2022 and EBITDA of 30 million, 1,300 employees), a leading company in Southern Italy specialized in the production of sneakers and bags, already a supplier to Dior.

The LVMH supply chain in Italy already includes, through various legal entities, tanneries in Tuscany such as Nuti Ivo (through the LVMH Métiers d'art division) and also companies specializing in special leather treatments such as ArtLab, as well as various manufacturers, both bags and footwear.

LVMH's upstream acquisitions concerned not only the world of leather goods but also the other businesses in which the group operates. For instance, LVMH has acquired a majority stake in the Platinum Invest group, which includes the companies Orest and Abysse, jewellery manufacturers based in France.

This acquisition followed that of the Pedemonte group in Italy in 2022, specializing in the manufacturing of luxury jewellery. Pedemonte (350 employees) was born in 2020 from the merger of several independent production laboratories, with decades of experience behind them with offices in Valenza, Valmadonna, in the goldsmith district that gravitates around Alessandria, and in Paris. In the same year, LVMH acquired a majority stake in tannery Heng Long in Tuscany, specializing in exotic leather, and a minority stake in leather and leather apparel manufacturer Robans located in Pisa.

Price and market ranges C&Ds

The increase in the categories covered and the expansion of product and service families makes any segmentation of brands based on price ranges anachronistic, useless and misleading. Luxury brands enter the business of cosmetics, eyewear or small leather goods at price points that are relatively affordable compared to their high-end offerings, although higher than the average price in the same category. This strategy is often used to attract a broader consumer base while maintaining a certain level of exclusivity and brand image. These products allow consumers to own a piece of the brand without the hefty price tag associated with mainline luxury products. Another similar concept widely discussed in marketing literature is 'masstige' (a blend of 'mass' and 'prestige'), often used to describe products that are positioned between mass-market and luxury goods. Masstige products offer higher quality and prestige than typical mass-market items, but are priced more affordably than traditional luxury goods.

A non-superficial view of this phenomenon shows how many of these products are fundamental to the brand's architecture to the point of pushing brands to control the design, production and marketing of the product as much as possible. The famous No 5 by Chanel, born in 1921 by the perfumer Ernest Beaux, is still today one of the best-selling perfumes in the world. It is a bouquet of 80 components, including the fundamental jasmine, made in Grasse through a process supervised by the brand.

Kering Eyewear, the eyewear division of the Kering Group (formerly PPR), was officially launched in 2014 to oversee the design, development and distribution of eyewear for several luxury brands within the Kering Group, including Gucci, Saint Laurent and Alexander McQueen.

Following the same rationale, Thélios, the joint venture between LVMH (Moët Hennessy Louis Vuitton) and Marcolin Group, was officially launched in 2017. Thélios combined the expertise of Marcolin, a leading eyewear company, with the fashion and luxury heritage of LVMH's brands to create high-quality eyewear collections. The joint venture was established to design, produce and distribute eyewear for several luxury brands owned by LVMH, including Louis Vuitton, Celine, Loewe and others. Over time, the brands of the luxury group slowly transferred the eyewear licenses from external suppliers to Thélios. In 2021, LVMH proceeded to acquire the 49 per cent of Thélios owned by Marcolin, and Marcolin instead the 10 per cent that LVMH owned in Marcolin, acquired upon the foundation of the joint venture. This operation allowed LVMH to further strengthen its presence in the eyewear sector by leveraging Thélios' Italian savoir-faire.

Another interplay between different markets and price ranges is that between luxury (haute couture) brands and mainstream or streetwear brands.

Mainstream fashion reflects the current styles, colours, patterns and designs that dominate the fashion industry during a specific period. These trends are often influenced by factors such as popular culture, media, celebrities and socio-economic developments. Mainstream fashion is accessible to a broad audience and is typically available at affordable price points. These clothing items and accessories are produced on a larger scale, making them widely available in retail stores, both physical and online. Mainstream is the opposite of timelessness; it is constantly evolving. Designers and retailers adapt their offerings based on changing consumer preferences. While there are global fashion trends, mainstream fashion can vary based on cultural and regional differences. Certain styles that are mainstream in one country or culture might not be as popular in another, reflecting the diversity of fashion preferences worldwide.

Streetwear is a distinctive style of fashion that originated from urban youth culture, particularly in the United States, during the 1980s. It represents a casual, comfortable and often eclectic approach to dressing, drawing inspiration from elements of sports, music, art and subcultures.

Streetwear emerged from the creativity of young urbanites, particularly in cities like New York and Los Angeles. It often embodies the rebellious and independent spirit of youth subcultures, including skateboarding, hip-hop, punk and graffiti art. Streetwear emphasizes comfort and wearability. It includes items like T-shirts, hoodies, sneakers, jeans and baseball caps. The clothing is typically loose-fitting and easy to move in, reflecting a laid-back style. Graphic designs, bold logos and unique patterns are common in streetwear. Graphic T-shirts, in particular, often feature artistic, political or cultural statements.

Celebrities, particularly musicians, athletes and social media influencers, often play a significant role in popularizing streetwear brands. Their endorsements and fashion choices influence trends within the streetwear community. Streetwear is not confined to a specific region or culture. It has become a global phenomenon, with enthusiasts and designers from various countries contributing to its evolution and diversity.

In recent years, streetwear has intersected with luxury, leading to collaborations between renowned luxury houses and streetwear labels. This crossover has blurred the lines between traditional luxury brands (like Louis Vuitton, Gucci and Balenciaga) and streetwear (such as Nike, Levi's or Supreme), creating a hybrid style often referred to as 'luxury streetwear'.

Gucci under the creative direction of Alessandro Michele is a prime example of a luxury brand embracing the streetwear phenomenon. Since Alessandro Michele (since replaced by Sabato Di Sarno in 2023) took the helm as the creative director of Gucci in 2015, the brand has undergone a significant transformation, embracing a more eclectic, unconventional and streetwear-inspired aesthetic. Under Michele's direction, Gucci incorporated streetwear elements such as bold graphics, oversized silhouettes, casual sneakers and vibrant colours into its collections. The brand also collaborated with artists and designers, creating limited-edition pieces and accessories that appeal to the streetwear culture.

Moreover, Gucci has actively engaged with youth culture and social media, leveraging platforms like Instagram and TikTok to connect with younger audiences. Alessandro Michele's designs for Gucci often feature a mix of high fashion and streetwear influences, blurring the lines between luxury and casual styles. This approach has resonated well with younger consumers, making Gucci a notable example of a luxury brand successfully embracing the streetwear phenomenon.

Miu Miu has climbed the rankings of the trendiest brands of the moment thanks to its leading-edge proposals and collaborations, including the one with New Balance for model 574 (see Figure 2.2).

FIGURE 2.2 The limited edition Miu Miu x New Balance sneakers

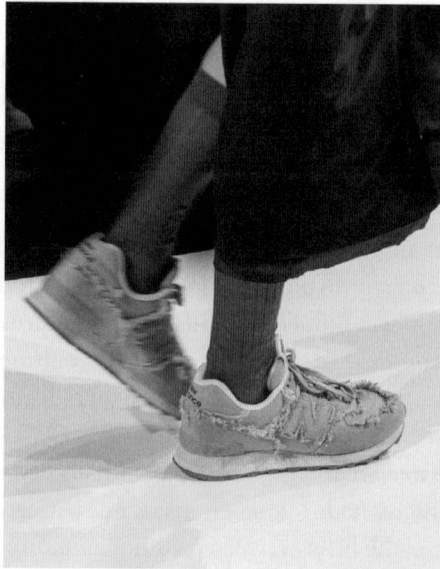

SOURCE Courtesy of Miu Miu

Many streetwear brands release limited edition or exclusive items, creating a sense of scarcity and exclusivity as a way to do trading up. Limited drops and collaborations with artists, musicians or other fashion labels are common in streetwear culture.

TRADING UP

The concept of trading up or premiumization is not merely about escalating prices; it involves enhancing the consumer's perception of a product. The concept of 'trading up' in business can refer to a company's strategic move to ascend within a market by targeting more upscale categories or consumer segments. Alternatively, it can describe a brand's effort to elevate itself from the commoditized competition, positioning itself in a more exclusive, premium niche.

This phenomenon is underpinned by an item's aesthetic appeal, the allure of exclusivity, the augmented performance, the artisanal touch, the packaging, the endorsement by VIPs, the genuine incorporation of the values of social and environmental sustainability and the emotional resonance it holds to align with the expectations of a more discerning and affluent clientele. The value is often augmented by word of mouth, especially from influential figures or through design by renowned creators. For instance, Diesel has carved a niche by infusing haute couture creativity into denim. Their approach, which includes limited-edition pieces adorned with luxury elements like Swarovski crystals, redefines denim as high fashion, commanding premium prices that far exceed the category's norms. This strategy is not just about the product but the status it confers, turning everyday apparel into covetable, status-symbol items. Diesel's 1DR bag, for instance, has risen to 'it-bag' status, becoming a highly sought-after item that balances gender-neutral appeal with accessibility under €500. This approach exemplifies how traditional materials, when combined with innovative design and exclusive, limited availability, can ascend into the realm of luxury.

Similarly, brands like Byredo and Aesop exemplify premiumization through intense fragrances and design-led, sensorial products, respectively. Their success is not just in the products but in the experiences and status they confer to the users. This approach to premiumization carefully balances increased pricing with the promise of exclusivity and enriched experiences, aiming to cultivate a perception of elevated status and desirability.

Levi's is a prominent example of a brand that has engaged in the process of 'premiumization' within the streetwear and fashion industry. The brand, known for its iconic denim jeans and casual wear, has introduced special collections and premium products to cater to a higher-end market in collaborations with renowned designers, and brands (like Valentino and Miu Miu). These limited-edition lines often feature unique designs, high-quality materials and special detailing, appealing to fashion enthusiasts willing to pay a premium for exclusive and collectible items. By using high-quality fabrics (like Japanese organic cotton) in exclusive collections, Levi's attracts consumers who are willing to pay a higher price for eco-friendly and luxurious materials. These items have a retail price up to three times higher than that of comparable models in the brand's assortment.

Ultimately, convergence also occurs between traditional luxury brands and brands that have made brilliant premiumization experiments. Products that were traditionally associated with commodities or fast-moving consumer goods (FMCGs) are being reimagined with luxury features. For instance, in addition to hand detergents from Aesop, yoga apparel from Alo and Lululemon with the use of high-end materials and features, creation of communities, adoption of selective retail strategies and production of limited-edition items and lifestyle products have created a new category of 'crossover luxury products'. Since 2019, Zara, a point of reference par excellence in fast fashion, has periodically offered around 100 limited edition pieces with fine materials such as cashmere and feather and sequin decorations which have a retail price of over €300.

Trading up in luxury can manifest organically through innovative approaches like Nespresso's luxurious take on coffee or through strategic acquisitions as seen with Procter & Gamble's purchase of SKII and Ouai. Ouai, founded by Jen Atkin, has rapidly ascended in the beauty sector, drawing in a younger, socially connected audience. Procter & Gamble's acquisition marks its first foray into the premium hair care space, complementing its existing portfolio and tapping into the robust growth of the prestige hair care market. With this move, P&G showcases its adaptability and commitment to evolving consumer trends and preferences.

The strategy of trading up through non-equity alliances like licensing has been exemplified in the mobile industry with collaborations between fashion brands and tech companies. Such partnerships have led to the creation of luxury phones that combine high-end fashion aesthetics with advanced technology, catering to a niche market that values both functionality and designer appeal. These alliances allow tech companies to enhance their products with the cachet of luxury fashion labels, while fashion brands extend their reach into new, tech-savvy audiences. The alliance between LG and Prada is a notable example of trading up through non-equity alliances in the mobile industry, blending high fashion with cutting-edge technology.

Channels C&Ds

In the recent past, online and offline has been considered by luxury brands as two distinct worlds. Today the customers want to transit from one channel to another without experiencing disruptions. For example, they can start browsing products on a mobile app, add items to their cart, and later complete the purchase on a desktop computer or in a physical store.

Additionally, a common behaviour along the consumer journey in the digital age has been called ROPO (Research Offline and Purchase Online) in marketing and retail literature. As online research and ecommerce became more prevalent, marketers and researchers noticed that many consumers were researching products or services online but still choosing to make their purchases in physical stores. In this scenario, the online research serves as a crucial part of the customer's decision-making process, but the transaction itself occurs offline. ROPO is a significant trend in today's retail landscape, highlighting the importance of online presence and digital marketing even for businesses that primarily operate in physical locations.

In the last four years, luxury brands have adopted a business approach that minimizes the distinction between online and offline and integrates various sales and communication channels to provide a seamless and unified customer experience. This new omnichannel approach, which has not yet been completed, should ensure that customers have a seamless and unified experience across all touchpoints, whether they are shopping online using a website or mobile app, visiting a physical store or interacting through social media or other digital platforms. Consistency and integration across all channels extend from branding to product information, to pricing, to promotions, and customer service is maintained.

Omnichannel strategy involves synchronizing inventory, customer data and operations across channels. This integration ensures that the business can fulfil orders, manage customer relationships and track inventory levels regardless of the channel used by the customer.

The omnichannel approach often leverages data and analytics to personalize customer interactions. Personalized recommendations, targeted marketing messages and tailored shopping experiences enhance customer engagement and satisfaction.

Omnichannel allows customers the flexibility to choose their preferred shopping channels and methods, catering to diverse consumer preferences. Whether customers prefer online shopping, in-store visits, mobile apps or a combination, omnichannel strategies accommodate these choices.

There are multiple advantages to being committed to an omnichannel strategy:

- Improved customer experience: Omnichannel strategies focus on enhancing customer satisfaction and preferences, leading to higher levels of customer loyalty and retention.

- Increased sales: By providing a seamless shopping experience, brands can capture sales from customers who engage through multiple channels, leading to increased revenue opportunities. By accessing multiple points of contact with the brand, upselling and cross-selling opportunities also increase.

- Enhanced efficiency: Integrated systems and processes improve operational efficiency, inventory management and order fulfilment. It is in fact possible to quickly move products between channels and countries based on demand, with a positive impact on customer satisfaction and inventory optimization.

- Better data insights: The adoption of a single CRM platform collects and generates valuable data insights, enabling brands to better understand customer behaviour and preferences, leading to more informed decision-making.

In summary, omnichannel is a customer-centric approach that prioritizes a seamless, consistent and personalized experience across all retail and communication channels, strengthening the relationship between brands and their customers.

The advance of online has represented a powerful accelerator of the modernization of traditional retail, pushing to find a new role for physical stores. These have become entertainment and communication platforms, far beyond a transactional role. This is why, as mentioned above, brands indulge themselves in finding all possible ways (including bars and restaurants) to spoil their customers, make their visit unforgettable and keep them in the store as much as possible, and also to collect data important for profiling purposes and making upselling and cross-selling attempts. This is how Dior inserts private luxury suites in Paris; in the Milan boutique, Cartier thinks of a welcome bar on the second floor and a private space on the third floor,

La Résidence; and Louis Vuitton will open its first hotel in Paris on the Champs-Elysée in 2026 close to its boutique. Further confirmation that the boundaries are now increasingly blurred.

Integration between the physical and digital environment is extreme at a time when retail has brought technology into stores in an increasingly pervasive way to revolutionize the consumer journey. The best example is the use of artificial intelligence (AI), augmented reality (AR) and virtual reality (VR) in stores. In 2020, Burberry carried out an important experiment with its Social Store in Shenzhen, a project in collaboration with Tencent which included interactive windows, a living sculpture reflecting the mirrored runway from the Burberry show, an immersive virtual space, a WeChat Mini Programme which brought the store to life through exclusive content and personalized experiences, audio guides, one-to-one appointments, table reservations and upcoming events and a playful digital animal character assigned to each customer that evolved the more they interacted with the space, with new characters and outfits to discover.

Cultural C&Ds

Originally, luxury was essentially associated with the world of manufacturing and creativity. Today the points of contact with the arts, music and culture are multiplying. The opportunities opened up by this magic blend have led many brands to invest in initiatives to support the arts, even beyond purely commercial purposes. Convergence blurs the lines between traditional art and commercial goods. This blend of luxury, arts and culture is analysed in depth in Chapter 4 of this book.

First, it is not rare to see artists creating limited-edition designs or artwork for luxury brands. Season after season, the iconic Lady Dior bag with its Cannage motif is revisited by artists from around the world. As the Dior website reports: '[it] is thus transformed into a unique work of art, merging heritage and creative visions through the most audacious interpretations' (Dior, nd).

The Galerie Dior, in the new store also designed by Peter Marino, is an original exhibition space that traces the history of the Maison from Christian Dior to his six successors: Yves Saint Laurent, Marc Bohan, Gianfranco Ferré, John Galliano, Raf Simons and Maria Grazia Chiuri. The gallery symbolizes the spirit of Parisian haute couture as much as it perpetuates the memory of this iconic address, revealing models, original sketches, archive documents and exceptional pieces.

LV realizes another type of union with art, in the direction of pop music and entertainment, placing Pharrell Williams as creative director in 2023. The connection with art is also tangible in the retail stores which become an important symbol for the brand's identity. The architect Peter Marino and Shohei Shigematsu, who is a partner at OMA New York, in charge of the redesign project of the Tiffany Landmark in New York, turned it into an art destination, where walking among the jewellery cases the visitor comes across around 40 works by Jean-Michel Basquiat, Anish Kapoor, Damien Hirst, Julian Schnabel, Rashid Johnson, Anna Weyant and Daniel Arsham. The stairs are centrally dominated by Daniel Arsham's bronze sculpture Eroded Venus of Arles from 2022.

Technology C&Ds

Technology has played an increasingly pervasive role in the world of luxury, involving the entire supply chain, from upstream to downstream.

Digital transformation has redefined the boundaries of luxury by offering a novel paradigm where advanced technologies intersect with the timeless allure of exclusivity and craftsmanship. This convergence between new technologies and luxury has originated an interesting area of 'digital luxury' that encompasses products or experiences that exist primarily in the digital realm. Digital transformation in luxury will be presented in Chapters 7, 8, 9 and 10 of this book, which highlight the relevance of new technologies such as artificial intelligence (AI) and non-fungible tokens (NFTs) as well as the use of gamification for customer engagement and sales generation. All these areas must in no way be seen as isolated since their strength is expressed in combined use.

In 2023, for example, the Kering group launched KNXT. It is a tech marketplace for NFTs where Madeline, a personal shopper powered by AI, guides customers through luxury goods available to purchase with crypto-currency ETH and exclusive NFTs by Kering brands (Gucci, Balenciaga, Bottega Veneta, Alexander McQueen, etc).

ARTIFICIAL INTELLIGENCE

In the world of luxury, where every detail matters, AI has emerged as a transformative force, supporting decision-making processes, customer analysis, engagement strategies and even design within the realm of luxury. The combination of AI and luxury can make decision making more accurate, allow a deep understanding of the desires of the discerning clientele in order to engage it and increase the degree and scope of personalization:

1   Accuracy in decision making and predictive analysis. AI algorithms analyse large data sets, predicting market trends and consumer preferences. Luxury brands leverage this predictive power to make informed decisions about inventory, pricing and product launches.

2   Understanding demanding customers. AI analyses customer behaviour, preferences and purchasing patterns, allowing luxury brands to segment their customers more effectively than in the past. By understanding different customer segments, brands can personalize marketing strategies and offers, improving customer satisfaction and loyalty. AI creates personalized customer experiences by recommending products, curating content and suggesting complementary items. This personal touch resonates deeply with luxury consumers, making them feel appreciated and understood, thus strengthening their emotional connection to the brand.

3   Engage luxury connoisseurs. AI-powered chatbots might provide immediate, personalized assistance to customers, answering questions and guiding them through product selection. Even brands that are rather reluctant to adopt new and very traditional technologies such as watchmaking are experimenting with new features to better interact with people. Audemars Piguet was among the first watch brands to experiment with chatbots in 2020 to visually explain the origins of the brand and its collections. Jaeger-LeCoultre (Richemont group) uses a chatbot to guide customers in choosing a strap or watch. The chatbot is also integrated into the brand's app and involves several steps that lead to an online purchase or search via store locator. In addition to the selection and purchase support function, the bot also offers connection to the brand's Instagram and YouTube channels, and the possibility of obtaining the official product catalogue or contacting the brand directly. Virtual assistants, equipped with natural language processing, ensure smooth interactions, improving customer engagement and satisfaction. Refinement of marketing strategies and creation of engaging contents are allowed by AI algorithms that analyse social media sentiment and trends, offering valuable insights into consumer perceptions.

4   Design assistance. AI-powered design tools generate design suggestions, enhancing creativity and accelerating the design process. These tools, which incorporate machine learning, start from historical designs, inspiring new creations while preserving the brand's aesthetic identity. Verganti, Vendraminelli and Iansiti (2020) suggest that AI facilitates the development

of solutions that are exceptionally tailored to individual users, achieving a high degree of personalization. These AI-driven solutions are not only potentially more creative, but also have the ability to continuously evolve and improve through learning iterations, adapting throughout the entire product lifecycle.

In the world of luxury, AI weaves a narrative of precision, personalization and deep understanding. By augmenting decision-making processes, digging deep into consumer desires, driving engagement and even contributing to the creative process, AI can contribute to the shift from a simple purchase into an unparalleled experience.

NON-FUNGIBLE TOKENS

In the ever-evolving landscape of luxury, NFTs have emerged as transformative entities, reshaping the luxury experience. NFTs, unique digital assets verified through blockchain technology, have transcended the realm of digital art and entertainment, infiltrating the domains of clothes, collectibles and immersive experiences. Artists and designers are creating virtual luxury goods – including artwork – granting buyers ownership rights. These items exist purely in the digital realm, diverging from traditional physical luxury goods. NFTs empower designers, artists and creators by enabling direct interactions with their audience. This trend democratizes art ownership and fosters a sense of community, blurring the traditional boundaries between creators, patrons and collectors.

Couture pieces, represented as NFTs, provide buyers with a truly unique ownership experience.

In 2021, Gucci sold its first NFT with an artistic 4-minute video titled Proof of Sovereignty by Lady PheOnix. Co-directed by former creative director Alessandro Michele, this video depicted the Aria collection by Gucci. The NFT was sold at Christie's for $25,000 and all proceeds from this sale were donated to Unicef USA to give access to anti-Covid vaccines internationally. In this way, Gucci reinforced its brand image through the storytelling in the NFT video and the new product line.

Gucci has certainly been pioneering in exploring the world of NFTs (and the metaverse in general) by joining forces with tech players like Arianee, an open-source protocol for digital certification of luxury goods, and Yuga Labs, the creators of the Bored Ape Yacht Club (BAYC) NFT collection. Gucci's partnership with Arianee resulted in the sale of virtual versions of sneakers that are unique pieces and authenticated using blockchain technology.

Luxury brands are leveraging NFTs to offer limited-edition digital collectibles, ranging from artwork to virtual accessories. These items, authenticated through blockchain, have become status symbols for digital connoisseurs. NFTs can also enable access to exclusive virtual experiences, such as fashion shows and product launches in the metaverse, blurring the lines between the physical and digital realms.

Last but not least, blockchain-backed NFTs enhance supply chain transparency in the luxury industry. By assigning NFTs to individual products, consumers can trace the origins and authenticity of their luxury goods, ensuring they are genuine and ethically sourced. This transparency reinforces trust between consumers and luxury brands, a vital aspect of the modern luxury market. The sensitivity of luxury brands to authenticity and traceability is so strong today that investments in blockchain technology are multiplying. The best example in this regard is that of Aura, a consortium created through the shared commitment and efforts of a pool of brands.

The Aura Blockchain Consortium was established in April 2021 by LVMH, Prada Group and Cartier, part of Richemont. Together with the OTB Group which joined in October 2021 and Mercedes-Benz in May 2022, it aims to develop and promote the use of an easily scalable single global blockchain solution open to all luxury brands worldwide, and to create a shared product verification and tracing system. This initiative derives from the need to provide consumers with additional transparency and traceability on one side, while on the other enhances the collective action to develop innovative solutions. The system was developed in partnership with Microsoft and ConsenSys, and LVMH brands, including Louis Vuitton, Bulgari and Hublot, have taken the lead in rolling it out.

The move follows a rise in interest from environmentally conscious consumers in the resale of luxury goods, which has spurred brands to establish an industry-wide blockchain system to guarantee authenticity. The system allows customers and sellers to access tamper-proof ledgers containing product information, including authenticity, ownership history, maintenance and provenance of materials.

The Aura Blockchain Consortium is governed as a non-profit, with any eventual proceeds reinvested in efforts aimed at enhancing customer relationships as well as brand protection.

GAMES AND GAMIFICATION

In the ever-shifting landscape of luxury, gaming and gamification have emerged as powerful tools to reshape the way brands interact with their clientele. Gamification means integrating game elements, such as points, badges, leaderboards and challenges into the real world, such as websites, applications or business processes. The objective of gamification is to improve user involvement, motivation and participation by exploiting the people's sense of competition, results orientation and rewards. Beyond the realm of entertainment, the principles of gaming have found a place in luxury, transforming customer experiences and engagement.

Gaming and gamification strategies are being employed by luxury brands, in combination with NFTs, enhancing consumer interactions in different ways, such as:

- Gaming collaborations. Luxury brands are increasingly partnering with renowned video games. For example, in 2019 Louis Vuitton (LV) collaborated with Riot Games to design a bespoke trophy case for the League of Legends World Championship. In games, players can purchase digital luxury items for their avatars, blurring the lines between the virtual and physical worlds. Gucci and Balenciaga have introduced digital collections within popular gaming environments, allowing players to express their style and status through meticulously designed virtual apparel and accessories. This fusion of luxury garment and gaming also introduces luxury craftsmanship to new generations. In 2023, Gucci went even further in offering an immersive experience, partnering with the online gaming platform Sand Box on the 'Cosmos' project to make its travelling (first stops in Shanghai and London) archive exhibition of the Maison accessible to all.

- Gamified shopping experiences. Luxury retailers are incorporating gamification elements into their online and in-store experiences. Gamified loyalty programmes, interactive product catalogues and AR try-on experiences create a sense of excitement and engagement for customers. Many brands like Cartier, Burberry and Gucci have introduced an AR shopping tool that allows users to visualize products in their real surroundings, enhancing the online shopping journey.

- Collectibles and limited-edition drops. Gaming-inspired collectibles and limited-edition drops have become highly sought after by luxury enthusiasts. Brands release limited quantities of exclusive items, creating a sense of scarcity and competition akin to gaming collectibles. These drops often leverage gamification mechanics, such as countdown timers. In July 2023, under the creative of Pharrell Williams, LV has included digital collectibles in the offering to break traditional design boundaries.

Shareholding C&Ds

In the past, about 30 years ago, governments and even the financial markets did not consider luxury that interesting; it was seen as a difficult world to approach and grow satisfactorily from an economic and financial point of view. For this reason, historically, there have always been individual entrepreneurs or families investing in luxury, and even when these companies opened their equity, the families maintained the control. Leading players and groups are basically privately owned: LVMH, Hermès, Chanel, Kering, Richemont, Audemars Piguet and Rolex are all in private hands, sometimes through foundations.

Family businesses weave narratives of passion, resilience and dedication; they have played a pivotal role in originating and shaping the narrative of luxury. They act as custodians of the brand heritage, preserving traditional craftsmanship and techniques passed down through generations. At the same time, they foster creativity and innovation while upholding the brand's essence. Prada exemplifies how family visionaries can combine tradition and innovation, while at the same time adopting modern managerial practices.

Family businesses often forge deep emotional connections with consumers. The story of Ferragamo, a family business turned global luxury brand, showcases how personal narratives can resonate with customers, fostering brand loyalty.

Over time, luxury private companies have carved out increasingly profitable niches on a global level, also expanding their range of action in terms of offering. They became world champions that even without a public support have ironically contributed to shape the image and reputation of leading-edge markets like France and Italy. This has made them interesting targets for investors of different types as well as for the financial market. In 2023, LVMH was the most valuable company in Europe with a market capitalization of €420 billion. Hermès positioned itself as the second leading brand in luxury, with a €200 billion market value.

Naturally, investment funds have set their sights on these realities, also finding how to support growth strategies along the supply chain, in retail or in production. In 2017, the CVC investment fund took over 80 per cent of Breitling from the Schneider family (who retained 20 per cent).

US-based private equity firm Apollo Global Management was the 100 per cent owner of Watches of Switzerland Group, the British retail chain publicly listed since 2019. In 2020, Apollo reduced the stake to 28.3 per cent. With 202 boutiques (under different retail brands) in Europe and America, Watches of Switzerland Group achieved 2023 revenues of £1,543 million (87 per cent from luxury watches).

Valentino is no longer in the hands of Valentino Garavani, but has been owned by Mayhoola, the investment fund of the Qatari royal family, since 2012 and Kering Group (which acquired 30 per cent of Valentino in 2023).

In 2018, Investindustrial (a private equity firm founded by Andrea Bonomi focused on buyouts of companies in Europe and North America) and Carlyle (a private equity, alternative asset management and financial services corporation based in the United States) announced the creation of a luxury design group that brings together a collection of complementary brands such as B&B, Flos, Arclinea, Fendi Casa and Lumen. This is actually the second luxury cluster, after Lifestyle Design (Poltrona Frau, Ceccotti, Cassina, Zanotta, Cappellini and Luxury Living), created in 2019 by the family business Haworth – already owner of Poltrona Frau since 2014.

Investments by financial institutions lead to more complex ownership and governance structures with a mixture of interests of different nature. They provide access to financial resources, influence corporate governance practices, enhance transparency and can contribute to the industry's overall stability and growth. The interaction between these financial entities and luxury companies often shapes the industry's strategies, competitiveness and long-term sustainability.

There are quite a few companies that have decided to access the capital market in recent years. Salvatore Ferragamo S.p.A., the Italian luxury goods company, has been publicly traded on the Milan Stock Exchange (Borsa Italiana) since 29 June. The main shareholders are still Ferragamo Finanziaria, which holds 57.78 per cent, and the Ferragamo family which has 10.69 per cent.

More recently, Zegna, like other historic luxury companies, has decided to strengthen itself financially to compete on the global market. On 20 December 2021, the Ermenegildo Zegna Group became a public company listed on the New York Stock Exchange, under the ticker 'ZGN'. The Zegna family retained control, holding 66 percent of the company, which had an initial capitalization of €2.4 billion.

Social C&Ds

The responsibility that falls today on luxury brands and groups is truly great given the image and economic strength they represent. Visibility also corresponds to responsibility. Luxury brands represent only 4 per cent of the diamond supply, but they have truly great value in terms of image, much higher than the economic value. Everything these companies do is evaluated positively or negatively subjectively by the audience. In 2023, the Arnault family (LVMH) decided to support the French food bank charity Restos du Coeur with a donation of €10 million (Richford, 2023). The objective was to help a non-profit organization in its daily activity of supporting people who need food, especially at a time of rising prices. Not everyone expressed favourable opinions about this spontaneous gesture, beyond commercial purposes; there was no shortage of people who strongly criticized it, believing that it would have been preferable not to communicate it in the newspapers.

Increasingly broad ethical, social and philanthropic interests have begun to converge on luxury brands, which have pushed towards the definition of important social responsibility strategies – this topic will be illustrated in Chapters 11 and 12. All luxury brands have put a lot of effort into philanthropy in the past, but this is not enough: they need to be transparent and communicate with the outside world. Companies like LVMH and Kering are setting standards in sustainable luxury, emphasizing the importance of environmental and sustainable practices by using eco-friendly materials, reducing carbon footprints and promoting ethical sourcing. They also experiment with unconventional materials such as lab-grown diamonds and vegan leather, challenging the traditional use of materials like natural diamonds and animal-derived leather in luxury goods.

This convergence merges luxury with environmental consciousness, appealing to socially responsible consumers. Environmental consciousness has indeed spurred significant global initiatives within the luxury world. Projects like Prada's 'Sea Beyond' and Panerai's 'Ocean Conservation' efforts reflect a growing commitment to sustainability and ecological preservation. These initiatives not only address critical environmental issues but also aim to set new standards for responsible luxury, demonstrating how global brands are actively contributing to a more sustainable future.

Social sensitivity in the luxury industry extends beyond environmental concerns, embracing diversity, equity and inclusion (DEI). Notable initiatives include the OTB Foundation's scholarships for talented young women, emphasizing education and opportunity. Additionally, the commitment to craftsmanship and its societal value is highlighted through educational programmes like Brunello Cucinelli's schools of craft and Bottega Veneta's leather school. These efforts showcase the industry's broader commitment to nurturing talent, preserving traditional skills and fostering an inclusive culture.

Takeaways

This chapter illustrates the concept of 'blurred lines' between markets, sectors, generations of consumers, social demands, business objectives, stakeholders, etc, creating convergences and divergences (C&Ds). C&Ds challenge traditional notions of luxury, emphasizing experiences, arts, technology, sustainability and social responsibility. As the luxury market continues to evolve, it's likely that more innovative concepts and categories will emerge, shaping the future of the business.

The convergence of previously separate concepts creates a new hybrid category, which, in turn, diverges from the existing clusters, leading to the emergence of innovative products, services or experiences. This dynamic interplay between convergence and divergence is what drives creativity, innovation and the evolution of various industries.

References and further reading

Aaker, D A (1996) *Building Strong Brands*, Free Press

Bain & Co (2023) Luxury Goods Market Study

Bertoli, R (2023) Ozwald Boateng reimagines Poltrona Frau classics, *Wallpaper**, www.wallpaper.com/design-interiors/ozwald-boateng-poltrona-frau-collaboration (archived athttps://perma.cc/3397-QFTT)

Burberry (nd) Burberry Open Spaces: Thomas's Café, https://row.burberry.com/c/burberry-open-spaces-shenzhen/#thomas-s-cafe (archived at https://perma.cc/DCU4-52AA)

Dalli, D, Colurcio, M and Marcati, A (2019) Making consumer engagement more effective: The impact of personalized benefit appeals on consumers' responses, *Journal of Retailing and Consumer Services*, **49**, pp. 251–62

Dior (nd) Dior Lady Art #6, https://www.dior.com/en_gb/fashion/womens-fashion/dior-lady-art-6 (archived at https://perma.cc/4YVR-NZTF)

Flamholtz, E and Randle, Y (2011) *Corporate Culture: The ultimate strategic asset*, Stanford Business Books

Gem & Jewellery Export Promotion Council (nd) Statistics, https://gjepc.org/statistics.php (archived at https://perma.cc/T9SD-HEWJ)

Gersick, K E, Davis, J A, McCollom Hampton, M and Lansberg, I (1997)
Generation to Generation: Life cycles of the family business, Harvard Business
Press

Hamel, G and Prahalad, C K (1994) *Competing for the Future*, Harvard Business
School Press

Han, Y J, Nunes, J C and Drèze, X (2010) Signaling status with luxury goods: The
role of brand prominence, *Journal of Marketing*, **74** (4), pp. 15–30

Kim, W C and Mauborgne, R (2005) *Blue Ocean Strategy: How to create uncon-
tested market space and make the competition irrelevant*, Harvard Business
Review Press

Kotter, J P and Heskett, J L (1992) *Corporate Culture and Performance*, Free Press

Lojacono, G (2021) The fundamentals of luxury, in G Lojacono and L Ru Yun Pan
(2021) *Resilience of Luxury Companies in Times of Change*, De Gruyter

Lojacono, G (2022) The fine line between localisation and cultural appropriation
in personal luxury goods: An exploratory study, *Strategic Change*, https://doi.
org/10.1002/jsc.2519 (archived at https://perma.cc/73HE-CYUB)

Nadelson, R (2020) The New York store where furniture is theater, *The New York
Times Style Magazine*, www.nytimes.com/2020/10/28/t-magazine/abc-carpet-
and-home-new-york.html (archived at https://perma.cc/QL2R-3YV2)

Palazzo Versace (nd) www.palazzoversace.ae/ (archived at https://perma.cc/
JU72-WBHC)

Richford, R (2023) Bernard Arnault pledges 10 million Euros to French food bank,
WWD, wwd.com/business-news/business-features/bernard-arnault-pledges-
10-million-euros-french-food-bank-lvmh-1235785748/ (archived at https://
perma.cc/28KC-A9SA)

Rosewood Hotels (nd) Asaya Fact Sheet, www.rosewoodhotels.com/en/hong-kong/
media/press-kit/asaya-fact-sheet (archived at https://perma.cc/5JF8-83TS)

Schein, E H (1985) *Organizational Culture and Leadership*, Jossey-Bass

Schroeder, J, Salzer-Mörling, M and Bjerke, B (eds) (2006) *Brand Culture*,
Routledge

Seares, E (2023) Luxury brands are snapping up suppliers: What are the pros and
cons? *Vogue Business*, www.voguebusiness.com/fashion/luxury-brands-are-
snapping-up-suppliers-what-are-the-pros-and-cons (archived at https://perma.
cc/3KTK-SLUE)

Sharma, P (2008) 25 years of family business review: Reflections on the past and
perspectives for the future, *Family Business Review*, **21** (4), pp. 357–65

Smith, E (2023) Watches of Switzerland shares plunge by a quarter after Rolex buys
retailer Bucherer, *CNBC*, www.cnbc.com/2023/08/25/watches-of-switzerland-
shares-plunge-by-a-quarter-after-rolex-buys-retailer-bucherer.html (archived at
https://perma.cc/84RL-4SP5)

Thomas, D (2007) *Deluxe: How luxury lost its luster*, The Penguin Press

Tushman, M L and Anderson, P (1986) Technological discontinuities and organizational environments, *Administrative Science Quarterly*, **31** (3), pp. 439–65

Verganti, R, Vendraminelli, L and Iansiti, M (2020) Innovation and design in the age of artificial intelligence, *Journal of Product Innovation Management*, **37** (3), pp. 212–27

3

Timeless yet timely: The paradox of luxury authenticity

GABRIELLA LOJACONO

The concept of authenticity resonates deeply in contemporary society, extending far beyond the parameters of luxury brands and the business world. It is a concept that captures the zeitgeist, reflecting the prevailing mood and sensibilities of our time. Authenticity today is not just a buzzword, but an ethos that underscores a collective yearning for genuineness in an increasingly complex world.

Before delving into the nuances of authenticity as it pertains to luxury brands – where it is often expressed through an alignment between values and actions and a consistency that bridges past, present and future – it's important to recognize that the quest for authenticity is a broader societal trend. It's seen in the choices individuals make daily, from the food they eat to the clothes they wear and the media they consume. There's an overarching desire for transparency, sustainability and ethical engagement, which are all facets of the authenticity diamond.

This societal shift towards authenticity brings with it a host of challenges and calls for profound reflection. In a landscape saturated with information and options, discerning the authentic from the superficial requires more than a keen eye; it demands a critical mindset. For individuals, this means navigating through a maze of marketing messages and social norms to identify what is truly aligned with their personal values. For businesses, particularly luxury brands, the challenge is to not only claim authenticity, but to embody it in every aspect of their operation – from design and production to marketing and customer engagement.

Authenticity in this context is dynamic; it is not static or monolithic. It is a living principle that evolves with the brand and its audience. A luxury brand's heritage is a treasure trove that informs its present and shapes its future. However, reverence for the past must be balanced with the agility to adapt to contemporary realities and anticipate future trends.

For luxury brands, therefore, authenticity is a delicate dance of truthfulness to one's history while also being responsive to the current cultural and market currents. It's about crafting a narrative that is coherent and resonant, one that honours the brand's legacy while also embracing innovation and change. This balance is critical in a world where consumers are increasingly knowledgeable and expect brands to not just perform, but also to participate in the broader societal discourse with honesty and integrity.

In essence, authenticity is as much about where a brand has been as it is about where it is and where it is going. It is the thread that weaves through the brand's narrative, holding together its identity. As we explore authenticity in the world of luxury brands, we are reminded that this concept is not confined to a corporate strategy but is a reflection of a wider, more fundamental human pursuit for realness in every aspect of life.

This chapter is crafted to highlight the intriguing balance that luxury brands must strike between two seemingly contradictory concepts: timeless and timely. Timeless refers to the enduring, classic and unchanging aspects of luxury brands. It's about the heritage, traditional values and the longstanding quality and craftsmanship that these brands represent. This element of timelessness is what makes a luxury brand iconic and revered across generations. On the other hand, being 'timely' suggests relevance, modernity and the ability to evolve with the times. It's about being current and resonant with contemporary tastes and societal shifts. For luxury brands, this means innovating, adapting to new markets or incorporating modern design elements without losing their core identity.

The chapter is well-grounded in empirical evidence, significantly benefiting from a research lab established at Bocconi University in Milan and funded by Gucci, part of the Kering Group, over a three-year period until 2021. This research lab likely provided a wealth of data and insights into organizational transformation and alignment to values.

In addition to this, the incorporation of structured and insightful interviews with prominent figures in the luxury industry adds a valuable practical perspective to this study. Interviews with Jacopo Venturini, CEO of Maison Valentino, and Leo Rongone, CEO of Bottega Veneta, offer a first-hand account of how top-tier luxury brands operationalize concepts like brand consistency and congruency. These leaders, being at the helm of their respective brands, provided unique insights into the strategic decision-making processes, brand management and the challenges and opportunities of maintaining brand authenticity in a competitive market.

This blend of academic research and real-world executive insights create a comprehensive and multifaceted understanding of authenticity in luxury.

Authenticity unveiled: Bridging societal trends and brand management

Authenticity suggests an allegiance to genuine values, an inclination towards simplicity and minimalism and a resistance to the superfluous. It's the philosophy of 'less is more' and 'quiet luxury' that guides this approach, shunning the ostentatious in favour of the understated. In ready-to-wear (RTW), this trend translates to a preference for classic silhouettes, neutral tones and logo-less patterns. This indicates a departure from conspicuous consumption and a move towards timeless, high-quality pieces.

In the realm of cuisine, this trend manifests in a return to authentic ingredients and preparation methods. Emphasis on local and organic produce, slow cooking and thoughtful plating reflects a deeper appreciation for the cultural and historical roots of various cuisines. The contributions of figures like Alice Waters and Carlo Petrini highlight the significant role that individuals and movements can play in reshaping global attitudes towards food, consumption and lifestyle. Their emphasis on organic food, sustainable agriculture and opposition to genetically modified organisms reflect a profound understanding of food as an integral part of our culture and identity, not just a basic necessity. The focus is not just on taste or nutritional value, but also on how food production affects the environment, how it reflects cultural traditions and how it can be a tool for social and environmental sustainability.

As an American chef and food activist, Alice Waters is a champion of organic, locally-sourced foods. Her approach goes beyond mere ingredients; it's about reconnecting people with the source of their food, fostering a deeper appreciation for the land and the labour that brings food to the table. Her influence in the culinary world has encouraged a shift towards more organic and sustainable practices in the United States and has had ripple effects in the global culinary scene.

Along the same lines, Carlo Petrini, an Italian culinary writer and activist, founded the Slow Food movement as a response to fast-food culture and the diminishing appreciation for local food traditions. The movement advocates for preserving traditional and regional cuisine and promotes farming of plants, seeds and livestock characteristic of the local ecosystem. It's a direct challenge to the industrialization of food, emphasizing the need to maintain biodiversity and ecological harmony.

This shift towards organic, sustainable and locally-focused food consumption is part of a larger trend towards authenticity and mindfulness in various aspects of life. It mirrors changes in other industries, where there is a growing emphasis on sustainability, ethical practices and a return to traditional methods or styles. The slow food movement is seen as a response to fast-paced lifestyles, promoting a deeper appreciation of food's origins, preparation and consumption.

This is a clear example of the concept of 'deceleration' proposed by Eckhart and Husemann in 2008. Deceleration isn't just about reducing speed; it's about enriching experiences, making more conscious choices and reconnecting with ourselves and our environments. It's a response to the recognition that constant acceleration and consumption are unsustainable, both for individual wellbeing and for the environment. As these authors suggest, understanding and embracing this need to decelerate can indeed be a successful strategy for businesses and a healthier approach for individuals and societies. The increasing pace of technological and social change has led to a collective feeling of being 'time-poor', driving a desire to slow down and reconnect with simpler, more authentic experiences. This concept of deceleration manifests in the impressive growth in yoga and wellness retreats that encourage a slowing down and reconnection with the body, or the popularity of digital detoxes, part of the package in some luxury hotels and resorts, where people take breaks from technology for a period of time.

Whether in fashion, beauty or food, this principle stands firm: creativity need not shout to be heard; it needs only to resonate with truth. Consumerism is often equated with opulence, and the current shift towards authenticity as a counter to that is particularly interesting. This trend is seen as a wake-up call to industries and individuals to focus on what is genuinely important.

This broader definition of authenticity aligns well with current trends across various industries and reflects a deeper cultural shift. Let's break down how authenticity encompasses connection with origins, minimalism and genuineness. Authenticity often involves a reverence for the past and a desire to preserve traditional values or methods. This can manifest in various ways, such as fashion brands embracing artisanal techniques or cuisines highlighting traditional recipes and cooking methods. In architecture and design, this might mean preserving historical elements or using materials and designs that are true to a specific time or place. Minimalism, in its essence, is about stripping away the unnecessary, to focus on what is essential. This aligns with authenticity as it involves a rejection of excess and a focus on the genuine value of objects, experiences and relationships. In fashion, this might mean choosing pieces that are timeless and well-made over trendy, disposable items. In lifestyle and interior design, it involves creating spaces that are free of clutter and which reflect a sense of calm and clarity.

Lastly, being genuine is at the heart of authenticity. It's about being true to oneself and one's values, and this is reflected in consumer choices, lifestyle and self-expression. In business, it translates into transparent practices, ethical production methods and products that deliver what they promise.

By incorporating these aspects into the concept of authenticity, we can understand it as not just a trend but as a holistic approach to life and business. This approach values history and tradition, simplicity and sustainability and honest self-expression. It's a response to the complexities and sometimes superficial nature of modern life, offering a more grounded and meaningful way to navigate the world. This redefined authenticity is indeed a powerful and resonant concept in today's society.

The concept of authenticity as a transformative force across industries, including design, architecture, personal development and leadership, is a powerful one. It suggests a comprehensive re-evaluation of values and practices to align more closely with principles of sustainability and genuineness. This trend seems to be a response to a deeper societal need for meaning and responsibility in all aspects of life, from what we wear to what we eat and how we live.

Authenticity, in the landscape of brand heritage and identity, is not a static or immutable state. It is a dynamic process that allows for growth and change while maintaining the core DNA that defines a brand's essence. The concept of evolution in the natural world provides a compelling analogy for the growth and transformation of luxury brands. Just as species evolve through genetic variations and adaptations to survive and thrive, luxury brands evolve through innovation and adaptation while staying true to their core identity.

Much like the unique genetic setup of an organism, each luxury brand has its own 'brand DNA' which comprises its core business, vision and values. This DNA sets the foundation for the brand's identity and its market positioning. In the context of a brand, 'mutations' can be seen as innovative ideas or creative designs that deviate from the norm. These innovations can arise from the reinterpretations of the brand's heritage by creative minds within the company. Just as mutations in nature can lead to new traits, these innovations can lead to new products, marketing strategies and customer experiences. Natural selection mirrors the market's response to a brand's offerings. Brands that align their products and experiences with consumer preferences and habits are more likely to succeed. Those that fail to resonate with consumers may fade away, similar to how traits that are not advantageous may disappear over generations.

As consumer preferences and societal trends change, luxury brands must adapt to maintain relevance and appeal. This might involve embracing sustainability, adopting new technologies or diversifying product lines to meet changing demands.

Over time, luxury brands may diversify their offerings or enter new markets, akin to the process of speciation. This can involve tailoring products to different cultures or launching new lines (or design) to cater to various consumer segments. At the same time, luxury brands often draw inspiration from different cultures and global trends. This exchange of ideas is similar to gene flow, where new influences can integrate with the brand's DNA, leading to a refreshed identity that still respects the brand's heritage.

Random events in the business world, such as economic downturns or shifts in leadership, can lead to unexpected changes in a brand's trajectory, much like genetic drift can alter the genetic diversity of a population.

In essence, for a luxury brand, evolutionary success means achieving a delicate balance between maintaining a consistent brand identity (staying true to the brand's DNA) and adapting to a changing world. Successful brands manage to evolve while retaining a clear lineage back to their original 'species', ensuring that their heritage remains an integral part of their contemporary narrative. This evolution is a sophisticated process involving the interplay of innovation, market forces and global influences. The brands that navigate this process successfully are those that manage to stay true to their core while dynamically adjusting to the new environments they encounter.

The theory of organizational ambidexterity as proposed by O'Reilly and Tushman (2011) is highly relevant to the analogy of evolution and luxury brand transformation. Organizational ambidexterity refers to the ability of a company to simultaneously exploit its current competencies while exploring new opportunities. In the dynamic world of luxury brands, the theory of ambidexterity provides a framework for understanding how companies can navigate the complexities of maintaining a prestigious heritage while also pushing the boundaries of innovation. Exploitation aligns with a brand leveraging its heritage, core values and established competencies – its 'genetic strengths'. This means continuing to refine the craftsmanship, service and quality that have defined the legacy, ensuring that the brand's timeless appeal and reputation are maintained and capitalized upon.

Exploration, on the other hand, corresponds with the mutation and adaptation aspect of evolution. It's about experimenting with new ideas, entering new markets or embracing emerging trends. For luxury brands, exploration is necessary to stay relevant and respond to changing consumer behaviours and market dynamics. It involves innovating product lines, adopting new technologies and sometimes redefining the brand experience, as illustrated in this book. In Valentino's case, exploration also means pushing the boundaries of creativity and finding new ways to define a retail strategy while putting the client at the centre:

> I believe that the term 'couture' is closely connected to creativity, another fundamental pillar of our Maison. Creativity, in my opinion, is a source of energy, a pulsating engine of action that should always be valued and promoted in all its forms across all sectors of the company, even in the seemingly less creative ones. It all starts with the alchemy and union between the work of Creative Director Pierpaolo Piccioli [replaced by Alessandro Michele in March 2024] and the strategic vision of the company. For me, this combination is essential and has been the key to the continuous success of the Maison over the years.

> Since my arrival in June 2020, I've implemented a new business model that puts the client at the centre. My vision is based on client-centricity and people-centricity, a multi-functional mindset that aligns multiple teams to establish a relationship of transparent and spontaneous trust with the client. This lasting bond aims to create an experiential journey within our reality, tapping into every possible touchpoint, both online and offline. Client-centricity embodies what I like to define as an 'experiential client journey' based, above all, on an emotional, empathetic and personalized approach for each client. Its goal is to offer a unique shopping experience that goes beyond a single purchase.

> In light of this, the new store concept launched globally in November 2022 offers a client journey inspired by Italian hospitality through a more intimate retail space. The store team accompanies the clients through the renovated boutiques, creating a ritual-like experience in a new home for the brand, an intimate place to welcome clients. This new perspective also led to an evolution and review of the right balance between wholesale and retail. We are progressively investing in the retail channel while continuing to work with selected wholesale partners who believe in the values of the Maison to develop high-level and mutually enriching projects. We have implemented our omnichannel approach that integrates online and offline experiences,

providing consumers with a direct and authentic relationship also thanks to the internalization of our ecommerce management platform, launched in February 2022. This enables us to maintain a seamless emotional connection with the client, which remains coherent across all touchpoints and throughout the entire purchase process.

In this context, the client adviser is a strategic figure in building, nurturing and managing relationships with the clients. Coordinated by the team manager, today they have a 360° vision and understanding of all product categories and the point of sale so that the client has a single point of reference who can empathically establish a bond and ensure their needs are met.

Jacopo Venturini (personal correspondence)

Just as energy and resources in the natural world are allocated efficiently for both survival and growth, luxury brands must also strategically allocate their resources. Investments must be balanced between maintaining excellence in current offerings (exploitation) and funding innovative projects that drive future growth (exploration).

A key learning from this analogy is that true authenticity embraces evolution, ensuring that the aesthetics, ethics and values that constitute a brand's foundation are not relics of the past, but living elements that breathe and grow within its current expressions.

Consider the term 're-signifying' introduced by Valentino, which poetically encapsulates this very ethos. It speaks to the brand's capacity to operate with relevance in both the present and the future, to be contemporaneous while carrying forward the symbols and values of its heritage into new eras, as explained by the CEO:

We have implemented a process of re-signification of the iconic codes of the brand, with its unmistakable history and heritage of values that it has carried with it since 1960, the year of its birth. In repositioning Valentino in its natural context as a Maison de Couture, we have reinterpreted its heritage by listening to the contemporary world and the needs and expectations of all our customers, harmoniously adapting it to today's reality and also giving space to the new generations.

Jacopo Venturini (personal correspondence)

This concept of 're-signifying' is a delicate dance between honouring the past and inventing the future, a *fil rouge* that is not discarded but rather reinterpreted and woven into the fabric of now.

To be authentic in luxury means to navigate the fine line between tradition and innovation, to kindle the flames of creativity without burning down the pillars of legacy. It is about finding that harmonious balance where innovation complements tradition, and evolution does not mean erasure. Then, authenticity is not the antithesis of change; it is the integrity with which a brand evolves while staying true to its heart.

The authentic thread: Weaving tradition and innovation in luxury

The journey of defining authenticity in luxury begins with a deep understanding of core values. These values are the bedrock upon which luxury brands build their identity. They resonate not just with the brand's heritage, but also appeal to the evolving sensibilities of their discerning audience.

Valentino's roots in haute couture are not just a historical note; they are the lifeblood of its brand identity and the beacon for its future. CEO Jacopo Venturini's vision to strengthen this core value of haute couture goes beyond the meticulous creation of exquisite, one-of-a-kind dresses. He wishes to infuse the philosophy of haute couture, which is all about craftsmanship, beauty and attention to detail, into every facet of the brand, transforming each client interaction into an experience that resonates with the grandeur and elegance of its couture heritage:

> Since I joined the company in June 2020, I have been working to reposition the brand in what I consider its natural place. I believe that Valentino is the most established Italian Maison de Couture. Haute couture goes beyond a dress and the meticulous care that goes into making it; it's about our daily relationships with our clients and lies at the core of our vision and business model. To me, 'Maison' is synonymous with intimacy, home, connections and the exchange of values, while 'couture' represents expertise, craftsmanship and personal relationships between premiers and clients. These two words embody Valentino's values, permeate our company culture and align with our unparalleled heritage and DNA. This translates into our daily approach to people. Hence, our shopping experience reflects the philosophy of couture clienteling, where clients are at the centre of everything we do, experiencing a personal and meticulously tailored relationship that embodies the couture values of our Maison, always with a focus on people-centricity and client-centricity.

According to Venturini, the philosophy of haute couture is a complex ecosystem of values extending far beyond creating couture gowns. It entails ensuring that the same level of care and personalized approach that goes into a couture gown is reflected in the ready-to-wear collections, in the ambiance of Valentino boutiques, the design of their website, the packaging of their products and the service provided by their staff. Incorporating this philosophy into daily life means that every garment, accessory and even client service interactions should reflect the essence of haute couture. It's the notion that each Valentino creation, no matter how small, is part of a larger narrative of luxury and exclusivity. It's about creating a seamless engagement that links every product and service to the core values of haute couture.

Consistency in staying true to these core values is the golden thread that runs through every facet of a luxury brand. Whether it's in product creation, marketing or customer service, this consistent adherence to core values is what builds and maintains trust and loyalty among consumers. It's a testament to the brand's authenticity, a quality that is highly valued by luxury consumers.

Gucci's recent evolution of its value statement in response to new societal trends, coupled with its aim to foster a more creative internal organization, is testament to the dynamic and responsive nature of authenticity in the luxury fashion industry. This strategic manoeuvre signifies an important shift, highlighting Gucci's keen awareness and adaptability to the changing societal landscape, while also showcasing its commitment to maintaining a genuine and relevant brand identity.

In recent years, the societal fabric has increasingly leaned towards values such as inclusivity, sustainability and a conscious approach to consumption. Gucci, recognizing these shifts, has adeptly adjusted its value statement to resonate with these emerging trends. This move goes beyond mere brand positioning; it reflects an acute understanding of Gucci's role in a broader social context. By aligning with these societal changes, Gucci reinforces its relevance and strengthens its position as a forward-thinking and responsible brand, keenly attuned to the zeitgeist.

The transition towards a more creative internal organization is another significant stride for Gucci. In the luxury fashion industry, where innovation and creativity are paramount, Gucci's initiative to nurture a workplace culture that encourages risk-taking, diverse perspectives and unconventional ideas is not just progressive but necessary. This creative thrust is likely to lead to groundbreaking designs and strategies that resonate with contemporary audiences, while still retaining the essence of Gucci's rich heritage.

Balancing respect for its heritage with the necessity to evolve and adapt is a delicate act that Gucci navigates with finesse. In updating its value statement and internal culture, Gucci is not just reinventing itself; it is reasserting its connection to historical roots while embracing changes that are vital for its continued relevance and authenticity in the eyes of modern consumers.

Moreover, in an era where consumers are increasingly informed and value-driven, Gucci's alignment with contemporary societal trends and its push for internal creativity serve to deepen its engagement with its audience. Today's consumers seek brands that offer not only high-quality products but also mirror their values and aspirations. Gucci's approach, therefore, is not merely a business strategy but a way to forge a stronger emotional bond with its customers, fostering a sense of loyalty and connection that transcends the traditional buyer-seller relationship.

In essence, Gucci's evolution of its value statement and its commitment to fostering a creative and responsive internal environment are reflective of a broader narrative in the luxury fashion industry. This narrative is about staying true to one's core values while dynamically adapting to the ever-changing world. It's about understanding that authenticity in luxury is not static but an evolving dialogue between the brand and its societal context. Gucci, in this evolving landscape, stands as a brand that not only understands the importance of this dialogue but also actively engages in it, ensuring its legacy and relevance for years to come.

Moving from the tangible to the intangible, effective storytelling becomes crucial (Chapter 6). Luxury brands like Bottega Veneta have mastered the art of weaving their values, heritage and vision into a captivating narrative. This narrative isn't confined to their products alone; it is reflected consistently across all touchpoints, creating an immersive experience for the consumer.

The growth of luxury brands around their core values is a delicate dance of evolution and adherence. Brands like Bulgari have shown how to grow into new territories (hospitality, leather goods, fragrances) and innovate while staying aligned with their essence. This involves not just introducing new designs or products, but evolving the customer experience and brand narrative to stay relevant and engaging.

The alignment of all stakeholders – employees, shareholders, customers, suppliers – with the brand's values is what makes a luxury brand genuinely authentic. This is evident in the case of Bottega Veneta. It's not just about proclaiming values; it's about living them. When every action, both internal and in the market, reflects these values, the brand is perceived as genuine, transparent and honest. This perception of consistency over time is what builds trust, resulting in customer and employee loyalty.

Choosing focus areas in the alignment, whether internal organization or market presence, is a strategic decision guided by these core values. Marco Bizzarri's tenure at Gucci exemplifies this. First, Bizzarri evolved the value statement in response to new societal trends, coupled with the aim to foster a more creative internal organization. This move went beyond mere brand positioning; it reflected an acute understanding of Gucci's role in a broader social context. By aligning with these societal changes, Gucci reinforced its relevance and strengthened its position as a forward-thinking and responsible brand, keenly attuned to the zeitgeist.

The transition towards a more creative internal organization is another significant stride for Gucci. Gucci's initiative to nurture a workplace culture that encourages risk-taking, diverse perspectives and unconventional ideas was not just progressive, but necessary.

The new value statement, emphasizing innovation, responsibility, diversity, excellence in execution and joy in work, was more than just words; it was a blueprint for transformation. From renovating shops to align these values with the market to appointing a creative director like Alessandro Michele, who embodied these values and spoke the language of the new generations, Gucci showcased a masterclass in alignment. Michele's role was pivotal, balancing respect for Gucci's codes with a modern evolution, perfectly embodying the balance between tradition and innovation that is crucial in luxury branding.

This narrative of authenticity in luxury is not just about the products or the heritage; it's about a brand's ability to stay true to its essence while navigating the changing tides of consumer preferences and market dynamics. It's about crafting a story that is as timeless as the products themselves. This approach to authenticity is what sets apart true luxury brands, turning them into symbols of not just status but of stories, values and a legacy that resonates with their audience.

Key dimensions of authenticity

To operationalize such an intriguing concept, it's essential to explore key dimensions that contribute to a brand's perceived authenticity. Authors such as Fisher-Buttinger and Vallaster (2008) and Burmann and Schallehn (2008, 2010) have made significant contributions in this field, identifying critical factors that foster authenticity. Their research highlights two fundamental dimensions: brand consistency and brand congruency.

Brand consistency

This dimension involves aligning the brand's values, strategy and vision with its brand architecture elements (Chapter 1), such as products, communication and overall brand experience. It's about ensuring that every aspect of the brand reflects and reinforces its core values and strategic vision. For instance, if a brand values sustainability, this should be evident not just in its marketing narratives, but also in its product design, packaging, supply chain practices and corporate policies. This consistency helps in building trust and credibility with consumers, as they see a brand that is true to its word across all touchpoints.

So, brand consistency is an outward-facing aspect. It's about manifesting the brand's core values in a tangible way that resonates with the audience. This external alignment is achieved through a cohesive narrative that is woven into every product, communicated in every marketing message and experienced in every retail interaction. It's how the brand presents itself to the world, ensuring that every touchpoint – from the design of a handbag to the ambiance of a boutique – speaks the same language of luxury, quality and exclusivity.

Bottega Veneta provides some interesting examples of this kind of alignment (Lojacono, 2023). For instance, authenticity within the world of collaborations isn't simply about shared aesthetics or interests; it extends to a profound alignment in philosophy and purpose. A prime example of this synergistic partnership is the collaboration between Matthieu Blazy and the visionary architect Gaetano Pesce for the September 2022 fashion show, showcasing the Spring/Summer 2023 collection. Their meeting was serendipitous, sparking a conversation about genuineness and the celebration of individuality – themes that deeply resonate with both creators. Pesce's creation of uniquely coloured resin chairs, each distinct from the next, culminated in an installation that was more than a backdrop for the fashion show; it was a powerful statement on diversity. The sentiment was so potently expressed that Pesce's impromptu inscription on the floor – 'This is a tribute to diversity' – captured media attention and underscored the event's homage to uniqueness.

Bottega Veneta, ever the custodian of enduring value, has taken a bold step to embody this principle tangibly. In an age where transience often prevails, Bottega Veneta's commitment to timelessness has led to the creation of the 'Certificate of Craft'. This lifetime warranty programme transcends mere customer service; it is a pledge of perpetual craftsmanship. Upon purchasing a bag, the client is endowed with more than just an accessory; they receive the assurance of longevity – a guarantee that, should their cherished item suffer wear, it can be restored to its former glory, even if that means a meticulous deconstruction and rebuilding by the artisans responsible for its original creation. During the restoration process, the client's connection to the brand is maintained through the provision of a courtesy bag, ensuring that the relationship between customer and brand is never interrupted.

This programme is a testament to Bottega Veneta's vision of luxury as an enduring presence in one's life, crafting pieces that are not just possessions, but lifelong companions.

Brand congruency

This dimension focuses on the internal alignment between a company's corporate values and its organization, particularly how these values are prioritized over short-term market trends in decision-making processes. It's about the coherence between what a brand professes and how it operates internally. This includes how a company treats its employees, its approach to corporate governance and its response to social issues.

Again, let's consider Bottega Veneta's artisanal mastery as not simply a matter of skill; it is a combination woven from passion, dedication and an innate understanding of the craft. The art of creating the perfect 'intrecciato' – the brand's signature weave – is not something every artisan possesses from the outset. To cultivate this unique skill set, Bottega Veneta has established the Alta Scuola di Pelletteria, affectionately known within the company as the Academia. This institution is a homage to one of the brand's foundational pillars: 'Labor et ingenium'.

The question then arises: how can this rich creative and productive ethos be translated from the ateliers to the boutiques, and ultimately, to the customers? It requires more than just passion and commitment. As Bottega Veneta believes, the essence of the brand must be carried forth by those who not only understand its values, but can also communicate them with a personal touch. Bottega place immense value on internal training, to impart the essence of the brand to sales associates. It's about sharing those pivotal messages that will ignite customers' imaginations, in the same way the founders of the company, Taddei and Zengiaro, envisioned.

Brand congruency ensures that a company doesn't just pay lip service to its values but lives them in its daily operations. It's a commitment to holding these values even when they might conflict with immediate market opportunities or trends.

Valentino, for instance, is putting a lot of effort into aligning its internal organization, from the realization process to sales staff, to achieve this goal:

> I would like to mention La Bottega dell'Arte, a training programme within the Maison in Rome aimed at preparing young talents to cover complex artisan roles. We are also taking care of our client advisers, who are becoming true ambassadors of the brand. From a broader perspective, our strategy is hinged around putting humans at the centre of everything. It is precisely through colleague-centricity that we value our employees, as a person and as a professional, so we train them and involve them in different steps of their path and growth to increase their sense of belonging and acquire new skills, always with a client-oriented perspective. This approach translates into a colleague-centric culture that supports client-centricity and creates a working and experiential environment of respect, inclusiveness and stimulation following the values that distinguish us.
>
> Jacopo Venturini (personal correspondence)

As we see, brand congruency focuses on the internal dynamics within the organization. It's about ensuring that the company's core values are not just slogans but are lived experiences within the corporate culture. This internal alignment targets every level of the organization, from the artisans in the ateliers to the executives in the boardroom. It's about creating a work environment where the brand's ethos is reflected in every decision, action and interaction among employees.

Both dimensions, congruency and consistency, are crucial in building and maintaining a brand's authenticity. In essence, while brand consistency builds the bridge between the brand and its audience, brand congruency fortifies the foundation upon which the brand is built. Both are crucial for a luxury brand's success – consistency ensures that the brand resonates with its audience, while congruency ensures that the brand remains true to its vision and values from the inside out.

This operationalization of authenticity thus serves as a guiding framework for brands aiming to establish a genuine, trustworthy and sustainable presence in their respective markets. Authenticity, in this sense, goes beyond just marketing or product design; it's embedded in the very fabric of the organization and is reflected in every decision and action. A brand that successfully integrates both brand consistency and congruency not only earns the trust and loyalty of its customers, but also sets a standard for ethical and responsible business practices.

Tradition as a source of authenticity

Exploring the concept of tradition as a source of authenticity in the luxury sector, it's vital to articulate how traditional practices, standards and values contribute to a brand's authentic identity. The work of Beverland (2006) and Beverland and Luxton (2005) is particularly instructive in this context, as they identify six key attributes of authenticity that are deeply rooted in tradition. Let's delve into each of these attributes and how they relate to tradition as a source of authenticity:

1 **Heritage:** Heritage is a cornerstone of authenticity in luxury brands. It involves a rich backstory and a legacy of craftsmanship and innovation. For a brand, its heritage is not just its history but a narrative that adds depth and character to its products and operations. Authenticity stems from how well a brand preserves and honours its heritage while also adapting to contemporary contexts.

2 **Stylistic consistency:** This attribute refers to maintaining a consistent aesthetic and design philosophy over time. Luxury brands often have a distinct style that becomes synonymous with their identity. This stylistic consistency, rooted in tradition, assures customers of a certain aesthetic experience, contributing to the brand's authenticity.

3 **Quality commitment:** A relentless commitment to quality, often derived from traditional methods and standards, is a hallmark of authentic luxury brands. This commitment might manifest in the meticulous selection of materials, artisanal production techniques or rigorous quality control processes, all of which are steeped in tradition.

4 **Relationship to place:** Many luxury brands are inextricably linked to a specific location or region, which influences their identity and operations. This relationship could be due to the origin of materials, the brand's founding location or cultural influences integral to the brand's products. The authenticity here is tied to the brand's connection and loyalty to its place of origin.

5 **Method of production:** Traditional methods of production, especially when they involve craftsmanship and artisanal skills passed down through generations, add a layer of authenticity. These methods often embody a brand's commitment to preserving skills and techniques that have historical and cultural significance.

6 **Downplaying commercial motives:** While commercial success is essential, authentic luxury brands often downplay overt commercialism in favour of emphasizing artistry, craftsmanship and customer experience (as

illustrated in Chapters 4–6). This approach aligns with traditional values where the focus was more on the creation of exquisite items rather than mass production.

In summary, tradition serves as a vital source of authenticity for luxury brands by anchoring them in a set of enduring values and practices. These six attributes – heritage, stylistic consistency, quality commitment, relationship to place, method of production and downplaying commercial motives – offer a framework for understanding how tradition informs and reinforces a brand's authentic identity. By adhering to these principles, luxury brands can maintain their unique position in the market, rooted in a rich tapestry of history and tradition.

Keeping the heritage alive: the role of archives

Historical and iconic products are essential to a luxury brand's DNA. They serve as a 'de-risking' strategy, especially in turbulent economic times, acting as a perennial substitute for seasonal items. These timeless pieces offer a source of stability and prosperity for the brand, becoming a platform for continuous inspiration. The archive is where these pieces, along with sketches and other creative artefacts, are meticulously preserved.

The function of an archive transcends mere storage; it is an integral part of the brand's creative and strategic foundation. By maintaining these archives, luxury brands can protect and honour their history and tradition, providing a rich source of inspiration for future collections and a strong connection to their past, which in turn reinforces the brand's authenticity and legacy.

Creative individuals within the brand, such as designers and product developers, often turn to the archive for inspiration. Here, they can engage with the brand's aesthetic vocabulary and grammar, which is critical for creating designs that are coherent with the brand's style and make it recognizable over time. By valorizing the archive, a brand ensures that its heritage remains a living part of its contemporary narrative and a wellspring of inspiration for new creations.

Under the leadership of Marco Bizzarri, Gucci embarked on a significant reorganization of its archive, by categorizing it around key iconic motifs flowers, distinctive hardware such as the lion head or horsebit, the emblematic web pattern in red and green, signature materials like leather and bamboo and the double G logo. In doing so, Gucci distilled the essence of its brand into recognizable symbols that have defined its aesthetic over the years. This approach allowed for a clearer narrative thread that connected past and present and it offered a rich source of inspiration for new designs that would resonate with contemporary audiences while remaining unmistakably Gucci.

The reimagined Gucci Museum in Florence followed this thematic categorization, moving away from a designer-centric display to one that highlighted the brand's iconic elements. This shift reflects a deeper understanding of how historical and cultural assets can be leveraged to tell a cohesive story – one that honours the brand's legacy while also demonstrating its dynamism and adaptability.

This strategic focus on iconic signs rather than individual designers emphasizes the continuity of Gucci's aesthetic language and allows for a more fluid interplay between different eras and creative visions. It is a celebration of the enduring symbols that have become synonymous with the Gucci name, ensuring that they continue to inform and inspire the brand's future trajectory.

The reorganization of the archive and the museum speaks to a broader strategy of maintaining a strong connection to the brand's roots while also encouraging innovation and evolution. By doing so, Gucci, under Bizzarri's guidance, illustrates the power of understanding and utilizing one's heritage to navigate the future – a principle that is central to the brand's continued relevance and success in the luxury industry.

Archives are more than just a nod to the past; they are a strategic asset. They serve as a powerful communication tool for the brand, supporting initiatives like exhibitions, books, reference materials and advertising campaigns. They also offer a space for educational initiatives for staff, store managers and executives, and can even act as a showcase for high-profile clients.

The practice of maintaining an extensive archive was pioneered by Yves Saint Laurent, who recognized the importance of preserving his couture pieces from the very beginning. Today, the Fondation Pierre Bergé – Yves Saint Laurent jealously guards an extensive collection that is currently showcased in the YSL Museum in Paris.

Christian Dior's archive, which began when Mr Arnault acquired the company, contains an impressive array of garments, accessories, sketches and press releases that date back to the brand's inception. The strategic inauguration of a new archive in 2017, on the occasion of Dior's 70th anniversary, was a move to sustain and celebrate the Maison's legacy with the level of care that haute couture demands.

The storied halls of Valentino's archive in Piazza Mignanelli, Rome, houses Mr Valentino Garavani's original sketches, alongside vintage dresses that preserve and transmit the brand's unique colours and techniques. This careful preservation ensures that the brand's history and tradition are not only maintained in excellent condition, but are also accessible for ongoing design projects and inspiration.

In the Valentino archive lies a treasure trove of the fashion house's illustrious past. Here, visitors can immerse themselves in the splendour of iconic pieces that not only defined moments in fashion history, but also underscored the brand's enduring legacy. Among these is the reproduction of the famous dress worn by Julia Roberts at the 2001 Academy Awards, a pivotal moment that signified more than just a Hollywood triumph. This second identical dress was made to commemorate this important moment, and it has been created to be kept forever among the great creations of the Maison. When Roberts ascended the stage to accept her Oscar for Best Actress for her role in *Erin Brockovich*, she did so in a vintage Valentino gown from the haute couture collection of 1992. This choice marked the inception of a new trend – the resurgence and appreciation of archive fashion.

The Valentino dress, with its timeless elegance, demonstrated that true style transcends the seasonal whims of fashion. It was a declaration of the enduring allure of Valentino's creations and a nod to the craftsmanship and vision that had sustained the house for decades. The archive, by preserving such pieces, serves as a beacon that illuminates the path from the past to the present, guiding the future of fashion.

Further enriching the narrative of the Valentino archive are pieces from the seminal White Collection of 1968, worn also by Marisa Berenson. This collection, a bold departure from the vibrant colours typical of the era, introduced a revolutionary concept – a logo crafted from the founder's initials. This elegant 'V' logo, a symbol that has since become emblematic of the Valentino brand, was reimagined by Pierpaolo Piccioli, blending the heritage with contemporary sensibility.

The archive thus stands as a confirmation of Valentino's profound impact on the world of fashion. It's a place where history is palpable, where the fabrics tell tales of red carpets and revolutions, where each stitch and silhouette speaks to a commitment to beauty that has stood the test of time. It's a repository not only of garments but of the brand's very soul – a soul that continues to inspire and define the essence of luxury and style.

Takeaways

Authenticity, as we have seen, is not a static quality but a dynamic interplay of values, actions and perceptions, both within a brand and in its engagement with the world.

At the heart of authenticity lies the alignment of a brand's core values with its actions. This alignment is not just about maintaining an image; it's about embedding these values deeply within the organization's culture and operations. Brands like Bottega Veneta, Gucci and Valentino have shown that authenticity involves a constant dialogue between maintaining a rich heritage and evolving with contemporary trends. It's about being true to one's legacy while embracing innovation and change.

The evolution of luxury brands, much like the evolution of species, involves adaptation and responsiveness to the environment. Just as species evolve through genetic variations and natural selection, brands evolve through innovation, market response and consumer engagement. This evolution is a delicate balance between leveraging one's heritage (exploitation) and exploring new opportunities (exploration). The success of a brand, akin to the survival of a species, depends on how well it navigates this balance, which is crucial for their continued relevance and success.

Additionally, the role of archives in luxury brands like Valentino and Dior underscores the importance of heritage as a source of inspiration and identity. These archives are not mere collections of past achievements; they are wellsprings of creativity and storytelling, linking the past to the present and future.

Lastly, the journey of authenticity is not solely the brand's; it involves the customer too. The transformation of core values into customer experiences, as seen in Bottega Veneta's approach to customer service and product longevity, is a testament to the brand's commitment to living its values.

In conclusion, authenticity in luxury brands is a multifaceted and evolving concept. It is about staying true to one's heritage while innovatively engaging with the present and future. It is about internal consistency and external resonance. Above all, it is about understanding that in the world of luxury, authenticity is not just a quality – it's a narrative that weaves through the very heart of a brand's identity.

References and further reading

Beverland, M B (2005a) Crafting brand authenticity: The case of luxury wines, *Journal of Management Studies*, **42**, pp. 1003–29

Beverland, M B (2005b) Brand management and the challenge of authenticity, *Journal of Product and Brand Management*, **14**, pp. 460–61

Beverland, M B (2006) The 'real thing': Branding authenticity in the luxury wine trade, *Journal of Business Research*, **59**, pp. 251–58

Beverland, M B (2009) *Building brand authenticity – 7 habits of iconic brands*, Palgrave Macmillan, New York

Beverland, M B and Luxton, S (2005) The projection of authenticity: Managing integrated marketing communications through strategic decoupling, *Journal of Advertising*, **34**, pp. 103–16

Burmann, C and Schallehn, M (2008) *Die Bedeutung der Marken-Authentizitaät für die Marken-Profilierung*, University of Bremen, Bremen

Burmann, C and Schallehn, M (2010) *Konzeptualisierung von Marken-Authentizität*, LiM, Bremen

Castellucci, F, Cillo, P, Lojacono, G and Rubera, G (2021) Gucci: An Industry – Changing Cultural Transformation, Case Study, Università Bocconi

Eckhart, G M and Husemann, K C (2018) The growing business of helping customers slow down, *Harvard Business Review*, https://hbr.org/2018/12/the-growing-business-of-helping-customers-slow-down (archived at https://perma.cc/C5M2-L5F6)

Eggers, F, O'Dwyer, M, Kraus, S, Vallaster, C and ldenber, S (2013) The impact of brand authenticity on brand trust and SME growth: A CEO perspective, *Journal of World Business*, **48**, pp. 340–48

Fisher-Buttinger, C and Vallaster, C (2008) *Connective Branding: Building brand equity in a demanding world*, John Wiley & Sons, London

Lojac+ono, G (2023) Authenticity in luxury to generate uniqueness, trust and loyalty, *Economics & Management*, **3**, pp. 34–37, https://emplus.egeaonline.it/en/61/archivio-rivista/rivista/3459151/articolo/3459197 (archived at https://perma.cc/JLL9-KPQT)

O'Reilly, C and Tushman, M (2011) Organizational ambidexterity in action: How managers explore and exploit, *California Management Review*, **53**, pp. 5–22, https://doi.org/10.1525/cmr.2011.53.4.5 (archived at https://perma.cc/5P22-56AC)

Yohn, D L (2017) Why your company culture should match your brand, *Harvard Business Review*, https://hbr.org/2017/06/why-your-company-culture-should-match-your-brand (archived at https://perma.cc/6GGN-4Q5Z)

4

Luxury, arts and culture: How luxury Maisons have become prominent cultural actors

CYRILLE VIGNERON

Luxury, as we know it, started to grow and expand in the 1970s and has since become a major economic sector. In the 70s and 80s, there was almost no connection between the art world and luxury. In countries like France, UK or Italy, culture was considered part of the national identity, a serious topic to defend and protect. During the negotiations about free trade, France argued that a 'cultural exception' could justify government subsidies to cinema, music, operas and more. Culture should not be seen as a commodity. Culture was definitely a public affair, too important to be left in private hands or left unprotected from the market law of supply and demand.

In 1984, Cartier challenged this point of view and became a pioneer with its Fondation pour l'art contemporain. Alain Perrin, its president at the time and a contemporary art lover, thought that the public sector was supporting art, but that the choices remained very conservative. Too little was done for living artists, whose work remained unknown and misunderstood. This foundation was a breakthrough, opening the way to private foundations dedicated to art. It played a key role to show that the private sector could be a positive contributor in this landscape. In the beginning, many remained sceptical, fearing that private interests might corrupt the art, and dilute culture into mercantilism. They were proven wrong. The foundation became a credible actor, and was followed by several important ones.

Fifty years later, the picture is entirely different.

European states continue to subsidize art and culture, but have limited budgets. As a consequence, they have not only welcomed private initiatives but have also become more open to cooperation between public and private. The collaboration between the Fondation Cartier pour l'art contemporain and the Milan Triennale is the best example of cooperation between private and public, across national borders.

In the meantime, luxury groups have also been more and more recognized as important cultural actors.

This chapter will analyse the links between luxury, art and culture, and their growing importance in expanding brand equity.

Luxury Maisons as cultural actors

In Europe, the traditional point of view was to make a distinction between major arts, highly valued, and minor ones or applied arts, less appreciated. Artists were valued higher than designers or artisans. Seven major arts, traditionally recognized in Western culture, are architecture, sculpture, painting, music, literature (including poetry and prose), theatre (performing arts) and cinema (film). These arts have been considered the highest forms of creative expression and have played significant roles in cultural and artistic developments throughout history. Minor or applied arts encompass crafts, floral arrangements, songs, pottery, culinary arts and many others. Consequently, artists received higher recognition compared to designers or artisans, reflecting a hierarchical valuation of creative work that distinguished between 'fine' arts and those considered more functional or practical.

In Japan, the distinction between major and minor arts is not as pronounced. Practices like Ikebana (floral arrangement) and the tea ceremony are regarded as art forms. This perspective reflects a broader appreciation for various expressions of beauty and skill, integrating them seamlessly into cultural and artistic traditions.

Architecture itself was seen as functional, and not considered a real art by itself. This has changed entirely. Famous architects are praised as major artists.

Countries were proud of their museums like the Louvre, the British Museum, the Rijksmuseum; proud of music institutions like the Royal Ballet, the Opera de Paris, La Scala in Milan, the Berlin Philharmonic orchestra, amongst others. They were not proud of luxury brands and their savoir-faire, which was even considered insignificant and frivolous.

Over time, applied arts became more and more recognized as an important part of national cultural heritages. The major Maisons have been gradually approached by public museums to stage their patrimony, attracting large audiences

A Dior exhibition at the Musée des Arts Décoratifs in Paris was viewed by more than 700,000 visitors. The Cartier exhibition Beyond Boundaries in Beijing received 600,000 visitors from all age groups. Watchmaking, jewellery, couture and even high gastronomy have become important cultural assets. Such exhibitions now contribute to a country's global image.

The Maisons with long traditions have also become part of art history. Cartier, Dior or Chanel play a role in the French applied arts, in the same way impressionist painters have contributed to France's art patrimony.

Prominent museums around the world produce exhibitions staging these Maisons, like Cartier in the Metropolitan Museum in New York or the Musée des Arts Décoratifs in Paris, Christian Dior in the MAD or Chanel in the Victoria & Albert museum in London.

Not all Maisons have a past rich enough to produce a major exhibition in such museums. The ability to do it defines the cultural stature of a Maison. Major exhibitions contribute to build solid brand equity. The capacity to host or be featured in a significant exhibition is a testament to a Maison's cultural significance and depth. These exhibitions are not merely displays; they are powerful narratives that weave the Maison's heritage, craftsmanship and artistic contributions. They play a crucial role in enhancing brand equity, solidifying the Maison's legacy and affirming its place within both the realms of high culture and the competitive luxury market.

The cultural world has evolved in its appreciation of savoir-faire

The general public shows a strong interest in seeing artisans at work, what they do and how they do it. They not only appreciate a watch, a dress or a handbag because it is beautiful, but because of all the skills it requires. It also applies to art, asking artists questions about their intentions as well as techniques.

The perception gap is closing between the seven major classic arts and other art forms, like cartoons, songs, cuisine, calligraphy, floral art or even tea ceremonies. Fashion shows have become art forms in themselves. Artisans are equally recognized as artists. Events like the French 'journées du patrimoine' where Maisons open their doors to visitors are increasingly popular.

The HomoFaber exhibition which takes place every other year illustrates this deep trend to celebrate what is now called *les métiers d'art*. In France the 'Maîtres d'art' are decorated by the minister of culture, similarly to the 'chevaliers des arts et lettres'. In a country which has always valued art and intellect more than manual work, this shows an important evolution of values and mindsets.

In this revision of values, creative designers have become stars. In particular, fashion houses rely on the reputation and style of their designer and artistic director. Karl Lagerfeld did a lot to grow Chanel's reputation. The strength of the French fashion sector has been to attract and integrate designers from all countries. Karl Lagerfeld, Azzedine Alaia, Phoebe Philo, Gabriela Hearst, Marc Jacobs, Alexander Wang and other designers from all origins can express their talent, be recognized and become stars.

At the beginning of the 20th century, Paris became the city where many artists gathered to find inspiration and be recognized. Today Paris plays the same role for designers.

In the mid 1990s, luxury was still insignificant on the public agenda. Other industries like nuclear energy, automotive, aeronautics and trains were subjects of pride and part of the economic-diplomacy agenda. Luxury did not really matter. Gradually, luxury has become a constituent of a country's image and reputation. Tourists' interest in France or Italy is now equally linked to beaches, historical cities and fashion streets. Paris and Milan are fashion capitals, and the Fashion Weeks are a constant magnet for global citizens.

Luxury and fashion in general is strongly associated with France and Italy, like watchmaking with Switzerland. A brand's country of origin is equally as important as the 'Made In' designation. 'Swiss-made' is a key element of branding for watches. Global brands with a luxury watch offering have them made in Switzerland, even if they were not 'born' there, like Cartier, Bulgari or Hermès. Some sectors have an equal reputation in multiple countries, like fashion in France and Italy. Jewellery is reputed in France, Italy and Switzerland.

Outside of Europe, the USA and Japan also have a strong tradition and reputation for jewellery, supported by famous brands like Tiffany or Harry Winston in the USA, and Mikimoto in Japan.

This recognized and perceived value is particularly important to justify prices. A watch manufactured in the Swiss Jura can be priced higher than the same one if made in France just a few kilometres away. Sparkling wine from Champagne can be priced higher than Franciacorta, even for similar quality.

The continuous interplay between culture and luxury

The interaction between a country's culture and luxury brands plays both ways. The brand's prestige contributes to the country's image and reputation, and the country's reputation for savoir-faire is a strong intangible asset for the brand. This is why countries, regions, sectors and brands commonly defend their heritage, savoir-faire and global appeal.

Through architecture and design, luxury is an important actor of city urbanism. In major cosmopolitan cities, luxury Maisons play an important role in shaping certain streets and avenues, which grow in prestige accordingly.

Milan via Montenapoleone, London New Bond Street, Paris Place Vendôme or Avenue Montaigne are luxury streets by essence. The fast development of luxury Maisons has pushed these Maisons to expand their footprint, and to build and decorate boutiques which are increasingly large and sophisticated. Working with world-famous architects, they contribute to improve the architectural interest of these cities.

In the cities of the world which do not have classified districts, brands construct from scratch entire buildings with spectacular facades, in collaboration with major names like Frank Gehry, Christian de Portzemparc, Jun Aoki and Sanaa, to name a few. In Seoul's Cheongdam road or Tokyo's Omotesando for instance, the luxury stores are part of the city archi-tours.

For about 30 years, the luxury Maisons tried to build a worldwide consistent image, by replicating the same store concept everywhere. As a consequence, luxury streets all tended to look the same. The recent trend is to better integrate each store in to its specific city environment. The Cartier Montenapoleone boutique is very Milanese and very different from the Rue de la Paix flagship. The Hermès Maison in New York Madison 706 is very different from the Hermès in Meatpackers, and in other cities in the world.

With this new trend, luxury Maisons contribute even more to enrich the diversity of the main cities of the world, becoming part of their urban style.

Another trend is to increase the size of the luxury flagship stores, and extend their functions to hospitality, cafés, restaurant, apartments or hotel suites where guests can stay. Some also include culture and art galleries. Luxury flagships transcend their initial mission to be a selling space, extending their cultural presence to art, culture and hospitality spaces. The recent Dior flagship Avenue Montaigne in Paris or Tiffany Landmark in New York illustrate this trend, with properties exceeding 10,000 square metres.

The luxury sector is thus not only an important part of a country's image, but has also become a significant contributor to its urbanism, architecture and style.

Luxury Maisons are closely linked to the world of art and cinema. Through their ambassador programmes and advertising campaigns featuring A-list celebrities, luxury Maisons have close ties with the cinema and entertainment business.

Red carpets and fashion shows are glamorous moments to style these celebrities with the fashion house's dresses and high jewellery parures. Product launches or boutique openings give the occasion to host spectacular parties with international pop stars entertaining the privileged guests.

A-class luxury Maisons contribute to the celebrities' image and stature, and these Maisons benefit in return from their influence on their followers. For luxury clients, luxury Maisons also become gateways to the world of celebrity.

Local ambassador programme also play an important role in connecting global Maisons to local clienteles, who expect these Maisons to be incarnated in someone familiar and relatable.

It is interesting to note that Korean K-pop companies actively encourage their growing stars such as BlackPink and BTS to become brand ambassadors, as part of their internationalization strategy.

These partnerships between brands and celebrities can turn bitter when one party or the other faces criticism, as happened for Dior with John Galliano and others recently. Brands as well as celebrities include deal-breaker clauses to protect their own image. Reputation is a critical currency for both. Partnerships help to grow this reputation, but can become a double-edged sword.

Some brands work directly with artists to design collections, which is a form of co-branding. LV was a pioneer in this respect, cooperating with Murakami Takashi and recently with Kusama Yayoi. However, this has not turned into a global trend, and some Maisons, including Chanel, Hermès and Cartier, refuse to use artists for their creations.

Another collaboration with artists is related to the store's design. Luxury Maisons work with famous architects and decorators. They often include artworks inside the boutique, to express the brand's modernity and link with art.

Luxury Maisons increasingly support art and culture through sponsorship, collaborations or private foundations (see Figure 4.1).

FIGURE 4.1 Strategic focus on arts and culture

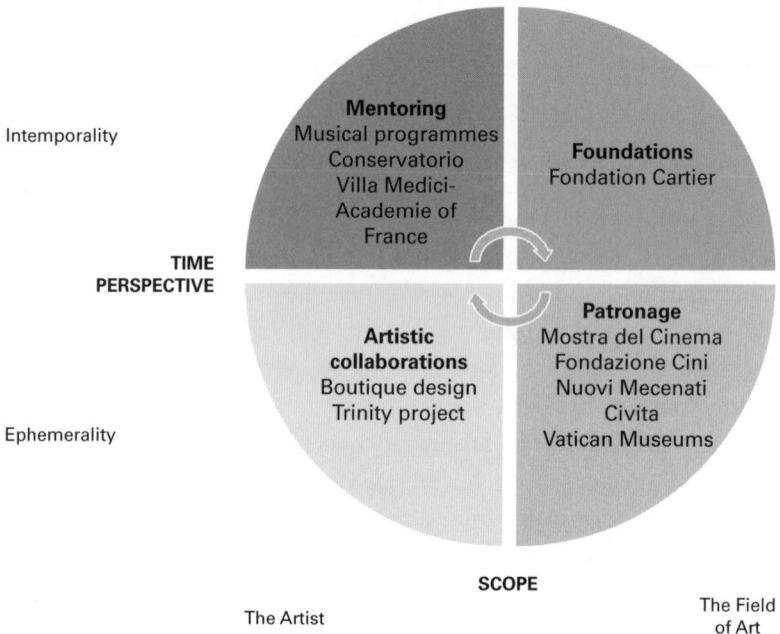

To map these involvements, the first axis to consider is time: ephemeral actions vs long-term commitments. Physical foundations, like Fondation Cartier pour l'art contemporain, Fondation Louis Vuitton, Fondation Pinault and Fondation Prada, to name a few, anchor commitments in the long term.

The second axis concerns the relationship with specific artists, or support for the field of art in general.

Combining these two axes identifies four quadrants, from ephemeral collaborations with individual artists to long-term commitments to the field of art. First-class Maisons increasingly make long-term commitments to art and culture. Patronizing the art and artists becomes a constituent of the luxury world.

Art is a window on the world. Working with artists is both a way to get inspiration and to connect with a different audience and public, including students and schools.

Some of these cultural actions can be directly linked to one general brand message, like the Rolex programme to endorse artists in the same way it endorses athletes, to celebrate talent and success.

Cartier has been a pioneer, creating the Fondation pour l'art contemporain in 1984, 40 years ago. Cartier expanded its involvement in recent years, through the Resonance programme to support young music interpreters.

Through its Foundation and other programmes, Cartier aims to support original creation and artists insufficiently recognized by the art business.

Recent trends include sponsoring new art forms, like Melanie Laurent's contemporary opera 'Eugenie's Tears' including VR scenes, or like Es Devlin's 'Come home again' installation in the garden of the Tate Modern in London. Artists who have worked with the Fondation also contribute to the scenography of jewellery exhibitions, including Hiroshi Sugimoto and Liz Diller.

As cinema and music become powerful business machines, luxury increasingly finds room to be part of it. Gabrielle Chanel has been featured in several movies; Chanel contributed to global success *Barbie*, being part of it beyond product placement; and Yves Saint Laurent has started to co-produce films.

Takeaways

This chapter outlines the evolving relationship between luxury, art and culture from the 1970s to contemporary times, highlighting the shift from a public to a more inclusive private-public partnership in promoting arts. Initially, the luxury and art worlds were separate, with cultural pursuits a source of national pride and heavily subsidized by governments, emphasizing the non-commercial aspect of culture. Cartier's establishment of Fondation pour l'art contemporain in 1984 marked a pivotal move towards engaging the private sector in art patronage, challenging the notion that culture should remain a public affair.

Over decades, luxury brands like Chanel, Dior and others have become recognized as cultural actors, collaborating with museums and artists, thereby contributing to their brand equity and cultural heritage. This reflects a broader acceptance of the luxury sector's role in cultural and urban development, showcasing a blend of commerce, art and public engagement.

Art and culture are key components of contemporary luxury. Prominent luxury Maisons are part of countries' cultural heritage through their savoir-faire. Their events, such as Fashion Weeks, are part of the cultural agenda.

They contribute to making city centres attractive in building beautiful boutiques which increasingly transcend their mission as a selling space.

By supporting more and more art creations in events, shows and films and through their long-term commitments to private foundations, they have become prominent cultural actors.

5

Experience-led luxury strategies: How brands are reshaping customer activation and engagement

GABRIELLA LOJACONO

This is the story of Audrey, a very important customer (VIC), painting a vivid picture of her experiences in the world of luxury retail and hospitality.

The missed birthday gift. Audrey decides to indulge in a luxury bag for her milestone birthday. She vividly recalls her excitement, discussing her desire with a warm, attentive client adviser who assures her of a place on the coveted waiting list. Yet, as months morph into a year, her anticipation wanes into disappointment. The associate's departure leaves Audrey's request forgotten, a symbol of her fading dream. Despite being promised by the client adviser that she would be put on the waiting list, the year passes with no follow-up. Visiting the boutique, she endures a long wait and unhelpful staff, leaving her gift-less and frustrated.

Undeterred, Audrey visits the boutique, her heart racing with hope. She finds herself amidst a sea of patrons, the minutes stretching into hours as she waits, unnoticed. Inside, the bustling staff glide past her with unseeing eyes, their hurried whispers echoing her growing sense of neglect. The shoe department, a suggested haven, offers no respite, only a stark reminder of her invisibility amidst the luxury she yearns to possess.

Her experience at the boutique becomes even more disheartening. After the long, unattended wait, a salesperson hurriedly suggests that Audrey checks the online inventory for shoes she saw on the shelves, citing the high demand and scarcity in-store. This impersonal advice contrasts sharply with the boutique's luxurious aura.

Nearly two years later, Audrey's lingering hope is extinguished by a cold, impersonal email. It informs her that her request for the bag cannot be fulfilled, and her place on the waiting list is unceremoniously removed, inviting her to start the process anew, and visit the boutique again. This dismissive communication, devoid of empathy, marks the final chapter of her disappointing quest with the luxury brand of her dreams.

The unattainable display item. Audrey's second quest leads her to a neighbouring boutique, where the vibrant buzz of the queue is punctuated by entertainers offering water and moving around with smart devices to set appointments to visit the store. Their smiles offer a fleeting comfort, but the inside reveals a stark reality – the objects of her desire, so tantalizingly displayed, remain just out of reach. The sales policy, a rigid gatekeeper, denies her the immediate gratification she seeks.

Advised that the luxurious bags on display might become available for purchase in a few weeks, she faces the predicament of having to visit the store weekly. Each visit is fraught with the hope that her desired item might be released for sale, and the anxiety that another, faster customer might claim it before her. This cycle of hope and uncertainty underscores the exclusivity and elusive nature of the luxury items she so desires.

Echoes of emptiness: The deceptive quiet of luxury retail. Audrey's narrative then shifts to a warm spring day, where the bustling city streets lead her to a seemingly empty boutique, a beacon of her desired purchases. Yet, entry is barred by a stern figure, her list of desires dismissed with a wave of indifference. The unwelcoming greeter, with a brusque gesture, informs her that everything is sold out and no assistance is available at the moment.

Contradicting the empty ambiance of the store, Audrey is advised to schedule an appointment for a future visit, preferably on a Monday or Tuesday in the next two weeks, to have any chance of finding what she seeks. This disheartening experience in the quiet store adds to her growing disillusionment with luxury retail service.

The exclusionary watch purchase. Her luxury journey takes her across borders, to the Emirates, in pursuit of a watch for her husband while travelling for business. Her decision to shop overseas is driven by the constraints of her busy schedule at home.

Here, she encounters a barrier of residency, her global lifestyle clashing with local exclusivity. Audrey is denied service due to not being a local resident, despite her frequent travels to the UAE, and not having a local credit card. In the foreign boutique, she faces a dismissive client adviser who, upon learning she isn't a local resident, coldly recommends she visits a local distributor instead. The rejection, sharp and unexpected, tinges her dream with a bitter realization of her outsider status. Back home, her request is filed but forgotten, leading her to opt for a different gift.

The online shopping ordeal. Online purchases turn into a hassle with delayed deliveries, incorrect orders and frustrating customer service interactions. Audrey's online shopping escapades add another layer of frustration to her luxury experience. In one instance, she excitedly orders and pays for a pair of trousers, admired for their exquisite cut and material, after seeing them on a friend. However, three weeks later, the trousers are a no-show.

Contacting customer service, she's met with vague promises of inquiries and follow-ups. Days later, with no update, a phone call reveals a startling fact: the order is pending due to stock shortages, awaiting more orders to justify a restock. Ultimately, her order is cancelled, the trousers discontinued, and a refund issued, sans apology.

In a similar vein, Audrey orders a skirt online. Despite meticulous attention to fit and size, what arrives is a pair of leather trousers, egregiously oversized. The ensuing ordeal involves a tedious exchange of emails, requests for photographic evidence of the mistake and a directive to return the wrong item before the correct one can be dispatched. She pleads for the originally ordered skirt to be reserved, but to no avail. A week later, she's informed of the return receipt but, simultaneously, that the skirt is now unavailable. Audrey's foray into online luxury shopping thus ends in a cycle of disappointment and unfulfilled desires.

The forgotten connection: A tale of lost personalization. In another chapter of Audrey's luxury experience saga, her relationship with a beloved brand undergoes a significant shift. Initially, Audrey enjoyed a deep connection with a client adviser who understood her preferences impeccably. This associate, beyond merely facilitating transactions, fostered a genuine relationship. She celebrated Audrey's milestones with personal messages and invitations to exclusive events and retreats, creating a truly bespoke experience.

However, this treasured relationship changes when Audrey is reassigned to different client advisers. The new associate, lacking the attentiveness of her predecessor, fails to recognize Audrey's disinterest in watches, a detail the former associate would have known. Despite Audrey's clear communication about her preferences, the new associate persists, sending her recommendations for exclusive watch collections and inviting her to related events. The new associate's oversight in recognizing Audrey's preferences and the lack of personalized communication starkly contrast with the empathetic, tailored approach of the previous associate.

The incomplete hotel experience. The tale continues with Audrey's hotel experience abroad, a supposed sanctuary from her disappointments. Yet, even here, the promise of luxury falls short.

After an exhausting wait at check-in, Audrey receives the key to her room but no explanation regarding the hotel and its services. During the hotel stay, Audrey is not informed about the hotel's enchanting rooftop bar, a discovery she makes too late to enjoy with her friends. The unnoticed rooftop, a hidden gem, becomes a bittersweet discovery – a perfect setting for her friends, now just a solitary reflection of missed opportunities.

The lost art of subtlety. Audrey's Saturday began with a sense of exclusivity as she was invited to a brand's showroom, an experience titled 'Behind the Velvet Rope'. The promise was a private audience with the design director, who would unveil the philosophy behind the new collection, narrate tales of inspiration and reveal mood boards and sketches – a peek into the creative sanctum. The atmosphere was electric with anticipation as Audrey, and a select few, were ushered into a space away from the commercial hum of the store floor. As the design director wove stories around each piece, Audrey felt the collection come alive. She could almost touch the muses behind the fabrics, the historical references in the patterns. The event felt like a connoisseur's gathering rather than a sales pitch – until the end.

As the narrative reached its peak, sales associates emerged, order forms in hand, transforming the experience into a transaction. They urged pre-orders, insisting on a 50 per cent deposit. The enchantment was broken. Audrey's Saturday morning, poised for delight, was marred by the unyielding sales drive. She declined; the memory of the day tarnished by the incongruous ending.

When personalization becomes impersonal: 'The WhatsApp conundrum'. Audrey's relationship with her dedicated sales associate started as a modern-day luxury fairytale. Messages were exchanged with care, gifts and thoughtful notes marked special occasions, making Audrey feel embraced and singularly esteemed.

But soon, the associate's messages veered from considerate to overwhelming. A barrage of images – hundreds at a time, every time – flooded Audrey's phone, an avalanche of new pieces that seemed less curated and more chaotic. The personal touch was lost in the mass marketing. Audrey felt reduced to just another contact in the sales associate's phone, her unique style unacknowledged. It was a digital downpour that washed away the bespoke nature of their interactions, leaving Audrey to navigate a sea of unfiltered choices. She longed for the refined curation of her early exchanges, where every selection was tailored, and every message felt handpicked.

The paradox of luxury: Navigating the maze of exclusivity and inflexibility. The climax of her story unfolds at a renowned spa. After a stressful period, Audrey eagerly calls to book some relaxing treatments, only to be met with an inflexible booking process. The spa insists on online reservations, not accommodating her immediate need or offering a personalized touch. Frustrated, Audrey forgoes her much-needed relaxation, highlighting the paradox of modern luxury: exceptional quality clashing with rigid customer service protocols.

Audrey's experiences across different luxury retail and hospitality scenarios vividly illustrate key lessons for some luxury brands. Her story, a blend of hope, frustration and revelation, offers a poignant insight into the complex world of luxury consumerism, as she navigates various luxury brands, encountering a series of disappointing experiences.

The takeaways are clear: brands should avoid neglecting customer needs, offering impersonal service, and creating unnecessarily complicated purchasing processes. Some experiences highlight a common tension in luxury brand interactions: the delicate balance between engagement and sales pressure. Brands that lean too heavily into sales can diminish the authenticity of the customer experience. In some stories, generic communication made her feel more like a target than a valued client. This serves as a cautionary tale against the misuse of communication channels in clienteling, such as WhatsApp, which should enhance the customer relationship, not burden it.

These narratives underscore the market's shift towards experiences that prioritize genuine connection and understanding over aggressive sales tactics. They serve as a reminder that the true essence of luxury is not the hard sell, but the creation of memorable experiences that respect the consumer's individuality and pace. Each episode in Audrey's journey highlights the importance of attentive, personalized customer care and the pitfalls of ignoring the nuances of luxury consumer expectations. Her story accentuates the value of understanding and recording client preferences for personalized communication and interaction. It serves as a reminder that luxury is not just about the product, but also about the unique, individualized experience each client receives.

Opting to use the term 'client adviser' instead of 'sales associate' aligns with the intention to emphasize a more consultative and immersive role for people on the sales floor. This distinction reflects a shift from a transactional to a relational approach, where the focus is on fostering a deeper understanding and appreciation of the brand's heritage, craftsmanship and values. Client advisers are seen as brand ambassadors who educate and guide customers through a personalized brand experience, helping them to connect with the ethos of the brand on a more significant level.

This role is especially pertinent in the luxury world, where purchasing decisions are often driven by emotional connections and an appreciation for the story and exclusivity behind the product and service. The use of 'client adviser' suggests an interaction with the client, offering advice and expertise that enrich the buying experience, ultimately cultivating long-term loyalty and engagement with the brand.

Differentiation through experiences along the customer journey

Understanding holistically the customer experience is akin to choreographing a ballet, where every movement contributes to the elegance of the performance. The customer's perception of value in the luxury domain is in fact meticulously sculpted through a series of interactions that extend well beyond the functional attributes of the product or service at hand.

This journey of perception formation is two-pronged. On one side, there is the tangible, functional value that aligns with the expected performance of the luxury goods or services – the very reason the client initiates the purchase. It is a measure of quality and the satisfaction of a specific need or desire. Simultaneously, there is an intangible element, the experiential value, that weaves through the purchasing process (and even after), capable of elevating or diminishing the perceived worth of the transaction (Zeithaml, Parasuraman and Berry, 1985). This experiential value is an alchemy of emotion, environment and engagement that, when expertly crafted, can significantly enhance the perceived value of the luxury experience. It's the difference between a simple transaction and a memorable event, where every touchpoint is an opportunity to either add a layer of delight or a point of friction.

The challenge and the art of luxury customer experience lie in harmoniously blending these functional and experiential elements to create a symphony of satisfaction that resonates with the client's deepest aspirations.

The concept of intertwining products, services, meanings and experiences suggests a harmonious and strategic blending of various elements to create value for the customer. This aligns with the perspective offered by Schmitt, Brakus and Zarantonello (2014) in their critique of the viewpoint that experiences provide more happiness than material possessions. Their work challenges the binary contrast between materialism and experientialism by suggesting that both can coexist and contribute to happiness in different forms – pleasure and meaning.

This consumer-experience model acknowledges that experiences can stem from both material goods and experiential services, each contributing to consumer happiness in distinct ways. It's not simply about choosing experiences over possessions, but rather how well a brand can integrate both to enhance consumer wellbeing. The role of brand experiences is pivotal in this model. It's suggested that brands can enhance consumer wellbeing by invoking specific types of experiences – sensory, affective, cognitive, physical and social – which mediate the relationship between consumption and happiness.

This section will guide the reader through the intricate dance of the luxury customer journey, touching upon some pivotal moments (Puccinelli et al, 2009), each interwoven with cognitive and emotional elements that are magnified in the world of luxury. Traditionally, the customer journey has been dissected into the phases of pre-purchase, purchase and post-purchase, a framework that inherently prioritizes the transaction. However, in our narrative, we transcend this commercial mindset by adopting a more holistic approach: pre-visit, during-visit and post-visit.

The concept of a 'visit' is preferred over a 'purchase moment' because it recognizes that a customer's journey isn't solely for immediate buying. Similarly, client advisers are encouraged to welcome clients with a long-term relationship-building approach, rather than being fixated on making an immediate sale. By redefining the journey in this way, we honour the multifaceted interactions between customers and brands, recognizing that the value of a visit isn't confined to the exchange of goods or services but is rooted in the richness of the experience itself. This approach underscores the importance of fostering deeper connections and understanding customer needs over time, aligning with the ethos of luxury brand experiences. This reconceptualization covers the entire breadth of the brand experience, valuing the customer's engagement at every touchpoint, regardless of a direct purchase.

The pre-visit phase

Pre-visit is the stage where anticipation builds, driven by the customer's curiosity, previous encounters or the brand's reputation. It's a dance of attraction, where the brand's allure is broadcasted, and the customer's intrigue is piqued.

This is the courtship of the consumer journey. Here, potential customers engage in a delicate dance of research across multiple channels, both online and offline. The influence of social and media contexts cannot be over-stressed; they are the music that sets the tempo for the dance. Think of a customer who discovers a high-end brand through an influencer's story or an artistically crafted advertisement – each touchpoint is a step in their journey towards the brand. A prospective customer experiences a luxury sports car while going to playing golf with a friend and decides to explore the possibility of purchasing one. After driving the car, he is inspired to research more about the brand and model.

He visits the brand's online platform to inquire further and uses a car configurator tool to visualize and customize his potential purchase. The customer eagerly anticipates follow-up from the dealership to receive more information and assistance in finalizing the dream car project.

Social influence as online exploration elegantly weaves into the pre-visit phase, acting as the invisible threads that guide the customer's initial steps. It permeates through word-of-mouth, the pervasive reach of social media and the subtle endorsements by figures of aspiration. This influence shapes desires, informs decisions and sets expectations, often before the customer even sets foot within the retail environment. It is here, amidst the social fabric, that the customer's perception of luxury begins to form, sculpted by the narratives and testimonials that resonate within their social circles.

The visit phase

The visit phase is the heart of the experience. It's where the customer steps into the brand's world, not necessarily with the intent to buy, but to interact, learn and feel. It's an immersive dive into what the brand stands for, a chance to touch, see and engage with the essence of the brand beyond mere products or services.

The visit is like the 'moment of truth', it is the crescendo of the customer's experience. It is where the customer and the brand's representatives perform in unison. Positive or negative perceptions hinge upon this interaction. A boutique that envelops the customer in exclusivity, with staff that choreograph every movement to cater to the customer's needs, can forge a lasting positive impression. When a client enters the store at Cartier, the sales assistant (once just a support for the client adviser) acts as the first point of contact, managing the flow of clients, assessing their needs and directing them to the appropriate area or personnel. This role has evolved to focus more on welcoming clients and enhancing their in-store journey from the moment they step in.

In luxury, the convergence with hospitality is not just influential – it's transformative. The essence of this revolution lies in managing touchpoints along the customer journey, inspired by the vocabulary and gestures of high-end hospitality. The experience is elevated, channels are unified, and retail is reimagined not as a physical space, but as a curated moment of delight.

Will Guidara's philosophy and transformation of Eleven Madison Park into one of the world's top restaurants had a central focus on the human element – that makes the distinction between service and hospitality. Guidara's journey from the restaurant's beginnings to becoming a beacon of hospitality illustrates the potential of genuine care in crafting an unforgettable customer experience. Here, it's not just about the food, or in broader terms, the product – it's about how customers are made to feel. The anecdote about the 'dirty water" hot dog magnifies this ethos – it demonstrates that creating memorable moments doesn't always require grand gestures but rather sincere attention to what the customer truly desires, even if it's as simple as a hot dog. The restaurant's team overheard guests' wish to try a New York City street hot dog and served a hot dog from a street cart in the upscale dining setting, turning it into an unforgettable highlight for the guests and exemplifying the restaurant's commitment to creating unique, joyous experiences. This act of hospitality showcases how personalizing service and catering to individual desires can leave a lasting impression.

At Eleven Madison Park, the Dreamweavers (team members dedicated to creating extraordinary, personalized experiences for guests) once creatively transformed a section of the restaurant into a whimsical seaside setting. This imaginative setup included a children's pool and beach chairs. The idea was to uplift a couple who had missed their flight to an island vacation, offering them an unexpected and delightful beach-like experience right in the restaurant. This inventive gesture encapsulates the extraordinary lengths to which establishments go to provide memorable experiences for their guests, especially when unexpected circumstances arise. Guidara allocated 5 per cent of the year's budget to finance the Dreamweavers.

CASE STUDY
Eleven Madison Park (EMP), New York

Hospitality is a sector where attention and care to clients have always been a focus point. There is a lot we can learn from how chefs, restaurants and restaurateurs run their business and to select just one case study is not an easy task. If you are wondering how a NY French brasserie, known for their seafood towers, became the number one restaurant in the world, the short answer would be: 'It's all about how they make you feel'. Obviously the food is impeccable, the atmosphere is magical and theatrical, the attention to detail is pushed beyond any imaginable boundaries, but it is how they make you feel that stick with you forever.

When chef Daniel Humm (chef of EMP) and Will Guidara (former GM of EMP) got the number 50 ranking in the 'Best 50 restaurants in the world' award, they took the perspective of being disappointed to be last, rather than being happy to be among the top 50. They used that emotion to do better and become better; they wanted to do something impactful in the industry to get to the number one spot in that list.

In interviews, Will has said that he started to vocalize his dream out loud and through that practice he realized that the way to the top was to 'Be unreasonable in pursuit of people, not food, not goods'. Inspired by his own personal experience, when his dad took him to the Four Seasons restaurant as a kid, he remembered how they made him feel, not specifically what he had for dinner.

And just like that, he decided to implement a service at EMP that was 'bespoke and over the top'. He wanted to go to unusual lengths to take care of people. He wanted to make people feel seen. He wrote two words on a napkin and those two words changed the hospitality industry forever: 'unreasonable hospitality'.

To put clients at the centre of the attention, and not food, in a restaurant business was an enormous shift, but Will knew that the food part was already taken care of by his brilliant partner and emerging young chef Daniel Humm, so as GM of the restaurant it was up to him to take care of everything else.

His unreasonable hospitality approach can be applied to any industry where there is a regular interaction with clients and where there is a need to bring joy to them.

Let's see how he put unreasonable hospitality into practice through some smart leadership techniques. And, since we are talking about a restaurant, let's see the ingredients of the recipe!

First of all, he realized that everyone working in the restaurant had to be on the same page. His main goal was to eliminate tension: the tension that there is very often between the people working in the kitchen and the people working in the dining room, and the tension that there was between the old guard and the newcomers. The old guard was composed of 'purists' of the hospitality industry, people who were used to a classic and traditional type of service, and the newcomers group was composed of 'disruptors', people thinking that you can have excellence without the 'stuffiness' of a traditional fine dining restaurant. There was a need to establish a real relationship between the two teams, and everyone had to work cohesively towards the common goal.

Will started to implement more meetings with the goal of articulating the vision and involving the teams to be part of it. He never wanted to sell his vision – he wanted a collaborative effort and individual contributions. At that point there were more or less 130 people on the team, and his idea was to have every single of them contribute creatively. The analogy he uses during interviews is one of a bank account: if only two people make deposits and all the people withdraw money, you will run out quickly. On the other hand, your account overflows if all the people make deposits.

The second ingredient was to look at the customer experience as a whole, breaking down every single step of the customer's journey, isolating every single customer's touchpoints and intentionally making every single one of them a 'little more awesome'. Starting from the moment you step into the revolving door at EMP, there is no visible podium. You only see a person standing there and greeting you by your name. No-one mentions what table number the hostess will bring you to, there is a seamless transition led by a pleasant conversation from the moment you step into the room to the moment you sit at your table. Seamless and joyful. That required more effort by the team – they had to learn sign language; they had to Google pictures of the guests so they could call you by your name the moment they saw you.

At EMP there are many magical moments when you feel special and seen, one of them is when they bring you to the kitchen for a special 'treat'. When you step into the kitchen in the middle of dinner service with probably 40 people working there you cannot hear a single sound of dishes clenching or pots moving around. You hear the buzz coming from the dining room, but in the kitchen there is an absolute sense of peace and the attention is all on you. If isn't that the perfect example of a well-oiled machine, I don't know what is!

Another ingredient of the recipe that Will worked on was to ask for 'more' and obtain it. 'More investments, more staff, better quality ingredients, more shifts…'. He wasn't afraid to take risks and he was very driven. What Will realized is that you cannot trick a *New York Times* restaurant critic into thinking you are a 4-star restaurant if you are not one. So, instead of putting on your best show only when the critic walks in, he wanted the restaurant to perform as a 4-star restaurant at every shift. For over a year, every night he pretended that one table was the 'critic's table' and that gave them the ability to stay in the frame of mind everyday and be consistently over the top.

When EMP got the 4th star from the *New York Times* critic, another ingredient emerged. Everyone was talking about the famous chef Daniel Humm and the owner Danny Meyer, with no mention of the GM, Will Guidara, but internally there was an absolute recognition of his efforts and the team's efforts. The goal of being a united team was achieved. The external communication was all about those two people bringing the restaurant to 4 stars, but internally the glory was shared and everyone's job was recognized as a fundamental piece of the puzzle.

SOURCE Guidara, 2022

This story can serve as a metaphor for luxury retail, where sometimes, against the grain of opulence, a simple, authentic connection can have the most lasting impact. In luxury retail, as in Guidara's restaurant, it's about crafting moments that resonate on a personal level, turning transactions into interactions, and customers into cherished guests. The concept of 'unreasonable hospitality' is particularly potent. It challenges the status quo and pushes for an extraordinary commitment to the guest experience. In the context of retail, this could mean personalizing the shopping experience to such an extent that it feels less like a sale and more like a personal curation of goods and services tailored to the individual.

Here are some takeaways and parallels that can be drawn for other luxury industries:

- **Personalized engagement**: Like the restaurant's approach of knowing guests' names and preferences as they walk through the door, luxury retail could use technology and client relationship management to anticipate and cater to individual customer needs.

- **Eliminating barriers**: Just as the podium was removed for a more personal greeting, luxury retail spaces can be designed to be more open and welcoming, removing physical and psychological barriers between clients and advisers.

- **Empowering teams with autonomy**: Similar to the Dreamweaver role at EMP, retail teams could be empowered to create unique customer experiences, giving them the authority to go above and beyond without needing managerial approval for every gesture.

- **Crafting experiences over transactions**: The focus should be on the overall experience rather than the sale itself. Each interaction should feel bespoke and intentional, much like a perfectly tailored piece of clothing.

- **Hosting over selling**: Sales associates, now client advisers or 'curators', should be seen as hosts of a journey within the brand's world, guiding customers through a narrative that intertwines product discovery with brand heritage and values.

- **Creating moments that matter:** Whether it's through a surprise gift, an unexpected level of service or simply remembering a client's significant life events, these moments can make a customer feel truly valued.

By applying these principles, luxury brands can forge deeper connections with their clientele, turning every visit into a memorable event and every purchase into a treasured acquisition. This level of care and attention can set a brand apart in a crowded luxury market, just as EMP stands out in the world of fine dining.

During his tenure as CEO of Audemars Piguet (AP), François-Henry Bennahmias pivoted the brand towards a 'People to People' strategy, which turned out to be particularly significant after the pandemic's onset. The approach, currently in place, is aimed to develop direct relationships with the clients, creating an unprecedented level of care and engagement. The strategy also has an impact in terms of organization, up to the commercial director becoming Chief Client Officer (CCO) to signify the shift from the traditional manufacturing and wholesale mindset to a new one deeply entrenched in human interactions.

The core principle, as expressed by the CCO Marco Viganò, is centred on the idea that AP 'is a manufacturing company created by people who share a passion with other people. This notion is about prioritizing sharing over transactions, where the joy of creation and the pleasure of customer interaction are inextricably linked. This translates into a selective direct-to-consumer distribution strategy, with less than a hundred stores worldwide, mostly under AP's full management and control.'

Investment in experiences rather than traditional distribution methods has been a cornerstone of this strategy, with the development of AP Houses. These spaces are conceived as a fusion of hospitality, retail and entertainment, often situated just off the beaten path where lower rents allow for more expansive and luxurious settings. The result is dual-faceted: customers enjoy enriched, memorable experiences and staff delight in a more pleasant working environment. The evolution towards 'retail hospitality' is a significant theme in this new operational method. This approach necessitates staff who are not only competent salespeople but also hosts – guardians of customer relations and crafters of experiences.

The locations of these AP Houses, like the inaugural one in Hong Kong's Queen's Road Central in 2017 or in London's New Bond Street, have become beacons of this approach, shifting the focus from high-traffic retail spaces to more intimate, experience-centred venues. Yet, the pursuit of excellence does not blind the brand to the reality of imperfection: 'There is the understanding that, in dealing with people, errors may occur and the emphasis is placed not on eliminating honest mistakes but on the grace with which they are handled. The "human aspect" of the business is celebrated, and teams are empowered to manage relationships, fostering resilience through recovery and response to imperfections' (Marco Viganò, personal correspondence).

This nuanced understanding of luxury service highlights that true excellence lies not in a flawless, mechanical execution, but in the authenticity of the human experience. It's a refreshing take on luxury that embraces the beauty of the imperfect, the personal and the genuine – a narrative that other luxury industries could draw inspiration from.

It's clear that at the core of this paradigm is humanity. Luxury is about creating memorable moments through attentive service and attentive care, where every interaction is valued and every emotion is considered. It's about recharging with each guest encounter and infusing each day with passion. The idea of having rituals that provide a kind of routine in the retail activity is perfectly consistent with the 'freedom in a framework' approach as articulated by the CCO of Audemars Piguet. The concept encapsulates a modern strategy in luxury retail that acknowledges the importance of human discretion within established guidelines.

This philosophy permits client advisers to allocate high-demand pieces (such as highly complicated timepieces or limited editions created in collaboration like the ones with Marvel or Travis Scott), based on a spectrum of qualitative factors rather than a simple first-come-first-served basis. This nuanced method takes into account the customer's profile, the relationships with the brand and the intention to wear and enjoy the timepiece rather than seek a financial gain through the acquisition of a valuable asset.

The objective is to develop a community of genuine enthusiasts and collectors which progressively become a vibrant part of the brand. CRM plays a significant role in guiding the allocation practices in order to ensure a consistent approach in the attribution of timepieces often in high demand, The process is designed to be transparent and accountable, limiting discretionary powers to prevent misuse or opportunistic behaviours.

It's not just about controlling supply and demand but mostly nurturing a long-lasting client relationship built on trust and mutual appreciation for AP's craftsmanship and heritage. Moreover, this strategy embraces the expansion of the brand appeal toward new clients, including segments that, despite not being the usual targets for traditional watchmaking, are in reality developing a genuine interest in complicated mechanical watches, such as female clients and younger generations.

The concept of 'freedom in a framework' thus reflects a delicate balance between giving client advisers autonomy to enhance customer relationships and maintaining a structure that ensures brand integrity and values are upheld. It's a sophisticated approach that respects the human aspect of retail while striving for excellence in client engagement and experience.

The elevated luxury journey during the visit phase unfolds in three key stages:

1 **Hosting the guest**: This initial encounter mirrors the warmth of entering a luxury hotel, a restaurant, a retail store or browsing a website with curiosity. It's an open invitation to engage, not necessarily with the intent to purchase, but to be immersed in the brand's aura. This stage is about fostering a sense of wonder and exploration. Client advisers act as curators, guiding guests through a gallery of heritage and innovation. They help guests unearth the narratives woven into each product and service, akin to collectors seeking out rare and meaningful pieces of art.

2 **Orchestrate the magic of discovery**: This stage delves deeper, offering a narrative about the brand's heritage and values. Here, customers explore the history and the ethos that inspire the brand to strive further, fostering a connection that may inspire a purchase or a deepened brand relationship. As guests traverse through the brand's history and offerings, client advisers cultivate a bespoke experience tailored to individual tastes and preferences. The connection is deepened through personal stories and shared values, reinforcing the brand's place not just in the market, but in the hearts of its clientele.

3 **Build the bond, cultivating continuity**: The culmination of the journey is the most critical – a decision of what to select from a restaurant menu, a purchase, a commitment to the brand's legacy. It's where the initial welcome and discovery converge into a meaningful decision. The final stage is about sealing the relationship with a memorable farewell that ensures continuity. This is not merely a conclusion, but a segue into an ongoing and emotional relationship, where guests leave with not just a product, but a piece of the brand's soul.

Luxury retail, borrowing from hospitality, transforms clients into guests and sales associates into client advisers, akin to curators in an art gallery.

This elevated journey full of immersive experiences transcends transactions, focusing instead on cultivating an emotional connection, much like collecting art pieces. In this reimagined retail experience, each phase is punctuated with careful attention to detail, mirroring the attentiveness of luxury hospitality.

The post-visit phase

Post-visit is about the echoes of the experience. It's the reflection, the conversations, the memories and the connections that persist. This stage focuses on the relationship's longevity, not merely on customer retention or repeat purchases. It's about nurturing a lasting bond that may, in time, lead to transactions as a natural progression of the relationship, rather than as its sole objective.

This is the encore of the customer journey. It includes all activities and services following the sale (or store/website visit), ensuring the performance lingers in the customer's memory. In luxury, this often translates to personalized follow-ups, exclusive aftercare services like watch overhauling or handbag restoration, each reinforcing the brand's commitment to excellence. The after-sales service package in luxury acts as the arms that continue to embrace the customer long after the initial purchase. It's not merely a service but a statement of enduring quality and a source of continued engagement – and revenue – for the brand.

Cartier's dedication to exceptional after-sales service is exemplified by its comprehensive 'Cartier Care Programme'. This service extends beyond a mere transaction – it's a testament to Cartier's commitment to customer satisfaction and maintaining the integrity of its timepieces. Customers who opt into the CRM programme can benefit from an extended eight-year warranty period, which comprises a two-year standard warranty plus an additional six years upon registration.

The process of after-sales service at Cartier involves a collaboration between three key roles within the store's ecosystem: the Service Associate (SA), the Client Adviser (CA) and the Technical Expert or Watchmaker. Each role plays a pivotal part in ensuring a seamless and efficient service experience for the client.

At the heart of Cartier's service is the 'Customer Service Bridge' (CSB), which serves as a vital link between the sales and service aspects of the customer journey. This integration ensures that clients receive a holistic experience that not only addresses their immediate service needs, but also fosters a long-term relationship with the brand.

Technology plays a crucial role in Cartier's service approach, particularly through its app, which is integrated with the brand's CRM system. The app enables efficient appointment management and provides a platform for clients to track their service history, make requests and maintain a wishlist, all while being connected to the Cartier database for a personalized experience.

In instances where more specialized care is needed, such as with heritage pieces or complex repairs, items are sent to Cartier's headquarters or designated platforms for expert attention. Even those pieces without serial numbers are treated with the same level of care, highlighting Cartier's respect for its products' longevity and heritage.

The Cartier after-sales service also educates clients about the technical aspects of their purchases, providing quotes and explanations for the services rendered. This educational approach empowers clients to understand and appreciate the craftsmanship behind their Cartier pieces.

In essence, Cartier's after-sales service is not merely a functional post-purchase process; it's a continuation of the brand's promise of excellence and a reflection of its ethos of creating lasting relationships with its clients through impeccable service and attention to detail.

The post-visit phase in the customer journey is an essential aspect of customer engagement and brand loyalty. It involves not just the brand's efforts to continue the conversation with the customer but also leverages the customer's active role in sharing their experience with others and providing feedback.

This stage is critical because it can transform a one-time buyer into a repeat customer and, even better, into a brand advocate. It's just the beginning of a relationship where customers become a storyteller of their own experience. The threads of referrals, online influence and feedback weave a pattern that extends the narrative beyond the initial purchase.

The culmination of Cartier's service journey is crystallized in the 'Barometro', a holistic feedback system that captures the client's comprehensive experience. This pivotal touchpoint allows clients to rate their encounter across various dimensions, reflecting the nuanced layers of their interaction with the brand. From the effectiveness of the storytelling about Cartier's storied past and present to the team's ability to engage and captivate through a well-woven narrative and the overall management of the interaction, the 'Barometro' serves as a guide for the brand's daily operations. This feedback is not merely numerical but is a narrative that Cartier values highly, as it provides insight into areas of excellence and opportunities for refinement. By engaging in this reflective exercise, clients contribute to an ongoing dialogue with Cartier, one that is instrumental in shaping an ever-evolving service landscape. The 'Barometro' thus becomes a strategic tool, guiding Cartier towards a perpetually elevated client experience.

Customers, now brand ambassadors, share their encounters with the world, their endorsements echoing in the vast halls of social media, influencing potential buyers. Their reviews, a compass for future improvements, become invaluable insights for the brand to refine and perfect the customer experience. What is around post-visit engagement emphasizes the symbiotic relationship between a brand and its customers, where each interaction contributes to a larger story of connection and community.

Harmonizing elegance, quality, excellence and empathy:
Crafting the quintessential guest experience at Mandarin Oriental

In luxury hospitality, the journey of each guest is a symphony meticulously composed from pre-arrival to departure, ensuring a seamless fusion of global excellence with local sensitivities.

The threshold for excellence has been elevated by the discerning modern customer. Today, flawless execution in every aspect is not an aspiration but an expectation. The minutiae of a guest's stay – from the temperature in the room to the scented and perfectly ironed sheets, changed twice a day, to the meticulous presentation of a gourmet meal – are perceived as baseline commitments rather than enhancements. Clean rooms, sumptuous cuisine and tranquil surroundings are no longer differentiators; they are prerequisites. Guests are connoisseurs of their own experiences, with a keen eye for detail and an appreciation for the subtleties that distinguish the remarkable from the merely satisfactory. It's in these nuances – a fitness centre that anticipates post-workout needs, a pool maintained at just the right temperature – that luxury hotels find their challenge and their opportunity.

This exacting standard extends to the culinary experiences offered. Exceptionality must permeate every bite and sip, with guests expecting not just good food but a gastronomic journey that excites and satisfies. Even perceived minor discrepancies, such as spatial constraints in communal areas or variations in amenities, can become focal points for feedback.

Mandarin Oriental exemplifies this blend, where the anticipation of guest needs begins with discreet yet thorough pre-arrival contact (around three days prior to arrival), gathering personal preferences to tailor experiences that resonate with the guest's cultural background and individual desires. The journey of a guest begins with pre-arrival anticipation, curated through meticulous research and personal outreach. The Guest Relation Team diligently mines CRM data and even peruse social media – respecting privacy and regulatory constraints – to gather insights into a guest's preferences and habits. Preferences are shared across properties, creating a consistent and customized experience regardless of location. The goal is to curate a highly personalized welcome that feels both warm and familiar.

Guest Relations plays a pivotal role in this pre-arrival phase, reaching out to guests to offer assistance and ascertain any specific needs or desires they might have for their upcoming stay. This outreach is not merely procedural but a foundational step towards building a stay tailored to each guest's preferences, from room type and dietary requirements – which informs not only the kitchen but also the in-room amenities tailored to delight each guest – to preferred activities and space organization.

Attention to detail is paramount. Tailor-made welcome amenities, based on the guests' likes and dislikes, await in the rooms. For example, a guest who loves berries but detests chocolate will find their favourite fruit beautifully presented and no chocolates around, enhancing their sense of being truly known and valued. If a guest is known to enjoy a post-flight spa treatment, they might find the appointment set upon arrival. Or, if they're returning from a run in the park, staff know the bath must be prepped with soothing salts. If the guest is a yoga lover, the room should be equipped with a mat and necessary equipment. It's these thoughtful touches that transform a stay into an experience.

Cross-selling is approached not as a mere sales strategy but as an essential service, ensuring guests have the opportunity to enjoy coveted experiences such as spa treatments or dining at in-house restaurants.

The approach to cross-selling extends beyond the confines of individual hotel properties, offering guests enriching experiences that encompass a broader geographical scope. In the case of Mandarin Oriental Milan, this strategy includes arranging exquisite excursions to their sister property at Mandarin Oriental, Lake Como. The opportunity to enjoy a boat trip on the picturesque Lake Como, complete with a sophisticated dining experience, is a perfect example of this. It's an offering that elevates the concept of luxury hospitality, allowing guests to indulge in unique adventures that blend the beauty of nature with the elegance and comfort associated with the Mandarin Oriental brand.

Upon entry, the warmth of recognition greets each guest as a standard of care. The staff are trained to ensure that within ten seconds of joining a queue, guests are warmly greeted, setting the tone for their stay. The check-in procedure, a blend of efficiency and personal touch, ideally unfolds in under five minutes for city hotels and ten minutes for resorts. The check-in process for VIPs, elegantly conducted within the privacy of the guest's room, is swift and personalized, respecting the guest's time and comfort, especially after long journeys. Empathy is the guiding principle for interactions – staff are encouraged to call guests by their name at least four times during any conversation, weaving a thread of familiarity and personal connection.

Staff are also trained to frequently check back with guests during their stay to anticipate needs, whether it's a top-up of water at dinner or a quick turnaround of laundry services.

At establishments like Mandarin Oriental, the golden rules are not just policies – they are the bedrock of the guest experience. The essence of luxury hospitality lies in meticulous attention to the fine details and an unwavering commitment to guest satisfaction, epitomized through a set of non-negotiable standards. Travellers find a sanctuary where efficiency meets luxury, with services, such as express garment services and flexible check-in times.

For leisure guests, the hotel transforms into a portal to local culture and relaxation, offering curated experiences like unique dining that deepen their connection with the destination. There's no value in suggesting a Michelin-starred venue or foreign cuisine if the customer wants to find unusual and simple places to enjoy local tradition. Whether it's arranging a private viewing of a fashion collection, coordinating a personalized tour of the city's hidden gems or providing an after-hours shopping experience in a renowned fashion store for guests seeking intimacy and personal attention, the goal is to enrich their stay with moments that are both culturally engaging and deeply personal.

Each guest interaction is an opportunity for service excellence with the contribution of all departments, from the front desk and concierge to housekeeping and maintenance, each playing their part in ensuring the guest's journey is smooth and delightful. Staff are trained to read cues, both spoken and unspoken, aligning service rhythm with the guest's pace, whether brisk for business needs or relaxed for leisure enjoyment. Attention to detail is paramount. Slippers are placed at the side of the bed that a returning guest prefers to sleep on; preferences for room amenities are remembered and acted upon without needing to be re-stated. These subtleties may seem minor, but they create a narrative of care and attention that guests carry with them long after their departure.

For those seeking the extraordinary, Mandarin Oriental crafts bespoke surprises that become the highlight of a stay, like finding a beloved football team's memorabilia in the room, or waking up to a panoramic view arranged as a last-minute surprise. It's these unexpected delights that spark stories guests will share and remember.

Mandarin's sports and adventure department goes beyond the usual concierge service, crafting bespoke excursions like a sunrise trek with a picnic breakfast at an off-the-beaten-path locale. These experiences aren't just about the activity; they're about immersing the guest in the destination's narrative.

Delightful treatment at Mandarin Oriental isn't reserved only for the few. Every guest has the potential to be surprised with a touch of the extraordinary. If guests mention an anniversary, they might return to their room to find a celebration waiting – a cake or a bouquet of their favourite flowers and pictures of beloved people around.

Loyal clientele is nurtured through personalized gifts and elevated amenities. For those who spend significant room nights with Mandarin, the bespoke touches range from monogrammed bathrobes to favoured brands of hats gifted as tokens of appreciation.

Engagement with guests is not confined to within the walls of the hotel. Digital concierge services allow a continual dialogue, where guests can express needs or make requests through platforms like WhatsApp, offering a level of convenience and personalization that aligns with modern expectations of luxury.

Quality assurance is constantly measured against internal and external KPIs. Immediate post-stay feedback is sought directly from guests, with the option of completing a survey which can be collated with public reviews on online travel and reservation platforms, allowing the hotel to measure guest satisfaction against the competition. LQA's undercover inspections provide objective evaluations, scoring the hotel on over 500 standards, from the tangibles of service delivery to the intangibles of engagement and emotional impact.

Behind the scenes, staff training is ongoing, ingraining the brand's values and the nuances of delivering a luxury experience that exceeds the benchmarks of the industry. Training is rigorous and continuous, with a focus on the brand's history and the high standards expected in every role. New hires are immersed in the culture of empathetic service, with an emphasis on the 'golden rules' that underpin every aspect of the guest journey, from check-in to check-out, and every moment in between.

Luxury in hospitality is no longer confined to tangible amenities; it's emotional resonance and the ability to anticipate and exceed expectations, crafting stays that guests cherish long after they have returned home. For VIP guests, these details are heightened. Prior knowledge of their likes, dislikes and habits allows the staff to curate unique experiences – a surprise gift related to a hobby, or a favourite drink waiting upon arrival. A guest known to enjoy a particular entertainment might find tickets awaiting them, alongside themed gifts to commemorate the occasion.

It's an artful resolution of the paradox between global branding and local relevance, where every detail, every service and every interaction weaves together to create a guest experience that is as memorable as it is uniquely personal, as culturally rich as it is comfortably luxurious.

Brand experience: Touchpoints, determinants and impact

In all phases of the customer journey there are multiple touchpoints, ie moments of interaction within these phases. For example, a customer planning a visit to a boutique might experience a series of meticulously designed moments: from scheduling an appointment, to being greeted upon entry, the waiting – if any, the test and trial of products, the payment process and finally the delivery. Each of these touchpoints is an opportunity for the brand to add value to the customer's experience.

In luxury, the plot thickens as many interactions between the brand and the customer are designed to build a relationship that transcends single, short-term transactions. For instance, a perceptive client adviser might use the knowledge of a client's travel schedule and interests to enhance the relationship. Knowing that the client is going to London on a business trip, the client adviser might arrange fast-track tickets to a sought-after exhibition, paired with a quintessentially English afternoon tea experience nearby in a 5-star hotel.

It's essential to recognize the ensemble cast influencing the customer experience (Lemon and Verhoef, 2016) along all touchpoints. From the brand's overarching communication strategies to the ambiance and personnel at the front end, to services provided online and offline, etc, each plays a pivotal role in the customer journey.

In personal luxury goods (PLG), the social milieu of a retail space is an integral part of the customer journey (see Chapter 6), shaping the ambiance and influencing purchasing decisions. It's here, within the elegant confines of a boutique, that the presence of other patrons and the nuanced interactions with staff can either enhance or detract from the luxury experience. The presence of and interaction with other customers, the attentiveness of staff from the warm welcome to the final payment, and the integration of technology all contribute to the atmosphere and experience (Roggeveen, Grewal and Schweiger 2020; Grewal et al, 2020).

Luxury brands have innovated to enhance service quality, with some investing in increased staffing to manage peak visitor traffic effectively. This approach not only mitigates congestion, but also elevates the overall customer experience. Additionally, targeted communication strategies have been employed to encourage appointments, reducing wait times. Some luxury brands have even adopted a dual-store model within the same city: one catering to general traffic, including tourists and another more exclusive space dedicated to VICs and local clientele – consider as an example the Gucci Salon concept accessible by VICs, with made to measure and made to order items, that debuted in Los Angeles in 2023 (Chitrakorn, 2023). This bifurcation ensures a more tailored and efficient service experience, reflecting a deep understanding of diverse customer needs and expectations.

Academic studies examining the impact of service design on waiting times in luxury retail reveal insightful strategies. Carmon, Shanthikumar and Freed (1995) illustrate that some psychological costs of waiting can be accounted for in the analysis of queuing systems, and that this may provide important recommendations for the service design.

The 2015 study by Tong, Nagarajan and Cheng provides insightful analysis into service quality in retail. It suggests that the service process is a sequence of steps, starting with a base service that forms the foundation, followed by additional steps that add further value. This structure highlights how different services contribute variably to value creation. The study primarily investigates the effects of local innovations in the initial service step on overall service times. Interestingly, it reveals that innovations can sometimes negatively impact critical service quality measures. This finding underscores the importance of considering local service peculiarities when implementing innovations.

Figure 5.1 depicts the relationship between luxury brand experience and its various influencing factors, as well as the impact on different brand-related dimensions.

FIGURE 5.1 Brand experience: determinants and impact

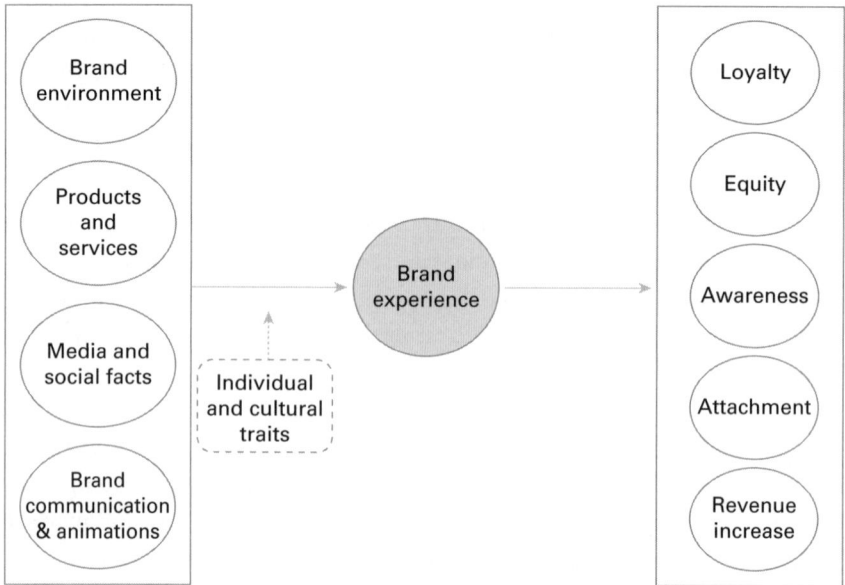

Brand experience is determined by the brand environment, media and social elements, brand products and services, the brand communication (including non-experiential information) and animation activities.

The concept of 'brand environment' encapsulates not just physical spaces like retail stores, hotels or restaurants, but also virtual settings like online platforms. 'Brand environment' conveys the holistic setting where the brand's essence and experience come to life, regardless of the location. It's a comprehensive term that includes any physical or digital space where a brand can interact with its audience and create immersive experiences.

The relationship between the four determinants and the brand experience is mediated by individual and cultural factors related to the client. The retail setting is also where cultural and individual factors come into play (Shavitt and Barnes, 2020), such as a customer's responsiveness to social cues or urgent personal circumstances. An illustrative example is a hurried customer who, despite informing the staff of her need for expedience, is delayed by the store's rigid packaging ritual. This scenario underlines the importance of recognizing and adapting to the immediacy of a customer's situation, ensuring that the luxury service is not only impeccable but also empathetic and responsive to their current context.

The perceived brand experience then influences brand loyalty, brand equity, brand awareness, revenue increase and brand attachment. Brand attachment, indeed, transcends the mere appreciation of a product or service. It's a profound emotional bond where customers feel an integral part of a family or community, sharing and embodying the same values as the brand. This connection goes beyond traditional loyalty; it's about identifying with the brand's ethos, its narrative and its vision. When customers see a reflection of their own values and aspirations in a brand, it fosters a sense of belonging and community. This deep, familial attachment not only influences their purchasing decisions but also drives them to advocate for the brand within their own circles, strengthening the brand's presence and impact in the market.

Incorporating the concept of expectations and satisfaction into the understanding of brand experience adds a crucial dimension to the narrative. Essentially, the customer's experience with a brand is not evaluated in isolation but is compared against the backdrop of their pre-existing expectations. These expectations can stem from past experiences, brand reputation, marketing communications or even word-of-mouth.

When a customer interacts with a brand, they subconsciously measure the actual experience against what they anticipated. This comparison plays a pivotal role in shaping their level of satisfaction. A positive discrepancy, where the experience surpasses expectations, can lead to high levels of satisfaction. Conversely, when the experience falls short of expectations, satisfaction diminishes. This level of satisfaction is a powerful driver of outcomes like brand loyalty, brand equity and brand attachment. Satisfied customers are more likely to return, make repeat purchases and become brand advocates. They also tend to have a stronger emotional connection to the brand, seeing it as a part of their identity. Therefore, managing and exceeding customer expectations (based also on brand's reputation and previous interaction with the brand world) is vital for fostering long-term customer relationships.

From storytelling to story-living

Luxury brands have already well understood the importance of fascinating storytelling surrounding their exceptional products and service. They leverage these genuine stories to embark in an emotional conversation with the audience. It's about crafting a compelling narrative that communicates the brand's values, history or product benefits to engage the audience emotionally and intellectually through various media (eg retail stores, online website, advertisements, social media or brand videos). Indeed, the art of storytelling is a pivotal component of the Cartier boutique experience. Clients stepping into the realm of Cartier expect a narrative journey that traverses the illustrious history of the Maison. The heritage of Cartier is not just about the luxury items it crafts but also about stories associated with each collection and the celebrated individuals who have donned Cartier's creations.

In Milan, every corner of the boutique, from the architectural marvel of the staircase reminiscent of a panther frolicking in an Italian marble quarry to the uppermost floor that evokes nature through the eyes of Stefano Boeri's design, there is a narrative to be told. The boutique itself, with its carefully chosen French lacquer and special materials, becomes a storyteller, inviting guests to immerse themselves in a multisensory encounter with art and culture.

The inclusion in the 'Barometro' (which collects feedback provided by clients after a store visit) of storytelling-related questions reflects the importance of narrative in the client experience. As such, client advisers are not merely staff but custodians of Cartier's lore, trained to share the heritage of the brand. This storytelling extends to the architectural features of the stores themselves.

Loro Piana's approach to storytelling is an essential aspect of their brand communication, focusing on creating a deep sense of desirability and connection with their clients. The art of storytelling for Loro Piana is about crafting narratives that resonate on a personal level, making their products feel indispensable, almost to the point where clients perceive them as something they cannot live without. By producing campaign materials that are akin to cinematic experiences, they aim to evoke emotions and desires that align with the aspirational nature of their brand. Their storytelling intertwines with client engagement, accounting for a significant portion of the customer experience. Loro Piana emphasizes the importance of building upon each product's desirability to ensure that it becomes not only desirable, but also genuinely attractive to their clientele.

By focusing on storytelling, Loro Piana not only communicates the unique attributes of their products, but also shares the brand's legacy, dating back to 1924; the rarity of its materials; the integrated chain that manages quality from source to client; the perfect harmony between tradition and innovation, investing significantly in R&D, crafting innovative fabrics like sophisticated linen blends and cashmere denim developed in Japan.

This approach to storytelling does not just tell a story; it invites clients to live and experience the narrative of the brand, making it a compelling part of their lifestyle.

Loro Piana, for instance, by showing people into mountain settings, not only narrates the story of its products but also encapsulates the essence of a lifestyle that their clientele can aspire to or see themselves in. Whether it's through experiencing the tranquillity of mountainous terrains or the joy of sledding down snowy hills, the brand is effectively associating its products with these high-quality experiences. Additionally, aligning with trends like cocooning, which emphasizes comfort and coziness in one's lifestyle, enhances this connection. By integrating their products into these narratives, Loro Piana can reinforce the desirability and lifestyle aspirations that their products embody. This multifaceted approach allows for a dynamic interaction between the brand and the consumer, where the product isn't just a purchase but a key to an aspirational lifestyle.

However, storytelling is not enough. It's a visible progressive move into a more immersive engagement strategy that goes beyond traditional storytelling by integrating the customer into the brand's world. As a happy ending, clients are invited to live and experience the narrative of the brand. They become a part of the story, often creating or influencing the narrative through their actions. This term has gained traction especially with the advent of virtual reality (VR), augmented reality (AR) and interactive marketing campaigns (Shankar et al, 2021). In this approach, the audience is no longer just consuming content; they are actively living it and making decisions that can change the story's direction. Brands using story-living invite customers to engage in experiences that embody the brand's ethos, allowing for a more personal, deeper emotional connection and more profound engagement.

Storyliving for a luxury and technical bike brand could manifest as an immersive brand experience that transcends traditional advertising. Rather than simply showcasing the bike's capabilities, the brand could craft an experiential journey that invites customers to be protagonists in their own adventure narrative, using the bike as their trusted companion.

Imagine a campaign where clients are encouraged to embark on curated expeditions, ranging from serene countryside rides to adrenaline-fuelled mountain treks. These adventures are designed to not only demonstrate the bike's technical prowess but also to engage the riders' senses and emotions. They could journey through picturesque landscapes, discover hidden historical sites or challenge themselves on renowned biking trails.

To deepen the connection with the brand, participants could be prompted to document their experiences, creating a personal diary of their journey. This diary would capture not only their physical travels, but also the personal transformations they undergo. From the exhilaration of conquering a steep climb to the fun during rides, or the quiet reflection during a solo journey at dawn – every entry would be a testament to the bike's role in their life's narrative.

As well, luxury sailing brands might invite prospects to participate in sailing challenges or organized trips. These companies provide an immersive experience that enhances the client's connection to the world of sailing. The events might include participation in prestigious regattas, exclusive sailing expeditions to exotic locations, or even hands-on sailing experiences under the guidance of skilled sailors. These activities not only allow customers to experience the thrill of sailing, but also foster a sense of community among brand enthusiasts.

These stories, once shared, form authentic, user-generated content that showcases the brand's impact on real lives. Through this strategy, the brand could build a community of storytellers and adventurers, with each client's tale contributing to the collective mythos surrounding these luxury bikes or sailing boats.

This form of story-living not only elevates the product, but also creates a bond between the brand and its clientele, as each personal experience becomes a shared chapter in the brand's ongoing legacy.

Crafting experiences at different levels

Experiences, wherever they are set and lived, are a powerful way to differentiate a brand from competitors, improving brand image and equity (Pine and Gilmore, 1998). The notion of customer engagement transcends the traditional confines of transactional interactions, elevating to an art form that orchestrates a symphony of experiences at various levels. These experiences are meticulously crafted, aiming to resonate with customers at the product level, brand level and through the routine touchpoints of daily operations.

At product level, customers are invited to discover the latest collections and products, creating a tangible connection with the brand's tangible offerings. Loro Piana, which eschews traditional fashion shows, has a distinctive approach in engaging clients at product level. Their strategy involves a collection that remains on the sales floor for an extended six-month period. This collection is segmented into different 'ways', where each month is dedicated to a particular theme or aspect of the collection. This methodology allows for a deeper exploration of the collection's narrative, with each 'way' being supported by its own set of campaigns, videos and storytelling efforts.

This strategy represents a holistic approach to product communication and commercial activation. It's a clear departure from the more common seasonal showcases of fashion, reflecting Loro Piana's commitment to timelessness over trendiness. Instead of a one-off event like a fashion show, Loro Piana's activations are designed to continuously engage with clients, allowing for an evolving conversation around the collection in store and out of store.

The brand level encompasses the non-commercial, the realm of events. Moncler's events showcase the ability to blend brand value communication and engagement with passionate audiences. In February 2023, Moncler held a London concert celebrating 'The Art of Genius', attracting 12,000 guests and achieving a global reach of over 10 billion, with 1.6 million livestream viewers. The event featured unique shows, including a robot peepshow and a live performance by Alicia Keys. Similarly, a Milan event in September 2023, inspired by glamping, featured Pharrell Williams and musician Tobe Nwigwe, drawing 5,000 attendees. Additionally, Moncler's 70th anniversary was marked by a large-scale celebration in Milan's Piazza Duomo, where 1,952 performers, clad in iconic Maya puffer jackets, presented a ballet in the rain to an audience of 18,000.

Experiences deeply entwined with the brand's essence might also offer a personalized and experiential journey. This dimension is about narrative and connection, designed to envelop top-tier clients in the brand's aura, often with a touch of exclusivity and prestige. For instance, the revered invite to a Valentino fashion show is a quintessential brand-level experience, offering a glimpse behind the velvet rope into the heart of the Maison's creativity. This is not merely an event, but a passage into the inner sanctum of Valentino's legacy.

Similarly, a private dinner, a curated visit to the brand's archives or an exclusive viewing of haute couture collections are all experiential threads woven into the fabric of the brand's relationship with its clientele. Jaeger-LeCoultre opens the doors to their manufacturing hub, allowing the public to book visits and engage with the heritage and craftsmanship that go into each piece. This approach not only showcases their technical prowess, but also strengthens the narrative of heritage and artisanal excellence.

These brand experiences may also encompass cultural and artistic engagements that align with the brand's identity. Valentino, in a collaboration with Magazzino Italian Art, showcased Schifano's artworks within its Madison Avenue store, merging the spheres of high fashion and fine art, creating a narrative that the brand is not only a purveyor of luxury but also a patron of the arts.

Another example is the partnership between Valentino and Triennale Milano for the 'Pittura Italiana Oggi' exhibition, which invites customers who harbour an appreciation for art into a dialogue with the brand, deepening the bonds through shared interests and passions.

Day-to-day operations cover the everyday engagement fuelled by a stream of fresh content, keeping the conversation between brand (typically through client advisers) and customer both lively and ongoing. In the day-to-day operational engagement, the pivotal role of client advisers emerges as the core of true clienteling (see Chapter 7). Their daily interactions with clients form the foundation of a personalized experience, fostering relationships that transcend transactional exchanges.

Client advisers are equipped with the skills and tools to maintain a continuous dialogue with clients. They utilize personalized messaging to reach out to individuals, ensuring that communication feels bespoke and attentive to each client's preferences and history with the brand. This personal touch is essential; it creates a sense of individual care and attention that reinforces client loyalty and satisfaction.

Moreover, the integration of technology, particularly branded apps, augments the clienteling strategy by offering a platform for both generic and highly personalized communication. These apps serve as a conduit for tailored recommendations, updates on new collections, and exclusive insights, allowing client advisers to enhance the client experience with a mix of curated content that speaks directly to the individual's tastes and interests.

Crafting experiences by building communities

The evolution from product-centric to customer-centric and now towards community-centric strategies reflects a deepening understanding of the dynamics of value creation and engagement in the luxury world. Initially, the focus was predominantly on the products themselves, emphasizing quality of services or craftsmanship and the exclusivity of the physical items. As markets became more competitive and consumers more discerning, the emphasis shifted towards a customer-centric approach, which prioritizes personalization, exceptional service and experiences tailored to individual needs and preferences.

Today, we are witnessing a further evolution towards community-centricity, particularly driven by the aspirations of new generations who seek not only personalized experiences but also a sense of belonging and shared identity. These community-centric strategies go beyond the individual to embrace groups of like-minded individuals who collectively appreciate the ethos, heritage and lifestyle that a brand represents. Atelier Chanel in New York, although open to the public, acts as a community hub where the brand and its most devoted customers can engage in a shared luxury experience. Set in the fashionable district of SoHo, this atelier is not just a shop but a place where beauty dreams become a tangible reality (Shatzman, 2019).

The distinction between the privileges of membership and an ordinary visit lies in the depth of engagement with the brand. Ordinary visitors might see the Atelier as a place to admire and purchase products, while members might view it as a portal to a deeper brand experience – one that offers them a continuous narrative with the brand's history, values and future. The idea behind creating the community is to foster a sense of exclusivity and belonging among Chanel brand enthusiasts. By becoming members, people are often given priority access to services, events or products that non-members might not receive. For example, membership privileges might include:

- early access to view and purchase new collections before they are available to the general public
- members-only events, such as launches or talks that are not open to the general public
- access to bespoke tailoring services, personalized styling sessions or one-on-one consultations with beauty advisers
- the opportunity to purchase limited edition items or member-exclusive products
- curated experiences
- a platform to connect with other like-minded individuals who share a passion for the brand and beauty, fostering a sense of community and shared experience

This transition to community-centricity is fuelled by the recognition that consumers are increasingly looking for ways to connect with others who share their interests and values. They desire platforms where they can interact, engage in meaningful activities together and celebrate their shared passions. Such community-driven initiatives not only deepen the relationship between the brand and its clientele but also amongst the clients themselves, fostering brand loyalty and creating a robust, self-sustaining ecosystem of advocates and ambassadors.

Brands like Ferrari are exemplifying this shift by creating experiences that allow customers to connect over shared passions, such as exclusive events or membership clubs that offer both personal and group benefits.

Experience-Led Strategy and community building at Ferrari

Ferrari, the iconic brand synonymous with luxury and performance, has redefined the paradigm of automotive-luxury excellence through its pioneering Experience-Led Strategy (ELS). Far beyond conventional offers in the luxury space, be it automotive, manufacturing or exclusivity, Ferrari places a dedicated premium on creating emotional connections, establishing enduring relationships, and fostering vibrant communities of passionate enthusiasts 'Ferraristi' (be these owners, prospects or overall 'aficionadi').

A key emphasis is on community building. Ferrari wants clients to feel a sense of belonging and connection to the brand. By providing diverse experiences tailored to individual preferences, be it performance cars, 'Classiche' classic cars, racing activities or specific organized driving-events, Ferrari aims to make each client an ambassador. The brand extends its influence globally through lifestyle stores, theme parks, museums, restaurants and international 'Ferrari Universe' events (including in Italy, Australia and Korea), reinforcing its presence and community-centric approach.

At the heart of Ferrari's groundbreaking strategy lies the direct communication with clients and the fusion of physical and digital communication. The brand actively cultivates a community-first approach, leveraging both digital and physical realms to engage clients (owners) and prospects (future owners). This integration between digital and physical is orchestrated seamlessly through the Ferrari mobile application.

The Ferrari app is a gateway to the Ferrari Universe, providing Ferrari owners and prospects with a direct channel to the brand. It goes beyond being a mere digital tool; it is an immersive experience that brings the essence of Ferrari into the palm of one's hand. Through the app, clients gain unprecedented access to their cars in a virtual garage – their current Ferrari vehicles, status on use and performance, reminders of activities regarding maintenance, 3D customization facilities, notifications about warranty expirations, shopping in 'My Store' and booking onto courses offered by 'Corso Piloti' (Ferrari driver courses include training in wet/limited adherence or snow and ice). The platform allows access to individual information to owners.

Ferrari SpA primarily operates through a B2B2C model, where the main relationship is between Ferrari and its subsidiary offices and their dealership network. These dealerships then interact directly with the customers. This structure highlights a two-step channel where Ferrari first engages in business-to-business (B2B) transactions with its dealerships, who in turn manage the business-to-customer (B2C) aspect, thus creating a combined B2B2C channel.

And last but not least, the biggest value-add for clients derives from content and insights which are typically not available outside this dedicated network: videos, product launches, invitations to private previews, premiere launch events, services and accessory offers including lifestyle and apparel, for example.

While the app is undeniably central to Ferrari's communication strategy, it is not an isolated entity. It acts as a catalyst for physical touchpoints, linking the virtual and real-world seamlessly. The app, for instance, facilitates personalized showroom visits, creating a tangible connection to the digital interactions. This synergy underscores Ferrari's commitment to making the brand experience holistic and immersive. This tailored communication ensures clients remain connected and eager to return to discover news and new offers.

The Ferrari Experience-Led Strategy hinges on the concept that experiences are not just events, but building blocks for enduring relationships. Ferrari is like the gatekeeper to an array of experiences, segmented into brand, on-road and on-track categories. Each experience is meticulously designed to create a lasting connection with the client, offering a personalized journey into the world of Ferrari that defies geographical constraints. At the core of this transformative strategy lies the idea of 'Experience Platforms' ideated centrally that go beyond borders, connecting enthusiasts globally.

BRAND EXPERIENCES

Ferrari orchestrates grand product launches, unveiling new models in spectacular fashion. The 'Universo Ferrari' platform, initiated in 2019, replaces traditional motorshows, offering clients personalized experiences in Maranello and in global roadshows (eg Sydney in 2022, Korea in 2023) where the full regional eco-system was deployed with the complete portfolio and limited edition vehicles, classics, after-sales service, driving experiences with key opinion leaders: long term collectors, owners, prospects and journalists, trade experts and lifestyle magazine publications. Financial analysts and investors and, of course, Ferrari CEO Benedetto Vigna and senior management are also in attendance.

Events like 'Casa Ferrari' (during race weekends or at luxury settings) create exclusive spaces for clients, turning celebrations and brand activations into memorable experiences. A concept of a 'home away from home', Casa Ferrari transforms third-party venues into exclusive spaces during events like festivals, Pebble Beach (USA) and Silverstone (UK). These spaces are tailored exclusively for Ferrari clients, creating an intimate and celebratory atmosphere.

ON-ROAD EXPERIENCES

Reserved for an even more select clientele who own a number of limited and one-off cars, the prestigious 'Cavalcade' is a curated five-day driving extravaganza set against stunning backdrops at the most prestigious locations worldwide. Locations include Italy of course, but also Morocco, the Middle East and Asia. To be there, these very important customers pay a significant entrance fee (€45,000 in 2023). The experience unfolds daily, keeping participants in suspense, with real-time updates and personalized photos available through the app. The event also incorporates a charitable dimension, reinforcing Ferrari's commitment to social responsibility.

Ferrari also pays homage to iconic races such as the 'Mille Miglia' and 'Targa Florio' (both are historic races, part of winning history or racing becoming an iconic facet to the Ferrari story) by organizing 'Tributes' that are open to all Ferrari owners. These one-day experiences, often in collaboration with racing organizations, allow participants to share in the thrill of historic events.

It's clear that within this expansive Ferrari Universe, experiences cater to varied tastes. While the iconic Cavalcade offers clients prestigious destinations, top-tier hotels and family-centric enjoyment, the Tribute events target those who crave the thrill of the race. Take, for instance, Ferrari's return to Le Mans after 50 years, a momentous victory immortalized in a one-day Tribute experience departing from Paris, traversing the Champagne region and sleeping in organized 'containers' to follow the race. It culminated in

Casa Ferrari hospitality at Le Mans – a journey that encapsulates the essence of Ferrari's racing legacy. This unique journey encapsulates the essence of Ferrari's racing legacy and its commitment to creating memorable, unconventional experiences.

Ferrari Tours are multi-day driving experiences, organized by regions or dealers, with open participation to all clients. In a nod to evolving demographics, Ferrari recognizes the increasing number of women driving its cars, even dedicating specific tours to female enthusiasts.

Introduced in 2023, the Legacy Tour celebrates iconic models of the past, such as the F40 (launched in 1987, the last model launched in the presence of Enzo Ferrari himself). Exclusively open to owners of these legendary cars, the tour creates a unique bond, blending nostalgia with the thrill of driving from one iconic location to another in the space of a few days and allowing bonding with fellow-owners and driving experiences (with your partners or friend) in a unique, privileged environment. Often the Italy-based events conclude at the Ferrari factory and Fiorano track, an opportunity to the cars to 'come home' and salute the production Classiche team in Maranello.

Lastly, there is the 'Test drive platform'. Ferrari invites clients and prospects to test the latest models. Having learned from the Universo experiences and the highly positive feedback from participants, Ferrari accelerated the driving experiences (on track and in special locations, including the Swiss Alps or French Riviera), allowing for recruiting new customers as well as the ideal moment for 'upgrades' of clients adding a V12 or Hybrid (SF90, 296GTB) powered car to their current V8.

ON-TRACK EXPERIENCES

The pinnacle of Ferrari's offerings includes the 'Effort Programme' providing exclusive access to top circuits, the GT racing programme for semi-professional racers and driving schools like 'Corsi Piloti' for skill enhancement. While not a racing programme, it offers a rare opportunity for clients to enjoy their cars in a controlled and exhilarating environment.

For those inclined towards competitive racing, Ferrari offers a GT Racing Programme, enabling semi-professional racers to compete globally. The annual Ferrari 'Finali Mondiale', the culmination of the racing programme, brings participants from various challenges together in a grand celebration including current and past F1 cars, the Le Mans 499P winning cars, different racing series cars as well as the complete portfolio range. It unites owners, fans and employees on a unique occasion. The Finali Mondiali are organized at different locations, including Mugello (in Tuscany, a track owned by Ferrari) as well as at Monza (near Milan), in Spain or the Middle East.

With 'Corsi Piloti', driving schools in Italy, the USA and China, Ferrari allows owners and prospects to enhance their driving skills, offering an immersive experience in high-performance vehicles. And with a dedicated attention to owners of 'Classiche' (cars built 20 years ago and older), Ferrari offers a specific driving programme which that bring clients to another era, driving in unconventional locations (track or road, including on frozen lakes in Finland). Note that the 'art' of driving a manual car is becoming rare, and mastering a 1950s or 1970s clutch-controlled car requires particular attention. So, Ferrari has developed a programme to 're-learn' this mastery, ensuring the enduring pleasure for owners and the general public alike.

Lastly, Ferrari Racing Days held regionally provide a local version of the Ferrari Mondiale, allowing clients to participate in the thrill of racing at circuits like Fuji in Japan.

In conclusion, Ferrari's success lies not only in crafting high-performance, exclusive cars but in curating unparalleled experiences and fostering a global community. By intertwining physical and digital interactions, prioritizing long-term relationships and offering diverse, personalized experiences, Ferrari transcends the traditional boundaries of automotive manufacturing, setting a benchmark for customer engagement in the luxury automotive industry.

The evolution of brand collaborations: From commercial hype to experiential depth

The landscape of brand collaborations has witnessed a significant transformation over the years, evolving from a more traditional and commercial focus to a contemporary approach that emphasizes experiential and brand-level engagements. This shift reflects a nuanced understanding of consumer behaviour and a strategic pivot towards long-term brand equity over immediate revenue generation.

In the past, brand collaborations often centred around creating a buzz within the industry, leveraging the collective appeal of brands to attract attention and drive short-term sales. These partnerships were typically between brands within the same sector – think of the fashion industry, where collaborations with names like Levi's and New Balance were not uncommon. The formula was straightforward: fuse the distinctive strengths of two brands to create a limited-edition product that would generate hype, draw crowds into stores and spike sales figures. This was a tactical move, a merchandising strategy that capitalized on the novelty of the partnership and the exclusive nature of the offerings.

However, as the market became saturated with such collaborations, the novelty began to wear off. Consumers started to seek something beyond the product; they craved a story, an experience, a connection with the brand that transcended the transaction. This marked the beginning of a new era for brand partnerships, one that favoured depth over width, meaning over mere visibility.

Today, luxury brands are increasingly engaging in collaborations that extend beyond their traditional boundaries, reaching out to players in the arts, cultural institutions, the hospitality sector and various associations (eg Unesco, Blu, One Ocean Foundation). These collaborations are more strategic, curated to enrich the brand narrative and provide an immersive experience that aligns with the brand's values and ethos. Rather than just co-branding a product, these partnerships aim to co-create experiences that resonate on a deeper level with consumers. In the grand scheme of luxury, it's clear that the engagement with customers is an ever-shifting paradigm, adapting to the dynamic nature of the customer base.

The decline of traditional brand-to-brand merchandising collaborations in favour of these multidimensional experiences can be attributed to a variety of factors. Consumers' increasing desire for authenticity and personal growth, the oversaturation of the market with limited-edition collections that no longer feel limited and the rise of social media as a space for consumers to seek and share unique experiences all play a part.

Luxury brands, with their rich histories and stories, are uniquely positioned to capitalize on this shift. They are able to leverage their heritage to offer something that goes beyond the material product – a sense of belonging to a tradition, an insider's glimpse into a world of craftsmanship or participation in a movement that reflects their personal values and aspirations.

A practical case could be a luxury fashion house collaborating with an artist to curate an exclusive exhibition within their retail space, transforming it into a cultural hub rather than a mere point of sale. Or, a high-end brand could partner with a luxury hotel to offer bespoke experiences that embody the lifestyle the brand advocates, thereby elevating the consumer's interaction with the brand to something more meaningful and memorable.

Consider the case of Valentino's partnership with Palazzo Avino. Here, the Italian house didn't just pop up within the historic confines of a 12th-century Ravello villa; it weaved its essence into the very fabric of the location. This summertime pop-up venture celebrated the 'Escape' 2023 capsule collection, but Valentino's vision encompassed a complete aesthetic infusion into Palazzo Avino's beach club, the Clubhouse by the Sea. This is a 'destination takeover' in its most holistic form – Valentino red splashed across the beach club, from 1950s-style umbrellas to yoga mats, all bearing the signature 'V' logo.

'Destination takeovers' like these reflect a sophisticated understanding of consumer desires. They're not just about selling products; they're about selling a lifestyle. For instance, guests at Palazzo Avino are treated to Valentino sunglasses and keychains, tangible mementos that extend the brand experience beyond the physical pop-up. It's an approach that speaks to a symbiotic relationship between brand and environment, where the essence of a locale is captured and expressed through the lens of luxury heritage.

These partnerships are not mere business ventures but carefully chosen alliances that augment the brand's narrative and deepen the customer's immersion into the world of luxury.

A profound example of how brands can transcend traditional boundaries leveraging on artistic collaborations is Jaeger-LeCoultre. Catherine Rénier, the CEO, emphasizes that purchasing a timepiece is akin to acquiring a piece of art. This sentiment is the foundation of their 'Made of Makers' project which collaborates with diverse artists to enrich the experience of their time-pieces.

Within this project, the collaboration with Nina Métayer, a celebrated pâtissière, is a remarkable instance where gastronomy meets craftsmanship. Métayer's creations for Jaeger-LeCoultre are more than just pastries; they are edible embodiments of the Reverso theme and the Golden Ratio, both central to Jaeger-LeCoultre's design philosophy. These pastries incorporate ingredients from the Vallée de Joux to evoke the natural beauty of Jaeger-LeCoultre's Swiss heritage. In the realm of music, as well, Jaeger-LeCoultre's partnership with British musician TØKIO MYERS to create a symphony for the Golden Ratio Musical Show exemplifies how sound can capture the essence of timelessness just as a watch does.

Furthermore, the alliance with Korean digital artist Yiyun Kang has taken the brand's narrative to a visual dimension. Kang's large-scale 3D-video sculpture 'Origin' is an artistic representation that mirrors the symmetry of nature and the artistry of the Reverso's design.

These partnerships demonstrate how Jaeger-LeCoultre transcends mere watchmaking to engage with the public on multiple sensory levels. It's about storytelling through craftsmanship, sophistication and the educational role the brand plays in the watchmaking industry.

Luxury brands have increasingly engaged with arts and culture, often extending their collaborations with cultural institutions. This trend has manifested in various forms such as temporary installations, exhibitions, cultural workshops and films.

An exemplary instance of this phenomenon was observed during Frieze Seoul 2023 (for a complete illustration, see Hu, 2023). Frieze Seoul, part of the prestigious family of Frieze art fairs, took place at COEX in the Gangnam district, bringing together influential art galleries and showcasing contemporary art alongside historical masterpieces. Coinciding with the fair, luxury brands like Acne Studio, Bottega Veneta, Chanel and Prada presented culturally immersive installations.

Chanel collaborated with the Yéol Korean Heritage Preservation Society, presenting 'Woobomanri: An Enduring Walk Toward Purity', an exhibition that highlighted traditional Korean crafts and fostered intergenerational artistic dialogue. The exhibition not only ran alongside Frieze Seoul but also during Seoul Fashion Week, enhancing its visibility and impact.

Prada, under the banner of Prada Mode, held a two-day event featuring site-specific installations by Korean filmmakers, fostering an ambitious vision of contemporary cinema. The event transformed KOTE into a multidimensional cultural hub, exploring themes of culinary culture, absence and mortality.

Bottega Veneta partnered with the Leeum Museum of Art for the solo exhibition 'Willow Drum Oriole' by artist Suki Seokyeong Kang, reimagining traditional Korean landscape paintings. Similarly, Acne Studios celebrated its printed magazine 'Acne Paper' with an 18th-edition launch at a local bookstore and a warehouse party, highlighting the brand's cultural engagement.

These initiatives by luxury brands are not just showcases of art and culture, but also serve as platforms for launching new products, hosting elite gatherings and reinforcing brand values. They offer an immersive experience that blends luxury with cultural enrichment, and underlines the significance of luxury brands as patrons and contributors to the global cultural landscape.

One size does not fit all: Localized experiences

Luxury brands have long been bastions of a particular kind of prestige tradition and craftsmanship that, from the country of origin, started to transcend borders. Yet, as these brands extend their reach into new territories, they encounter a landscape rich with diversity of local cultures, tastes and preferences that demand more than a one-size-fits-all approach. The art of localization becomes not merely an operational necessity but a narrative that unfolds in the alleys of global markets, telling a story of adaptation, respect and integration.

Localization is the process whereby companies adapt their products, services and business strategies to fit the specific cultural, social and legal needs of a target market. It allows them to establish a presence that is culturally sensitive, legally compliant and strategically aligned with the local market's unique characteristics and needs. Localization helps companies meet the specific needs and expectations of local consumers, which can differ significantly from one country to another. At the same time, they must ensure their operations comply with local laws and regulations. Localization also helps companies avoid cultural insensitivity or legal issues that can arise from not understanding the local context.

Consider the journey of Burberry. Once known for its classic trench coats, the British brand faced a turning point when it looked to the East (Lojacono and Pan, 2021). Japan presented an opportunity, albeit with a twist: the clientele was predominantly female, petite and lived under the warm rains of Asian summers. Burberry's response was as elegant as it was strategic – they crafted lighter raincoats tailored for Japanese summers, which soon adorned the wardrobes of stylish women across Asia. This move was more than product adaptation; it was a dialogue with a culture, a statement that said, 'We see you, we understand you, and we are here for you'.

But localization extends beyond the product; it encompasses the entire brand experience. When Bulgari ventured into the vibrant and complex Indian market, it learned a hard lesson in cultural nuance. Its initial failure in the early 2000s was a sobering reminder that trust and heritage are the cornerstones of the Indian jewellery market – a realm dominated by family-run jewellers with generational clientele. Bulgari's resurgence in 2014 came with a renewed respect for Indian tastes and traditions (Bryson and Atwal, 2017). The Italian luxury house not only introduced designs with a local flavour, infusing around 20 per cent of its products with yellow gold and bridal motifs, but also reinvented the retail experience with opulent private rooms, catering to the Indian predilection for discretion and personalized service.

The challenge for luxury brands is to weave their identity into the fabric of each locale without losing the essence that makes them globally desirable.

Sephora's misadventure in Japan serves as a cautionary tale. In 1999, the beauty giant entered the Ginza district with a flourish, only to exit three years later. Their stores, laden with perfumes, clashed with the Japanese predilection for skincare and subtlety, revealing a disconnect with local consumer behaviour.

Modern luxury brands, armed with these lessons, now engage in a more narrative form of localization. They tell stories through their store designs which echo local architecture and culture while preserving their brand's soul. They collaborate with local artists and influencers, becoming patrons of regional creativity and style. They harness digital platforms, not only to sell, but to create immersive experiences that resonate with local sensibilities.

The story of localization is one of continuous evolution. It's about luxury brands, like Bulgari, Cartier and Louis Vuitton, becoming fluent in the language of the markets they enter – whether it's through the curated ambiance of their stores, the exclusive nature of their services or the local craftsmanship they showcase. It's about transforming the unfamiliar into the intimate, turning every store visit into a homecoming, no matter where that store might be. This is the new chapter in luxury experience – where localization is not an afterthought but the core of a brand's global strategy, ensuring that their global journey is marked by a series of meaningful local engagements.

This delicate process is akin to a brand immersing itself into the cultural milieu of a new locale, understanding and embodying the particular ethos, traditions and preferences that define the country. It's about crafting a narrative that resonates deeply with local consumers while maintaining the brand's intrinsic values and global appeal. That's the reason why the term 'contextualization' is more effective than 'localization' to evidence a subtle, but critical distinction: it's about brands positioning themselves within the correct frame of reference, ensuring their story is told in a way that's both globally consistent and locally relevant.

Today, all luxury brands craft a global presence marked by local relevance, ensuring that the brand's narrative is not lost in translation but is instead enriched by each market's unique fabric. Where brands like Gucci, Tiffany and Burberry have become adept storytellers, 'contextualization' serves as a guiding principle. It's not about redefining the brand for each market but about contextualizing its essence so that it becomes a part of the local context – distinct, valued and cherished. This is the nuanced art of localization: a symphony of global elegance played out on a diverse array of local stages.

Let's delve into how luxury brands can, and do, adapt along different facets of their operations: communication, products, services, retail strategy and store interiors.

Communication

Luxury brands curate their marketing strategies to echo the local heartbeat. This means using platforms that are the daily bread of local consumers, such as WeChat in China or KakaoTalk in South Korea, to create digital narratives that engage and entice. It's about leveraging the prevalence of mobile-first societies in Asia, for instance, to offer seamless online experiences that culminate in the physical elegance of their stores.

Effective localization in communication means aligning with local narratives. It's about the resonance of a brand's story within the cultural context, which could be achieved by collaborating with local influencers and celebrities, like Chanel's endorsement by South Korean actress Park Shin-Hye, or featuring product names and messages that reflect local idioms and sentiments.

Products

Adaptation here is both subtle and significant. It might mean Louis Vuitton crafting leather goods in India to capture the essence of local craftsmanship while infusing it with their iconic design language. Or it could be the likes of Chanel or Hèrmes creating Lunar New Year capsule collections that pay homage to regional celebrations and shopping patterns. Or brands like Tom Ford offering fragrances with oud, the precious oil, in the Middle East.

In 2022, Cartier collaborated with Japanese fashion designer Chitose Abe of Sacai to reimagine the iconic Trinity ring. This unique fusion resulted in a capsule collection of six pieces that debuted at Paris Fashion Week. The collection modifies the scale and proportion of the original Trinity design, offering a fresh perspective on a classic. This reinterpretation includes oversized bands in bracelets and rings that extend across multiple fingers, infusing traditional elegance with contemporary flair. This creative venture reflects the brand's willingness to integrate local influences and cultural diversity into its timeless designs. The collection was primarily marketed in select locations worldwide, focusing on Asian countries and the UK, thus catering to diverse cultural tastes and preferences.

At the product level of engagement, collaborations between brands serve as a potent tool for communicating specific narratives to wider audiences. These collaborations often involve intertwining the distinctive qualities of both brands to create a unique offering that resonates with a particular market segment or geographic locale. A prime example of this is the collaboration between the Italian luxury brand Valentino and the Japanese label Porter-Yoshida & Co. This partnership saw the melding of Valentino's iconic design language with Porter-Yoshida & Co's renowned craftsmanship. The result was a special collection that highlighted Porter-Yoshida & Co's signature nylon fabric, a material revered for its durability and style, which was married with Valentino's vibrant patterns and designs. This collection was specifically tailored to appeal to the Japanese market, showcasing a blend of Italian luxury and Japanese functionality. The collaboration was pre-launched in Japan, with strategic locations such as Porter-Yoshida & Co Omotesando and a pop-up store at Isetan Shinjuku – places that are ingrained in the local fashion landscape and resonate with the Japanese audience.

These carefully chosen venues underscore the importance of cultural relevance and proximity to the consumer, ensuring that the products are not only physically accessible but also contextually connected to the audience. By leveraging the strengths of both Valentino and Porter-Yoshida & Co, the collaboration succeeded in creating a product experience that was deeply rooted in material excellence and geographic specificity. It communicated a message of innovation and cross-cultural partnership, appealing to a clientele that values both the aesthetic heritage of Valentino and the functional elegance of Porter-Yoshida & Co. This targeted approach at the product level exemplifies how luxury brands can engage with customers by offering them something that is culturally pertinent.

Services

Exclusivity and personalization are the cornerstones of luxury services. Bulgari exemplifies this with its Indian foray, offering private shopping experiences that cater to the Indian culture's appreciation for privacy and family heritage in luxury purchases. Similarly, concierge and consignment services in the Middle East cater to the ultra-wealthy who demand discretion and bespoke experiences. Staff at prestigious hotels are trained to be culturally astute, recognizing and respecting the diverse traditions, dietary restrictions and lifestyle habits of guests from across the globe.

Whether it's avoiding meat products for guests from India, avoiding alcohol for guests from the Middle East or ensuring a selection of herbal teas for guests from East Asia, each preference is meticulously noted and catered to.

Retail strategy and store interiors

Brands today are not bound to replicate the same experience across all locations. Instead, they are adept at infusing local culture into their boutiques, creating bespoke experiences that resonate deeply with the locale. This strategy is pivotal in ensuring that the brand resonates with the local audience, reflecting their tastes, cultural nuances and preferences. Cartier is a prime example of how luxury brands are adapting to local cultures and environments to enhance the customer experience. Cartier stores worldwide showcase an alchemy of local materials, decorative elements and colours that speak to each area's distinctiveness.

Cartier's approach to using their stores as vehicles for communication is demonstrated by their unique pop-up in Japan. Inspired by the local ubiquitous 'Kombini' concept, Cartier reimagined everyday items through the lens of luxury, thereby elevating the mundane to the extraordinary. That space was not only Instagram-friendly but also a place for community, enjoyment and purchase of specially developed products. This pop-up offered a playful and engaging environment, serving as a new experiential direction for client advisers and customers alike.

In Mykonos, a seasonal Cartier boutique was conceived to resonate with the local vibe – laid-back yet luxurious, with a Greek artist's collaboration, it appealed to a younger audience, effectively rejuvenating the brand's clientele. This boutique was not just a place to shop, but a destination to experience the brand amidst the laid-back luxury of the Mediterranean.

Every boutique is a unique chapter in the brand's narrative. Whether it's the seaside-inspired interiors of the Cannes boutique or the design-centric renovation of Milan's flagship, each Cartier store is a reflection of its environment, yet undeniably Cartier in essence.

Whether it's the silver tones in Bulgari's London hotel that nod to the city's silversmith heritage or the vibrant aesthetics of a Gucci store in Seoul, these spaces tell a story that's culturally rooted yet unmistakably aligned with the brand's ethos. Gucci Gaok (from the Korean word for 'traditional home) is the flagship store in the vibrant and eclectic Itaewon neighbourhood of Seoul. It is a nod to the brand's efforts to integrate local architectural and cultural elements into the store's design which includes mosaic-like ceramics and rounded staircases. The store's mosaic walls infuse the space with colours and vibes reminiscent of the 1970s nightclub aesthetic. The store provides unique features, such as the presence of two VIP spaces furnished with wooden boiseries, sumptuous chairs and a carpet, offering a more private and exclusive environment for discerning clients which adds an exclusive club-like feel to the shopping experience.

The store's facade, designed by renowned Korean artist Seung Mo Park, features a unique 'Hwan' (Illusion) theme, representing a dark forest to symbolize the illusion of nature. This design consists of over 100 steel panels, each comprising 13 layers, and aims to explore the interplay between light and shadow. This facade not only adds to the aesthetic appeal of the store but also reflects on contemporary environmental concerns, emphasizing the existence and non-existence of nature. Gucci's localization is not just limited to the physical aspects of the store, but extends to the selection of local celebrities or influencers as brand ambassadors.

Through these multifaceted adaptations, brands not only navigate, but also thrive in the local landscape, turning the potential 'liability of foreignness' (Denk, Kaufmann and Roesch, 2012; Zaheer, 1995; Mezias, 2002) into a strategic asset. The concept of liability of foreignness (LOF) refers to the extra challenges and costs that multinational enterprises face when operating in foreign markets, compared to local companies. These challenges can arise due to a lack of familiarity with the local market, cultural differences and the need to comply with different legal and regulatory systems. Major sources of LOF are:

- unfamiliarity hazards that result from a lack of local market knowledge, including cultural, social and business norms
- relational hazards that arise from difficulties in managing internal and external relationships in a foreign environment, such as with employees, suppliers or customers
- discrimination hazards that occur when a foreign firm is treated unfavourably by local stakeholders or governments, which could be due to consumer preferences for local products or for political reasons

These liabilities can affect a brand's performance in the foreign market, including its profitability, efficiency and survival chances. The impact of LOF can vary based on factors such as cultural and geographical distance, the level of the firm's international experience and the competitiveness of the foreign market.

This challenge involves adapting to local market peculiarities, often incurring additional costs associated with aligning brand strategies with diverse cultural, regulatory and operational environments. While this alignment is essential for long-term success and relevance in international markets, it can initially reduce return on foreign sales (ROFS) as brands invest in understanding and integrating into local contexts.

Takeaways

The stories of Audrey's journey in the retail world are woven with a thread of caution for luxury brands: the art of customer engagement is delicate and the leap from personalized storytelling to sales can be a chasm too wide if not navigated with finesse.

The detailed narrative of brand experience illustrated the layered approach to customer engagement in the luxury world, highlighting the intricate planning and diverse strategies employed to create experiences that go beyond the transactional, fostering long-lasting relationships with clientele. Today's competition in luxury is about creating lasting memories and emotional connections, showing that while luxury products are the medium, the true essence of luxury lies in the emotions and memories crafted not only within the walls of each retail store. In a world where products can be quickly imitated, the curated brand experience becomes the ultimate differentiator that can't be replicated. Borrowing from the meticulous standards of luxury hospitality, brands should ensure operational excellence, where attention to detail and anticipation of customer needs are the norm.

Brand-level experiences are the pinnacle of engagement, reserved for those who have not only the means but the desire to delve deeper into the brand's ethos, history and vision. It's an elevated form of clienteling where customers are not just buyers, but connoisseurs, each experience serving to fortify the relationship between the individual and the brand.

It's an era where customers are invited to not only observe, but to participate and co-create. This evolution marks a movement away from passive engagement to active experience, where clients don't just recount the brand's history; they live it, shape it and pass it forward.

Building and nurturing communities around the brand is essential. Luxury brands should foster connections through exclusive events, insider access and platforms where like-minded individuals can interact, share and form a loyal tribe.

Luxury experiences should be sensitive to cultural subtleties, adapting to local customs and preferences without diluting the brand's heritage. This balance ensures relevance and resonance across diverse markets.

By focusing on these core tenets, luxury brands can ensure their experience-led strategies are robust, resonant and reflective of the high standards their clientele expect and deserve.

References and further reading

Borghini, S, Diamond, N, Kozinets, R V, McGrath, M A, Muñiz, A M and Sherry, J F (2009) Why are themed brandstores so powerful? Retail brand ideology at American Girl Place, *Journal of Retailing*, **85** (3), pp. 363–75

Bryson, D and Atwal, G (2017) *Luxury Brands in China and India*, Palgrave MacMillan

Carmon, Z, Shanthikumar, J G and Freed, T (1995) A psychological perspective on service segmentation models: The significance of accounting for consumers' perceptions of waiting and service, *Management Science*, **41** (11), pp. 1806–15

Chitrakorn, K (2023), Gucci's new London flagship targets 'true luxury' customers, *Vogue Business*, www.voguebusiness.com/consumers/guccis-new-london-flagship-targets-true-luxury-customers (archived at https://perma.cc/C54Z-2QKC)

Denk, N, Kaufmann, L and Roesch, J-F (2012) Liabilities of foreignness revisited: A review of contemporary studies and recommendations for future research, *Journal of International Management*, **18**, pp. 322–34, https://doi.org/10.1016/j.intman.2012.07.001 (archived at https://perma.cc/LQ2B-T58Z)

Grewal, D, Noble, S M, Roggeveen, A L and Nordfalt, J (2020), The future of in-store technology, *Journal of the Academy of Marketing Science*, **48** (1), pp. 96–13

Guidara, W (2022) *Unreasonable Hospitality: The remarkable power of giving people more than they expect*, Optimism Press

Haron, A J (2016), Standardized versus localized strategy: The role of cultural patterns in society on consumption and market research, *Journal of Accounting & Marketing*, **5**, pp. 1–4

Hartman, K and Spiro, R (2005) Recapturing store image in customer-based store equity: A construct conceptualization, *Journal of Business Research*, **58**, pp. 1112–20, https://doi.org/10.1016/j.jbusres.2004.01.008 (archived at https://perma.cc/84BX-KR58)

Hu, D (2023) K-pop stars, luxury labels join frieze Seoul to celebrate Korea's booming art scene, WWD, https://wwd.com/eye/lifestyle/frieze-seoul-luxury-k-pop-2023-jennie-blackpink-bts-1235806805/ (archived at https://perma.cc/LV3K-G3WC)

Keller, K L (1993) Conceptualizing, measuring, and managing customer-based brand equity, *Journal of Marketing*, **57** (1), pp. 1–22, https://doi.org/10.2307/1252054 (archived at https://perma.cc/SZ4J-KXCA)

Kozinets, R, Sherry, J, Storm, D, Duhachek, A, Nuttavuthisit, K and DeBerry-Spence, B (2004) Ludic agency and retail spectacle, *Journal of Consumer Research*, **31**, pp. 658–72, https://doi.org/10.1086/425101 (archived at https://perma.cc/PEN4-BZUG)

Lemon, K N and Verhoef, P C (2016) Understanding customer experience throughout the customer journey, *Journal of Marketing*, **80** (6), pp. 69–96, https://doi.org/10.1509/jm.15.0420 (archived at https://perma.cc/U34K-GYH6)

Lojacono, G and Pan, L R Y (2021) *Resilience of Luxury Companies in Times of Change*, De Gruyter

Mezias, J M (2002) How to identify liabilities of foreignness and assess their effects on multinational corporations, *Journal of International Management*, **8**, pp. 265–82

Pine, B J and Gilmore, J (2013) The experience economy: Past, present and future, in J Sundbo and F Sørensen (eds), *Handbook on the Experience Economy*, Elgar

Puccinelli, N M, Goodstein, R C, Grewal, D, Price, R, Raghubir, P and Stewart, D (2009) Customer experience management in retailing: Understanding the buying process, *Journal of Retailing*, **85** (1), pp. 15–30, https://doi.org/10.1016/j.jretai.2008.11.003 (archived at https://perma.cc/2EUS-8Y4E)

Roggeveen, A L, Grewal, D and Schweiger, E B (2020) The DAST framework for retail atmospherics: The impact of in- and out-of-store retail journey touchpoints on the customer experience, *Journal of Retailing*, **96** (1), pp. 128–37, https://doi.org/10.1016/j.jretai.2019.11.002 (archived at https://perma.cc/BR69-DJ2P)

Schmitt, B, Brakus J J and Zarantonello, L (2014) From experiential psychology to consumer experience, *Journal of Consumer Psychology*, **25** (1), pp. 166–71, http://dx.doi.org/10.1016/j.jcps.2014.09.001 (archived at https://perma.cc/Z3J9-YBAM)

Shankar, V, Kalyanam, K, Setia, P, Golmohammadi, A, Tirunillai, S, Douglass, T, Hennessey, J, Bull, J S and Waddoups, R (2021) How technology is changing retail, *Journal of Retailing*, **97** (1), pp. 13–27, https://doi.org/10.1016/j.jretai.2020.10.006 (archived at https://perma.cc/5THQ-KKA7)

Shatzman, C (2019) Chanel opens a beauty wonderland with its first Atelier Beauté in New York, *Forbes*, www.forbes.com/sites/celiashatzman/2019/01/24/chanel-opens-a-beauty-wonderland-with-its-first-atelier-beaute-in-new-york-city/ (archived at https://perma.cc/D5YP-E753)

Shavitt, S and Barnes, A J (2020), Culture and the consumer journey, *Journal of Retailing*, **96** (1), pp. 40–54, https://doi.org/10.1016/j.jretai.2019.11.009 (archived at https://perma.cc/6K65-HXUR)

Tong, C, Nagarajan, M and Cheng, Y (2015) Operational impact of service innovations in multi-step service systems, *Production and Operations Management*, 25, pp. 833–48, https://doi.org/10.1111/poms.12508 (archived at https://perma.cc/8K39-BC6D)

Verhoef, P, Lemon, K, Parasuraman, A P, Roggeveen, A, Tsiros, M and Schlesinger, L (2009) Customer experience creation: Determinants, dynamics and management strategies, *Journal of Retailing*, 85, pp. 31–41, https://doi.org/10.1016/j.jretai.2008.11.001 (archived at https://perma.cc/W62B-J36P)

Yoo, B and Donthu, N (2001) Developing and validating a multidimensional consumer-based brand equity scale, *Journal of Business Research*, 52, pp. 1–14, https://doi.org/10.1016/S0148-2963(99)00098-3 (archived at https://perma.cc/7W43-23MZ)

Zaheer, S (1995) Overcoming the liability of foreignness, *Academy of Management Journal*, 38, pp. 341–63

Zeithaml, V, Parasuraman, A P and Berry, L (1985) Problems and strategies in service marketing, *Journal of Marketing*, 49 (2), pp. 33–46, http://dx.doi.org/10.2307/1251563 (archived at https://perma.cc/UGT2-CGKL)

6

Seamless retail: Bridging the digital and physical divide

GABRIELLA LOJACONO

The in-store experience at Cartier transcends the usual retail interaction, transforming into a theatrical stage where luxury and artistry play the leading roles. The boutique windows become a canvas for storytelling, where precious items like emeralds are presented in a way that honours their grandeur, narrating a tale of their origins and allure. For instance, envision a window transformed into a lush landscape, each pane offering a view into the verdant countries from which the emeralds hail, capturing the essence of their birthplace.

Then there's the tale of the Tutti Frutti ring for a very important customer (VIC) – a piece that doesn't just sit on a cushion but is celebrated amidst an elaborate display of vibrant fruits, mirroring the colourful medley of precious stones that adorn it. Such displays are not merely visual; they convey the brand's dedication to creating an emotional connection with their clientele, making each visit a memorable event.

The boutique's role extends to hosting and planning for a variety of experiences. For example, a Cartier boutique might be envisioned as a festive space, where the store's façade sets the stage for a personal moment like a crafted window display for a birthday surprise, or the entire store is transformed into a romantic setting for a proposal. These moments, where the personal stories of clients intertwine with the brand's legacy, create lasting memories that enhance the customer's journey with the brand.

Behind the scenes, Cartier's artisans, like watchmakers and high jewellery designers, are often brought into the limelight, providing a face to the exquisite craftsmanship that goes into each piece. These experts, typically shrouded in the mystery of their workshops, step forward to share their knowledge and skill, adding an authentic touch to the luxury experience. This humanization of the craft provides customers with a unique opportunity to appreciate the intricate work that defines Cartier's offerings.

Memory creation is at the heart of the luxury experience. Cartier's approach to boutique experiences is strategic and thoughtful. An illustrative example is Cartier's use of the Kintsugi technique, which transforms broken ceramics into works of art with golden seams, symbolizing resilience and beauty. The use of the Kintsugi technique speaks to resilience and renewal, connecting with clients on an emotional level after challenging times like the pandemic and deepening their bond with the brand.

The boutique's atmosphere in Milan is further enriched by the inclusion of a bar – an elegant space where clients can relax and savour moments with the Cartier team. This area serves as a 'distress zone' for those coming in for repairs or simply seeking a convivial atmosphere. It's where the transactional nature of retail is set aside, fostering relationships that extend beyond the purchase.

Special events, such as intimate lunches within the Résidence area or book presentations that delve into the worlds of jewellery and art, provide an exclusive ambiance that blends retail with hospitality. These occasions are often tailored to the clients' personal milestones, such as family gatherings or birthday celebrations, curated by the brand to offer an unparalleled, culturally rich experience.

Each of these elements – the window displays, the expert interactions, the hospitable bar and the exclusive events – compose a narrative that elevates the essence of Cartier.

Furthermore, Cartier's approach to boutique experiences is strategic and rooted in storytelling. The stores are not static showcases, but active, engaging spaces where events, parties and even quiet moments of contemplation are anticipated and facilitated by thoughtful interior design.

Each Cartier store, whether in Milan's design-centric precincts or the historical avenues of London, Tokyo, Rome or Venice, presents a unique atmosphere. These are more than mere retail spaces – they are bastions of the brand's living history, designed to offer experiences that resonate with the local culture and the distinct preferences of the city's denizens. The case of Cartier testifies that retail stores, as mentioned in Chapter 5, have a pivotal role in generating continuous engagement and provide memorable experience. The Cartier retail boutique exemplifies the multifaceted nature of luxury stores, serving not just as a point of sale but as a venue for diverse brand experiences.

This chapter will explore the various functions of such retail stores that transform their space for product showcases, special events, exhibitions, pop-up concepts, interactive animations and tailored customer experiences. Each role will be illustrated to demonstrate how boutiques become a dynamic platform for customer engagement and brand storytelling.

The luxury retail experience becomes a meticulous blend of commercial moments and 'animations' that elevate the customer journey into a realm of shared values, cultural enrichment and unforgettable memories. It's a world where every touchpoint, every event and every collaboration is an opportunity to reinforce the brand's narrative and deepen the customer's connection to the brand they cherish.

In essence, the modern luxury boutique is far from being merely a retail space – it's transformed into a moment where exceptional service meets cultural resonance, where every corner is an invitation to inspiration and every interaction a potential for local social connection. These boutiques have become dynamic stages where the spectacle of heritage and the authenticity of storytelling blend harmoniously with the local culture's distinct rhythm. These spaces are designed not just to showcase the brand's legacy and values but to echo the local heartbeat, to resonate with the community's ethos. They are places where the paradox of blending global prestige with local relevance is artfully navigated. Here, the richness of the brand's origins and the respect for the local milieu coexist, creating a narrative that's both universally admired and personally meaningful.

In the digital era, replicating the richness of in-store experiences online presents a unique challenge. This chapter delves into the role of online platforms in luxury retail, examining how they can complement and enhance the tactile allure of offline encounters. It explores strategies for imbuing digital interactions with a human touch and creating a seamless retail landscape where online and offline realms are not mere extensions but integral, harmonious components of the brand experience. The focus is on crafting a cohesive journey for consumers, where each touchpoint, physical or virtual, is thoughtfully designed to evoke emotion and provide value, ensuring that the essence of luxury is felt at every stage.

In this scenario, 'seamless retail' refers to the integration of online and offline retail channels to create a unified, cohesive shopping experience for customers. This concept aims to eliminate any disconnect between a brand's physical stores and its digital presence. It involves synchronizing various aspects like inventory, customer service, pricing and marketing across both channels. The goal is to provide a consistent experience, whether a customer shops in a physical store, on a website or through a mobile app, ensuring convenience, personalized service and a frictionless transition between online and offline interactions.

From point of sale to point of experiences

In the contemporary retail landscape, the luxury boutique has evolved from a mere point of sale into a multifaceted point of experience. This transformation signifies a shift from a standardized retail format to a locale-specific concept, where each store is not only a gateway to the brand's offerings but also a platform for community engagement and immersive experiences through different forms of 'animation'.

'Animations', in the context of luxury retail, refers to a series of dynamic, engaging in-store events and activities designed to create an immersive brand experience for customers. These can range from product demonstrations and interactive displays to themed events, workshops and personalized services:

1 **Product demonstrations**: Introducing new products through live demonstrations, allowing customers to experience the features and benefits first-hand, often enhanced by expert guidance. Stores frequently orchestrate events to unveil new collections, inviting their most valued customers to exclusive cocktail receptions where the ambiance and décor are meticulously crafted to echo the thematic essence of the latest shows. At such events, the narrative woven by the brand's creative minds is articulated not just through the clothing on display but through a comprehensive sensory experience that may include visual elements, music and even olfactory cues that align with the collection's theme. Guests are not mere spectators but are invited to step into the brand's world, engaging with the designers or brand ambassadors who guide them through the inspirations, materials and creative processes that birthed the new line. It's an intimate preview, an advance showing of the collection before it becomes available to the broader public. In this exclusive setting, guests are also afforded the privilege of placing pre-orders for pieces they connect with, thereby ensuring they are among the first to own the latest from the brand. Such retail experiences underscore the brand's dedication to creating a personal relationship with their clientele, recognizing and catering to their desire for exclusivity and early access. These immersive events are a testament to the brand's

recognition of retail spaces as platforms for engagement that go beyond mere transactions, fostering a deeper connection between the consumer and the brand narrative.

2 **Interactive displays and immersive digital experiences**: Using technology such as augmented reality (AR) or touchscreens for customers to explore products in an engaging way, often leading to a deeper understanding and appreciation of the brand. In February 2022, LVMH Moët Hennessy Louis Vuitton Japan and SoftBank Corp embarked on a strategic collaboration to revolutionize luxury retail experiences. This partnership focuses on integrating advanced technologies like VR and 5G to create immersive customer interactions both in-store and online. These initiatives allow customers to connect with the brand's heritage and craftsmanship through innovative storytelling and digital platforms, marking a significant leap in the digital transformation of LVMH Japan's customer services.

3 **Themed events**: Hosting events that align with seasonal collections, brand milestones or cultural celebrations, which often involve decorations, special guests and limited-edition products.

4 **Workshops and masterclasses**: Offering exclusive sessions where customers can learn new skills or gain knowledge related to the brand's expertise, such as perfume blending seminars or fashion styling workshops.

5 **Exhibitions**, which can be temporary, like the special 'Cartier Tank. A Journey Through Time', or permanent, like the sculptures and paintings decorating the Tiffany Landmark on Fifth Avenue. In May 2023, Valentino's new flagship store in Paris marked its grand opening with a special collaboration. Artist Gioele Amaro, known for his work with Valentino Re-Signify, showcased his significant pieces within the Avenue Montaigne boutique. In addition, Amaro created an exclusive artwork specifically for the event, which was featured on a prominent billboard along Avenue de l'Opéra, blending art with fashion in an immersive retail experience.

6 **Personalized services**: Providing bespoke services such as monogramming, engraving or custom fitting that add a personal touch to the shopping experience.

7 **Artistic collaborations**: Partnering with artists or designers to create unique store installations or capsule collections, adding a layer of exclusivity and cultural engagement.

8 **Pop-up experiences:** Setting up temporary, experiential spaces that offer customers a unique brand experience, often highlighting a specific product or collection. These temporary spaces can be transformed into enchanting venues for hospitality receptions like breakfasts or brunches, which serve as a platform for the brand to showcase its values and lifestyle proposition. Imagine stepping into a pop-up space during the holiday season that has been transformed into a winter wonderland. Guests are greeted with the warm aroma of spiced beverages and an array of gourmet pastries. The setting is not just about showcasing products but about creating a memorable experience that resonates with the luxury and attention to detail for which the brand is known. A Christmas brunch, for instance, could feature a sumptuous spread of seasonal delicacies and fine foods that reflect the brand's sophistication. During the event, guests could mingle with brand ambassadors, client advisers and fellow aficionados in a relaxed atmosphere, fostering community and brand loyalty. Moreover, these events can be tied to exclusive previews of holiday collections, or limited-time products. The combination of a unique shopping experience with the pleasure of a convivial meal elevates the concept of retail beyond its traditional boundaries. It's a holistic approach, where every aspect of the pop-up space is designed to leave a lasting impression on the guests, drawing them deeper into the narrative and lifestyle that the brand epitomizes. In essence, incorporating elements of hospitality such as brunches into a pop-up strategy during Christmas or other peak times provides a dual benefit: it delights and engages current customers, and also serves as a beacon for potential new customers drawn in by the allure of the brand's hospitality.

9 **Secluded events** on the occasion of a special client's celebration. As seen in the Cartier opening case, such experiences are carefully crafted to surprise and engage a specific clientele. The surprise might be as intimate as a private birthday celebration within the boutique's VIP room, with a special window display arranged just for the occasion, transforming a personal moment into an unforgettable brand experience. Or it could be as grand as closing the boutique for a marriage proposal, complete with a photographer to capture the moment, underscoring the brand's commitment to customer delight.

All in-store 'Animations' serve to not only entertain and educate customers, but also to deepen the relationship between the brand and its clientele, ultimately enhancing brand loyalty and driving sales. They turn the store into a destination, a place where shopping is not just about acquiring new items but about enjoying memorable, shareable experiences. So, luxury boutiques are now envisioned as spaces where customer-centric and community-centric approaches thrive. They are places where people congregate to not only engage with the products but to connect, share and participate in the brand narrative. The retail environment transitions from product-focused to customer-focused, prioritizing the creation of a community around the brand's values and enhancing the lifetime value of the customer.

Each boutique can embody different roles, using the different 'Animations', morphing to meet the specific needs and cultural context of its location:

- **Centres of heritage and culture**: Boutiques are museums of the brand's legacy, offering patrons a deep dive into the history and values that shape the Maison's identity. Each product is presented not just as an item for purchase but as a narrative piece with its own unique story and place within the brand's rich tapestry.

- **Conduits for community and connection**: These spaces are designed to foster community, acting as gathering spots where loyal customers and new enthusiasts alike can share their admiration for the brand and engage with its ethos.

- **Platforms for personalized experiences**: Luxury boutiques might be crafted with the foresight to adapt to various events, transforming into spaces for intimate gatherings, exuberant celebrations or serene settings for private viewings.

- **Stages for engagement and entertainment**: The modern boutique is a versatile arena where the brand's narrative comes alive, hosting events that range from educational sessions to festive parties, all aimed at deepening the customer's connection to the brand. In this immersive environment, craftsmanship is not hidden but celebrated. Artisans, integral to the retail tableau, are seen crafting and restoring products, providing a window into the soul of the brand's artistry. For instance, at Tiffany's landmark New York store, an exclusive atelier – revealed only to select guests on special occasions – allows guests to witness the magic of creation and restoration. Similarly, at Cartier, horology experts not only tend to timepieces with meticulous care but also emerge from their workshops to engage with clients, offering personalized explanations of the services rendered. Through this approach, brands invite customers not just to shop, but to partake in a shared journey, to become not only consumers, but members of a living, breathing story that unfolds within the store's walls.

Blending these roles into a cohesive narrative stands as a testament to the brand's adaptability and commitment to customer-centric experiences. Beyond service, luxury boutiques can become cultural havens, akin to libraries rich with the brand's heritage or museums showcasing the storied past and contemporary artistry of the brand. These spaces are designed to inspire, to stir the imagination and to foster a deeper connection with the brand's narrative.

Five short examples might illustrate the distinctive in-store experiences provided: each brand transformed their retail space into a captivating world that transcends mere shopping. Sabyasachi's Indian boutiques marry cultural heritage with fashion, creating museum-like sanctuaries that tell a story with every artifact and garment. Amorepacific in Korea, on the other hand, offers a beauty journey that fuses advanced technology with serene aesthetics. It stands as a pioneering example of retail innovation, blurring the lines between a beauty store and an immersive sanctuary. Its flagship store is not just about shopping – it's a holistic experience that invites visitors to interact with beauty on a deeply personal level, in a space where industrial meets serene. Here, sustainable practices meet cutting-edge technology, as personalized beauty services powered by AI become a highlight. The store is a haven for engagement, learning and connecting with the essence of the brand through its garden, workshops and specially curated product libraries.

Ader Error's spaces surprise with avant-garde designs that challenge conventional retail norms, whereas Gentle Monster's stores immerse visitors in otherworldly art installations that redefine eyewear shopping. Ader Error's visionary retail spaces defy the ordinary, serving as a crossroads of unisex fashion and immersive art. With a philosophy of 'But Near Missed Things', the brand curates a shopping experience that's akin to an art gallery, infusing mystery and a sense of discovery. Spaces like the Seongsu-dong store, with its black hole impact theme, and Sinsa's Space 3.0, where changing rooms unveil hidden worlds, embody Ader Error's commitment to surprising and engaging customers. These stores aren't just shops; they're exploratory journeys into fashion's new frontier.

Gentle Monster's SKP-S store in Beijing redefines the retail landscape with its 'Digital-Analogue Future' theme, offering a glimpse into a life on

Mars with innovative art and technology. The space, complete with futuristic installations like robotic sheep and Mars-inspired sculptures, captivates visitors with a narrative that weaves excitement for the digital with nostalgia for the analogue. The experience is crowned by NUDAKE, where the culinary arts meet the brand's creative storytelling, making SKP-S a beacon of experiential retail.

Lastly, Glossier's US locations emphasize tactile and digital harmonization, focusing on spaces that feel more like a beauty playground than a traditional store. Each brand invites customers into a curated experience, making their visit a memorable exploration rather than a simple transaction.

Indian elegance in retail: Sabyasachi's museum-style fashion haven

Indian designer Sabyasachi Mukherjee has crafted a unique retail experience that blends the aesthetics of a museum with the allure of a fashion store. This experience is vividly showcased in the brand's largest store, which opened in Kala Ghoda, Mumbai. This space, spread across 25,862 square feet and encompassing four floors, is housed in a historic 19th-century building.

The store's design reflects his memories: travel souvenirs, rare artefacts and found objects that resonate with Mukherjee's childhood in Kolkata. Every corner of the store is filled with a curated selection of items, ranging from vintage cabinets, hand-carved tables, Chinese glazed ginger jars and Art Nouveau-style urns to brass sculptures and Durga busts. This eclectic mix creates an ambiance of regal Indian maximalism, with elements like life-sized animal figures and mother-of-pearl tables adding to the charm. Sabyasachi's approach to store design is hands-on, and he is known to personally direct each detail.

This meticulous attention to detail is evident in the New York store in the West Village and the flagship store in Kolkata. In Mumbai, the ground floor features a permanent exhibition area where archival pieces from collections like 'Bater' are displayed, adding a museum-like quality to the retail space. The store's ambiance is further enhanced by a carefully curated playlist, ranging from Leonard Cohen to Lata Mangeshkar, which adds a lyrical dimension to the shopping experience. Mukherjee's personal stories and inspirations, reflected in annotations and mood boards throughout the store, offer insights into his creative process and influences.

Sabyasachi's design philosophy is deeply rooted in the idea of paradoxes, as he enjoys creating spaces and products that resonate with both traditional and contemporary sensibilities. His favourite aspects of the store are often the most understated yet significant ones, like the parakeet faucets in the restroom that symbolize the beauty of the handmade. Mukherjee's vision extends beyond fashion design. He sees his brand as a broader expression of craft, with ventures into handbags, jewellery, beauty, fragrances and even hospitality. In essence, Sabyasachi's stores offer more than just a shopping experience; they are immersive environments that encapsulate the essence of his brand, blending art, history and fashion in a unique and compelling way.

Amore Seongsu: A tranquil beauty oasis for personalized services in Seoul's urban canvas

Amore Seongsu in Seoul presents a unique example of an experiential store that goes beyond traditional retail concepts, transforming shopping into an immersive and interactive experience. This flagship store of Amorepacific, a leading global beauty and skincare conglomerate, is situated in the industrial area of Seongsu-dong, eastern Seoul. It stands out as a tranquil oasis amid its surroundings, offering a stark contrast to the busy urban setting.

Originally a car repair shop, the Amore Seongsu space has been repurposed to create a serene garden landscape that harmonizes with the industrial neighbourhood. This flagship location is much more than a mere showcase for Amorepacific's diverse product range. Instead, it serves as an experiential hub, inviting visitors to deeply engage with the brand and its offerings.

Amore Seongsu is notable for its commitment to sustainability, aligning with Amorepacific's mission of '2030 AMORE Beautiful Promise'. This includes goals like using 100 per cent renewable energy at all global production sites and incorporating recycled or bio-based plastics for 30 per cent of its packaging by 2030.

Upon entering, visitors are enveloped in a comforting forest-like scent, with the garden visible through the windows. The store features a cleansing room where customers can prepare their skin for testing products at the beauty library. This library showcases an extensive range of over 1,500 products from Amorepacific's brands.

One of the store's key attractions is its custom beauty services, such as the Hera Silky Custom Match service, which uses AI technology and a robot developed in collaboration with KAIST to create customized foundation shades. This service, along with the Lip Picker service for custom lip tints, offers personalized experiences that are both innovative and engaging.

The store layout is designed to guide visitors through various stages of skincare, with different zones for each step. The central garden area enhances the serene atmosphere, creating a sense of comfort and connection with nature.

Amore Seongsu also hosts various events and classes, such as makeup classes, flower arrangement workshops and perfume-making sessions, adding another dimension to the concept store experience.

Ader Error: Mystery and sense of discovery

Ader Error, a South Korean fashion brand, has garnered attention for its unique approach to retail space design. The brand, shrouded in mystery and designed by an anonymous collective, was founded in 2014. It stands out for its unisex fashion and a distinctive blend of art, design and installation in its stores. Ader Error's retail philosophy is encapsulated in its motto 'But Near Missed Things', reflecting a focus on the unconventional and the unexpected.

The brand's approach to store design is twofold: some locations emphasize exhibition, while others focus on connection between the physical and digital world. Their setting immediately sets the tone for an experience akin to an exclusive art exhibition rather than a conventional retail space.

At the Ader Error brand store in Seongsu-dong, visitors are greeted with a space designed to resemble the aftermath of a black hole's impact. The interior design elements are reminiscent of astronaut rooms, complete with equipment and a sense of exploration. Following the Sinkhole Room is the 'Archive Room', which is reminiscent of kinetic media art. This space symbolizes communication between dimensions and features archive balls, adding to the otherworldly and interactive nature of the store. The Z Gravity Room takes the experience further by creating a realm where gravity seems to have lost its grip. Here, visitors are immersed in an environment that depicts astronauts docking in space, representing the stillness before a breakthrough in creative thought. One of the most striking spaces is the Dimension Craft Ship Room. It features a spaceship-like metal structure with water gushing beneath it, giving a strong impression of being in an alternate, otherworldly space. The store also includes a second floor that feels like a contemporary art gallery. Here, the blend of fashion and art is seamless, showcasing Ader Error's iconic pieces in a setting that is both intimate and expansive.

At Space 3.0 in Sinsa, the journey begins with a surprise element – changing rooms that lead to unexpected spaces. One changing room opens to reveal a 'noraebang' (Korean karaoke room), offering visitors an entertaining break from shopping. Another room transforms into a cozy space with a bunk bed and a projector screening a film of a moving train, creating an immersive and relaxing environment. To reach the in-store coffee shop, visitors navigate through a corridor designed to resemble a hotel hallway, adding to the store's unique and exploratory atmosphere. These elements are not just visually engaging but also interactive, inviting visitors to engage with the space in a personal and memorable way. The store's design encourages exploration and discovery, making each visit a unique adventure.

Ader Error's 'plugshops' represent a more abbreviated version of Ader Error's sensory experience found at brand stores. These spaces, though smaller and more focused than the brand stores, still offer a unique and unconventional artistic design approach to retail. The plugshop in Songpa-gu, located in Lotte Worldmall, is an example of this concept. It's designed to foster organic connections and interactions in myriad spaces, free from the constraints of a specific platform. The space features artistic and functional elements like a metallic cocoon with speakers and artistically crafted furniture, which includes the unique 'Persistence of Time Chair' and other thought-provoking installations. A mannequin is sitting at the entrance with an elegant pose as if observing passers-by; the other one is bent over and seems to be looking under the raised floor in search of something, his head is covered by the hood of the sweatshirt.

Ader Error's retail spaces are not just about shopping; they are destinations where art, design and fashion intersect. These stores offer visitors an opportunity to engage with the brand in a deeply personal and memorable way, blurring the lines between retail, art and experiential design.

Gentle Monster SKP-S: A visionary retail odyssey

Gentle Monster, a South Korean eyewear brand, has been a trailblazer in the world of experiential retail, a concept that prioritizes immersive, interactive experiences over traditional product displays. Their innovative approach to retail, especially in collaborations like the one with SKP Beijing, underscores a shift in how brands engage with consumers in physical spaces.

In the partnership with SKP Beijing, Gentle Monster developed a unique format known as SKP-S. This concept goes beyond the traditional retail store, blending art, technology and fashion into an immersive experience.

One of the most striking features of this collaboration is the 'Future Farm' installation. This avant-garde set-up envisions a world where machines and AI reflect on the past by creating an analogue virtual reality. The installation includes lifelike robotic sheep that move and breathe, symbolizing a bridge between the digital and analogue worlds.

The theme of the SKP-S retail space, 'Digital-Analogue Future', presents a futuristic vision of human life on Mars. The space is divided into different areas, each offering a unique experience. Along with the Future Farm, the mall features a variety of thematic installations and artworks, such as a 3D carving machine, depictions of human habitation on Mars, Mars Rovers, space capsules and a variety of sculptures. These elements are designed to draw visitors into a narrative about the future, blending elements of fear and excitement associated with the digital world with nostalgia and remorse for the analogue past.

The final area of this innovative retail space includes Gentle Monster's dessert brand, NUDAKE. Here, visitors can indulge in unique culinary creations, adding yet another layer to the multi-sensory experience.

Gentle Monster, renowned for their theatrical retail spaces, has ventured into the olfactory arts with Tamburins' debut perfume collection. Their Seoul exhibition spans a multi-story venue, blending art installations and immersive soundscapes to create an experiential journey through scent. Embodying Gentle Monster's signature fusion of art and commerce, Tamburins' flagship stores echo this ethos, transforming shopping into a gallery-like encounter. The collection, themed 'solace: a handful of comfort', invites introspection and conveys the brand's spiritual identity, extending Gentle Monster's influence from visual to sensory storytelling.

Glossier LA: The digital-infused beauty haven

Glossier, a beauty brand well-known for its digital-first approach, has also created a unique in-store experience, particularly in its flagship store in Los Angeles which opened in 2021. This experience highlights a blend of digital and physical elements, setting it apart from traditional cosmetics stores which often appear cluttered and product-heavy.

In the Glossier LA store, the layout is clean and ordered, showcasing products on aesthetically pleasing pink counters. This minimalist approach to product display makes the store environment feel more serene and less overwhelming compared to typical cosmetic stores that are usually crowded with products.

A key feature of the Glossier in-store experience is the integration of digital technology to enhance customer service. Store assistants are equipped with smart devices connected to the warehouse. This system streamlines the shopping process; once a customer chooses a product, the order is quickly processed, and the product is delivered to them in the store, personalized with their name on the bag. This efficient use of technology not only speeds up the purchasing process, but also adds a personal touch to the shopping experience.

Glossier's approach in its LA store exemplifies how digital technology can be seamlessly integrated into a physical retail space to create an efficient, personalized and aesthetically pleasing shopping experience. This strategy reflects a broader trend in retail where brands are looking to combine the best of digital and physical worlds to cater to the modern consumer's desire for both convenience and a unique in-store experience.

Sabyasachi, Amorepacific, Ader Errors, Gentle Monster and Glossier exemplify how retail spaces can evolve into destinations for immersive brand experiences which combine retail with art installations and thematic experiences, representing a significant shift in retail philosophy. It's not just about selling products; it's about creating a memorable experience that resonates with customers on a deeper level. By blending product exploration with personalized services, art exhibits or educational events, they transform the act of shopping into an enriching journey that resonates with customers on multiple levels. The return on investment significantly hinges not only on sales, but on the creation and dissemination of authentic media content, which is increasingly shared across multiple channels. This strategy is particularly effective in the current retail landscape where creating immersive, memorable experiences is essential.

Freedom within a framework: Retail rituals and golden rules

The journey from welcome to farewell is a choreographed performance where every act is significant, every moment is an opportunity to enchant, and every guest leaves feeling like a valued collector of not just goods but experiences and memories.

It is a space where every moment is an opportunity to deliver the extraordinary, where the human touch and the relentless pursuit of perfection coalesce to redefine what luxury means in retail.

This approach emphasizes the importance of emotional connections, ritualized excellence and the seamless blend of retail and hospitality principles to create a luxury retail experience that is both human-centric and operationally sublime.

Incorporating daily rituals of excellence, akin to a morning brief or a team huddle, ensures continuous improvement and maintains a high standard of service. The new luxury retail journey is a balanced choreography between emotional intelligence and structured rituals. These rituals are the underpinning of luxury retail's commitment to excellence:

1 **Morning brief:** Each day begins with a convergence of minds and spirits. Here, the team shares a collective breath before diving into the day's rhythm, aligning on opportunities that await and the challenges that might unfurl. In the sanctum of the store, before doors swing open to welcome guests, there is a quiet buzz as the team assembles. The agenda for this gathering is precise: to forecast the ebb and flow of the day's tides. The morning brief is an anticipatory map, charting the expected arrivals of specific clients and VICs, each with their individual preferences and requests that the team meticulously prepares to fulfil. Leaders and advisers alike engage in an exchange of information – who has booked appointments, the distribution of workload and how best to orchestrate the allocation of spaces within the store to ensure each client feels they are entering a personalized sanctuary of luxury. This prelude to the day's symphony includes a review of directives from headquarters, acting as a compass for the team's endeavours. New product highlights are discussed, showcasing the latest offerings that might ignite the desires of the clientele. Price adjustments, if any, are carefully noted, ensuring that each team member is armed with the most current and accurate information, ready to navigate discussions with finesse and confidence. In these moments, the team also primes itself for the unexpected – for luxury retail thrives not just on scheduled appointments, but on the serendipity of walk-ins and spur-of-the-moment desires. The morning brief, therefore, is not just about preparation, but also about cultivating a mindset of agility and grace under the spontaneous demands of luxury service. As the team disperses, carrying with them the shared understanding and collective purpose fostered by the morning's convergence, the stage is set.

2 **Floor (collaborative) mentorship:** A dynamic practice of guiding teams in real time, addressing errors and providing support, emphasizing the constant evolution of service. Team members observe and engage with

their peers in a dynamic exchange of insights and refinements. This process celebrates the wisdom of shared experiences, where suggestions are not critiques but gifts of knowledge, offered to enhance the collective performance and enrich the client's journey.

3 **Periodic team touch-bases:** Regular reflections with the team in store and at HQs level ensure lessons are learned and strategies for improvement are set for the coming period.

It's clear that at the core of this paradigm is humanity. Luxury is about creating memorable moments through attentive service, where every inter-action is valued and every emotion is considered. It's about recharging with each guest encounter and infusing each day with passion.

The idea of having rituals that provide a kind of routine in the retail activity is perfectly consistent with the 'freedom in a framework' approach as articulated by the Chief Client Officer at Audemars Piguet. The concept encapsulates a modern strategy in luxury retail that acknowledges the importance of human discretion within established guidelines. This philoso-phy permits client advisers to allocate high-demand pieces such as those from coveted collaborations (like those with Marvel) based on a spectrum of qualitative factors rather than a simple first-come-first-served basis. This nuanced method takes into account the customer's profile and history with the brand to ensure that these exclusive items are acquired by genuine enthusiasts who value and intend to cherish them rather than resell them for a profit. Such allocation practices are governed by a CRM committee and at times may even require validation from the CEO, particularly for excep-tional collaborations, ensuring a controlled and deliberate distribution of key and 'hot' references.

The process is designed to be transparent and accountable, limiting discretionary powers to prevent misuse or opportunistic behaviours. It's not just about controlling supply and demand, but also about nurturing a brand-client relationship that is built on trust and mutual appreciation for the craftsmanship and heritage of the brand's offerings. Moreover, this strategy includes a vision for expanding the brand's appeal along strategic goals, specifically targeting segments such as female customers for sophisticated mechanical watches, which traditionally may have been more male-oriented.

The concept of 'freedom in a framework' thus reflects a delicate balance between giving client advisers autonomy to enhance customer relationships and maintaining a structure that ensures brand integrity and values are upheld. It's a sophisticated approach that respects the human aspect of retail while striving for excellence in client engagement and experience.

The renaissance of retail: The rise of pop-up stores

A retail revolution has been unfolding since the turn of the millennium – a shift from the monotony of static storefronts to the vibrant dynamism of pop-up stores. The early 2000s witnessed consumers' growing ennui with traditional retail; they craved something more – a retail environment that wasn't just a place to shop, but a destination offering inspiration and excitement.

Flagship stores, in the chronicle of retail evolution, can be seen as catalysts for the experiential dynamics that pop-up stores would eventually come to embody later. They set the stage for the immersive experiences that pop-up stores would build upon.

Flagship stores, emerging in the late 20th century, have transcended traditional retail boundaries, evolving into immersive brand temples. These directly operated spaces, more than revenue centres, embody the brand's full identity, creating a 'retail spectacle' and enriching the customer experience (Kozinets et al, 2002, 2004). They significantly influence brand attitude, attachment and equity. Brand attitude reflects a consumer's general appreciation of a brand (Borghini et al, 2009); brand attachment represents the cognitive and emotional bond a consumer forms with a brand (Park, MacInnis and Priester, 2008); and brand equity and awareness denotes the value derived from consumer perception of the brand (Yoo and Donthu, 2011; Keller, 1993).

These stores served as the foundation from which the pop-up store concept would later evolve.

While flagship stores were permanent, they introduced consumers to the idea of retail as an event – an idea that would become central to the pop-up store strategy.

As retail continued to evolve, brands sought to replicate the immersive experience of flagship stores but with a novel twist. The pop-up store format allowed brands to create similar engagements in a more flexible, ephemeral manner, aligning with the rapidly changing consumer interests and the growing demand for novelty and exclusivity.

The pop-up store is thought to have originated from various predecessors – guerrilla marketing tactics, seasonal themed stores and the small designers seeking to captivate the public's attention without the confines of a permanent space (Surchi, 2011; McIntyre, Melewar and Dennis, 2016). This novel retail format captured the imagination of consumers and the media alike, with its ephemeral nature turning shopping into an event, a performance that piqued curiosity and attention (De Lassus and Anido Freire, 2014).

Leading this retail revolution was designer outlet Vacant, a trailblazer in the art of temporary stores. Vacant's unique approach took the world by storm in 2003, introducing a series of boutiques that would materialize in vacant city shops across New York, London, Paris and Berlin, existing for only a month at a time. Vacant distinguished itself by offering a well-curated shopping experience. Their shelves were curated with limited edition items, treasures that couldn't be found in traditional stores, creating a sense of urgency and rarity. These pop-up boutiques weren't just about shopping; they were about discovery and being part of an elite group in the know. Interested customers were drawn into a secret network, with details of the store's whereabouts revealed solely through email alerts to those who had subscribed to Vacant's database.

Notably, avant-garde Japanese fashion house Comme des Garçons launched their own version of the pop-up store. These boutiques were even more enigmatic, with no phone listings and devoid of any traditional signage, discreetly nestled in the backstreets of Berlin. Their business model was revolutionary, eschewing conventional retail wisdom by planning to shut down after a successful year regardless of profitability. Comme des Garçons' stores have since appeared in various global locales, including Barcelona, Singapore and a one-month stint in Tokyo, each time creating a buzz of anticipation and exclusivity.

These early pop-up boutiques laid the groundwork for what has become a global retail phenomenon, intertwining the allure of exclusivity with the spontaneity of impermanence, and forever altering the landscape of modern shopping.

Brands quickly recognized the strategic advantages of pop-up stores. They became vehicles for market testing and building brand awareness, providing a low-risk stage for experimenting with new products or concepts before a wider release. The temporal aspect of pop-up stores created a unique value proposition – exclusivity through scarcity (Catalano and Zorzetto, 2010).

The essence of pop-up stores transcended mere transactions. They evolved into experiential spaces where consumers could immerse themselves in a brand's narrative, engage in a sensory journey and form a personal connection with the products on display. These temporary installations became stages for storytelling, where every element, from design to product selection, was part of a cohesive tale designed to enchant and engage (De Lassus and Anido Freire, 2014). The pop-up phenomenon in luxury took on various forms, from temporary stores in travel destinations (so called 'resort pop-ups') to unexpected activations in city centres, to creating shop-in-shop experiences in department stores, to combine shopping with entertainment.

Loro Piana has been engaging for years in unique city activations that deepen the brand's narrative and resonate with cultural nuances. Their approach during Milan's Design Week exemplifies a strategic intertwining of brand ethos with local and international cultural threads – most notably, the rich Japanese aesthetics. Loro Piana ventured beyond the confines of their boutiques to curate encounters with Milanese and international visitors. The brand seized the pulsating energy of Design Week to showcase its profound appreciation for Japanese culture. A flower kiosk and a traditional Japanese bakery popped up amidst the urban landscape, inviting passersby into a sensory dialogue with the brand. The kiosk, an ephemeral space nestled at the intersection of Via Manzoni and Via Montenapoleone, swathed in the brand's signature elegance, became a visual metaphor for growth and beauty, mirroring the brand's growth from textile mastery to a lifestyle emblem.

Equally, on Via dei Giardini, Loro Piana provided a taste of Japan with *wagashi kasutera* sweetened with honey and matcha, traditional confections that mirrored the brand's attention to craft and heritage. This activation was not merely a nod to culinary delight, but a sophisticated expression of Loro Piana's commitment to sustainability and artistry – principles shared with Japanese culture. The *wagashi kasutera* were presented in packaging wrapped in furoshiki, using exquisite fabric remnants from Loro Piana's collections, offering a sustainable and luxurious takeaway that extends the life of their textiles. These special activations were not just about product visibility or temporary sales opportunities; they were about enriching the customer experience, creating a lasting memory.

The Acqua di Parma Caffè Milano exemplifies a refined foray into the experiential retail trend, where luxury brands curate spaces that extend their ethos beyond products to create a holistic brand experience. Situated within the Grand Hotel de Milan's esteemed restaurant Caruso, the pop-up caffè was a temporal homage to the launch of the Colonia C.L.U.B. fragrance, embodying the Acqua di Parma spirit of shared enjoyment and sophisticated leisure.

The caffè's design harmonized the brand's signature motifs with the sumptuous elegance of the restaurant, offering a multisensory journey through carefully curated spaces. The indoor lounge, veranda and outdoor area each offered a unique atmospheric narrative, all unified by the distinctive Acqua di Parma yellow and the superior craftsmanship of Italian design, featuring contributions from Poltrona Frau and Manifattura Geminiano Cozzi.

These spaces weren't mere backdrops; they were interactive stages that facilitated a cultural and communal experience. Clients could indulge in Sicilian-inspired cuisine and workshops that varied from perfume artistry to the creation of bespoke bouquets, all while being enveloped in the essence of Colonia C.L.U.B. This clever integration of product, place and practice spoke to the brand's understanding of luxury as a comprehensive lifestyle.

Notably, the caffè served as a community hub, inviting a diverse audience to engage with the brand's narrative. From children's workshops celebrating Father's Day to literary and photographic mosaics workshops, Acqua di Parma transformed a marketing initiative into a vibrant cultural salon. The pop-up caffè's multi-layered approach – pairing Italian culinary delights with craft and design workshops – not only heightened brand visibility but also strengthened consumer relationships by fostering a sense of community. This aligns with a growing trend where luxury brands leverage hospitality to transcend transactional relationships, aiming to create enduring bonds with consumers through shared experiences and values.

Furthermore, Acqua di Parma's approach reflects a strategic understanding of omnichannel marketing, integrating physical experiences with digital interactions through innovative elements like the QR code on sugar packets, leading to a charity-supporting video game. This seamless blend of in-person and digital engagement underscores the brand's adaptability and commitment to contemporary communication methods.

Pop-up stores have undergone a remarkable metamorphosis, transcending their initial incarnation as ephemeral retail or activation spaces, often located in coveted travel destinations, to become sophisticated, brand-immersive environments. Initially conceived as transient destinations for the sale of exclusive, limited-edition products, these pop-up ventures have increasingly embraced a holistic approach to consumer engagement, merging retail with elements of entertainment and hospitality. This evolution has witnessed pop-up stores morphing into integrated shop-in-shop experiences within department stores, where they serve not only as points of sale but also as vessels for brand storytelling, particularly in regions where a brand aims to deepen its market penetration.

This phenomenon could be aptly termed 'store takeovers', where the influence of a brand extends far beyond the confines of traditional retail setups.

Loro Piana's retail strategy includes store takeovers, as seen in their collaboration with Harrods in 2023, a striking example of brand storytelling brought to life through immersive visual design. The iconic façade was adorned with gilded brass arches and turquoise boiserie, creating a spectacle that turned heads and drew people in. The use of floral and jacquard motifs, elements from the Spring Capsule Collection itself, allowed for a seamless transition from the outer architectural beauty to the inner thematic experience.

These are not mere pop-ups, but complete transformations of a retail space that mirror the brand's narrative including a powerful communication.

In Paris, for the Spring/Summer 2022 Collection, Valentino adopted multiple pop-ups at Le Carreau du Temple, each location hosting exclusive products and events that resonated with the Maison's modern ethos. This is a transformative approach to retail, one that invites consumers to step into a world where every interaction is an opportunity for the brand to manifest its values in a tangible, personal and visually arresting manner.

Different pop-up strategies serve varying objectives when it comes to customer engagement. Temporary activations, such as kiosks or street carts, are particularly effective for generating buzz and word of mouth. They are dynamic, accessible and often unexpected, catching the attention of passersby and potential customers with their novelty. These pop-up experiences are designed to intrigue and draw in a crowd, sparking conversations and encouraging people to share their unique encounters on social media or through personal networks.

On the other side of the spectrum are store takeovers, which tend to target an audience that's already well-versed in luxury consumption. These are not just casual shoppers but are often loyal clients of the department store or patrons of other luxury brands.

In their most advanced iterations, pop-up stores are now seamlessly blending with leisure environments, offering fully-equipped beach setups replete with brand-aligned bars and restaurants, catering to consumers' desire for relaxation. Similarly, within the hospitality industry, brands are curating not just the retail space but also influencing the design aesthetics and furnishing of hotel common areas, thus extending the brand experience into every touchpoint of a guest's stay. These curated experiences are becoming increasingly significant as brands strive to create deeper connections with consumers. Loro Piana's takeover of La Réserve à La Plage beach club in St Tropez and Marc Jacobs' reinvention of the Surf Lodge are examples of brands crafting memorable encounters that resonate with their audience's aspirational lifestyles.

Dior has indeed pioneered the amalgamation of commerce and leisure, seamlessly weaving the fabric of its brand into the dream destinations. The Dior Riviera pop-up concept serves as a quintessential case study of this trend, where the brand's narrative unfolds across idyllic settings from the azure allure of seafronts to the serene majesty of mountain retreats. The Dior Riviera collection, envisioned by Maria Grazia Chiuri, stands as a sartorial tribute to 'la dolce vita', a cherished sentiment of the brand's founder, Christian Dior. This line draws inspiration from the lush landscapes and vivid hues of Provence, bringing forth an array of garments and accessories that encapsulate the essence of the sun-kissed Mediterranean. The iconic toile de Jouy is reimagined in a palette that whispers of endless summer skies and tranquil seas, gracing everything from the Lady D-Lite to the Dior Book Tote.

Dior's deftness in creating ephemeral retail havens is evident in their selection of locales for the Dioriviera pop-ups. These destinations, chosen for their emblematic charm, have hosted the brand's summer capsules, allowing clients to indulge in an immersive Dior experience.

The Dioriviera pop-ups have been more than mere points of sale; they are sanctuaries where fashion, art and leisure converge. The Capri resort pop-up of 2020, nestled within the Riccio Restaurant & Beach Club, was a marvel where the brand's aesthetics danced in harmony with the local culture, offering a retail experience that could only be accessed by the sea's embrace. Similarly, the 2022 Dior pop-up spa at Hotel Splendido in Portofino was a temple of beauty and wellbeing, commanding stunning views of the Ligurian Coast.

Dior has not limited its footprint to the Italian Riviera; the brand has graced global locales with its presence, ensuring that each pop-up is a distinct narrative thread that contributes to the brand's history. Whether it's the beachside grandeur of Nammos at Four Seasons Resort in Dubai or the mystical allure of Mykonos, each Dioriviera installation is an ode to the brand's heritage, interpreted through the lens of the locale's unique character.

These pop-ups are not just retail spaces, but a celebration of the Dior ethos – a harmonious blend of tradition and innovation, where limited-edition collections serve as coveted treasures for the brand's discerning clientele. They are events in their own right, where the act of shopping is transformed into an experience that engages, delights and leaves a lasting imprint on the memory.

In essence, the Dioriviera pop-ups encapsulate the art of storytelling through retail, where each pop-up is a chapter that enriches Dior's narrative. They speak to the luxury consumer's desire for exclusivity and experience, striking a delicate balance between the brand's global identity and the local culture, thus embodying the spirit of 'glocalization' (the blend of globalization and localization to acknowledge the importance of global outreach while emphasizing the necessity of respecting and integrating local differences). These activations are more than just a seasonal venture; they are a testament to Dior's vision of fashion as a living, breathing entity that thrives on the new and the now while remaining steadfast to the timeless allure that is quintessentially Dior.

This pivot towards integrating retail with entertainment and hospitality signifies a bold move to infuse lifestyle elements into the brand identity, ensuring that every interaction with the brand is memorable, enjoyable and deeply ingrained in the consumer's psyche. It's a testament to the brand's commitment to not just exist in a space, but to animate it, to transform it, and ultimately to own the complete ambiance of the luxury experience.

Experience-enhancing technologies

For the younger demographic, luxury retail stores morph into dynamic playgrounds. They become experimental labs where digital integration meets traditional retail, creating hybrid spaces that cater to a generation that values both the physical touchpoint and the digital interface. Here, customers can interact with cutting-edge technology, participate in unique digital experiences, or simply revel in the social atmosphere of the brand's physical embodiment (see Chapter 10).

The integration of advanced technologies into the luxury environment is a multifaceted strategy that aims to enhance customer experiences and streamline operations, both in physical stores and online. The key technological advancements that are shaping the future of luxury retail might include:

- **Artificial intelligence (AI)**: AI is used for a multitude of functions in retail such as providing personalized recommendations, enhancing customer relationship management, increasing potential cross- and up-selling, optimizing supply chains and managing inventory (Davenport et al, 2020; Shankar, 2018).
- **Cloud and micro-cloud computing**: These technologies offer scalable and cost-effective solutions for data storage and processing especially for CRM purposes.

- **Internet of Things (IoT)**: The IoT connects various devices and sensors, allowing for improved inventory management and customer engagement through interactive, digitized services (Ng and Wakenshaw, 2017).

- **Mobile technologies**: With consumers spending more time on mobile devices, retailers are investing in mobile-friendly platforms for research, purchase execution and order tracking.

- **Virtual reality (VR), augmented reality (AR) and mixed reality (MR)**: These technologies create immersive and interactive shopping experiences, blending the physical and digital worlds to enhance customer engagement (Tan, Chandukala and Reddy, 2022).

Brands and retailers are facing with decisions about which technologies to invest in and how to implement them effectively. Key considerations include the impact on customer experience (Hoyer et al, 2020), alignment with the brand's identity, need to develop organizational capabilities, individual technology acceptance, competitors' adoption of similar technologies, regulation changes and the potential for increased sales and customer loyalty – while challenges in adopting these technologies can include high costs, complexity and the need for significant changes in company culture and processes.

Luxury brands and retailers must also consider the privacy and ethical implications of using certain technologies. The adoption of these technologies affects not just customers, but also employees, suppliers and retailers, and might require careful management and strategic planning.

The future of technology in luxury retail will likely see an increased blending of physical and digital experiences and a continued emphasis on personalization and convenience. The key to successful technology integration lies in creating a seamless and engaging customer journey that leverages these technologies while remaining true to the brand's heritage and values. As technology continues to evolve, luxury retailers must remain agile and innovative to stay ahead in a competitive and rapidly changing landscape.

The seamless brand retail landscape for a unified experience

Initial academic studies predominantly focused on offline channels, online channels and direct marketing channels, with Verhoef, Neslin and Vroomen (2007) exploring 'research shopping' behaviour, where consumers research in one channel and purchase in another. However, as the digital landscape evolved, particularly with the rise of mobile channels, the retail environment underwent a disruptive change. New channels began to dismantle traditional barriers such as geography and consumer knowledge, prompting a need for retailers to rethink their competitive strategies (Brynjolfsson, Hu and Rahman, 2013).

The transition to omnichannel retailing brought about a blurring of lines between channels, with firms and customers using them interchangeably and simultaneously. This shift made it challenging to control channel usage and raised the issue of showrooming, where customers search for information in-store while simultaneously searching for better offers on their mobile devices.

Within this omnichannel context, researchers have expanded the conceptual scope to include search, display, email, affiliates and referral websites as separate channels. The focus has shifted to a more synergetic management of numerous available channels and customer touchpoints to optimize the customer experience and performance across channels.

Verhoef, Kannan and Inman (2015) propose that future research should delve deeper into omnichannel issues, posing specific questions such as the impact of individual customer touchpoints on retail channel performance and how the integration of mobile channels within stores affects purchase behaviour and store performance. They advocate for a thorough investigation into whether integration across various touchpoints and channels indeed results in stronger retail performance. Furthermore, they suggest that new research should model choice behaviour of multiple channels and touchpoints simultaneously to understand the driving forces behind customers' simultaneous choices. There is also a need for more experimental and econometric research to address the retail mix across channels, exploring the effects of marketing mix instruments used across touchpoints and channels on channel performance and understanding the drivers of showrooming behaviour.

For the luxury sector specifically, these research directions offer a wealth of opportunities to explore how the unique aspects of luxury retailing – such as personalized service, exclusive brand experiences and customer-brand relationships – interact within an omnichannel strategy. Investigating these areas could yield insights into how luxury brands can effectively manage customer experiences across diverse touchpoints to enhance brand performance and deepen customer loyalty.

The shift to omnichannel retailing has indeed become a norm in the industry, especially in the last few years where the need for digital transformation was accelerated. Luxury brands have demonstrated agility by actively embracing innovation to stay ahead in a rapidly evolving marketplace. This trend highlights the proactive stance of luxury brands in integrating digital technologies with traditional retail practices to offer seamless customer experiences across all channels.

This rapid pace towards digitization and integration of channels is not just about adopting new technologies, but also reflects a broader change in mindset. Luxury brands are recognizing the importance of being where the customer is, whether in a physical store or online, and ensuring that the brand experience is consistent and high-quality across all touchpoints. The accelerated move towards omnichannel strategies is often driven by changing consumer behaviours, where customers now expect a fluid shopping experience. For example, they might want to browse products online, try them in-store, place an order on their phone and choose where and how they pick up their purchases. In response, brands have not only improved their online presence but also integrated their online and offline channels to create a more cohesive, customer-centric approach.

'Seamless retail' (SR) encapsulates the concept of providing an integrated experience across various brand touchpoints. To effectively convey the idea of harmonizing different aspects of a brand – from in-store interactions to online presence, customer service and beyond – to create a cohesive and consistent experience for the customer, SR seems a more innovative and fitting choice in the scenario described in this book.

'SR for unified experience' distinguishes this approach from traditional concepts like omnichannel, emphasizing the unity and consistency of the customer experience. It highlights the importance of every interaction working in concert to deliver a singular brand narrative to today's sophisticated consumers, regardless of the platform or channel or touchpoint. This term can be particularly powerful in the context of luxury brands, where the customer experience is paramount. It suggests a sophisticated, holistic approach to customer engagement, underlining the commitment to excellence and attention to detail that customers expect from high-end brands.

In the modern retail landscape, SR strategies have erased the boundaries between offline and online shopping, providing customers with an integrated shopping experience. Consumers no longer need to consciously choose between physical and digital stores. They can navigate effortlessly across platforms, with each channel being a complementary part of a cohesive journey. This holistic approach ensures that whether a customer is browsing online, using a mobile app or visiting a brick-and-mortar store, the transition is fluid and consistent, reflecting the brand's unified presence across all touchpoints. SR, therefore, represents the evolution of multi-channel strategies, focusing on a smooth, uninterrupted customer journey and reflecting the brand's adaptability to the interconnected nature of modern consumer behaviour and unified experience.

The omnichannel menu

The agility of luxury brands in these innovation efforts underscores their capacity to rapidly adapt to new consumer demands and market conditions, ensuring that they not only retain their existing clientele but also appeal to new customer segments who value the flexibility that omnichannel solutions provide.

A seamless integration of online and offline channels is crucial to maintain a unified brand image. This omnichannel approach centres on the customer's perspective, ensuring brand messaging and CRM strategies are consistent across all platforms, including multi-brand and department stores, retail outlets and digital channels. Key events like fashion shows serve as platforms to differentiate customer engagement levels, from VIP invites to wider audience presentations in boutiques. Parallel online activities, like newsletters, Instagram posts and TikTok and YouTube videos, complement these offline initiatives creating contents at brand and product level.

TikTok has become a significant platform for luxury brands to engage audiences. Brands like Prada and Gucci have successfully leveraged TikTok, achieving notable media impact value (based on reach, relevance, engagement and sentiment) through active engagement and content creation. Meanwhile, some brands, although not actively posting on the platform, still maintain a presence through content shared by influencers and celebrities. This approach allows them to benefit from the platform's reach and influence without direct involvement, demonstrating TikTok's versatility in brand marketing strategies.

The CRM system isn't just a database; it's integral to retail marketing, aligning with product development and understanding client preferences to enhance the relationship with the brand (Chapter 7).

To effectively merge online and offline retail channels, understanding their KPIs is crucial. Sales are driven by traffic, conversion rates and average order value. Online traffic is influenced by paid and organic search, newsletters and social media. 'Paid search' refers to the use of search engine marketing (SEM), which involves purchasing ads on search engines like

Google. 'Unpaid' methods, such as search engine optimization (SEO), rely on optimizing content, using keywords and enhancing website design to naturally rank higher in search engine results pages (SERPs) without direct payment for placement.

Organic methods aim to naturally attract visitors and increase visibility based on the quality and relevance of the content. Organic traffic is considered valuable because it is driven by genuine interest or search intent, leading to potentially higher engagement and conversion rates.

Geographical considerations play a role when expanding online presence, involving language, customs and regulatory differences. Online conversion is influenced by the range of products and services offered, mirroring the physical retail experience.

A broad product assortment increases the likelihood of online sales conversions. However, a larger inventory increases the risk of excess stock. An omnichannel approach, integrating online and offline inventories, helps manage this by offering a broader range without overstocking. Pricing control is crucial, especially on multi-brand platforms, to avoid global price disparities.

The integration of online and offline channels in luxury retail goes beyond basic services, encompassing aspects like visual merchandising and customer relationship management (CRM). Visual merchandising online should mirror that of physical stores and window displays, ensuring a consistent brand image. When a new collection launches, both online and in-store should feature the same visual presentation. Moreover, customer databases should be unified across channels, creating a comprehensive master database that includes information about both in-store and online shoppers. This integrated approach helps ensure a seamless and consistent customer experience across all brand touchpoints.

Omnichannel services, like in-store availability checks, returns in store, click-and-collect, click-and-reserve, pre-orders and private appointments, create a seamless experience across online and offline channels, enhancing customer service and experience. This approach makes the online channel feel like another branch of the store, providing consistent service and experience across all customer touchpoints.

In the study by Gao and Su (2016), the researchers developed a model to analyse the impact of a 'buy online, pick up in-store' (BOPS) system on retailer strategy and customer behaviour. Their model highlights how BOPS influences consumer choice by offering real-time stock information and reducing shopping inconvenience. Their findings suggest that BOPS is not equally beneficial for all products; in particular, it may not be profitable for high-selling in-store items. Additionally, while BOPS has the potential to attract new customers, shifting existing online customers to in-store pickup might reduce profit margins if in-store fulfilment is less cost-effective.

The principle of 'unity of stock' impacts on customer satisfaction and it is based on fluid collaboration between warehouse and retail teams to fulfil orders regardless of whether a customer shops in-store or online.

The key distinction customers usually notice is the human element present in physical retail which is absent online. While the brand essence, the product quality and the customer profile remain consistent across channels, the challenge lies in transmitting the brand's values, heritage and energy through the digital interface without the benefit of human interaction.

Bottega Veneta, for instance, is proactive in addressing these challenges, notably by integrating content creation closely with retail experiences. Bottega involves multiple departments – from merchandising to creative teams – ensuring that storytelling is cohesive and compelling across all touchpoints. This strategy includes curated content that resonates emotionally with customers, using powerful copywriting and visuals to evoke the brand's essence on the website.

Furthermore, Bottega Veneta is actively working to bring a human touch to online shopping. They offer personal shopping advice, and advisers reach out to customers, providing a sense of human connection. Bottega Veneta is keen on keeping the online shopping experience enticing and exclusive, suggesting strategies like online-exclusive products or early collection launches. They have also come to understand that certain product categories, such as gifts or home collections, may perform better online due to their suitability for ecommerce.

Valentino's move to enhance the digital customer experience with the human touch aligns with this growing trend of luxury brands seeking to replicate the personalized service of in-store shopping within the online environment. The introduction of client advisers dedicated to the brand's website is a strategic effort to provide tailored assistance and a more intimate shopping experience to online customers, particularly top spenders. By having client advisers who manage digital customer portfolios, Valentino is aiming to bridge the gap between the convenience of online shopping and the bespoke service traditionally associated with luxury retail. These advisers assist customers in navigating the site, informing them about new product drops and offering help beyond the typical chat function. This personalized service is designed to make online shopping more accessible, engaging and tailored to individual preferences and needs.

With resources spread across regions such as EMEA (Europe, the Middle East and Africa) and North America, Valentino is ensuring that this elevated level of service is consistent and widespread. The advisers not only serve to enhance the online shopping experience but also to create a sense of community and loyalty through unique experiences like exclusive events and services such as personalized style consultancy. This strategic initiative, which was rolled out in the first quarter of 2023, emphasizes the brand's commitment to providing a seamless and enriched online journey, ensuring that even the most discerning clients receive the attention and expertise they would expect from an in-store visit, all from the comfort of their own digital devices. It's a clear indication that luxury brands are increasingly prioritizing digital innovation to meet the high expectations of their clientele.

Retail environment: Offline vs online expectations

In discussing the relevance of retail environment, understanding customer expectations and behaviours in both online and offline environments is crucial. Hult et al (2019) provide a comprehensive study that, while not exclusively focused on luxury, offers valuable insights that could be particularly intriguing when applied to the luxury sector.

The research suggests that clients harbour higher expectations of offline (brick-and-mortar) experiences than online shopping. This is attributed to the direct interaction with sales assistants and the immersive, well-orchestrated store environment. Customers perceive a lower risk in physical stores, expecting a more reliable shopping experience, with access to personalized information and assistance in tailoring products and services to their needs. The tangible interaction in-store enhances the perceived quality of products.

Physical stores also cater to the experiential aspect of shopping. Customers often view visiting a store as a leisure activity, a personal treat that offers enjoyment and fun. This contrasts with the online shopping experience, which is perceived as efficient but riskier, especially regarding product originality and matching online descriptions.

Hult et al highlight transaction security and privacy concerns prevalent in online shopping (Nepomuceno, Laroche and Richard, 2014). These security concerns in online shopping lead some customers to adopt a ROPO (research online, purchase offline) approach, where they research products and compare prices online but make the actual purchase in a physical store. This is also evidenced by Verhoef, Kannan and Inman in their influential 2015 article on the omnichannel retail environment.

Choosing to shop in-store can entail additional costs, such as time spent on parking and waiting. However, these are often offset by the desire for quality time and the significance of the purchase. Conversely, the convenience and comfort of shopping from home are major factors driving online shopping. Verhoef, Kannan and Inman discuss the concept of 'switching costs' – the perceived cost of changing from one shopping mode to another. Online, these costs are reduced through systems that save purchase histories and customize search and payment processes. In contrast, the lock-in effect in offline stores is driven by familiarity with the store and exceptional treatment by sales staff. Additionally, both online and offline retailers enhance customer retention by offering privileges based on accumulated spending and customer loyalty tiers.

Applying these insights to the luxury sector could reveal unique patterns and preferences, offering valuable strategies for enhancing customer satisfaction and loyalty in both digital and physical retail spaces.

In online customer experiences, the traditional goal of achieving customer satisfaction has evolved into a quest for customer delight (Bartl, Gouthier and Lenker, 2013). This shift is driven by the recognition that delight, characterized by an intense emotional response to unexpectedly positive service performances, can significantly amplify behavioural outcomes such as loyalty and purchase intentions. Key actions brands can take to delight and surprise their customers online, based on insights from academic and empirical studies (Oliver, Rust and Varki, 1997; Venkatesh, 2000; Arnold et al, 2005; Barnes, Beauchamp and Webster, 2010; Bleier, Harmeling and Palmatier, 2019), are:

- **Exceed expectations**: Delight arises from surpassing customer expectations in an unexpected and surprising manner. Brands must aim to go beyond the industry's average service level to evoke this response.

- **Optimize website quality**: Individual website quality factors should be finely tuned to foster delightful experiences. These factors include informativeness, usefulness, response time and entertainment value.

- **Enhance sensory appeal and emotional engagement**: Incorporate emotional and hedonic elements into the website to engage consumers on a deeper level beyond transactional interactions.

- **Create entertainment and positive user experiences**: Move beyond task-related purposes and design websites that offer positive, memorable experiences, periodically renovated, that could lead to word of mouth and repeat visits.

- **Measure and utilize delight and surprise**: Understand how consumers perceive different website quality factors in terms of their capacity to induce delight and surprise, and leverage these insights to improve website interfaces and functionalities.

- **Align offline and online experiences**: Ensure that the brand's core values, storytelling and customer experience are consistently reflected across all channels, aligning both the content team's and the design team's efforts.

- **Invest in website development**: Recognize that upfront investment in website development can result in positive returns by elevating the customer's online experience and increasing purchase intentions.

- **Focus on real consumer interactions**: Collect actual consumer feedback to understand immediate attitudes and behavioural intentions, facilitating a more consumer-centric approach to online engagement.

By addressing these points, brands can craft online environments that not only satisfy customers but also delight them, fostering a stronger emotional connection and encouraging loyalty and advocacy. The nuanced understanding of delight, distinct from satisfaction, underlines its strategic importance in the competitive landscape of online retail.

In some academic contributions, new technologies, and especially AR, have been confirmed as powerful channel integrators as well as facilitators of better online experience. In particular, the research by Hilken et al (2017) contributes to our understanding of how AR can transform how customers perceive products within their own environment. Hilken et al concentrate on how AR technologies are used by firms to augment online service experience and enhance customer value perceptions. Based on situated cognition theory, the authors propose that AR creates a more authentic and situated experience by providing users with simulated physical control over products and environmental embedding, which effectively places the product in the user's own context. Spatial presence is identified as a key mediator in this process. It describes the user's sensation of being present in the augmented environment, which in turn promotes decision comfort and increases the perceived value of the online experience.

The study also discusses that the effectiveness of AR varies depending on the customer's information processing style. Specifically, AR has a greater impact on those who prefer verbal information processing, as the visual simulations offered by AR complement their processing style. Moreover, the positive effects of AR on decision comfort are somewhat moderated by privacy concerns. Users who are more concerned about how their data is collected and used may feel less comfortable with the decision-making process, despite the presence of AR.

Brand.com platforms serve a broader purpose in brand-building, particularly among younger consumers who may use online resources primarily for brand exploration rather than direct purchasing. This is substantiated by research conducted at Bocconi University with 196 MSc students in luxury management. The survey highlighted that only 12 per cent of these students purchase or plan to purchase luxury items online, aligning with the observed trend that the weight of online sales for many luxury brands remains a fraction of their overall revenue.

This indicates that luxury brands are leveraging online platforms to shape brand perception and influence, nurturing potential customers through immersive content and brand storytelling. The online experience is crafted to reflect the brand's values and aesthetics, providing a digital extension of the in-store experience or even driving a visit to the store.

Thus, the focus is not solely on converting online visits to immediate sales but on fostering long-term relationships and loyalty. Online platforms become a touchpoint for discovery, engagement and education about the brand's heritage and offerings, which may eventually lead to purchases in physical stores where the tactile and personal aspects of luxury shopping are unrivalled (Pauwels et al, 2011).

The omnichannel paradox: Balancing integration with channel-specific exclusivity

The tension between full integration of retail channels and the provision of unique channel-specific features can indeed be considered a paradox, especially when catering to diverse needs and audiences. The dual in the omnichannel landscape is about achieving a seamless customer experience across all channels while also leveraging the unique strengths and exclusive offerings of individual channels to meet varied consumer expectations.

In the omnichannel retail landscape, maintaining coherence across different channels is crucial to avoid confusion and ensure a seamless customer experience. While diversifying merchandise and services across online and offline platforms can offer exclusivity and cater to specific consumer segments, it also runs the risk of creating a disjointed brand image in the eyes of the consumer.

It is not uncommon for brands to launch exclusive capsule collections or limited editions that are available only online or in physical stores. This strategy can generate excitement and a sense of urgency among customers, but it can also lead to confusion if not managed carefully. Customers might struggle to understand why certain products are not available across all channels, leading to potential frustration.

Similarly, the product assortment often varies between online and offline channels, with online platforms sometimes offering a curated selection rather than the full range available in stores. This discrepancy needs to be communicated effectively to prevent customer disappointment when they are unable to find specific items online that they have seen in-store.

Additionally, the return and reimbursement policies can vary significantly between online and offline purchases. Online shopping often comes with more flexible return policies due to local regulations that protect ecommerce consumers, allowing for easy returns and refunds. However, return policies for in-store purchases may be more restrictive, potentially leading to dissatisfaction among customers who expect the same level of service across all channels.

For luxury brands, where customer service and satisfaction are paramount, it is essential to carefully consider these differences. They must strive for transparent communication about product availability and return policies to manage expectations and maintain trust. As the omnichannel environment continues to evolve, luxury brands need to harmonize their strategies across channels to deliver a consistent and high-quality experience that upholds the brand's reputation and values.

Being direct with wholesale

Omnichannel strategy, particularly in the context of wholesale, requires a holistic approach that integrates all channels, ensuring consistent brand messaging and customer experience. For emerging or smaller brands, wholesale can be a critical avenue for expansion and reaching new markets. Integrating wholesale into the broader strategy involves ensuring partners are aligned with the brand's values and narrative. This can be achieved by treating wholesale relationships with the same care as direct retail channels, providing comprehensive training, clear communication guidelines and leveraging technology to ensure brand consistency. Best-in-class brands excel by nurturing these relationships, ensuring that intermediaries become brand advocates, effectively conveying the brand's message and upholding its standards.

Brands like Moncler or Rolex recognize the importance of the wholesale channel as a direct touchpoint to consumers, valuing the 'sell-in' approach – how products are introduced to wholesale partners – as much as the 'sell-out'. From the brand's perspective, wholesale has a strategic role, and it may be worthwhile to:

1 Experiment with hybrid business models, like a more direct influence over shop-in-shop operations within department stores or travel retail environments by enhancing the partnership with wholesalers. This strategy does not require owning a concession, but focuses on structuring a stronger collaborative relationship to exert control and align brand representation more closely with your standards.

2 Explore new product categories on a smaller scale to see readiness to go beyond traditional offerings larger scale.

3 Test new partners before moving into concessions and increase the level of risk, without a substantial initial investment.

An active and curated approach to wholesale can allow for direct relationships with consumers, even by intermediated but selective channels (ie a reduced number of doors). This might involve partnering with renowned department stores, engaging in digital collaborations and crafting unique pop-up experiences that connect with local communities and reflect the brand's innovative spirit.

Assessing the experience-led and seamless retail strategies: A roadmap

In this era of heightened competition and discerning consumers, the imperative for luxury brands to perpetually refine and reassess their experiential positioning relative to direct competitors cannot be overstated. The Experience-Led Strategy Assessment, a three-step evaluative odyssey developed and honed by Bocconi over 10 years, is more than a roadmap – it is an indispensable compass for navigating the ever-evolving retail landscape. This journey begins with the strategic segmentation technique and definition of strategic groups, scrutinizing the interplay between business models and market dynamics. It advances into a deep dive into product portfolios, juxtaposing a brand's merchandise strategy against its rivals. The culmination of this voyage is a meticulous analysis of the retail experience, a critical audit that dissects and examines every customer touchpoint.

The methodology presented in this section transcends conventional analysis, representing a holistic and dynamic approach that demands continuous vigilance and adaptation. It is the weaving of a brand's narrative with the threads of innovation, customer insight and market foresight. By rigorously applying this approach, brands can ensure that their story – one told through products, places and experiences – resonates with potent relevance and authenticity.

To conclude, the Experience-Led Strategy Assessment is not simply a capstone of academic insight. It is an actionable testament to the transformative power of strategic vigilance. For the brand, it heralds an era where the alchemy of analytics and creativity ensures that their narrative is not just told but is also lived, felt and cherished by their clientele. Let this be not merely the end of this chapter, but the beginning of an enduring commitment to self-assessment, improvement and experiential distinction.

Embarking on the journey of strategic positioning and brand experience assessment, the initial step, *Step 1*, is crucial. It involves segmenting the competitive landscape into strategic groups defined by their analogous strategies and operational approaches. In this segmentation, brands are dissected and categorized based on a spectrum of strategic dimensions as elucidated by Michael Porter in *Competitive Strategy* (1980). These dimensions, which include product range, iconic pieces, core business, degree of diversification, geographical scope, distribution channels and vertical integration, are not merely classifications – they serve as the axes of strategic differentiation and as indicators tied to the industry's key success factors.

Within the design industry, for instance, we may discern distinct strategic groups by examining the degree of vertical integration – contrasting the deeply integrated operations of a firm like Natuzzi with the more 'editorial' approach of Kartell. Similarly, examining the geographical scope reveals a clear demarcation between export-driven entities like Natuzzi and Boffi and domestically-focused firms such as Scavolini.

Exploring the cashmere industry further illustrates the multifaceted nature of strategic groups. Companies like Loro Piana and Brunello Cucinelli, which may have cashmere as their core business, are set against those for whom it's a peripheral offering. The analytical process requires listing these companies and then determining the two pivotal strategic dimensions that will distinguish one brand from another, mapping them onto a framework that clusters them into coherent strategic groups. This mapping is instrumental in illustrating the landscape and highlighting the flag cases – those examples that define or defy the categories.

Beyond the tangible strategic dimensions, a brand's market perception, influenced by consumer sentiments and competitive positioning, is equally critical. Perceptive mapping, a technique that plots brands on a perceptual scale based on consumer impressions, complements the strategic group segmentation. It offers insights into how consumers differentiate between brands that might otherwise appear similar in strategic terms. This dual-layered approach provides a comprehensive picture of competitive standing, informing strategic decisions and enabling a brand to navigate and position itself effectively in a competitive market.

Together, these elements form the foundation of Step 1, setting the stage for a nuanced and detailed examination of the product portfolios and retail experiences that will follow in subsequent steps.

Step 2 of the Experience-Led Strategy Assessment focuses on the merchandising aspect, where brands are dissected and compared at a product category level. This granular approach to competitive analysis is vital for brands to understand not just their position in the market, but also their competitors' product strategies.

The process begins with selecting key product categories from three directly competing brands. Brands are then compared based on a variety of dimensions that include, but are not limited to, entry price, core price, average price, the range and types of products offered, style, the number of stock keeping units (SKUs) and the ratio of carry-over items to seasonal or fashionable products. This stage goes beyond mere numerical comparisons. It delves into the nuances of product offerings such as limited editions, capsules, collaborations and pieces exclusive to online or offline channels. It examines the products' market performance, considering sold-out items, bestsellers, pre-orders and waiting lists. This is crucial for identifying the brand's strengths and potential weak spots in its offering, which in turn enables the formulation of strategies for new collections and product launches.

The objective is to pinpoint opportunities for differentiation and innovation. For instance, if a gap is identified in the market for a product category at a certain price point, or there's a demand for a style not currently being offered by any of the brands, these insights can be leveraged to fill those gaps and meet unaddressed customer needs.

The outcome of this analysis should be presented in a format that is both accessible and informative. Well-organized tables and clear visuals, such as pictures of the products, are essential for conveying complex data in an understandable way. This not only aids in merchandising strategy discussions but also prepares for presentations to other departments (eg the creative team, the marketing team, the retail and sales team, etc).

In essence, Step 2 is a comprehensive merchandising audit, providing a clear view of where a brand stands in relation to its direct competitors and highlighting actionable insights for product development and strategic positioning.

Step 3 is the retail experience assessment – the retail safari – which is as much an anthropological expedition as it is a commercial one. It requires one to dive into the ecosystem of the store, online and offline, to observe, interact and unearth the nuances of the brand experience. Where expectations soar as high as the skylines, a systematic and immersive analysis of the retail experience is paramount. As we prepare to delve into the final and most granular step of the Experience-Led Strategy Assessment, it's imperative to approach this retail safari with a blend of curiosity and critical acumen. This methodical exploration is not just about observing the overt; it's about perceiving the nuances that define excellence and exclusivity in the luxury market.

Our journey begins at the precipice of expectation, where we, as discerning observers, step into the shoes of the most demanding customers, preparing our narrative and list of questions to challenge people on the salesfloor. The store is not merely a physical space but a theatre of brand storytelling, where every element, from window display to the warmth of the welcome, contributes to a compelling narrative; these are the areas of assessment.

As we cross the threshold into the sanctuary of luxury, we are armed with a detailed checklist, designed to dissect and analyse the multifaceted layers of brand interaction. We are not just passive onlookers but active participants, engaging with the environment, querying the staff, and interacting with the digital interfaces that bridge the physical divide.

The store (as the brand's website) itself becomes a crucible for innovation, where each brand's commitment to excellence is silently scrutinized under the lens of our comprehensive evaluation. We seek to unearth the subtleties of brand strategy, the alignment of product and presentation and the digital dynamism that connects with a global clientele.

See the box on the next page for the eight areas of investigation to support a thorough analysis.

RETAIL EXPERIENCE ASSESSMENT

1 Windows and visual merchandising:
   a. Identify the number and types of items displayed.
   b. Note any pricing strategies or promotional tactics.
   c. Understand the story or value proposition being communicated.
   d. Look for the use of digital displays and their content.

2 Store environment and layout:
   a. Observe how queue and waiting times are managed and the customer flow.
   b. Hotspots identification: Determine areas with the highest customer traffic.
   c. Product placement: Assess how products are organized and grouped (by aesthetics, themes, category, etc).
   d. Fixtures and furniture: Evaluate the design and functionality of racks, shelves, etc.
   e. Interior aesthetics: Note the design choices, ambiance and overall feel.
   f. Sensory aspects: Consider music, scent and lighting and their impact on the experience.
   g. Store layout: Analyse spacing and ease of navigation.
   h. Mannequins and displays: Observe styling and representation.
   i. Density: How many products are exhibited in a given space (measure by counting number of steps).

3 Staff interaction and service:
   a. Staff count and appearance: Note the number of staff and their attire.
   b. Greeting and engagement: Evaluate the welcome ceremony and initial interactions.
   c. Customer service attitude: Assess the staff's approach to customer service.
   d. Brand affinity: Sense the pride and knowledge staff have regarding the brand.

  e. Digital tool usage: Observe if and how staff use digital tools to enhance service.

  f. Product knowledge: Check the staff's familiarity with both in-store and online offerings.

4 Customer demographics and behaviour:

  a. Customer profiling: Estimate the number of customers and categorize them (locals, tourists).

  b. Appearance and branding: Observe customer attire and potential brand loyalty.

  c. Engagement: Watch how customers interact with the products and staff.

5 Product assortment and placement:

  a. Category analysis: Evaluate the breadth and depth of product categories.

  b. Material and trend analysis: Identify the fabrics and trends on display.

  c. SKU variety: Count the number of models and sizes available.

  d. Origin labelling: Check for country-of-origin tags.

  e. Price points: Document the range of prices across important categories.

  f. Traceability: Look for innovative product tracking and authenticity verification.

6 Service and hospitality:

  a. Customization services: Identify if customization options are clearly offered.

  b. Hospitality services: Observe the quality and type of hospitality offered.

  c. Sales ceremony: Evaluate the sophistication of the selling ceremony with technology.

  d. Feedback mechanisms. Note the presence and type of feedback systems.

  e. Assess CRM (customer relationship management) and KYC (know your customer) tools.

7 Omnichannel integration:

a. Online-offline synergy: Evaluate how online and in-store experiences are integrated.

b. Wholesale-retail connection: Observe the connection between different sales channels.

8 Technological intensity and impact:

a. Assess on a scale of 1–5 the adoption and integration of technology in-store and online such as:

i. innovation in product discovery

ii. natural language processing (eg bots) for customer interaction

iii. machine vision and visual search for product search and selection

iv. products availability on new media (eg the metaverse), AR/VR

b. Evaluate the current and future impact of these technologies on customer experience.

Each area must be meticulously documented, with managers collecting as much data as possible, including customer interactions, staff service levels and the physical presentation of products. This retail safari will conclude with a synthetic grading from 1 to 5, reflecting the overall retail experience's effectiveness and technological advancement, providing a clear depiction of the brand's current standing and areas for potential growth. Competing brands can be benchmarked on a radar map along these eight dimensions.

Throughout this journey, as brands are mapped and strategies are outlined, the focus shifts to the customer's perception – the ultimate measure of a brand's success. This assessment extends beyond the tangible; it's an endeavour to understand the resonance of a brand within the hearts and minds of its consumers.

In this final paragraph, the narrative comes full circle, tying together the analytical with the emotional, the strategic with the perceptual. The Experience-Led Strategy is not just a framework; it's a philosophy, one that champions the customer experience as the cornerstone of brand legacy and success. It's a reminder that in luxury, the battle is won not by price points or product features alone but by the value perceived, the memories created and the relationships forged.

Takeaways

As we conclude this chapter, let's carry some insights, reminding us that, in the end, luxury is not just about having, it's about feeling. The role of stores transcends traditional selling, becoming vibrant hubs of brand experience. This chapter underscores the importance of a seamless retail presence, merging online and offline realms to offer customers a fluid, consistent experience across channels. It emphasizes innovative technology integration, enhancing, not replacing, the human touch in luxury encounters. Employees, as brand ambassadors, play a pivotal role, their expertise and passion vital in enriching the customer journey. Pop-up stores emerge as dynamic, strategic tools, offering temporary yet impactful brand interactions.

Reflecting on Audrey's journey in Chapter 5, the chapter advocates for continuous refinement of retail strategies, ensuring they align with evolving customer expectations and deliver memorable, personalized experiences. This narrative journey through luxury retail underscores the transformative power of stores in crafting enduring brand connections.

In the context of luxury brand strategy, evaluating and refining experiential positioning is crucial. The three-step Experience-Led Strategy Assessment developed by Bocconi aids in this process. The first step involves segmenting competitors into strategic groups, based on various operational and strategic dimensions. The second step is a detailed analysis of product portfolios, comparing the brand's merchandise strategy with competitors. The final step involves a comprehensive audit of the retail experience, examining customer interactions across all touchpoints.

This methodology is a blend of brand narrative, innovation, customer insight and market foresight, crucial for maintaining relevance and authenticity in the luxury market. It encourages continuous assessment and improvement in strategic positioning and customer experience, ensuring that the brand's story is not just told but experienced and valued by its clientele.

References and further reading

Abhijit, G, Dhruv, G, Praveen, K K, Haenlein, M, Schneider, M J, Jung, H, Moustafa, R, Hegde, D R and Hawkins, G (2021) How artificial intelligence will affect the future of retailing, *Journal of Retailing*, **97** (1), pp 28–41, https://doi.org/10.1016/j.jretai.2021.01.005 (archived at https://perma.cc/V997-9Q7Q)

Argo, J J and Dahl, D W (2020) Social influence in the retail context: A contemporary review of the literature, *Journal of Retailing*, **96** (1), pp. 25–39, https://doi.
org/10.1016/j.jretai.2019.12.005 (archived at https://perma.cc/GN2Z-3Q6M)

Arnold, M J, Reynolds, K E, Ponder, N and Lueg, J E (2005) Customer delight in a
retail context: Investigating delightful and terrible shopping experiences, *Journal
of Business Research*, **58** (8), pp. 1132–45

Barnes, D C, Beauchamp, M B and Webster, C (2010) To delight or not to delight?
This is the question service firms must address, *Journal of Marketing Theory
and Practice*, **18** (3), pp. 275–84

Bartl, C, Gouthier, M H J and Lenker, M (2013) Delighting consumers click by
click: Antecedents and effects of delight online, *Journal of Service Research*,
16 (3), pp. 386–99, https://doi.org/10.1177/1094670513479168 (archived at
https://perma.cc/5ET8-EMR3)

Bleier, A, Harmeling, C and Palmatier, R (2019) Creating effective online customer
experiences, *Journal of Marketing*, **83** (1), https://doi.org/10.1177/
0022242918809930 (archived at https://perma.cc/77PN-Z4MD)

Borghini, S, Diamond, N, Kozinets, R V, McGrath, M A, Muñiz, A M and Sherry, J
F (2009) Why are themed brandstores so powerful? Retail brand ideology at
American Girl Place, *Journal of Retailing*, **85** (3), pp. 363–75

Brynjolfsson, E, Hu, Y and Rahman, M (2013) Competing in the age of omnichannel retailing, *MIT Sloan Management Review*, **54**, pp. 23–29

Catalano, F and Zorzetto, F (2010) *Temporary Store: La strategia dell'effimero*,
Franco Angeli

Costa, M and Cattaneo, A (2010), *Il temporary shop: nuove forme di comunicazi-
one e vendita in sintonia con lo spirito dei tempi*, Lupetti

Davenport, T, Guha, A, Grewal, D and Bressgott, T (2020) How artificial intelligence will change the future of marketing, *Journal of the Academy of Marketing
Science*, **48**, pp. 1–10, https://doi.org/10.1007/s11747-019-00696-0 (archived at
https://perma.cc/8A9F-MTX6)

De Lassus, C and Anido Freire, N (2014) Access to the luxury brand myth in
pop-up stores: A netnographic and semiotic analysis, *Journal of Retailing and
Consumer Services*, **21** (1) pp. 61–68

Gao, F and Su, X (2016) Omnichannel retail operations with buy-online-and-pick-
up-in-store, *Management Science*, **63**, https://doi.org/10.1287/mnsc.2016.2473
(archived at https://perma.cc/3HNA-DBDQ)

Grant, R M (2021) *Contemporary Strategy Analysis*, Wiley

Haron, A J (2016), Standardized versus localized strategy: The role of cultural
patterns in society on consumption and market research, *Journal of Accounting
& Marketing*, **5**, pp. 1–4

Hilken, T, de Ruyter, K, Chylinski, M, Mahr, D and Keeling, D I (2017)
Augmenting the eye of the beholder: Exploring the strategic potential of
augmented reality to enhance online service experiences, *Journal of the Academy
of Marketing Science*, **45** (6), pp. 884–905, https://doi.org/10.1007/s11747-017-
0541-x (archived at https://perma.cc/5XSS-XF7T)

Hoyer, W, Kroschke, M, Schmitt, B, Kraume, K and Shankar, V (2020) Transforming the customer experience through new technologies, *Journal of Interactive Marketing*, **51**, pp. 57–71, https://doi.org/10.1016/j.intmar. 2020.04.001 (archived at https://perma.cc/5VBK-WRJU)

Hult, G T M, Sharma, P, Morgeson, F and Zhang, Y (2019) Antecedents and consequences of customer satisfaction: Do they differ across online and offline purchases? *Journal of Retailing*, **95** (1), pp. 10–23, https://doi.org/10.1016/ j.jretai.2018.10.003 (archived at https://perma.cc/A3TY-9A8M)

Keller, K L (1993) Conceptualizing, measuring, and managing customer-based brand equity, *Journal of Marketing*, **57** (1), pp. 1–22, https://doi.org/ 10.2307/1252054 (archived at https://perma.cc/SZ4J-KXCA)

Kozinets, R, Sherry, J, DeBerry-Spence, B, Duhachek, A, Nuttavuthisit, K and Storm, D (2002) Themed flagship brand stores in the new millennium: theory, practice, prospects, *Journal of Retailing*, **78** (1), pp. 17–29

Kozinets, R, Sherry, J, Storm, D, Duhachek, A, Nuttavuthisit, K and DeBerry-Spence, B (2004) Ludic agency and retail spectacle, *Journal of Consumer Research*, **31**, pp. 658–72, https://doi.org/10.1086/425101 (archived at https:// perma.cc/75JR-V4WJ)

Laroche, M, Yang, Z, McDougall, G and Bergeron J (2005) Internet versus bricks-and-mortar retailers: An investigation into intangibility and its consequences, *Journal of Retailing*, **81** (4), pp. 51–267, https://doi.org/10.1016/ j.jretai.2004.11.002 (archived at https://perma.cc/SV6J-YJ3R)

Lemon, K N and Verhoef, P C (2016) Understanding customer experience throughout the customer journey, *Journal of Marketing*, **80** (6), pp. 69–96, https://doi. org/10.1509/jm.15.0420 (archived at https://perma.cc/U34K-GYH6)

McIntyre, C, Melewar, T and Dennis, C (2016), *Multi-Channel Marketing, Branding and Retail Design: New challenges and opportunities*, Esmerald Group Publishing Limited

Murray, K and Schlacter, J (1990) The impact of services versus goods on consumers' assessment of perceived risk and variability, *Journal of the Academy of Marketing Science*, **18**, pp. 51–65, https://doi.org/10.1007/BF02729762 (archived at https://perma.cc/ZJT6-AM92)

Nepomuceno, M V, Laroche, M and Richard, M-O (2014) How to reduce perceived risk when buying online: The interactions between intangibility, product knowledge, brand familiarity, privacy and security concerns, *Journal of Retailing and Consumer Services*, **21**, pp. 619–29, https://doi.org/10.1016/j. jretconser.2013.11.006 (archived at https://perma.cc/XH4E-9ZPC)

Neslin, S A, Grewal, D, Leghorn, R, Shankar, V, Teerling, M I, Thomas, J S and Verhoef, P C (2006) Challenges and opportunities in multichannel customer management, *Journal of Service Research*, **9** (2), pp. 95–112, https://doi.org/ 10.1177/1094670506293559 (archived at https://perma.cc/MEL9-72XU)

Ng, I and Wakenshaw, S (2017) The Internet-of-Things: Review and research directions, *International Journal of Research in Marketing*, **34**, https://doi. org/10.1016/j.ijresmar.2016.11.003 (archived at https://perma.cc/QU2V-HNQ4)

Oliver, R L, Rust, R T and Varki, S (1997) Customer delight: Foundations, findings, and managerial insight, *Journal of Retailing*, **73** (3), pp. 311–36

Park, C, MacInnis, D and Priester, J (2008) Brand attachment: Constructs, consequences, and causes, *Foundations and Trends in Marketing*, **1** (3) pp. 191–230, http://dx.doi.org/10.1561/1700000006 (archived at https://perma. cc/83HR-GZUE)

Pauwels, K, Leeflang, P S H , Teerling, M L and Huizingh, E K R (2011) Does online Information drive offline revenues? *Journal of Retailing*, **87** (1), pp. 1–17, http://dx.doi.org/10.1016/j.jretai.2010.10.001 (archived at https:// perma.cc/69FJ-N72U)

Pine, B J and Gilmore, J (2013) The experience economy: Past, present and future, in J Sundbo and F Sørensen (eds), *Handbook on the Experience Economy*, Elgar

Porter, M E (1980) *Competitive Strategy*, Free Press

Shankar, V (2018) How artificial intelligence (AI) is reshaping retailing, *Journal of Retailing*, **94**, pp. vi–xi, https://doi.org/10.1016/S0022-4359(18)30076-9 (archived at https://perma.cc/T7DZ-ZE2S)

Surchi, M (2011) The temporary store: A new marketing tool for fashion brands, *Journal of Fashion Marketing and Management*, **15** (2), pp. 257–70

Tan, Y-C, Chandukala, S R and Reddy, S K (2022) Augmented reality in retail and its impact on sales, *Journal of Marketing*, **86** (1), pp. 48–66, https://doi.org/ 10.1177/0022242921995449 (archived at https://perma.cc/84Q9-AETF)

Venkatesh, V (2000) Determinants of perceived ease of use: Integrating control, intrinsic motivation, and emotion into the technology acceptance model, *Information Systems Research*, **11** (4), pp. 342–65

Verhoef, P, Kannan, P K and Inman, J (2015) From multi-channel retailing to omni-channel retailing, *Journal of Retailing*, **91**, https://doi.org/10.1016/j. jretai.2015.02.005 (archived at https://perma.cc/DRU4-Y4TY)

Verhoef, P C, Neslin S A and Vroomen, B (2007) Multichannel customer management: Understanding the research-shopper phenomenon, *International Journal of Research in Marketing*, **24** (2), pp. 129–48, https://doi.org/10.1016/j. ijresmar.2006.11.002 (archived at https://perma.cc/YD2A-7K2B)

Yoo, B and Donthu, N (2001) Developing and Validating a Multidimensional Consumer-Based Brand Equity Scale, *Journal of Business Research*, **52**, pp. 1–14, https://doi.org/10.1016/S0148-2963(99)00098-3 (archived at https:// perma.cc/M39Q-Y3F8)

7

How to build a 360° view of the customer to nurture personalized relationships

GABRIELLA LOJACONO

The integration of client experiences with strategic data utilization forms the cornerstone of customer relationship management (CRM). This chapter delves into the critical practice of collecting, analysing and applying both quantitative and qualitative client data to craft engaging strategies that not only retain loyalty but also transform potential visitors and lesser-engaged clients into very important customers (VICs). We will explore the criteria for effective client segmentation, methods to track and enhance client journeys across their lifetime, and actionable strategies for engagement.

Central to this discourse is the role of advanced CRM platforms, the burgeoning influence of AI and machine learning, and the advent of clienteling 2.0 applications. These technologies are pivotal in linking corporate strategy with on-the-ground client interactions, empowering client advisers to play a key role in cultivating successful, long-lasting client relationships. This chapter aims to provide a comprehensive understanding of these dynamics, underscoring the significance of technological enablers in augmenting the luxury experience.

In navigating the complexities of global CRM strategies, luxury brands face the challenge of disparate data regulations across regions. For instance, a European client like our Audrey may encounter service discrepancies in a Japanese store due to regional CRM limitations, which hinder the sharing of her purchase history and preferences; she is treated like a new customer even though she is a VIC of the brand. Such fragmentation jeopardizes the seamless omnichannel experience that brands strive for.

Moreover, China's stringent Personal Information Protection Law (PIPL), surpassing Europe's General Data Protection Regulation (GDPR) in restrictiveness, mandates that customer data remain local, with explicit consent required for international transfer. This raises a critical question: if similar regulations are adopted across Asia, how will luxury brands maintain a cohesive customer service model without infringing on these laws?

Brands must address these regulatory constraints, emphasizing the need for a system that respects local laws while providing a unified view of the client's journey to authorized personnel (eg the store manager), thus fostering both compliance and superior customer service.

The advent of sophisticated data collection and analysis through AI and machine learning marks a revolutionary shift in CRM strategies. These technologies facilitate a transformation from a 'one-to-many' approach to a 'one-to-one' or 'ad personam' paradigm. This allows for bespoke communications, engagements and experiences that are finely tuned to the individual preferences and behaviours of each client, laying the foundation for advanced clienteling. This personal touch is not just an enhancement but is at the core of modern CRM systems, elevating the customer journey to unprecedented levels of personalization.

Connecting front of house with back of house: Six golden principles

The journey into the heart of CRM and clienteling unfolds as a narrative of deep connections and personalized experiences. To better understand the new frontier of customer relations and engagement, it's useful to weave in threads from past chapters into an illustration of the premise of seamless integration between the back-end systems and front-line interactions. CRM stems from six pivotal concepts that form the foundation of a sophisticated strategy, bridging the gap between the meticulous analytics of the back office and the personalized art of front-end customer engagement.

The first tenet is **connection**. It transcends the physical interaction in-store, advocating for a relationship that doesn't end at the point of sale but evolves into a dynamic and ongoing conversation, ensuring customers never feel the frustration of an impersonal experience.

The 'connection' concept emphasizes the need for compromises. Brands face choices: allowing clients to wait outside, ensuring a ready and attentive welcome inside, or having them enter immediately only to possibly wait for assistance. Then, busy clients might prefer expedited service; others leisurely browse, absorbing the brand aura. These scenarios underscore the necessity for retail teams to strategize the best balance that aligns with their brand identity and maximizes client satisfaction. Waiting becomes a part of a curated journey, transforming retail from sales generators into architects of experience. Client advisers seek to preempt any disconnection that could arise from a disjointed retail experience. This entails creating a harmonious journey where clients feel valued and attended to, without unnecessary delays or impersonal treatment.

Personalization forms the second guiding principle, where each client is acknowledged and celebrated – no two customers are alike, and the CRM strategy reflects this through individualized attention that echoes throughout their journey with the brand. Each client's preferences and desires are uniquely catered to, crafting individualized experiences that resonate on a personal level. This approach transcends standard retail offerings and enters the world of bespoke service, where every detail is attuned to the client's expectations and brand universe.

In a post-pandemic world, the focus has shifted towards engaging more with the **local customer base**, acknowledging their value not just as an alternative to tourists, but as the core of a sustainable business model. This approach ensures that local customers are not overlooked but are instead seen as essential to the brand's success.

Synchronizing Enterprise Resource Planning (ERP) and CRM is the fourth area of awareness and attention. Integrating ERP with CRM streamlines operations from product data management to customer interactions, bridging the gap between client relationships and operational efficiencies.

An ERP manages product details and inventory costs, while a CRM tailors this information to enhance customer relations. Together, they form an interconnected system that optimizes both inventory management and customer satisfaction. An ERP system's meticulous data management dovetails with CRM's client-centric insights, orchestrating a symphony of optimized supply chains and personalized customer experiences.

The golden principle of '**one stock**' represents the fifth concept to bear in mind. Breaking down barriers between different stock locations, one stock provides customers with access to products regardless of their geographical location.

The concept of one stock within the luxury retail space speaks to the ambition of creating a customer-centric, fluid system that transcends borders. It's about reshaping the retail ecosystem to operate as a global network of interconnected fulfilment centres. This strategy entails leveraging metropolitan delivery services as a concierge to enhance the convenience for urban customers, allowing the seamless movement of products (and returns) to match the ebb and flow of local demand. At a global level, it's a strategic redistribution of inventory, minimizing stockpiles in one region while addressing potential shortages in another, ensuring that whether a customer shops in Milan or Tokyo, the brand experience remains consistently exceptional and responsive.

By knitting these aspects together, a luxury brand ensures that the journey from back-end inventory management to front-line customer engagement is seamless, resource-efficient and deeply customer-centric.

In the ethos of **omnichannel strategy**, the sixth guiding principle, luxury brands transcend mere cross-channel service (like 'pick up in store' or 'book an appointment') to embody a fully integrated omnichannel identity. This means every client interaction, whether online, in-store or via mobile, is cohesive and consistently informed. Integrating once-separated databases for products, sales and clients is essential to unlock opportunities along the consumer journey. While technology acts as a facilitator for these integrations, the real value comes from custom solutions tailored to the brand's unique vision and business model. Partnerships with technology providers like Salesforce or Oracle can offer robust platforms, but the strategic implementation must align with the brand's identity, business model and customer experience goals to truly enhance clienteling and maintain a competitive edge.

Advisers are empowered with comprehensive client histories, akin to a Google for customer profiles, enabling them to provide personalized experiences seamlessly. The brand's commitment extends to acknowledging advisers' efforts in client engagements, ensuring that their contributions are recognized and rewarded, thereby motivating them and aligning their achievements with the brand's overarching vision and business strategy.

For advisers, maintaining motivation is critical, as their client interactions directly impact sales and brand loyalty. Consider Audrey's scenario: she engages deeply with Marc, the adviser in Paris, for two hours during the Easter holidays trying on various items. Then she inquires about new ones in London, only to make her final purchase online at home at midnight from the sofa. This fluid consumer journey highlights the need for a system that credits advisers for their role in the sales process, regardless of where the sale is completed. Brands must craft these systems to ensure advisers like Marc feel valued and recognized for their contributions, integrating comprehensive client histories into the brand's operational framework to foster a truly omnichannel brand ethos.

The integration of data and personalized client services in luxury retail has significantly impacted key performance indicators. Interviews with several luxury brands reveal that through effective stock management and leveraging sales associates' insights, they've managed to reduce inventory levels by up to 10 per cent, thereby improving operating margins. Additionally, they've streamlined the checkout process, enhanced transaction speed and increased accuracy. Sales associates, equipped with comprehensive purchase history and client data, have been pivotal in raising the average transaction value, enabling more targeted recommendations and effective cross-selling strategies. This rich blend of human expertise and data analytics underscores the transformative power of informed, personal client engagement in driving retail success.

Data acquisition and client segmentation

The inception of a luxury brand's CRM strategy begins with the critical step of data acquisition, which has evolved from paper forms to digital registrations through smart devices and QR codes. This initial collection of traditional demographic data is a gateway to the dynamic and continuous profiling of clients. This allows to segment customers into groups based on personal attributes – such as age, gender, nationality, residence and interests – and transactional data, like purchase history, yearly spending, monetary value and purchase frequency.

Leveraging transactional data for client segmentation is a first important step. By plotting spending frequency against total spend, four distinct customer segments emerge: those who make frequent low-value purchases, single high-value purchasers, aspirational one-time buyers and consistent big spenders. Customized engagement strategies, such as targeted programmes, CRM activities and special events, are crafted to shift buying behaviours within these segments – for instance, encouraging infrequent shoppers to visit more often, or increasing the spend of lower-value clients through personalized experiences. This strategy also integrates with merchandising by notifying clients about complementary products, like a newly launched jacket matching previously purchased trousers, or targeting specific interests.

The CRM strategy for luxury brands, epitomized by Valentino, is a nuanced pyramid where data is the foundation for client segmentation. This pyramid is structured into usual tiers, with very, very important customers (VVICs) at the apex, descending to very important customers (VICs), aspirational clients and the broad base of existing and potential clients. At Valentino, more than 60 per cent of clients are Millennials, although the majority of the spending is in the hands of the over-40s. This segmentation is not static; it's a fluid lifetime view, acknowledging that client spending can vary annually.

The significance of VICs is underscored by their contribution to sales, with a VIC often having a minimum spend of around €50,000 at luxury brands and around €10,000–€12,000 at department stores and wholesale digital platforms. These top-tier clients, representing around 3–5 per cent of the total number, can account for 30–40 per cent of a brand's total sales, reflecting their crucial role in the business's financial success. Understanding and catering to the needs and preferences of these clients is essential for sustaining and growing a luxury brand's revenue.

The role of technology in CRM has transcended mere transactional analysis. The data journey flourishes by incorporating 'engagement' details like spending patterns, email opened, site visits and interactions on the brand. com that are also critical in shaping an appealing ecommerce strategy. With CRM 3.0, a singular database captures every interaction across digital platforms, creating a holistic view that informs targeted strategies. The CRM platform is enhanced with qualitative insights from sales associates.

AI becomes a robust analytical tool, predicting sales trends and demands, and offering personalized customer experiences based on historical data. AI based on AA (Advanced Analytics) can be a digital assistant, providing service and sales support and, responding to queries. It integrates various data points such as purchase history, colour preferences, age, location and purchasing behaviour to deliver tailored recommendations, thereby acting as a composite piece of software that enhances the shopping experience. These systems can analyse large datasets, identify patterns and make decisions or recommendations in a way that mimics (and integrates) human intelligence, leveraging machine learning and other sophisticated statistical techniques.

Client advisers contribute to this rich data collection, annotating profiles with qualitative notes that capture the nuanced preferences of each client – such as a client's affinity for some drinks – thus enabling personalized engagement strategies. Incorporating qualitative notes into the CRM via a smart app enhances the data's richness, aiding in personalization. When a brand introduces a new line for pet lovers, say a collection tailored for dog owners, the clienteling app becomes an invaluable tool. For instance, sales advisers can utilize the app to initiate targeted campaigns. If a client is identified in the CRM with a #dogs tag, indicating their interest in pet-related products, the adviser can share this curated campaign with them. This not only personalizes the shopping experience, but also capitalizes on the customer's known interests to introduce them to new, relevant products.

Geo-enrichment analytics provide insights into a customer's locale-based potential, guiding tailored strategies to convert and engage. Incentivizing client advisers to capture these qualitative nuances fosters a culture of internal entrepreneurship and customer-centric service.

This amalgamation of a variety of data underpins two fundamental pillars: a comprehensive understanding of the client to deliver exceptional service, and a robust omnichannel approach that ensures a seamless customer management experience from the point of registration.

At Valentino, sophisticated segmentation leverages advanced analytics, employing over 150 variables that feed into a data lakehouse, enabling refined insights through business intelligence and machine learning algorithms. Such segmentation recognizes the fluidity of customer engagement, acknowledging that not all clients maintain consistent spending habits year on year.

In a world where data is the currency of personalization, the meticulous process of segmenting clients allows luxury brands to craft bespoke experiences that resonate with the lifestyle and aspirations of each individual. The data-driven insights not only track high spenders but also identify clients with growth potential, ensuring that customer relationships are meticulously cultivated and valued beyond mere transactions.

Onboarding and nurturing: Clienteling to keep the client engaged

Luxury brands are leveraging AI and machine learning to elevate their CRM from a broad 'one to many' approach to a refined 'one to one' strategy. Client engagement begins immediately after the first store visit. Within days, an onboarding process is initiated to warmly welcome the client in the brand's world. This process might include personalized communications through digital tools, ensuring a connection is maintained. These communications may include a reminder of items they showed interest in, or an invitation to exclusive events.

Subsequently, both automated and manual communications are employed to nurture this relationship. Automated systems might send a thank-you message or product recommendations, while advisers can make personal calls or send custom videos. Non-automated interactions allow for tailored gestures, based on data-driven insights.

Brands like Valentino exemplify this approach by using the clienteling app SmartXP that facilitates these interactions, ensuring advisers are equipped with the information needed to personalize each client's journey and foster long-term engagement. The app ensures continuous client engagement celebrating personal moments and fostering a deeper connection. Over time, the system schedules prompts for further touchpoints, ensuring the client feels valued and connected. This tailored approach reflects customer-centricity where every interaction is a step towards a stronger client-brand relationship.

Clienteling transcends mere message exchange; it's a dual-channel dialogue where listening is as critical as speaking. This approach fine-tunes each interaction, strengthening the bond with every contact and ensuring that the client feels heard and understood. It's about shaping a client-centric journey that evolves with their feedback and preferences, fostering a deeper, more meaningful connection.

Brands employ a nuanced contact strategy that aligns with the brand ethos while efficiently utilizing resources. Client tiers from VVICs at the pinnacle to VICs and the broader base of the pyramid receive varying degrees of personalized engagement. For VICs, Valentino offers personalized interactions through a clienteling app managed by advisers, one-to-one communications via platforms like WhatsApp and WeChat, and bespoke invitations to exclusive events like private fashion shows or access to the brand's archives. These high-value clients enjoy extraordinary gestures, collaborations and invitations that reflect their status. Aspirational clients are engaged with broader-reaching methods such as platforms like WhatsApp, WeChat and Line, newsletters, app push notifications and SMS/MMS messages, tailored to regional preferences, ensuring relevance and a sustained connection across different client tiers.

For the broader client base, the goal is to elevate their experience, using both digital and in-person interactions to potentially move them up the pyramid. Meanwhile, data is synthesized at HQs, with insights disseminated to client advisers via apps, informing targeted campaigns like holiday gifting, ensuring advisers are equipped to engage clients proactively and personally.

Valentino is enriching the digital shopping realm by deploying Online Private Advisers to craft personalized experiences for nurturing important clients. These advisers curate bespoke digital lookbooks and provide exclusive online pre-access, enhancing the luxury fashion journey. This omnichannel strategy, blending personal touch with digital convenience, is part of Valentino's wider effort to maintain engagement and anticipate client needs in the fluid world of high fashion.

Post-purchase follow-ups, AI-driven product recommendations and intention-to-rebuy strategies keep the client active in their journey, enhancing the bond beyond mere transactions. This approach is pivotal in nurturing long-term relationships, creating a couture experience that resonates with each client's unique journey.

The compelling case of Cartier's boutique tours in Milan showcases the importance of capturing the interest of new generations and expanding a prospect database. This strategy highlights how demographic data alone is insufficient for modern clienteling. Cartier's approach involved inviting the general public to demystify the luxury shopping experience through guided tours, starting with an online registration that seamlessly bridged digital engagement with a physical journey. By offering a personalized experience and a parting gift, Cartier succeeded in attracting young prospects, illustrating that luxury is ageless.

This initiative underscores the need for rich, diverse data collection, emphasizing quality over quantity to avoid overwhelming prospects with irrelevant follow-ups. The case exemplifies a strategic pivot towards long-term relationship building, leveraging technology to enrich data within privacy boundaries, setting a foundation for targeted client engagement and efficient resource allocation.

The journey of the client in luxury automotive has many entry touch-points, starting from the initial inquiry, often made to dealerships that act as gatekeepers to the prestigious ownership experience. Ferrari, for example, has a detailed system in place that begins with these inquiries. Engagement strategies often hinge on creating an exclusive community feel. For instance, leveraging referrals from existing clients and pre-owners who can invite friends to join brand events or test drives serves as an effective touchpoint. The HQs closely monitor follow-ups to ensure every prospect receives attention, especially when a model is sold out and alternative options must be proposed. This ensures that the potential buyers' journey with Ferrari doesn't end at a sold-out notice, but is just the beginning of a relationship with the brand that values each individual's unique aspirations and desires.

The preliminary data collected from these first touchpoints is pivotal for crafting a tailored engagement strategy, which may include updates on upcoming models, exclusive events and test drives, keeping the dream and anticipation alive even during a waiting period for the next available model. Keeping communication channels open and providing regular, value-added interactions ensures that interest remains piqued until the opportunity for purchase arises.

Ferrari's approach exemplifies the importance of maintaining a luxurious experience from start to finish, ensuring every interaction is as exceptional as the vehicles they craft.

Ferrari's CRM strategy exemplifies meticulous client segmentation and management, all facilitated by an advanced Oracle-based platform. The dealer is the linchpin in this system, tasked with ensuring engagement and responsiveness, aided by tools for detailed profiling and data-driven actions. Dealers navigate a complex landscape of long waitlists (around three years) and customer service, with the end goal of maintaining loyalty and enhancing the ownership experience. Dealers are guided by specific protocols to ensure brand consistency, focusing on local events and personalized offerings rather than product launches. With 80 targeted campaigns a year and an intelligent data platform, Ferrari's marketing strategy is finely tuned to engage customers through their journey, maintaining a sophisticated and exclusive brand narrative.

Post-sale focus, with activities ranging from maintenance (main dealers' business) to upselling to exclusive car customization, Ferrari's approach centres on a long-term vision, creating a community where passion for the brand fosters a sense of exclusivity and belonging.

Data provided by Ferrari in Maranello highlights the significant revenue generated from upselling and customization services. Upselling and tailored services are lucrative avenues for dealers, evidenced by the 25 per cent profit margin (on an average value of €4,000 per car) from a substantial car inventory park. With customization alone contributing approximately €1 billion to Ferrari's dealer turnover, the strategy of offering personalized options has proven financially rewarding. Performance metrics among dealers vary, indicating a diverse approach to these services. This focus on customization and upselling not only drives profit, but also enhances customer loyalty and brand value.

Ferrari's VVICs are brand ambassadors recognized for their behaviour, commitment and engagement with the brand, not only on the purchasing value. They enjoy exclusive benefits that include previews of new models before public release, as experienced during private events like the SP1-SP2 preview in Maranello. Ferrari ensures tailored maintenance solutions for their vehicles, further enhancing the ownership experience. Ambassadors are also invited to participate in special events and advanced driving courses, fostering a deeper connection with the brand. This strategy underpins Ferrari's goal of establishing personalized, one-to-one communication with its most dedicated clients.

CRM-based clienteling

Providing tailored recommendations and fostering intimate communication with clients is increasingly facilitated by innovative shopping and clienteling apps.

In 2019, two Italian tech entrepreneurs with a background in luxury, fashion and sportswear created Luce, a retail app utilized by over 16,000 Kering associates globally. It has been lauded as a groundbreaking digital tool within Kering's portfolio of luxury brands, including Gucci, Saint Laurent, Bottega Veneta and Balenciaga, streamlining retail operations and enhancing clienteling efforts. In the past, clienteling relied on common customer-facing tools like WhatsApp and WeChat, which didn't integrate well with internal systems like inventory or customer preferences. Now, with advanced clienteling apps like Luce, there has been a transformative shift. These apps enable the seamless connection of databases, providing sales associates with a comprehensive view of product ranges and real-time availability. This integration allows for more personalized customer interactions and efficient management of inventory, creating a more connected and insightful retail experience.

The same Italian tech entrepreneurs in 2022 launched Alpha, a connected clienteling app offering personalized stylist services and shopping suggestions directly to the client. Alpha's innovative approach as a cross-brand app revolutionizes luxury retail by enabling seamless, connected clienteling and personal service across various high-end brands. It differentiated itself from alternatives that primarily serve sales associates to notify news and send greetings on the occasion of special celebrations. The app allows for a detailed client profile enriched with preferences and interactions, enhancing the adviser-client relationship. It reflects the seamless blend of in-store and digital experiences, resonating with the fluid lifestyle of modern luxury clients and anticipating the integration of metaverse experiences into personal shopping (Robinson, 2022).

Alpha's entry into the digital clienteling space was a game-changer for luxury, offering a cohesive personal service experience that extended beyond the limitations of single-brand apps.

The development of Alpha underscores a strategic recent shift towards nurturing relationships with VICs that are showing an increase across brands and channels. As an example, the growth of VICs at Mytheresa.com was +25.3 per cent in Q2 of FY23 and +26.2 per cent in Q1 FY23, as compared to the prior year period (from the Mytheresa website).

Luxury brands are leveraging clienteling apps to enhance the shopping experience. Burberry's 'R message' extends omnichannel capabilities, allowing associates to engage customers remotely. Neiman Marcus acquired Stylyze for personalized outfit recommendations, while Farfetch partnered with Wishi to scale personalization. Seer, working with Saks, The Webster and Harvey Nichols, helps create shoppable suggestions. Seers is a technology provider for luxury retailers, enhancing the clienteling experience. Their platform assists retailers in creating personalized shopping suggestions that mirror magazine layouts. This service enables sales associates to offer a tailored, high-end shopping experience, fostering deeper connections with top-tier clients and aiming to transform occasional buyers into regular spenders.

In London, Browns has innovated a unique approach to clienteling with an app featuring a 'connected retail layer'. Sales associates can scan a QR code to access a customer's in-app wishlist, making personalized product recommendations and even sending items the customer considered during a visit. This sophisticated system enhances the in-store experience and streamlines the purchase process, allowing transactions to be completed via mobile, demonstrating an integrated, customer-centric approach to retail (Bain, 2022).

Other clienteling apps like BSPK (which interfaces with the Salesforce and Shopify platforms and is used by luxury corporate clients like Louboutin), and traditional shopping apps like The Yes (acquired by Pinterest), The List and Nate (available only in some countries), also contribute to this evolving landscape, each offering varying degrees of personalization and client engagement (McDowell, 2022).

Ferrari has crafted a unique digital experience through its app, focusing on curated ecommerce and exclusive experiences that cater to its discerning clientele and excited prospects. This platform is part of a centralized communication system that carefully balances content delivery with customer preferences. The Ferrari app represents a strategic advancement in engaging clients and prospects, offering a direct communication channel beyond the reach of independent dealers. The app allows clients to view their cars in a virtual garage, access a 3D configurator for personalization (which is then shared with the dealer for further refinement in the showroom) and receive notifications about warranty expirations. It also serves as a portal for direct communication, sharing videos, product launches, services and event information. Clients can explore content, make discoveries or book experiences like the 'Corso Piloti' driving course, enhancing their engagement and streamlining their experience with the brand.

The effectiveness of these digital tools is heightened when combined with the personal insights and nuanced understanding that client advisers have of their clients. The apps can distribute communications en masse, yet when used by a client adviser who understands the client's unique preferences, the technology becomes a powerful extension of personalized service.

Cartier's approach to maintaining and nurturing client relationships is embodied in their innovative use of the My Client app, a powerful tool connected to their CRM system. This app is an essential asset for client advisers, offering a range of customizable communication templates for targeted outreach. Whether it's for general updates or personalized messages, the app facilitates seamless communication with clients, enhancing the Cartier experience. It also plays a strategic role in activation strategies and meeting specific KPIs, such as expanding market share in watches. Advisers can access data to identify clients who purchase jewellery but not watches, engaging them with tailored communications and cross-selling initiatives. The app's capabilities extend to managing events and commemorating special occasions like birthdays or purchase anniversaries, adding a personal touch to client interactions.

Additionally, the app is used to encourage and track feedback through the 'Barometer', a system that rates client experiences and identifies areas for improvement. This feedback mechanism is critical in ensuring service excellence and client satisfaction. Cartier's meticulous approach to client management, blending personalized communication with strategic sales initiatives, demonstrates their commitment to a rich, engaging client experience on a day-to-day basis.

In this operational engagement layer, it's the nuanced, human touch of the client advisers, complemented by the smart use of technology, that truly embodies the essence of luxury clienteling. It's about creating a seamless and continuous relationship with clients, where every interaction is an opportunity to affirm the client's value to the brand and to reinforce their emotional connection to the Maison.

Prevention strategies to keep customers loyal

Modern CRM systems, powered by AI and machine learning, enable luxury brands like Valentino to transition from static client segmentation to dynamic engagement strategies. These systems can predict and prevent customer churn by analysing behaviour patterns and sociodemographic data, allowing for timely, tailored re-engagement actions.

In the context of CRM strategies, the focus is on prevention and managing the customer's lifetime engagement with the brand. The CRM tools are pivotal in identifying patterns, such as a recurring customer's absence for a year or two. This triggers the marketing team to re-engage with the customer through targeted strategies to encourage their return, thereby avoiding a sense of abandonment. If the customer returns, it's crucial to have preserved their complete purchase history to tailor the re-engagement efforts effectively and reinforce their connection with the brand.

So, when a pattern shifts – a high-frequency client suddenly pauses their visits or their spending wanes – the model raises an alert. The sales adviser, now informed, isn't just reacting; they're reaching out with a personalized touch, perhaps a special invite or a query about the client's needs, drawing them back into the fold.

The sensitivity and intuition of human interaction are pivotal here for collecting add-on information. In-store conversations allow for the gathering of nuanced data about clients' preferences and lifestyles. Sales associates can discern not only clients' brand affinities and spending habits, but also detect subtle shifts in their life that may affect their interest in luxury shopping. Being in touch with the client is helpful to gauge their interest levels in competing brands. Such interactions can reveal shifts in clients' affinities, potentially indicating a reallocation of their luxury spending towards other brands, which could signify changes in market trends or client needs.

This human element is crucial, as it guides the understanding of a client's evolving relationship with luxury brands and enables a more personalized and empathetic approach to client engagement. This information helps to tailor better brand's strategies and maintain client loyalty in a competitive landscape.

Potential VIPs are identified through a data mosaic, comparing new client traits with those of established VICs, focusing attention where the promise of loyalty glimmers.

Client advisers might identify high-potential clients by recognizing patterns common to valuable customers, facilitating targeted activation initiatives to nurture potential VICs. This proactive, predictive approach to clienteling represents a significant evolution from traditional, descriptive CRM methods.

This strategy isn't just about retention; it's about nurturing the potential, about crafting narratives that bind the clients more closely to the brand, through personalized gestures and content that resonate with each individual's unique story.

Looking ahead: Cutting-edge advancements in customer analysis and interaction

The key to enhancing the customer experience lies in the confluence of expert sales associate training and the strategic use of data. With the advent of AI, the future points to an ecosystem where sales associates, equipped with voice recognition technology, can access a customer's purchase history and preferences without the barrier of screens. Pronouncing a customer's name and surname initiates the retrieval process, while standardized queries allow for seamless interaction. This hands-free approach also applies to capturing client feedback or notes, where the associate can dictate details, freeing them from the screen and fostering a deeper, more personal customer engagement. This enables a more human connection, where eye contact and personal interaction are not sacrificed for data retrieval from a device.

In the meantime, appointments become a strategic touchpoint – structured and prepared, they allow for personalized engagement, whether in-store, at home or during exclusive events.

This blend of traditional clienteling and cutting-edge tech enriches customer relationships while optimizing the retail journey, aligning with the brand's vision of personalized, attentive service where every interaction is an opportunity to deepen the relationship and enhance the brand experience.

The future of luxury retail may involve advanced smart face recognition systems with sensors to analyse in-store dynamics like window traffic, customer conversion and shopper demographics. This data, when mapped and integrated with store performance metrics, can identify patterns such as a particular age group's purchasing behaviours. Emphasizing security and privacy, a 'zero trust' approach would ensure such systems operate on automation, processing aggregate statistics without compromising individual client details, thus aligning with privacy standards and enhancing store efficiency.

Takeaways

The 'back of house' – the operational systems like ERP – and the 'front of house' – client-facing activities – are being harmoniously synchronized. This marriage is underpinned by the quintessence of connection: creating seamless experiences for clients beyond the transactional. It's about fine-tuning operations, from inventory management to bespoke client interactions, while adapting to the post-pandemic market where local clientele gain prominence. Technology now enables the vision of 'one stock', where purchase possibilities are boundless, transcending the confines of a single store. Omnichannel prowess is not just about offering varied services, but embodying a brand ethos where client information flows ubiquitously, ensuring every touchpoint is informed and every client interaction is deeply personalized through well-orchestrated clienteling initiatives.

Data analysis for client segmentation should not only focus on annual metrics (the last 12 months) but to consider the entire lifetime value and engagement of a client. This longitudinal perspective allows for a deeper understanding of a client's behaviour, preferences and potential value over time, fostering more strategic and personalized clienteling efforts that resonate on a more individual level. It's about recognizing the full narrative of a client's journey with the brand, beyond the confines of a solar year.

Technology is a powerful enabler providing new ways of collecting and valorizing data to ideate effective strategies to nurture the relationship with clients. These strategies have tangibly improved key performance indicators like stock rebalancing, inventory levels, checkout times and the accuracy of client service. It would celebrate the sales associates, armed with data, who now have the power to elevate the customer experience through personalized recommendations and strategic cross-selling, thereby boosting the average transaction value and cementing the relationship between clients and brand.

References

Bain, M (2022) Luxury's customer experience is getting a tech upgrade, *Business of Fashion*, www.businessoffashion.com/articles/technology/state-of-fashion-technology-report-luxury-brands-customer-experience/ (archived at https://perma.cc/G5N4-7LET)

McDowell, M (2022) Inside the new look digital clienteling tool, *Vogue Business*, www.voguebusiness.com/technology/exclusive-inside-the-new-look-digital-clienteling-tool (archived at https://perma.cc/C6DL-G2YH)

Robinson, R (2022) Alpha's connected clienteling app is the latest tech tool aimed at improving retail experience, *Forbes*, www.forbes.com/sites/roxannerobinson/2022/02/07/alphas-connected-clienteling-app-is-the-latest-tech-tool-aimed-at-improving-retail-experience/ (archived at https://perma.cc/U6VQ-7ZDU)

8

Emerging trends in customer relationship management

GUIDO TIRONE

Customer relationship management (CRM) has evolved significantly over the years, becoming one of the pillars within the strategy book of a luxury company. This chapter analyses the evolution of CRM and emerging trends, from the collection of customer data and creation of customer profiles to leveraging data through analytics and artificial intelligence (AI) to create omnichannel engagement via customer-centric marketing, all while taking advantage of new cloud-based solutions.

Introduction to customer relationship management

CRM is a strategic approach that companies leverage to manage all their interactions with current and potential customers. The objective is to improve relationships with the customer by creating seamless interactions that will help satisfy hidden customer needs while also growing the business (Salesforce, 2023a). To know customers, companies must create, capture and deliberately mine the river of customer data.

The individualized person-to-person relationship that constitutes most luxury experiences today cannot scale, but a new model that leverages AI and algorithms, in combination with the human element, will deliver the connection and intimacy a customer craves to more people through a CRM system. It removes barriers between company and customer allowing a better under-standing of customer needs, and identifies the proper channels and timing for interactions. Additionally, it streamlines processes while improving profitability.

The significance of CRM in contemporary business

In today's highly competitive business landscape, CRM plays a crucial role in enhancing customer loyalty, improving customer retention and increasing sales and marketing efficiencies.

CRM allows companies to build stronger relationships with their customers. By understanding customer preferences and behaviours, companies can tailor their products, services and marketing efforts to meet individual needs, and ultimately increase customer loyalty (Anderson, Fornell and Mazvancheryl, 2004). CRM strategies are also used to reduce churn and improve customer lifetime value (CLV) by deploying personalized communications and targeted promotions (Reichheld, 1996). CRM systems can help sales and marketing teams work more efficiently. They can segment customers based on their behaviours and preferences, enabling highly targeted marketing campaigns. This leads to improved lead generation and conversion rates (Sheth and Parvatiyar, 1995).

The historical evolution of CRM

The historical evolution of CRM can be divided into four different phases, reflecting the growing importance of data-driven customer management, the expansion of CRM functions beyond sales use cases and the adaptation to technological advancements. As customer expectations continue to evolve, CRM is likely to undergo further transformations in the future.

PRE-COMPUTER ERA (BEFORE THE 1980s)

Before the advent of computers, companies handled customer relationships using manual methods. Pen and paper did the initial job of recording customer data, but as companies reached scale it became a task too challenging to handle. Then came the Rolodex, invented in 1956 to organize customer contact information such as name, address, phone number and other details. While better than manual recording, those rudimentary tools only allowed companies to focus on individual relationships and lacked the data-driven approach of modern CRM.

ORIGIN OF CRM (1980s–90s)

As technology advanced, the 1980s saw the development of the contact management system, which allowed customer information to be stored in a database, driving the emergence of database marketing. This was the first step towards more organized customer data management with companies starting to leverage early computer systems to store customer information, enabling more efficient direct marketing and customer segmentation.

In the 1990s, CRM began to evolve with the introduction of Sales Force Automation (SFA) software. SFA focused on automating daily, repetitive, sales-related tasks, such as lead tracking, contact and opportunity management. This new software improved sales efficiency and laid the foundation for CRM as we know it today. Towards the late 1990s, CRM evolved to include other areas such as sales, marketing and customer service, giving birth to the concept of operational CRM. Companies could now manage interactions and track customer history more effectively (Payne and Frow, 2005).

TRADITIONAL CRM SYSTEMS (2000s–2010s)

Traditional CRM emerged in the early 2000s as a system that enhanced customer data management, allowed for the automation of sales and marketing tasks and helped manage interactions across the customer lifecycle. The core of this CRM model is expressed in the standardized performance that uses input data as a basis. The main objective of traditional CRM is to improve customer relationships in order to retain customers and drive sales growth (Dearmer, 2023).

Traditional CRM is typically deployed on-premises, meaning they are installed and run on servers managed by IT teams within an organization. The systems focus primarily on collecting customer data from various channels (POS, the company's website, telephone, email, live chat, marketing materials, etc) so that it can be leveraged to improve the relationship of the company with their customer.

The benefits of traditional CRM are the ability to provide organized systems for storing and retrieving customer data and allowing the tracking of sales activities, while also providing detailed insights into customer behaviour, enabling companies to formulate effective marketing strategies. In addition, the on-premises nature of traditional CRM gives companies full control over their data, which can be critical for organizations with stringent data security requirements. Some of the biggest challenges of traditional CRM are a complex user interface that can be difficult to navigate, limited integration capabilities with other digital platforms and a significant upfront investment for software purchase and installation with ongoing costs for system maintenance and upgrades.

MODERN CRM SYSTEMS (POST-2010s)

Modern CRM is the most recent evolution in the field. The systems are also referred to as cloud-based CRM because they leverage the latest cloud, mobile, application programming interface (API) and database technologies to make themselves available from anywhere and at any time. While they share traditional CRM's objective of streamlining customer interactions and data management, modern CRM systems are able to meet the specific needs of each unique company at a predictable and fair cost. Modern CRM systems are also able to prioritize user experience by featuring an intuitive design that facilitates ease of use, reducing the learning curve for team members.

Modern CRM systems are built to integrate seamlessly with other digital platforms, including social media and other third-party applications, broadening the scope of data collection and customer engagement. Modern CRM systems provide an expanded set of tools such as AI capabilities, advanced analytical tools and marketing automation.

The core principles of CRM

The core principles of CRM (understanding the customer, integration and analytics) are the cornerstone concepts that each company needs to successfully implement and maintain a CRM system aimed at creating lasting customer relationships while also achieving a company's business objectives. Despite the evolution in technologies and ever-changing business dynamics (from the Covid-19 pandemic to de-globalization), these cornerstones have remained consistent over time.

Understanding the customer

To achieve the objective of improving customer relationships, CRM systems need to first understand the customer's need. This means CRM systems must be centred around the customer, starting with the creation of a 360-degree view of each customer. Companies are using advanced data collection and processing methodologies that leverage AI and machine learning (ML) to collect data about each customer interaction with the company (purchase history, online/offline interactions, call centre calls, etc) and create a single customer profile. While this was almost impossible to achieve at the beginning of the 2010s, advances in computer processing and identity mapping have allowed the consolidation of customer interactions despite their origins from different data sources.

Once a comprehensive customer profile is created, companies can acquire a better understanding of the customer needs which in turn they can leverage to tailor the products and services offering to those needs, and thus increase customer lifetime value. To achieve its full potential, however, it is important that a company continuously work on increasing the breadth of the customer profile, as new touchpoints are introduced and customer behaviours evolve. Companies at the forefront of customer-centricity actively seek input from customers and welcome feedback to improve their understanding of their customer's needs.

Integration

For CRM systems to achieve their full potential, the breaking down of silos and integration across departments is required. One of the biggest challenges for companies to solve is how to engage with the customer in a consistent way independent of medium or channel. With the increasing number of touchpoints available, and responsibilities for those touchpoints spread across different teams within an organization, the only way for a CRM system to ensure consistent messaging and a unified approach to customer interactions is by integrating all customer-related activities independent of their origins.

This requires different departments such as marketing, sales, customer service and the supply chain to cooperate in the implementation and maintenance of CRM systems. Once those barriers are removed, teams will reap the benefits of automating repetitive tasks and streamlining processes, freeing up time for more valuable and rewarding tasks.

Analytics

Equally as important in achieving CRM systems' full potential is the use of advances in analytics and artificial intelligence (AI) to augment the decision-making process. For decades, companies have tried to leverage customer data to understand customer behaviours, and to identify trends and pain points in the customer journey to generate incremental value with improvements. While this process relied on rudimentary analytics and instincts for a long time, advances in analytics and AI have allowed data-driven insights to guide the decision-making process. This has resulted in the creation of more effective marketing strategies and improved customer experiences that reflect a better understanding of customer needs at scale.

Companies that excel in this area deploy a continuous feedback loop strategy that consists of:

- collecting customer data throughout the journey
- leveraging advanced analytics and AI to analyse performance and find areas of opportunity
- deploying A/B or multi-variate testing to identify the right customer experience
- enhancing the customer experience

One important element in the process is the use of personalization at scale, which offers tailored customer experiences (one to one) in the form of personalized marketing communications, product offerings or service interactions.

The importance of data and technology in CRM

Data and technology have been central to the success of modern CRM, by playing a vital role in gathering, managing, analysing and utilizing customer information to improve customer relationships and drive business growth.

At the heart of a CRM system is data collection, processing and storage. Obtaining data about each customer interaction throughout the journey is a necessary step to fully understand customer behaviours and needs. Advances in technology, digitalization and the Internet of Things (IOT) have facilitated the collection of customer data through a proliferation of data sources, resulting in the creation of a torrent of information.

There are four types of data that companies are interested in obtaining: identity, quantitative, qualitative and descriptive. **Identity data** is any information that enables an individual to be uniquely identified, usually collected via POS systems, online transaction databases, clienteling or social media profiles. **Quantitative data** is measurable operational data of customer interactions with a company, usually collected via online and offline tracking or third-party pixels. **Qualitative data** is attitudinal, motivational or opinion data, usually collected through a questionnaire. Finally, **descriptive data** is additional profile information covering family and lifestyle details, usually obtained with partnership through external companies.

All customer data is stored and consolidated in the CRM database with the use of advanced analytics and identity mapping, allowing the creation of a single customer profile. This 360-degree view of the customer allows companies to understand each customer's history and needs comprehensively, resulting in the tailoring of marketing messages, product recommendations and customer service interactions to the individual preferences of each customer.

Technology also played a crucial role in the advances of modern CRM. First, it allowed the automation of daily repetitive tasks across multiple departments, from data entry to lead tracking and scheduling. This automation streamlines operations, reduces errors and frees up time for employees to focus on more value-added tasks. CRM technology also enhances the quality of customer support by providing agents with easy access to relevant information and allowing companies to engage with customers across multiple communication channels, such as email, social media, live chat and mobile apps.

Second, advanced analytics tools enabled companies to fully take advantage of the customer data they were collecting by better identifying trends, patterns and correlations. Data-driven insights help guide the decision-making process, improve the customer experience and create targeted marketing efforts. The deployment of predictive analytics has allowed companies to forecast customer behaviour, such as predicting which customers are likely to make a purchase or churn, which in turn allows companies to be proactive in their customer engagement tactics.

In addition, advanced analytics tools have allowed companies to leverage cluster analysis for customer segmentation. Cluster analysis is a data analysis technique that identifies meaningful, naturally occurring groups within a dataset and distinguishes them as clusters. These clusters are used to discover hidden relationships in data based on specific characteristics. This approach to segmentation has helped further tailor marketing strategies to different customer groups, improving the relevance of marketing efforts (SurveyMonkey, 2023).

Challenges faced in implementing a CRM system

CRM systems promise significant benefits to companies wanting to implement them, from a better understanding of the customers to tailored interaction and maximization of CLV. There are, however, several challenges that companies need to overcome in order to successfully build and maintain a CRM system and obtain the expected return on the investment. The easiest way to overcome those challenges is to acknowledge and address them before and during the implementation process.

While we have already discussed the importance of data for CRM, ensuring data quality and accuracy is a fundamental challenge in the successful implementation of a CRM system. Given the increasing use of data-driven insights to guide the decision-making process, it is imperative that the data leveraged to generate those insights is accurate and truly representative of the customer population. Inaccurate, partial or outdated data can undermine the effectiveness of the CRM system by creating a partial or inaccurate customer profile and ultimately result in non-relevant recommendations.

In addition to data quality and accuracy, data integration is another obstacle to overcome. With the proliferation of data sources, companies now have access to vast amounts of customer data. For value to be extracted, it is crucial that customer data is integrated under a single customer profile. Advanced analytics tools, identity resolution techniques and careful planning can be used to generate a unified customer view and break silos.

The next challenge considers the human aspect of CRM. To fully extract its potential, employees within an organization need to embrace the new system. Without proper documentation and change management, users can be reluctant to embrace new CRM tools or processes, which can lead to underutilization or even failure of the CRM system. Change management strategies are the best tool to overcome this obstacle, starting with effective communication of the benefits of CRM highlighting the automation of repetitive tasks and the increase in time available for value-add tasks. Comprehensive training and support for employees is vital to ensure they adapt to new processes and tools.

CRM implementation can be costly. A disorganized and inexperienced implementation can overrun a budget and strain resources. The first step to avoid this is to clearly define the CRM strategy, starting with an alignment of goals and objectives for the project, as well as how the benefits are going to be measured to evaluate their contribution to overall business goals. To avoid unanticipated expenses and lack of cost control, a budget needs to be established with processes to regularly monitor expenditures.

Finally, a clear customization strategy needs to be developed. Modern CRM systems can be highly customizable; however, companies occasionally fall into the trap of over-customization to meet specific business needs that then result in limited use cases. Over-customization can lead to complications, increased maintenance costs and a more challenging implementation process. A clear customization strategy that prioritizes modifications based on business value is the best approach to overcome this obstacle.

Emerging trends in CRM

Customer data analytics

Customer data analytics play a crucial role in understanding, managing and improving customer relationships by allowing companies to identify patterns and trends across customer profiles. This results in data-driven insights that inform the decision-making process and tailor effective interactions with the customers.

Customer data analytics starts with the generation, collection and storage of customer data across each touchpoint in the customer journey, with an emphasis on volume and diversity. More comprehensive and diverse customer profiles provide better training for AI models. Data is then aggregated and curated to create a 360-degree view of the customer.

Advances in data collection and storage have allowed CRM to reach its fullest potential. The introduction of data lakes in the early 2010s provided a more flexible and scalable way to manage and analyse data right when companies were facing an explosion of data from various sources. A data lake is a centralized and scalable repository that allows organizations to store vast amounts of raw and unstructured data in its native format. Unlike traditional relational databases, they are designed to accommodate a wide variety of data types, including structured data (tables and databases) and unstructured data (text documents, images, videos and logs). The data in a data lake is often stored in a flat architecture without a rigid structure, making it highly flexible and capable of handling vast volumes of diverse and unstructured customer data.

By centralizing data from various sources, including social media, customer interactions and transaction histories, data lakes enable companies to gain a holistic view of their customers which allows for more personalized marketing, improved customer service and data-driven decision-making.

Once the data is collected, stored and aggregated, predictive analytics allow companies to extract value from the data. Statistical algorithms and ML techniques are leveraged to predict future customer behaviours and preferences based on historical data on customer interactions. While the number of applications for predictive analytics is elevated, they usually tend to fall into one of three buckets: customer acquisition, customer retention and maximization of customer lifetime value:

- **Customer acquisition**: Predictive analytics can be used to enhance customer acquisition efforts by enabling companies to identify and target potential customers more effectively. One of the common strategies under this umbrella is lead scoring, which consists of ranking potential leads based on their likelihood to convert into customers. Predictive analytics assesses lead characteristics based on the customer profile and lookalike modelling to assign a score to represent the probability of converting a customer, while also suggesting the most relevant strategy to convert that customer. This allows sales teams to prioritize their efforts on high-potential leads with a more customized and effective interaction.

- **Customer retention**: Customer churn prediction is one of the highest-yielding values related to customer retention. The strategy consists of leveraging predictive analytics to analyse historical data on customer behaviours to predict the probability of each customer churning. Once a customer is flagged as having a high risk of churning, next-best-action modelling can be used to implement targeted interactions and communications aimed at re-engaging the customer and avoiding the churn.

- **Maximization of customer lifestyle value**: Both customer acquisition and customer retention strategies are dependent on an accurate prediction of CLV in order to identify which tactic is more relevant for a given customer. Leveraging historical data on customer behaviour and various models, such as regression, machine learning (ML) and time-series analysis, predictive analytics allows companies to make predictions about a customer's future behaviour and purchasing patterns calculating CLV for each customer, independently of the stage in the customer lifecycle. Expected CLV can be used to optimize acquisition campaigns, by comparing the cost to acquire a customer with the expected value to identify how the marketing budget is best spent. Expected CLV can also be used for retention and cross-selling strategies, by identifying customers that have a higher likelihood to purchase and deviation from the expected CLV.

As companies increasingly rely on vast datasets to better understand and engage with their customers, data privacy and ethics have become a key element in CRM strategies. It is each company's responsibility to uphold the privacy of individuals' data and adhere to ethical standards in data collection, analysis and usage. This has led to the creation of CRM ethics, which refers to the principles and guidelines that govern the responsible and ethical use of customer data and interactions within CRM practices.

Customer privacy is one of the central elements of CRM ethics: companies must be diligent in securing customer data and ensure that sensitive information remains confidential. Compliance with data protection laws across the world is essential, with the most prominent laws being the General Data Protection Regulation (GDPR) and the California Consumer Privacy Act (CCPA). Ethical CRM practices include obtaining informed consent from customers for data collection and usage, the need for transparency in data handling and the option for customers to opt in or opt out of data collection.

In addition, security measures must be in place to protect customer data from breaches and unauthorized access. Encryption, access controls and regular security audits are crucial for maintaining data privacy. Upholding data privacy and ethical standards in CRM is not only a legal requirement, but also contributes to safeguarding an organization's reputation and fostering customer loyalty. Organizations that prioritize data privacy and ethical CRM practices are better positioned to create long-lasting, mutually beneficial relationships with their customers.

Artificial intelligence and machine learning

CRM has evolved from a static data repository into a dynamic, customer-centric system that relies on personalization, automation and data-driven decision-making. This evolution couldn't have materialized without the advent of AI and ML, which played a pivotal role in the transition from traditional to modern CRM, becoming a cornerstone of the latter.

AI is what allows companies to mine through their vast customer database to identify and predict customer purchasing patterns and preferences. Those insights can be leveraged to inform the decision-making process or train ML algorithms to create highly personalized experiences for each customer. Personalization can involve the tailoring of product recommendations or the customization of marketing messages via content or collaborative filtering. Both use cases are rooted in ML algorithms that continuously refine their suggestions based on a customer's evolving preferences and the real-time data they generate.

This level of personalization not only improves customer satisfaction, but also leads to higher conversion rates and increased revenue, as customers feel more valued and understood by the companies they interact with. This level of personalization is not only revolutionizing how companies engage with their customers, but also elevating the effectiveness and customer-centricity of CRM systems.

AI and ML also allowed the creation of automated customer service via chatbots and virtual assistants, aimed at enhancing customer interactions, streamlining processes and delivering personalized 24/7 customer support. This has transformed the status quo for customer service and relationship management. Leveraging AI and natural language processing, chatbots are now able to engage with customers in real-time, properly handling customer inquiries and assist in issue resolution. This around-the-clock customer support eliminates the need for customers to wait for business hours for conflict resolution and in turn increases customer satisfaction.

In addition, by automating routine and mundane customer service tasks, chatbots and virtual assistants are freeing up human agents to focus on more complex and higher value-added tasks. Chatbots are highly scalable and can initiate follow-up actions, such as scheduling appointments or processing orders, resulting in significant cost savings and higher employee satisfaction.

Another crucial characteristic of chatbots and virtual assistants is that they can be seamlessly integrated with CRM systems, ensuring that the data collected and customer interactions are recorded and accessible for future reference and analysis. While chatbots and virtual assistants have been central to the advancements in modern CRM, it is fundamental to strike a balance between automation and human interaction, ensuing that customers have access to human agents when necessary, especially for complex inquiries and issues.

Another critical use case of AI and ML in CRM is sentiment analysis, also known as opinion mining. This analysis is a process that involves the automated assessment of customer feedback, social media interactions and other unstructured data to gauge customer sentiment and derive actionable insights that can be used to improve CLV. Sentiment analysis leverages natural language processing (NPL) and ML algorithms to identify and analyse sentiment expressed in customer communications and categorize it into different buckets (positive, negative, neutral) allowing a company to gain valuable insights into how customers feel about their products, services or brand.

Companies leverage sentiment analysis tools to continuously monitor social media platforms for mentions, comments and conversations related to a brand or product. By analysing the sentiment behind these mentions, companies can gauge public perception and respond promptly to both positive and negative feedback. AI and ML techniques are also employed to analyse customer comments, reviews and survey responses to identify trends and patterns in customer sentiment. Those insights are then leveraged to inform strategic decision-making and help companies align their offerings with customer expectations. By understanding customer sentiment, companies can tailor their interactions and marketing efforts to resonate with their audience, leading to increased engagement and loyalty.

One of the strengths of sentiment analysis is the capacity to detect potential problems and negative sentiment early, enabling a company to take proactive measures to address customer concerns before they escalate. Companies that harness AI and ML for sentiment analysis gain a competitive edge by responding effectively to customer sentiment, leading to higher customer satisfaction and retention.

Omnichannel engagement

An omnichannel strategy offers a seamless customer experience across the entire customer journey, which is obtained by integrating each offline (physical store, radio, print, etc) and online (website, app, social media, email, etc) touchpoint into a single system. This strategy provides a comprehensive view of the customer while also engaging with the customer in a way that reflects how customers want to engage with the company, and not company organizational charts.

Customer behaviour has evolved with the advent of the digital age. According to Google research, 90 per cent of multiple device owners switch devices daily, utilizing three devices on average to finish a task (Gevelber, 2013). It is no surprise that a customer journey could start on a desktop computer, continue on a mobile device and be completed in person at a physical store. Increased adoption of IoT will only increase the complexity of such journeys. Companies need to adapt to this and define new strategies that take into consideration the fragmentation of the customer journey, which can be achieved through a unified and comprehensive omnichannel experience where all channels and platforms work together (Mohan, 2022).

Customers expect a consistent, personalized and convenient experience across the purchasing journey, independent of the channel they engage with.

Whether they talk with a call centre agent, visit the website or follow on social media, they want a consistent and personalized experience. This presents a big challenge for companies that requires the breaking down of barriers across departments and the integration of systems. The role of CRM is to create a unified view of the customer to infuse customer interactions with personality and empathy, which are crucial differentiators for the modern customer who has already come to expect convenience, speed and consistency.

CRM allows companies to collect and analyse customer data from various sources and create customer profiles and personas that reflect their needs and goals. Once a clear picture of customer segments is drawn, the next step is to define the customer journey across all touchpoints. CRM systems are then used to track and measure customer journey performance and to identify gaps, opportunities and challenges that affect satisfaction and retention.

An important step in the definition of the journeys is the optimization of channel strategy to deliver a seamless customer experience. This means for each segment and stage of the journey identify the right timing and channel that is relevant to the customers and ensures consistency and continuity. Channel strategy needs also to be aligned to the different customers segments by tailoring content, offers and messages.

Social CRM is the integration of social media channels into CRM systems. Starting in the late 2010s, CRM systems have been able to support social media alongside traditional channels so customers can interact with companies via their preferred channels. This ultimately resulted in better customer service and greater marketing insight gathered from customer social media data. Social CRM makes it possible for a business to communicate with customers using the channel of their choice, whether by phone, text, chat, email or social media. Leveraging those interactions, a social CRM system helps companies gather richer, actionable insights about customer sentiment on their company, their brand and specific products or services.

The insights gathered can be used by companies to optimize service levels and the multi-channel customer experience. Companies can act more quickly, respond more effectively and even anticipate customers' upcoming needs. By enabling companies to track social interactions with customers using the same sophisticated tools as they use for other touchpoints, companies can deliver faster, more complete resolutions to customer service cases across the whole business, resulting in happier customers (Salesforce, 2023b).

The role of mobile application CRM systems has also grown since the late 2010s. Mobile CRM delivers a full CRM experience on smartphones, tablets and other internet-enabled devices. It enables sales, marketing and customer service teams to access and manage key information in real time, wherever they are. The mass migration of internet users from desktop to mobile devices means people now expect real-time information to be available from anywhere, the same applies to CRM systems. Post-pandemic office dynamics and the increase in hybrid and remote work means employees are no longer 'tied' to their desks; they're working on the go. Sales team members travel between offices and locations to meet with prospects. Field agents need access to schedules and work orders even when they're not in the office.

Beyond the obvious benefits of allowing employees more flexibility in their work environment, customers also benefit from having mobile CRM availability for your organization. A mobile CRM app can help ensure that your customers are always getting the best service available. Employees have access to real-time updates and vital information, meaning they are fully equipped to provide clients with the reliable information they need, at speed. With mobile CRM software, mobile devices such as tablets and smartphones can deliver all the classic functionality of a system hosted on a laptop or desktop computer, but with the added benefits of on-the-go access via cloud computing. In effect, users should be able to run their business from their phone (Salesforce, 2023c).

Customer-centric marketing

Customer-centric marketing consists of shifting the focus away from pushing products or services to delivering value and exceptional experiences by understanding and meeting the customer's needs. Central to the marketing strategy is not the maximization of sales at all costs, but the ability to be the best at knowing, anticipating, tailoring and delighting the customer in their needs. This strategy emphasizes the importance of centralizing growth around the customer needs by building trust and fostering loyalty, knowing that it will ultimately fuel success in the long run (Gupta, 2023).

Storytelling is a powerful tool to engage customers, convey the brand message and inspire action; however, it also comes with challenges. The first challenge for effective storytelling is the need to understand the customer, the target market, hidden needs, friction points and goals. CRM can help companies overcome this challenge by leveraging customer profiles to create stories that are tailored to the different segments. The second challenge is to craft a clear and compelling message that aligns with a company's identity and brand. CRM will help deliver this message in a consistent and relevant way across all touchpoints. CRM and AI are the only avenues for companies to engage in storytelling at scale (Linkedin, 2023a).

Customer centricity cannot be achieved without loyalty, especially in a competitive and saturated market. Loyalty programmes are the strategies used by companies to reward their loyal customers, keep them engaged and increase their loyalty over time. For a loyalty programme to be successful it is important for companies to understand who the most loyal and profitable customers are, and what are the drivers behind it. CRM systems allow companies to leverage the torrent of data on customers to create and deliver the perfect loyalty programme.

The first step in the creation of loyalty programmes is the definition of loyalty tiers, which reflect the different layers in the loyalty pyramid and the value of each. AI and ML have improved the scoring of customers by identifying the drivers of loyalty at different levels and for different segments. The next step is to create loyalty campaigns aimed at engaging customers with the programme. CRM systems allow the automation of loyalty campaigns, by setting up triggers and workflows that send targeted and relevant communications and offers at the right time and through the right channel.

CRM can also be used to integrate a loyalty programme with other systems and platforms, such as third-party apps, social media platforms, payment and reward providers. This will enable a company to have a holistic and consistent view of their customer data and deliver a seamless and omnichannel loyalty experience (LinkedIn, 2023b).

CRM in the cloud

The advent of cloud computing allowed CRM systems to reach their fullest potential in the late 2010s. Cloud-based CRM systems leverage the latest cloud, mobile, API and database technologies to make themselves available from anywhere and at any time through the internet. For a traditional CRM system, companies will host and operate the servers and network that house the customer database, paying and managing all resources needed to run the system in addition to the upfront implementation costs. By contrast, in a cloud-based CRM system, the cloud provider manages all the infrastructure to host and run the system, allowing companies to avoid the upfront and maintenance costs associated with the infrastructure. The company will access the CRM system through a web-based application or dashboard through an internet connection.

This type of cloud-based infrastructure has many advantages, one of the most important being scalability and flexibility. Scalability in cloud computing refers to the ability to increase or decrease resources as needed to meet changing demand. Data storage capacity, processing power and networking can all be scaled using existing cloud computing infrastructure. The increase in resources can be achieved rapidly and easily with almost no downtime, since the cloud providers already have the infrastructure in place. With traditional CRM, this process would have taken weeks or months of work and incurred tremendous expense (VMware, 2023).

Cloud-based CRM systems are also cost-effective. Traditional, on-premises CRM systems demand substantial initial investments in hardware, software licenses and IT infrastructure. They also require ongoing maintenance and upgrades, which can be both time-consuming and expensive. Cloud-based CRM solutions, on the other hand, reduce these financial burdens. With cloud CRM, there are no hefty upfront costs for hardware or software licenses. Instead, companies pay a subscription fee, which typically includes maintenance and updates.

This subscription-based model allows organizations to budget more effectively and allocate their resources to other critical areas of their operations. Moreover, the elimination of on-premises hardware and software maintenance significantly reduces the total cost of ownership, making cloud-based CRM a more cost-effective solution over time.

Cloud-based CRM solutions prioritize data security, which is crucial in today's world of increasing cyber threats and stringent data protection regulations. These systems are designed with robust security measures to safeguard customer information and sensitive business data. Features like data encryption, regular security audits and multi-factor authentication help protect against data breaches and unauthorized access. Furthermore, cloud CRM providers invest heavily in compliance with data protection regulations, such as GDPR in Europe or the Health Insurance Portability and Accountability Act (HIPAA) in the US healthcare industry. By adhering to these standards, companies can mitigate the risk of costly fines and damage to their reputation.

In addition to data security and compliance, cloud-based CRM systems offer advanced backup and disaster recovery solutions. In the event of a data loss or system failure, organizations can be rest assured that their data is safely stored and can be quickly restored, minimizing downtime and potential business disruption.

Takeaways

This chapter has explained how CRM systems have evolved over time and why they have become central in a company's strategy playbook. The ability of CRM to create a 360-degree view of the customer that encompasses all interactions between a customer and a company (offline and online), and to leverage this data to inform and manage customer relationships, has allowed companies to improve relationships with the customer by creating seamless interactions that will help satisfy hidden customer needs while also growing the business.

The chapter also analysed the emerging trends in CRM, starting from the collection of customer data and creation of customer profiles, to leveraging data through AI and ML to create omnichannel engagement via customer-centric marketing, all while taking advantage of new cloud-based solutions.

However, it is important to recognize that trends are constantly evolving. The CRM landscape is constantly changing and new trends and technologies are on the brink of emergence. To maintain a competitive advantage, it is fundamental for companies to continue experimenting and find new ways to improve customer relationships.

References

Anderson, E W, Fornell, C and Mazvancheryl, S K (2004) Customer satisfaction and shareholder value, *Journal of Marketing*, 68 (4), pp. 172–85

Dearmer, A (2023) Traditional CRM vs. new CRM: Uncovering the best fit for your business, *Teamgate*, www.teamgate.com/blog/old-vs-new-crm/ (archived at https://perma.cc/Y4EU-Q26X)

Gevelber, L (2013) The shift to constant connectivity, www.thinkwithgoogle.com/marketing-strategies/search/shift-to-constant-connectivity/ (archived at https://perma.cc/7M5Z-KNBV)

Gupta, S (2023) 3 practical steps to execute a customer-centric marketing strategy, *Gartner*, www.gartner.com/en/digital-markets/insights/customer-centric-marketing (archived at https://perma.cc/9JJ7-UGYD)

LinkedIn (2023a) What are the challenges of using storytelling in Content Marketing? www.linkedin.com/advice/0/what-challenges-using-storytelling-content-marketing (archived at https://perma.cc/UG8Q-SZLL)

LinkedIn (2023b) How do you use CRM to identify and reward your most loyal and profitable customers? www.linkedin.com/advice/0/how-do-you-use-crm-identify-reward-your-most-loyal (archived at https://perma.cc/9KJ6-5H6E)

Mohan, S (2022) The role of CRM in an omni-channel strategy, *Kapture CRM*, www.kapturecrm.com/blog/role-of-crm-in-an-omnichannel-strategy/#2_Integrate_and_Collaborate_with_Modern_Tools (archived at https://perma.cc/9T45-B8HS)

Payne, A and Frow, P (2005) A strategic framework for customer relationship management, *Journal of Marketing*, **69** (4), pp. 167–76

Reichheld, F F (1996) *The Loyalty Effect: The hidden force behind growth, profits, and lasting value*, Harvard Business Review Press

Salesforce (2023a) CRM 101: What is CRM? www.salesforce.com/crm/what-is-crm/ (archived at https://perma.cc/5QES-GL7V)

Salesforce (2023b) What is social CRM? www.salesforce.com/eu/learning-centre/crm/social-crm/ (archived at https://perma.cc/3MWM-M54T)

Salesforce (2023c) What is mobile CRM? www.salesforce.com/eu/learning-centre/crm/mobile-crm/ (archived at https://perma.cc/MQU5-MVXM)

Sheth, J N and Parvatiyar, A (1995) Relationship marketing in consumer markets: Antecedents and consequence, *Journal of the Academy of Marketing Science*, **23** (4), pp. 255–71

SurveyMonkey (2023) How cluster analysis identifies market and customer segments, www.surveymonkey.com/market-research/resources/how-cluster-analysis-identifies-market-and-customer-segments/ (archived at https://perma.cc/R53L-N9PV)

VMware (2023) What is Cloud Scalability? www.vmware.com/in/topics/glossary/content/cloud-scalability.html?resource=cat-34491101#cat-34491101 (archived at https://perma.cc/H7VA-27SH)

9

How to optimize spend and evaluate success

GUIDO TIRONE

Optimization plays a crucial role in the luxury industry, contributing to various aspects of business operations and customer experiences. This chapter analyses the significance of optimization in the luxury industry, from understanding the luxury customer to allocating budget across different channels, to the definition of key performance indicators and leveraging analytics and machine learning for evaluating success and implementing real-time adjustments.

The significance of optimization in the luxury industry

Optimization in the luxury industry is a multipronged strategy that goes beyond operational efficiency, ranging from maintaining brand reputation to ensuring operational efficiency, all while delighting the customer. The strategy encompasses preserving the essence of luxury and adapting to changing market dynamics while ensuring that the brand remains synonymous with exclusivity and exceptional quality. Achieving this balance contributes to long-term brand loyalty and sustained success in a highly competitive market.

The significance of optimization in the luxury industry is profound, touching on various aspects critical to its success. Efficient supply chain management, streamlined production processes and precise inventory control are imperative to maintaining the unparalleled quality and craftsmanship synonymous with luxury brands. In the digital age, optimizing online platforms ensures a seamless and secure customer experience, fostering a sense of exclusivity in ecommerce transactions. Marketing optimization, driven by data analytics, enables targeted campaigns that resonate with the discerning tastes of luxury consumers, contributing to brand loyalty.

Furthermore, optimization extends to international logistics, sustainable practices and data security, safeguarding the brand's reputation and customer trust. In essence, optimization is the foundation that sustains the delicate balance between tradition and innovation, ensuring that luxury brands continue to thrive in a dynamic and competitive market.

Market trends and challenges

Optimization trends and challenges in the luxury industry are continuously evolving to address the changing landscape of consumer preferences, technological advancements and global market dynamics. The luxury industry is navigating a complex landscape where optimization trends are intertwined with challenges. Adapting to technological advancements, addressing consumer concerns and maintaining the essence of luxury are key considerations for brands in this space. However, despite the changing landscape some trends have remained at the centre of optimization, and are forecast to continue to play a crucial role for years to come:

- **Digital transformation and ecommerce optimization**: The luxury industry has increasingly embraced digital platforms. Ecommerce optimization, including user-friendly interfaces, personalized experiences and secure transactions, has become a crucial trend. Optimizing online channels enables luxury brands to reach a global audience, providing a seamless and exclusive digital experience (RTB House, 2022).

- **Data-driven personalization**: Data analytics and AI-driven technologies are being leveraged to personalize customer experiences. This includes personalized recommendations, targeted marketing campaigns and customized services. Personalization enhances customer engagement, fosters brand loyalty and aligns offerings with individual preferences (Adaptive Creative, 2023).

- **Supply chain optimization**: Luxury brands are optimizing their supply chains for efficiency and flexibility. This includes real-time tracking, demand forecasting and strategic partnerships. Streamlined supply chains reduce costs, improve product availability and ensure the timely delivery of luxury goods.

- **Technology integration for customer engagement:** Luxury brands are increasingly integrating technology such as augmented reality (AR) and virtual reality (VR) for immersive and interactive customer experiences. Tech integration enhances engagement, particularly in online and offline retail spaces, providing a unique and memorable brand interaction (Cappasity, 2023).

To be successful with their optimization strategies and to take advantage of the above trends, companies will need to address some challenges. The first challenge luxury brands face is the ongoing dilemma of balancing tradition and heritage with the need for innovation to stay relevant in a rapidly changing market. Striking the right balance is critical to maintaining the timeless appeal of luxury products while adapting to contemporary consumer expectations.

Data security and privacy concerns also play an important role. With their increasing reliance on customer data for personalization, luxury brands must address concerns related to data security and privacy. Ensuring robust data security measures is crucial for maintaining customer trust and compliance with regulations. Lastly, adapting to shifting consumer values will be a main driver of success. Shifting consumer values, including a greater emphasis on sustainability and ethical practices, pose a challenge for luxury brands. Brands need to adapt and communicate their commitment to these values to remain appealing to a changing consumer base.

Understanding the luxury customer

Understanding the luxury customer is a complex endeavour that involves delving into various facets of their demographics, psychographics, behaviours and preferences. The process to achieve this involves a combination of market research, data analysis and a deep appreciation for the unique characteristics and preferences of this customer base.

The first step in the process is conducting market research aimed at understanding the key demographic characteristics of the customer, including income levels, age groups, geographic locations and cultural nuances. Psychographic variables are also considered by delving into the customer lifestyles, values and aspirations to better understand their motivations for purchasing luxury items, and how the customer base defines luxury.

Once demographic and psychographic data is collected, the next step is the creation of detailed customer personas, resulting in archetypal luxury customers that properly reflect their preferences, behaviours and challenges.

The last step is the use of analytics and machine learning to analyse consumer behaviour, from purchase patterns to preferred channels of engagement, and responses to marketing initiatives. Social listening is another fundamental approach to better understand the customer, monitoring social media platforms and online forums to understand conversations and sentiments surrounding luxury brands. Social listening provides insights into customer opinions, trends and influencers. Similarly, actively seeking and analysing customer feedback is key to success. It is critical to pay attention to reviews, comments and testimonials to understand customer satisfaction, preferences and areas for improvement.

Understanding the luxury customer is a competitive advantage, allowing companies to anticipate the customer's needs with impeccable customer services. By understanding the customer's expectations, companies can anticipate needs, provide seamless service and resolve issues with a high level of sophistication.

In conclusion, understanding the luxury customer is not merely a strategy but a prerequisite for success in the high-end market. By delving into the intricacies of their preferences, values and aspirations, luxury brands can create a nuanced and compelling brand identity that resonates with their target audience. This deep understanding forms the foundation for building trust, fostering loyalty and delivering the exceptional experiences that define the world of luxury.

Market segmentation and targeting

In the complex marketing landscape, the principles of market segmentation and targeting emerge as indispensable strategies for success. These twin pillars empower companies to navigate the diverse needs of their customer base, enabling relevant communication and efficient resource allocation. The luxury industry, characterized by exclusivity, craftsmanship and aspirational allure, demands a nuanced approach to marketing. Market segmentation and targeting are pivotal strategies that luxury brands employ to resonate with their customer base and expand their reach while maintaining an aura of exclusivity.

Luxury customers are not a homogenous group, but represent diverse lifestyles, values and aspirations. For this reason, when defining market segmentation, it is important to use methodologies that recognize the diversity of the customer base as well as the different use cases that they are going to be deployed for. One approach leveraged by companies to achieve this balance is the combination of multiple methodologies when defining market segments:

- **Demographic segmentation** examines age, income, occupation and other key demographic factors, and can be leveraged to cater to different age groups with tailored messaging and product offerings, to align pricing and promotional strategies with varying income brackets and to recognize the distinct needs of professionals, entrepreneurs and other occupational groups.

- **Psychographic segmentation** analyses consumers based on lifestyle, values and aspirations and can be leveraged to group customers based on shared attitudes and interests, to craft campaigns that resonate with specific personality types and to understand and appeal to customers' aspirations and long-term goals.

- **Geographic segmentation** examines geographical factors such as longitude, latitude, weather, etc, and can be leveraged to tailor marketing efforts to the unique characteristics and preferences of different regions, to recognize the impact of weather on consumer needs and preferences, and also to adapt messaging to align with local cultures and traditions.

- **Behavioural segmentation** analyses quantitative data from transactions, digital platforms and other touchpoints and can be leveraged to separate the customer base into different cohorts, based on engagement, with the aim of customizing marketing approaches, crafting strategies for brand loyalists versus those open to trying new products, and adapting promotions for different occasions and events.

Personalization and customization have become key trends in luxury marketing. Consumers, accustomed to tailored experiences, seek products and services that reflect their individual preferences. Sustainable practices have also emerged as a significant segmentation factor. Eco-conscious consumers now form a distinct segment, influencing purchasing decisions based on a brand's commitment to sustainability.

The importance of targeted marketing in the luxury industry

In the luxury industry, where exclusivity, sophistication and a deep understanding of the customer are fundamental, targeted marketing emerges as a strategic pillar for achieving success. The importance of precision in reaching and engaging with the right audience is even more important in the luxury industry where discerning tastes and a desire for personalization reign supreme.

Targeted marketing is not just a strategy for luxury brands; it's a fundamental approach that shapes the very essence of the luxury experience. By understanding the unique characteristics of their customer base, luxury brands can navigate the delicate balance between exclusivity and accessibility, create personalized connections and position themselves as purveyors of not just products, but exceptional experiences. In a landscape where precision is synonymous with luxury, targeted marketing emerges as the cornerstone for sustained success and unparalleled brand resonance.

Luxury is synonymous with exclusivity. Targeted marketing allows luxury brands to maintain an aura of exclusiveness by specifically catering to a niche audience. By tailoring campaigns to resonate with a select group that aligns with the brand's values, the allure of exclusivity is preserved, enhancing the brand's desirability. Luxury brands also have a distinct identity and narrative. Consistency is vital for creating a strong brand image and reinforcing the values that define the luxury brand. Targeted marketing ensures that the brand message remains consistent and resonant with the chosen audience.

Targeted marketing also enables brands to delve into the intricacies of consumer behaviour, from understanding their preferences and aspirations to predicting purchasing patterns. This in-depth comprehension is crucial for crafting meaningful and impactful campaigns. Luxury consumers are not merely transactional, their behaviours are deeply nuanced and multifaceted. But luxury is not just about products, it's also about the experience. For this, targeted marketing allows brands to tailor experiences to the unique preferences of individual consumers. Personalization allows companies to elevate the overall consumer experience and foster a deeper connection via personalized communications, exclusive events or customized product recommendations.

Marketing in the luxury industry often involves substantial investments, the use of targeting ensures that these resources are allocated efficiently by directing efforts toward the segments most likely to engage and with higher customer lifetime value. The precision achieved through targeting allows brands to optimize return on investment and maximize the impact of marketing campaigns. As the digital landscape evolves and its relevance becomes increasingly significant, luxury brands must navigate online spaces without compromising their sophistication. Targeted digital marketing ensures that the brand maintains a refined and tailored presence in the digital realm, reaching the right audience through channels like social media and online advertising.

Budget allocation in the luxury sector

In the complex world of the luxury sector, where opulence, exclusivity and timeless allure define the landscape, the importance of strategic budget allocation cannot be overstated. Every allocation of resources in the luxury sector is a carefully calculated investment in maintaining and elevating the brand's prestigious image.

From high-end marketing campaigns that weave compelling narratives of sophistication to the creation of artisanal masterpieces that embody craftsmanship, each budgetary decision is a declaration of commitment to excellence. The allocation of funds for luxurious in-store experiences, where ambiance is as crucial as the products themselves, and the meticulous preservation of heritage further solidify the brand's identity.

In an era where digital presence is indispensable, resources are judiciously directed to create seamlessly sophisticated online platforms that reflect the brand's essence. Ultimately, strategic budget allocation in the luxury sector is an artful blend of tradition and innovation, ensuring that every investment contributes to the perpetuation of a brand's legacy and the cultivation of an enduring connection with its unique customer base.

Allocating budget for marketing channels

Strategic allocation of resources for marketing initiatives is the compass that guides companies through the dynamic landscape of consumer engagement. In an era where the customer journey includes dozens of offline and online touchpoints, the optimal distribution of resources across channels is key to success. Allocating budgets requires a meticulous understanding of the target audience, industry nuances and overarching marketing objectives but also an optimization process aimed at continuously improving efficiencies.

From the digital ecosystem encompassing social media, content marketing and online advertising to traditional channels like television and print, each allocation is a calculated investment. Furthermore, earmarking funds for influencer collaborations, events, analytics tools and customer relationship management ensures a holistic approach. The art lies in finding the optimal balance, where resources are strategically directed to channels that resonate most effectively with the target audience, fostering brand visibility, engagement and, ultimately, business success.

Traditional and digital marketing are two divergent yet integral approaches to conveying brand messages and engaging with audiences. Traditional marketing, rooted in established mediums like print, television and radio, relies on one-way communication to reach a broad audience. While it offers a tangible and often local presence, the costs associated with production and distribution can be higher and measuring its impact can be challenging. In contrast, digital marketing leverages online platforms, embracing the interactive and dynamic nature of the digital landscape. Through channels such as social media, content marketing and SEO, businesses can achieve a global reach while precisely targeting specific demographics.

The flexibility of digital marketing allows for varied budget options, and its robust analytics provide detailed insights into campaign performance. The choice between traditional and digital marketing hinges on factors like the target audience, campaign goals and available resources, with an integrated approach often proving the most effective strategy for modern businesses.

The role of influencer marketing

In the contemporary landscape of digital marketing, the role of influencer marketing has emerged as a transformative force, acting as a catalyst for brands aiming to connect authentically with their target audience. Influencers, with their dedicated and engaged followers, offer a unique bridge between brands and consumers. Beyond the conventional advertising sphere, influencer marketing harnesses the trust and relatability influencers have cultivated with their audience. By collaborating with influencers, brands tap into a vast and diverse audience base, often reaching niche markets that may be challenging through traditional means. Influencers bring a distinctive authenticity to brand endorsements, weaving product or service recommendations seamlessly into their content. This role extends beyond mere promotion, it encompasses content creation, social media amplification and fostering meaningful engagement.

The agility of influencer marketing allows brands to stay nimble in the dynamic realm of social media, adapting to trends and maximizing visibility. In essence, influencer marketing is not just a promotional strategy but a dynamic channel that leverages the influence of trusted figures to create genuine connections and drive brand success in the digital age.

Influencers, particularly those entrenched in the luxury sphere, bring a unique blend of credibility and authenticity to brand endorsements. Their carefully curated content, often featuring opulent products and experiences, serves as a powerful conduit to convey the aspirational story that underpins luxury. Crucially, influencers possess the ability to engage directly with their audience, creating a personalized connection that resonates with the desires of affluent consumers. Collaborating with influencers ensures access to affluent demographics, amplifying the brand's reach while maintaining a sense of exclusivity.

Additionally, influencers adeptly navigate the digital landscape, leveraging their platforms to showcase the intricate details, quality and artistry that define luxury goods. In a world where image and perception are paramount, influencer marketing emerges as an indispensable strategy for luxury brands, cultivating a narrative of desirability, sophistication and an unspoken invitation to partake in a lifestyle synonymous with luxury.

Data-driven decision making

In the ever-evolving landscape of the luxury world, data-driven decision-making is an indispensable pillar, reshaping the paradigm of how high-end brands operate and cater to their exclusive clientele. At the heart of this transformation is the profound understanding that data analytics provides the nuanced preferences, behaviours and aspirations of luxury customers. The sophisticated understanding of the customer is key in defining strategies across different business areas, from the customization of products and services, to ensuring that each offering aligns seamlessly with the discerning tastes of the target audience.

The use cases of data analytics extend beyond personalized experiences to include strategic areas such as inventory management, marketing initiatives and pricing strategies. Luxury brands leverage data to optimize campaigns, identify the most effective channels and even dynamically adjust pricing based on market dynamics. This meticulous approach not only enhances operational efficiency, but also contributes to the creation of bespoke experiences, solidifying the brand's image as an arbiter of sophistication and exclusivity. In the luxury world, where precision and personalization are paramount, data-driven decision-making emerges as a pivotal tool, enabling brands to navigate the complexities of a dynamic market and craft offerings that resonate with the essence of luxury.

Data and analytics allow companies to understand the intricacies of consumer behaviour, preferences and trends which have become a necessity in the current competitive landscape. Analytics serves as a guiding light, offering insights that empower luxury brands to anticipate and meet the ever-evolving expectations of their high-net-worth clientele.

Leveraging analytics for insights

Predictive analytics in luxury marketing is a game-changing strategy that empowers high-end brands to understand, anticipate and cater to the evolving needs and preferences of their customer base. By leveraging sophisticated algorithms and machine learning models, luxury brands can analyse the trove of historical data on purchase patterns and engagement with the brand to build detailed customer profiles and make informed predictions about future trends, consumer behaviours and market dynamics. This approach enables brands to stay ahead of the curve, forecasting shifts in demand, identifying emerging trends and relevant storytelling, and even predicting which products or services will resonate most with their target audience.

Different use cases and business areas benefit from the use of analytics and insights. Demand forecasting consists of the use of predictive analytics to help companies forecast demand for specific products or styles, allowing them to proactively adjust production and inventory levels to meet consumer expectations, those anticipating trends. Predictive models can also assist with personalization and tailoring of experiences, by analysing individual consumer data to anticipate preferences and behaviours. Luxury brands can use this information to create personalized shopping experiences, from curated product recommendations to exclusive offers.

Similarly, analytics can be leveraged for the planning and optimization of strategic events, by forecasting attendance, gauging interest in specific themes or collaborations and optimizing the overall event experience for attendees.

Analytics are also a crucial element of marketing and price optimization. The use of predictive analytics can help increase campaigns' precision, by guiding marketing strategies in identifying the most effective channels, messaging and influencers for specific audience segments, ensuring that the marketing efforts better resonate with the luxury consumer base. Predictive analytics can also aid luxury brands in dynamically adjusting pricing strategies based on various factors, including market demand, consumer behaviour and competitive pricing. This ensures that pricing aligns with perceived value and market conditions.

Finally, predictive analytics can be leveraged to anticipate market trends and innovations. By analysing data on consumer preferences and market trends, predictive analytics assists luxury brands in staying ahead of emerging styles and innovations. This insight is invaluable for maintaining a leading position in the ever-evolving luxury landscape.

Measuring the impact of marketing campaigns

Measuring the impact of marketing campaigns is a critical aspect of optimizing strategies, allocating resources effectively and ensuring the highest return on investment. Accurately measuring marketing campaigns offers insights into the effectiveness of marketing strategies by understanding which campaigns the customers better react to. This data-driven approach not only allows businesses to allocate resources more efficiently and adapt campaigns in real-time but also provides a comprehensive understanding of consumer behaviour and preferences. Ultimately, the importance of measuring campaign impact lies in its ability to provide informed decision-making, optimize future strategies and demonstrate the tangible value marketing efforts bring to the overall success of the business.

When measuring marketing campaigns, several key metrics and methodologies are employed to gauge the success and effectiveness based on the campaign's nature and its objectives:

- **Website and app metrics**: used to monitor the performance of digital platforms and the marketing campaigns driving traffic to them, these types of analytics are essential for understanding customer behaviour on digital platforms, optimizing user experience and making informed decisions. The type of metrics included in this category range from traffic metrics (visits, page views, etc) leveraged to evaluate traffic to a platform, to engagement metrics (time spent on site, bounce rate, etc) leveraged to evaluate the engagement of the traffic, to conversion metrics (conversion rate, cart completion rate, etc) leveraged to evaluate the quality of traffic. Those metrics allow us to identify which campaigns drive the most traffic and also which campaigns drive the most engaged and qualified traffic, which is fundamental in the optimization of marketing campaigns (Ketchum, 2019).

- **Email campaign metrics**: used to monitor the health of the email list, which is the list of customers that subscribed to receive email communications from a company. Monitoring those metrics allows a company to gather insights into how subscribers are interacting via emails and help marketers refine strategies for better engagement and conversion. Email campaign metrics are divided into different buckets (Davey, 2023):

- o delivery metrics (delivery rate, email bounce rate, etc) are used to understand if a campaign was successfully delivered to subscribers and to identify possible issues with invalid email addresses

- o open metrics (open rate, unique opens, etc) and click metrics (click-through rate, unique clicks, etc) are used to evaluate engagement with email campaigns by identifying subscribers that opened or clicked on a campaigns

- o conversion metrics (conversion rate, transactions, etc) are used to evaluate the effectiveness of a campaign in converting the subscriber into a customers

- o subscribe/unsubscribe metrics are used to understand the health of the email list and the relevancy of email communications

- **Social media metrics**: used to collect insights into the performance and impact of a brand's presence on various social platforms. Like email campaign metrics, social media metrics are also divided into different buckets. Engagement metrics (likes, comments, shares, etc) are used to evaluate audience engagement with different campaigns, and reach and follower metrics (reach, followers, impressions, etc) are instead used to understand brand visibility (Newberry, 2023).

- **Evergreen metrics**: used to evaluate the success of marketing campaigns in a consistent way independent of a campaign's nature and objectives. Those metrics are the most common and important for optimization decisions, as they allow fair comparison across campaigns and are standardized in their calculation for external stakeholders to be evaluated:

- o Cost per acquisition (CAC) is used to calculate the cost of acquiring a new customer, which allows a company to identify the most effective initiatives for driving activation.

- o Customer lifetime value (CLV) estimates the total value a customer will bring to the company over his/her lifetime, which allows a company to identify the most effective initiative for driving high-quality activation.

o The ratio of CLV and CAC identifies the campaigns that can bring in high-value customers at the lowest cost (Matar, 2023).

o Repurchase rate is used to evaluate how loyal and engaged customers are. It is a key metric in ecommerce and retail that measures the percentage of customers who make a repeat purchase from a business within a specified period.

Another important element in the evaluation of marketing campaigns is the attribution model selected. Marketing attribution models are methodologies used to assign value to the various touchpoints in a customer's journey that lead to a conversion or sale. These models help businesses understand which marketing channels and interactions contribute most effectively to their goals. The selection of an attribution model that is not able to correctly evaluate the customer journey may result in incorrect optimization decisions.

The evolution of attribution models since the 2010s has been significant, starting from the use of first-touch or last-touch attribution, where all the credit is given to the first or last touchpoint, to linear or position models where the role of other channels in the journey was partially recognized, to multitouch attribution (MTA) which considers the entire customer journey and assigns credit to multiple touchpoints based on their influence, offering a comprehensive view of the customer journey, acknowledging the role of multiple interactions.

MTA that leverages AI and machine learning is the preferred model in the luxury industry, as it allows us to properly understand the role and influence that each touchpoint (offline or online) plays in the complex luxury industry consumer journey.

Real-time adjustments

Real-time adjustments driven by analytics represent a dynamic and responsive approach to marketing strategies, allowing businesses to adapt swiftly to changing conditions and optimize campaign performance.

The first step in the process is data monitoring which utilizes analytics tools to continuously monitor relevant data sources, such as website analytics, social media metrics or campaign performance. Alert and notification are then implemented to automatically alert stakeholders of significant changes or anomalies in the data. To fully take advantage of real-time adjustments companies also need to be able to perform an immediate evaluation of the incoming data by analysing the performance of ongoing campaigns in real-time allowing marketers to identify what is working and what needs adjustment.

The second step in the process is the creation of a dynamic content optimization (DCO) strategy, which involves tailoring the content of a campaign or webpage dynamically based on various data points, user behaviour or contextual information. The goal is to deliver personalized and highly relevant content to individual users, enhancing the user experience and improving campaign performance. To achieve this, companies need to create an experimentation culture that allows them to continuously conduct real-time A/B and multivariate testing; the goal is to collect feedback from the customers and conduct experiments to remove any friction and improve the customer experience. To be successful, companies need to create a continuous loop where they collect feedback from the customers, test new ideas via experimentation, implement successful ideas and start learning again.

DCO is one of the main strategies that fall under the experimentation umbrella. This strategy is employed in digital marketing and advertising to personalize and optimize content and messages based on customer data, behaviour and contextual factors. The primary goal is to deliver more relevant and engaging content to individual customers, thereby enhancing the overall user experience and improving campaign performance. The goals are achieved through the conduction of real-time A/B and multivariate tests of different content variations to identify the most effective messaging, visuals or call to action (Amazon, 2023).

Social media optimization (SMO) is a set of strategies and techniques aimed at maximizing the visibility and performance of a brand or individual on social media platforms. The goal of SMO is to increase brand awareness, engage with the target audience and drive traffic to the brand's digital assets. The first strategy is profile optimization, which ensures profile completeness by validating that social media profiles are fully filled out with accurate and up-to-date information and consistent branding by validating that profiles are using consistent branding elements, such as logos and profile pictures, across all social platforms.

A hashtag strategy is the strategic use of hashtags on social media platforms to enhance the discoverability, reach and engagement of content. Hashtags are keywords or phrases preceded by the '#' symbol that categorize content and make it searchable. Optimizing hashtags involves selecting and using them strategically to maximize their effectiveness in reaching the target audience, by using relevant and trending hashtags to increase the discoverability of content and by creating and promoting branded hashtags to foster community engagement.

Posting schedule optimization involves determining the most strategic times and frequencies to share content on social media platforms for maximum visibility, engagement and impact. Each social media platform has its own set of optimal posting times, influenced by factors like the target audience's behaviour, time zones and platform algorithms. This strategy helps determine the optimal times when the target audience is most active and schedule posts accordingly, but also how to maintain a consistent posting schedule to keep the audience engaged (Tien, 2023).

Website optimization involves the strategic improvement of various elements on a website to enhance its performance, user experience and overall effectiveness in achieving business goals. Optimizing a website is a multifaceted process that encompasses both technical and non-technical aspects. Performance optimization focuses on optimizing the performance of the digital applications powering the website to obtain an advantage in performance and improve SEO rankings and also conversion. Optimizing images, using browser caching and minimizing HTTP requests helps improve page load times, utilizing a content delivery network (CDN) to distribute content across servers helps reduce latency, and ensuring that the website is mobile-friendly and responsive across various devices and screen sizes helps reduce friction.

User experience optimization is leveraged to create intuitive navigation by designing a clear and intuitive navigation structure to help users find information easily; create clear calls-to-action (CTA) by placing prominent and clear CTAs to guide users toward desired actions; and streamline forms, minimizing the number of fields to improve user interaction.

Conversion rate optimization (CRO) is the most important strategy under the website optimization umbrella, and is the systematic process of enhancing a website or landing page to increase the percentage of visitors who take a desired action, such as making a purchase, filling out a form or subscribing to a newsletter. CRO involves analysing user behaviour, testing different elements and implementing improvements to boost the overall conversion rate.

Similar to website optimization, mobile app optimization is the process of enhancing the performance, user experience and visibility of a mobile application to increase downloads, user engagement and overall satisfaction. It involves various strategies and techniques to ensure that the app meets the expectations of users and performs well on different devices.

Performance optimization focuses on speed and responsiveness by optimizing the app's loading time and responsiveness to ensure a smooth user experience and minimizing crashes by regularly testing and debugging the app. User interface and experience enhancements focus on ensuring a user-friendly and intuitive interface that aligns with mobile design principles, streamlining navigation and maintaining a consistent design language throughout the app for a cohesive user experience. Push notifications optimization personalizes communication based on user preferences and behaviour, optimizes the timing and frequency of push notifications to avoid being intrusive, and clearly communicates the value or benefit in push notifications to encourage engagement.

Customer journey mapping (CJM) is a visual representation of the end-to-end experience a customer has with a brand or product, from initial awareness through the entire lifecycle of engagement. It involves capturing every interaction, touchpoint and emotion a customer may experience, providing businesses with insights to enhance the overall customer experience. Customer journey optimization (CJO) involves the strategic enhancement of every touchpoint and phase within the customer journey to improve overall customer satisfaction, increase conversions and foster long-term loyalty. It's a holistic approach that combines data analysis, technology and customer-centric strategies.

This strategy starts with omnichannel integration by ensuring a consistent and seamless experience across all channels, both online and offline, and by coordinating messaging and promotions across various touchpoints. Real-time interaction management is used to implement real-time content personalization based on user behaviour and preferences, and triggered messaging by sending timely and relevant messages at critical points in the customer journey. Feedback loops and continuous testing are then leveraged to optimize touchpoints across the entire journey (Qualtrics, 2023).

Evaluating return on investment

Evaluating return on investment (ROI) in the luxury industry is paramount for ensuring that resources are allocated effectively and that business initiatives contribute to overall profitability and brand value. Unlike conventional sectors, the luxury market is characterized by intangible elements such as brand prestige, exclusivity and unparalleled craftsmanship. Assessing ROI in this context involves a meticulous examination of various factors. Beyond traditional metrics like sales and revenue, considerations delve into the realms of brand equity, customer engagement, and the creation of unique and memorable luxury experiences. The impact of exclusive partnerships, innovations in craftsmanship and sustainable practices on the financial bottom line and brand perception is carefully scrutinized. Ethical considerations, digital presence and the efficacy of marketing strategies play pivotal roles, while global expansion efforts and technological integrations contribute to the holistic assessment. ROI in the luxury industry extends beyond financial gains, encapsulating the preservation and enhancement of brand desirability, reputation and the enduring allure that distinguishes luxury enterprises in a competitive market.

Developing KPIs

'Luxurious metrics' refers to a set of performance indicators and measurements uniquely tailored to evaluate the success and impact of initiatives within the luxury industry. These metrics go beyond conventional business metrics and are designed to capture the distinctive characteristics and values associated with luxury brands and products. Luxurious metrics may include factors such as brand equity, exclusivity, craftsmanship recognition, client retention rates and the success of personalized and customized offerings. These metrics aim to quantify elements that contribute to the intangible and aspirational aspects of luxury, providing insights into the effectiveness of strategies that enhance brand desirability, customer loyalty and the overall prestige of a luxury enterprise. In essence, luxurious metrics offer a specialized framework for assessing the unique and high-end dimensions of success in the luxury industry.

Brand equity measures the impact of investments into brand equity and perception by assessing the intangible value and strength of a brand in the minds of consumers. This can be done by measuring how easily consumers recall the brand without prompts (unaided) and with prompts (aided), by using perceptual maps to visually represent how consumers perceive the brand in comparison to competitors, or by assessing how well a brand retains its existing customer base.

Exclusive clientele growth is a critical metric for businesses, especially in the luxury industry, where creating and sustaining an aura of exclusivity is often key to success. This metric focuses on expanding the customer base, but with a deliberate emphasis on attracting and retaining high-value, discerning clients. The first step is defining the exclusive clientele by clearly identifying the characteristics that qualify customers as part of the exclusive clientele (spending habits, loyalty, brand affinity, net worth, etc). The second step is to create market segmentation that reflects those criteria and track the size and engagement of this population over time.

Luxury experience metrics are key performance indicators (KPIs) designed to measure and evaluate the quality and impact of the customer experience within the luxury industry. As the luxury sector places a premium on providing unique and exceptional experiences, monitoring and optimizing these metrics is essential. Customer satisfaction is usually evaluated by conducting regular surveys to gauge overall satisfaction with the luxury experience or by measuring net promoter score (NPS), which assesses the customer's likelihood to recommend the luxury brand or service to others.

Personalization effectiveness measures how well a business tailors its products, services and experiences to the individual preferences and needs of its customers. In the context of the luxury industry, where a premium is placed on bespoke and exclusive offerings, personalization is a key element of creating a unique and memorable customer experience. Its effectiveness is measured by evaluating customer engagement with different features and CLV.

Finally, exclusivity perception assesses how customers perceive the exclusivity of the luxury brand. This is usually done via surveys or by measuring the impact and desirability of limited-edition or exclusive offerings.

Takeaways

In the intricate landscape of the luxury industry, the pursuit of excellence necessitates a strategic and meticulous approach to optimizing spend and evaluating success. As brands navigate the realms of discerning consumers, exclusive collaborations and evolving market dynamics, the importance of dynamic budgeting, innovative KPIs and optimization strategies becomes paramount.

This chapter has illuminated the pathways for luxury brands to craft and refine their spending strategies, emphasizing the need for a judicious allocation of resources, the continuous evaluation of success metrics and the creation of optimization strategies across all areas of the business. The process starts with the understanding of the luxury consumer through market research and analysis of quantitative data available, to define market segmentation and targeting of content and messaging. The importance of precision in reaching and engaging with the right audience is even more important in the luxury industry where discerning tastes and a desire for personalization reign supreme.

Data and analytics are then leveraged to allocate budget and measure the impact of campaigns, leading to different optimization strategies that evolve around a feedback loop and continuous optimization.

By embracing innovation, technology integration and a commitment to customer experience, luxury brands can not only optimize spend effectively, but cultivate a lasting legacy of distinction and desirability in the ever-evolving world of luxury.

References

Adaptive Creative (2023) The rise of data-driven personalization in the fashion industry, *LinkedIn*, www.linkedin.com/pulse/rise-data-driven-personalisation-fashion-industry-appetitecreative/ (archived at https://perma.cc/QZL5-T9EL)

Amazon (2023) Dynamic creative optimization (DCO): Definition, examples, tips, https://advertising.amazon.com/library/guides/dco-dynamic-creative-optimization (archived at https://perma.cc/QZL5-T9EL)

Cappasity (2023) How immersive tech helps luxury brands improve in-store experience, https://cappasity.com/how-immersive-tech-helps-luxury-brands-improve-in-store-experience/ (archived at https://perma.cc/QZL5-T9EL)

Davey, L (2023) 10 email marketing metrics you should be tracking in 2024, *Shopify*, www.shopify.com/blog/email-marketing-metrics (archived at https://perma.cc/5V5G-XM3J)

Ketchum, R (2019) A new way to unify app and website measurement in Google Analytics, *Google Blogs*, https://blog.google/products/marketingplatform/analytics/new-way-unify-app-and-website-measurement-google-analytics/ (archived at https://perma.cc/9F9S-C4LU)

Matar, M (2023) Achieving sustainable growth: Navigating CLV and CAC, *LinkedIn*, www.linkedin.com/pulse/achieving-sustainable-growth-navigating-clv-cac-miona-matar/ (archived at https://perma.cc/9F9S-C4LU)

Newberry, C (2023) 17 social media metrics you need to track in 2024, *Hootsuite*, https://blog.hootsuite.com/social-media-metrics/ (archived at https://perma.cc/XRD9-3B7K)

Qualtrics (2023) Customer journey mapping 101: Definition, template & tips, www.qualtrics.com/experience-management/customer/customer-journey-mapping/ (archived at https://perma.cc/8VBJ-AXG6)

RTB House (2022) Digital transformation of top luxury brands, https://blog. rtbhouse.com/digital-transformation-of-top-luxury-brands/ (archived at https:// perma.cc/K4XL-XCQL)

Tien, S (2023) 13 easy ways to tackle social media optimization, *Hootsuite*, https:// blog.hootsuite.com/social-media-optimization/ (archived at https://perma.cc/ C9QE-MFBP)

10

New technologies and the future of customer experience

LAURA RU YUN PAN

There hasn't been a time when technology has played a more important role than it has today. Almost every single luxury brand has undergone some form of digital transformation, from Ferrari's partnership with Qualcomm (Ferrari S.p.A, 2022) creating a digital cockpit to Louis Vuitton's latest soulbound token NFTs (Louis Vuitton, 2023). New technologies are inevitably a source of innovation that continually generates value to both the companies and their customers.

This sentiment is shared by the major players in the industry. Since 2016, LVMH has been an advocate for technological innovation by becoming a founding partner of the VIVA Technology conference in Paris. Every year, LVMH launches their innovation prize where they shortlist several tech start-ups and provide them with the resources to scale. The start-ups they work with are mostly technologically driven and fall under several categories, from omnichannel and ecommerce to artificial intelligence (AI) and blockchain technology. In the same vein, Kering Group has also launched KNXT, an internal technology incubator that is experimenting with new technologies such as Web 3.0 and generative AI.

As the world becomes more technologically connected, the luxury industry understands that they can no longer sit on the sidelines and wait for the best ideas to enter their sector. Rather, they need to be the innovators and explorers. Today, the luxury industry has become one of the largest investors in new technology, with numerous use cases that have both failed and shown promise. In this chapter, we explore some of the emergent technologies that have recently been introduced to further enhance the customer experience, and how they will change the way we interact with luxury goods and services.

Traceability and authenticity with connective technologies

Connective technologies refers to a broad category of technologies designed to facilitate communication, collaboration and seamless connectivity of devices, systems, people and products. This technology plays a crucial role in creating networks, enabling data exchanges and improving interoperability across various platforms. In the mid-2010s, the term Internet of Things (IoT) emerged as a buzzword, but no one really knew what it represented.

Fast forward to the early 2020s, and many of these technologies are already embedded within our products, services and systems. Some of the more common connective technologies we see in the luxury industry are wireless communication protocols (radio-frequency identification (RFID) and near field communication (NFC) technology), cloud computing, blockchain technology, application programming interfaces (APIs) and AI, to name a few.

When it comes to traceability and authenticity, the most prominent tools used in industry are RFID and NFC. RFID is an automatic digital identification technology, a form of wireless communication that uses electromagnetic fields to automatically identify and track items. The RFID system's hardware collects data such as the position of the product, time and date, at any given time throughout its lifecycle. This allows the software to recognize it and provide the administrator with a view of the product's progress, from production to distribution and sales. The technology has been around since World War II, but was not widely adopted until the early 1970s when it was used by the New York Port Authority as a toll device (Landt, 2005). Around the 2010s, RFIDs became a popular solution in commerce and supply chain management due to the system's ability to precisely trace all the storage phases, from the outflow of goods to the incoming of products, sorting and inventory management. Due to its wireless tracking, however, it is often deemed inappropriate, thus making NFC more desirable.

NFC is rooted in RFID technology but there are a few points of differences. Unlike RFID, NFC is a short-range wireless technology that enables communication between two electronic devices over a shorter distance of no more than 4 cm (1.57 in). NFC is much weaker and offers a low-speed connection, which means closer proximity is required for the information to be read.

Most modern smartphones are equipped with a NFC reader, and contactless payment systems like Apple Pay and Samsung Pay utilize this technology. This shift has also revolutionized the adoption of NFC technology. In the past, NFC could only be read through a dedicated device – think about a hotel room key which is NFC enabled, and the door lock is the reader. Now that smartphones have the ability to act as a reader, it has opened up the opportunity for new digital customer experiences.

Almost all NFC technology used in the fashion industry has the following services:

- **Tracking engine**: With this low range wireless technology, the tracking engine is responsible for low level logging of user provenance. It can detect whenever an NFC tag is read and takes basic information about the interaction, such as device type, geolocation, occurrences, etc (if and when authorized by the customer).

- **Authentication service**: A newer version of NFC tags, known as 'Crypto Tags', are encrypted, configured and serialized tags. They utilize a secret key that encrypt and stores the data onto the blockchain. Once the tag is scanned, it matches the information with the blockchain to verify the cryptographic hash is correct. In addition to this, it also incorporates the rolling code, much like the one-time passcode (OTP) you receive from your bank. The URL within the tags is generated as in Figure 10.1. This type of authentication is the most secure way to have authentication verification, as previous versions of NFC tags have little security against replication or unauthorized verifications to happen. To increase the security behind this technology, there is also the possibility of adding timestamps in the redirect once the tag is scanned. This timestamp can be matched to determine if the operation has been performed within a specific timeframe – the same way a one-time passcode (OTP) from a banking transaction works.

- **Engagement component**: An optional feature where the NFC tags allow brands to create an extended digital experience by leveraging intuitive web graphic composers. These engagement features include changing product ownership, sales campaigns or styling tips, as well as an education element which can provide customers with the product's provenance and manufacturing steps.

FIGURE 10.1 How smart tags work by combining a unique ID and one-time token

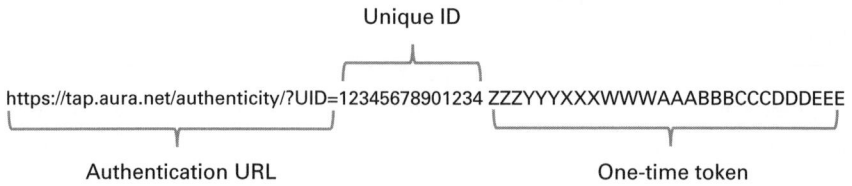

Unique ID

https://tap.aura.net/authenticity/?UID=12345678901234 ZZZYYYXXXWWWAAABBBCCCDDDEEE

Authentication URL   One-time token

SOURCE Courtesy of Temera

The ability to combine wireless communication protocols and blockchain technology, by companies such as Temera, which is a partner of Aura Blockchain Consortium, aims to help tackle the authenticity problem luxury companies are continually facing.

Battling the product authenticity problem

According to the OECD, the fake goods industry is estimated to constitute over 3.3 per cent of global trade (Organisation for Economic Co-operation and Development, 2018), with a value of $4.5 trillion. In 2020, Statista reported sales of over €1.9 billion worth of watches and jewellery, and €1.6 billion worth of handbags and luggage, were lost through counterfeit goods (Sabanoglu, 2022). This value will continue to rise over the coming years, and will pose a big problem for the luxury industry.

So far, luxury conglomerates have invested in various solutions to combat counterfeiting, from sophisticated tech solutions such as RFID tagging to lobbying government to seize and destroy counterfeit import and export. Many of these approaches have not resulted in anything fruitful. In addition to this, luxury companies are also protecting themselves through their teams of lawyers with anti-counterfeiting legal action. For example, LVMH alone employs over 60 lawyers and spends around $17 million annually to avoid losing out to the fake market (Wisdom International Patent & Law Office, 2020).

One of the key technologies that has emerged as a potential solution is blockchain technology. In 2018, a spokesperson from Alibaba, the Chinese tech giant, which had just launched their luxury ecommerce platform Luxury Pavilion that year, stated that they were considering the use of blockchain technology as a way to track and manage authenticity. The novel concept was not yet widely considered by most luxury brands, but just 12 months later, LVMH had quietly announced their partnership with Microsoft Azure and blockchain consultancy Consensys to pilot a project titled Aura Blockchain Consortium.

The initial concept drawn up in May 2019 was that LVMH would utilize the Ethereum blockchain to make it possible for their consumers to not only access product history and proof of authenticity, but also allow their brands to track and trace their products and services, from raw materials to the point of sale, all the way to the second-hand markets (Consensys, 2019).

Aura Blockchain Consortium did not officially launch until April 2021, when Cartier (together with Richemont Group) and Prada Group joined as members of the consortium. Of the three luxury conglomerates, Prada Group was one of the first of the three to roll out their use case since the brand had already been using RFID and NFC technologies in all their products. In June 2022, Prada products arrived in stores with a new paper tag indicating that their products are traced and authenticated using the Aura blockchain. The idea behind it is that when a product is purchased, the customer can scan a QR code or NFC chip and claim ownership of the product. In a few simple steps, it will certify the authenticity of the product and allow them to access all of the product's information.

The certificate of authenticity generated is said to live digitally forever. This also helps with the after-sale process, as the owner of the product can take it back to the store for maintenance without producing a paper receipt. The sales associate will simply scan the NFC chip to get all the information required to proceed to the next steps. In addition to this, when the item is later sold to the secondary market, the product can be instantly verified as genuine without raising much doubt. And the transfer of ownership is also easily done by adding the new owner's details digitally, atop its previous owner's, thus building a record of ownership. All of this is registered and recorded on the blockchain, which is secure and immutable, meaning it cannot be hacked or changed.

The process described above has always been cumbersome and shadowed by doubt. Over the years, we have seen countless cases of customers of pre-loved luxury goods accusing retailers of selling them a fake. In 2021, an article from *Forbes* stated that The RealReal, a very popular pre-loved luxury retailer, has been battling fakes and lawsuits. Kestenbaum (2021) argues that The RealReal had not provided enough resources to ensure its authentication process is credible, taking its turnaround time into consideration, when compared to other authenticators where they have a team dedicated to the craft. Now imagine that the authentication process is as simple as scanning a chip embedded into the product, and the information can be matched to the seller and the brand. Not only would this cut down on time spent and resources needed, but it would also ensure counterfeit goods can be eradicated from the process.

While the second-hand market is often seen as the main beneficiary of this technology, counterfeit goods are slowly making their way into direct retail through unsavoury methods. In May 2022, it was reported that a Louis Vuitton boutique in Changsha, China had sold a fake bag to a customer. The French luxury house was brought to court, and it was later found that the bag was indeed a fake. While Louis Vuitton has denied the allegations and stands by their belief that they have never sold any fake goods through its own retail network (Zhang, 2022), they do not know how this could have happened. Some assume that the fake bag may have re-entered the direct retail through a return.

Having interviewed a number of sales associates, it was found that most of them are not trained to authenticate a return product. In most cases, a mandatory authentication process is not even stipulated in their standard operating procedures. If we combine that with the high turnover and high demand for customer service, there is little to no time for such a thorough process for product returns. However, if authentication can be done in less than a minute, not only does this protect the brand from encountering a similar issue to Louis Vuitton, but it can also further enhance the customer experience.

The Digital Product Passport

Clothing tags. We know they serve a purpose, but they limit the amount of information the manufacturer can provide. Some clothing labels have multiple layers, and this can become quite heavy and, or distort the shape of the clothing. However, as consumers become more concerned about the composition of materials used and pay more attention to care instructions, clothing tags are ineliminable.

Moreover, the conversation around sustainability and the extension of a product's lifecycle is increasing in significance. Not only are consumers alarmed about the upstream processes, such as raw material sourcing, manufacturing and distribution, but the need for better clarity and transparency throughout the entire value chain is also relevant. Thus, many brands have turned to Digital Product Passports.

Digital Product Passports are a repository of a product's information and generally consist of a product's upstream lifecycle, such as the design and provenance information. They could also include features embedded for the downstream lifecycle, such as styling tips, care instruction or repair services, as well as history of ownership. All of these services are accessible via a discrete QR code or NFC tag sewn into the product. Both the brand and the customer are able to simply scan the code or tag with their smartphone to access all the information.

EON, a small tech company based in New York and founded in 2016, is leading this digital transformation. In 2021, EON started working with ecommerce giant Yoox Net-a-Porter or YNAP (YNAP, 2020) to provide an innovative shopping experience across its private label collections. Through the clothing label, customers can unlock a number of services such as styling advice, repair advice and eventually recycle and resell guidance. It also provides the customers with greater visibility of the product's provenance, which includes the design process and fabric information. According to Federica Bertolani, Sustainability Manager at YNAP:

> [The] Digital Product Passport can unlock a world of potential for extending the lifespan of our wardrobes. This technology provides opportunities for customers to engage more deeply with their luxury and fashion products – see how they have been made, where they have come from and, eventually, enable them to be more easily passed onto a new owner. We see a future where Digital Product Passports will have an important part in helping us shift mindsets around longevity and circularity. (EON, 2021)

YNAP is not the only company that believes in this. Sustainability driven brands such as Pangaia, Gabriella Hearst and Chloé are also heavily invested in this technology. In July 2022, Vogue Business (Webb, 2022) stated that one of the major issues for brands tackling the product lifecycle problem is that brands have no visibility or knowledge of what happens the minute a product leaves the store. Unlike the automotive or luxury watch industry where regular servicing is recommended, when it comes to fashion, there is no traceability.

To further reinforce the concept that Digital Product Passports are going to become the norm, Loro Piana, one of LVMH's ultra-luxury brands, has also introduced this technology for their Gift of Kings® product range (LVMH, 2023). In March 2023, Loro Piana and Aura Blockchain Consortium jointly announced that they are entering a new era of traceability. A QR code that is currently placed on an external clothing tag (with plans for it to be incorporated into the actual product) will provide a full story of the garment, highlighting each step in the production chain, and how it morphs into the final product. Once the customer purchases the product, a digital certificate is generated by the Aura Blockchain Consortium that guarantees not only the end-to-end traceability of the garment, but also authenticity of the product.

The Gift of Kings® range is made from the most prized merino wool, where Loro Piana have worked with a small number of sheep herders across Australia and New Zealand. Loro Piana's vertical supply chain provides a clear provenance of the product, ensuring the customer is able to not only learn about the exquisite wool, but also pass it down to a new owner and extend its lifecycle.

Outside of the fashion industry, Salone del Mobile, the most important furniture trade show which takes place in Milan every year, introduced a Digital Product Passport in 2023. The Passport consists of a certificate of authenticity and a one-of-one NFT, all of which are stored on the block-chain. MyLime, the company providing the technology, explains that each furniture will be fitted with three points of verification: a QR code, a serial number and a RFID chip (Salone Milano, 2023). Next a digital twin is created and released as an NFT, all of which are part of the Digital Product Passport.

In November 2023, WWD reported that Mugler too, has introduced this feature, with a twist. Leveraging French start-up Arianeé's technology, Mugler aims to not only provide authentication and traceability, it will also act as a 'digital engagement platform', reported to give users access to behind-the-scenes content, event invitation and early access to sales campaigns (Templeton, 2023). Similarly, the Aura Blockchain Consortium is also doubling down on this service, suggesting that a range of other benefits can be explored, apart from the aforementioned services. For example, waste management, e-warranty and insurance, digital twins, community building and more.

As of now, Digital Product Passports are still a novel technological solution. However, it is possible that they could become an industry-wide norm. As of 24 January 2024, the European Commission has issued three publications relating to the enforcement of DPPs, which suggests that the regulation should come into effect between 2026 and 2027, and an aim to have most products covered by 2030. The European Commission has teamed up with

CIRPASS in leading the execution of DPPs across Europe. As of now, they are focusing on three key areas:

1 textiles and fashion
2 car batteries, consumer electronics and construction products
3 food, food packaging and other packaging

The main goals are sustainability-focused and adhere to initiatives such as the Circular Economy Action Plan (CEAP) and the Ecodesign for Sustainable Products Regulation. Today, over 30 luxury brands have engaged with traceability solution partners to commence their DPP plan. This new regulation has created an inevitable adoption of technology. And, while blockchain is not mandated as part of the EU regulations, connective technologies such as RFID, NFC and QR codes would emerge as the industry standard.

CASE STUDY:
How Bulgari is extending its customer journey with NFC

When it comes to the adoption of innovative technologies in the luxury industry, Bulgari is ranked at the top. In 2010, fellow LVMH brand Fendi was one of the first to embed RFID technology into their bags, replacing the hologram stickers they introduced in 2004. The RFID chips are stitched into the bag and can be read by a device in store. Despite this, it is rarely used in-store or by third party authenticators, who still rely on the serial numbers embossed on the leather tags. Over the years, the Innovation & Transformation Director at Bulgari, Ennio Piccirillo, had looked at various technologies to solve the industry's authentication problem and understood that while utilizing RFID or NFC as an authentication tool is great, there are also opportunities to further develop the customer experience.

In 2019, Bulgari introduced the first digital interaction leveraging NFC technology, the Bulgari Touch (Bulgari, 2019). Created to establish a personalized one-to-one relationship with its customers, the Bulgari Touch is an additional platform on top of its existing authentication tool, which provides a range of engaging features such as a photo booth with special stickers and filters, access to product information or exclusive collections, styling inspiration, videos, editorials and games, to name a few. To access these features, the customer has only to tap their smartphones on the product tag or the base of the handbag. The embedded NFC chip in their leather goods and soft accessories, like handbags, wallets and scarves, is now able to extend the experience beyond the product itself.

The Bulgari Touch was designed to remove the need for physical documentation to confirm the product's authenticity, as this can often be lost, faked or switched. The luxury industry is well aware that expert counterfeits or 'superfakes' come with a range of documentation, as well as receipts that can often pass off as the real thing. This has been exposed by creators on TikTok showing off superfakes that come with authenticity certificates, as well as purchase receipts from the boutique, both of which are forgeries.

By leveraging the Aura blockchain, the details of the product and their eventual owners will be registered on the distributed ledger and kept securely. The NFC chip, which is usually hidden beneath the brand logo, is assigned a unique identifier (UID) and is linked to a specific product that can be verified by Bulgari's enterprise resource planning (ERP) system. The action either confirms or denies a product's authenticity if the code matches the one on their system. Since this information is proprietary, it prevents counterfeiters knowing the UID of any given product (Temera, 2019).

In an interview with Mr Piccirillo, he mentioned that the Bulgari Touch was created to solve a number of issues in the luxury retail sector. While product authenticity is the most obvious problem, other operational processes should also be considered. The two he highlighted were:

- helping sales associates with product information, details of the product supply chain and inventory management
- simplifying aftersales service, which has been described previously

For Bulgari, it was important to explore all the possibilities a technology could offer. Considering the investment placed in the redevelopment of the manufacturing process and implementation of the technology, it should not be seen as a novelty or nice-to-have, but rather something that serves a principal purpose, in this case confirming authenticity of a product, as well as a way to help their sales team better engage with their customers.

Web 3-enabled loyalty and customer relationship management (CRM)

'Web3' (also known as Web 3.0) has become a very popular catchword since the mid-2020s. The term was first coined by computer scientist Gavin Wood, one of the co-founders of the Ethereum blockchain, and describes the newest iteration of the internet (Kharpal, 2022).

The concept of Web3 is focused on decentralization, blockchain technology and handing power back to the users. Some common Web3 products include non-fungible tokens (NFTs), cryptocurrencies and smart contracts, to name a few. It is prophesized to change the way we use the internet, and luxury companies are at the forefront of this technology.

The first generation of the internet, or Web 1.0, was the static web which we experienced from the 1980s to the early 2000s. This version of the internet is characterized by its one-way communication where information was posted, and users were limited by the way they interact or participated in enriching the information. The next version of the internet, Web 2.0, is something we are most familiar with. It is characterized by social media, user-generated content and a shift towards two-way communication. This version of the internet is heavily focused on centralized tech companies, sometimes referred to as FAANG (Facebook and Meta products, Amazon, Apple, Netflix and Google) in a position of control, while users are often the contributors of information.

The future version of the internet, as hypothesized by tech enthusiasts, Web3 is characterized by an eventual departure from the current centralized web, where dominant tech companies still hold substantial control over user data, and move into a decentralized model where the individual is empowered to have greater control and ownership of their personal information. Not only that, the principle behind Web3 is also to empower co-creation. Think of it as a socialist movement, where the exchange of information is regulated and owned by the community as a whole.

Currently, the luxury industry has launched the most projects in the Web3 space. These include collectible NFTs, decentralized metaverses and smart contracts. While many might think that luxury's leap into the world of Web3 may have seem impetuous, many top leaders believe that such innovation is inevitable, and that they must look at new ways to communicate and engage with their audiences. Particularly now, as the landscape for data collection is shifting rapidly.

The landscape for data is changing

When the Cambridge Analytica scandal broke in 2018, it was reported that Meta (formerly known as Facebook) was illegally selling user data for profit and sentiment manipulation (Confessore, 2018). Since then, governments around the world have become particularly cautious about how personal data is being handled.

On 25 May 2018, the European Union enacted the General Data Protection Regulation (GDPR) (European Parliament and Council of the European Union, 2016). It is comprehensive privacy legislation that aims to govern how the personal data of individuals located in the EU may be processed and transferred. This meant that companies must stipulate in a clear manner what data they are collecting, why they are collecting it and how they plan to store and process the data collected. This includes explanations of whom the data is shared with, how long the data will be stored and how they intend to protect the collected data.

While the GDPR has made strides in protecting internet users in the EU from the illegal sale of their data, the EU government is pushing for even more scrutiny. The Digital Markets Act (DMA) or Regulation 2022/1925 entered into force on 1 November 2022 and was enforced on 2 May 2023 (Sunderland et al, 2020).

One of the key features of the DMA is to bar big tech companies from monetizing information about phone users, prohibiting them from using and selling the data they have collected about a person through apps or in-built features. Examples of such data include information about sleep patterns or screen time, which are often features of smart devices. In a TED Talk presented by Kashmir Hill and Surya Mattu in Vancouver, Canada, titled 'What your smart devices know (and share) about you', they highlighted that most smart devices are not only telling you information about your lifestyle patterns, but feeding this back to their parent company (the company that produces that device) (Hill and Mattu, 2018).

It seems logical as to why the EU has introduced the DMA, but this will have a significant impact on large corporations that depend on Meta's data goldmine as a tool for targeted marketing. As companies can depend less and less on big tech to provide them with consumer insights, they will have to revert back to obtaining this information themselves.

Luxury companies are the most well positioned for this shift, due to the following factors:

- **Strong brand identity**: A luxury brand's strategy is often defined by its DNA. Its well-defined brand identity allows their message and perception to be clear in the consumer's mind. For example, almost anybody has heard of the brand Prada, even if they are not a customer of the brand. They would also associate Prada with a specific price point, knowing its luxury positioning.

- **Close customer relationship**: Luxury brands compared to other retailing brands have retained robust records of their customers. Since most interactions between the brand and the customers are personalized, it allows the brand to collect a wider range of information. This includes their purchase history, stores visited, duration of their relationship with the brand, their birthday and product preferences.

- **Data collection tools**: Before walking out of a luxury transaction, customers are usually asked to fill out a customer information card, which adds to their CRM database. Every luxury brand treasures its CRM database, as it is able to segment its existing customers. Moreover, they are able to use their purchase history and preferences to hone in on how to better cater to these customers.

- **High-end customer segmentation**: Luxury brands cater to a niche consumer group. The smaller customer base allows the brands to ignore the noise and focus on understanding consumer preferences, behaviours and expectations.

While luxury companies have established a reliable way collect first party data, they still need to rely on certain third-parties to provide richer data that can inform their communication and strategy. Data points such as spending, travel and even dietary behaviours fall outside the purview of first-party data collection. However, as tech companies get scrutinized further by governments, luxury companies may need to find other ways to enrich their own data collection.

Gamifying data collection

Gamification is the process of applying game mechanics and principles into a non-game context. For example, coffee loyalty programmes where after purchasing nine coffees, you can get the 10th one for free. The aim is to take elements like competition, rewards, points and achievements, then integrate them into activities or processes that can promote a sales cycle. In this case, we are looking at how companies are using these triggers to obtain data directly from their customers.

Since gamification taps into our natural inclination to play and compete, always wanting to get a better score or unveil the next stage, it is an effective approach. In some existing brand-led loyalty programmes, such as Luisa Via Roma's privilege programme, you are able to earn points by creating a profile and entering your personal information. More points can be earned if you share posts on social media to flaunt your purchases from the platform. These incentives, which usually turn the points collected into monetary value, are quite effective in convincing the consumer to give up certain resources.

In 2009, an app called Foursquare was founded, which gained a lot of popularity in the early 2010s. The idea behind Foursquare is to utilize the global positioning system (GPS) technology in your phone and claim a location by 'checking in' there. The more check-ins executed, the more likely they are able to earn rare badges, which is the goal of the game. The crux of Foursquare's success is its 'Mayor' title, where you are battling with other people to gain the most check-ins at a particular location to claim the title. The motivation behind this is to allow Foursquare to properly verify your location through principles behind the sharing economy. Even Starbucks partnered with the app, where you would be offered a $1 discount on your next order if you are able to show that you hold the mayor title of the store you are visiting.

Little did we know, Foursquare's gamified experience essentially created an ecosystem that collected geolocation data, which was sold as a service to other companies. Today, when you are tagging a location on Instagram or Facebook, all of this data was collected through Foursquare's gamification strategy.

In addition, gamification can also create an engaging customer experience. This innovative approach is currently being trialled by Lufthansa Airline's Miles & More programme, Uptrip. The process starts by encouraging their customers to scan their boarding passes; based on the flight details, the system allows you to pick two collectible cards. Each card comes with a corresponding reward, such as free lounge entry, extra miles earned, an on-board wi-fi voucher, upgrade opportunities or even instant frequent flyer status upgrade. These cards can also be traded between family members and friends. The aim behind it is to encourage consumers to choose Lufthansa as their preferred airline, as there are significantly more perks than their competitors (Lufthansa, 2023). For Lufthansa, it also allows them to better understand who their customers are, what they desire most from their flying experience, and who they are interacting with when trading cards. The data collected can be used to further improve their service and offering in the future, as well as formulating accurate targeted marketing.

If we can combine the lessons learned from Lufthansa's Uptrip and Foursquare, luxury companies are able to turn their retail locations into gamified checkpoints. This not only brings traffic to the stores, but also allows brands to map the travel patterns and experiential preferences of their customers.

Could NFTs transform personalized customer experience?

According to Richemont Group, almost all of their specialty watch brands have stuck to an 'appointment only' retail structure after Covid-19 distancing measures. This means customers are discouraged from entering a store without having previously making an appointment. This approach has also been adopted by ultra-luxury brands such as Hermès, Chanel, Goyard and Loro Piana. There are a number of reasons for this:

- **Luxury experience, not a marketplace:** Between 2019 and 2022, luxury consumption surged by 10 per cent, excluding the slowdown caused by Covid-19 (Bain & Co, 2022). Combine this with the emancipation from lockdowns, and many luxury brands suddenly became overwhelmed with customers. What differs a luxury brand from fast fashion is the attention and care their sales team are able to provide to their customers, as well as a comfortable and relaxing environment in their retail stores. Hence, luxury retail must maintain a certain level of experience, by not transforming into a marketplace.

- **Resource planning:** In flagship stores, they can have a team of up to 80 sales associates at any given time. However, retail stores come in varying sizes, and it could become overwhelming for the sales team if there are too many customers to serve. Luxury brands with smaller retail spaces, particularly in speciality watchmaking, can probably serve up to three or four clients at any one time. By setting appointments, it allows the team to manage their schedules, as well as to not turn customers away due to their lack of capacity.

- **One-to-two:** For most luxury companies, their retail operations handbook typically stipulates that a customer should not be left alone during a sales journey – for example, when the sales assistant has to go into the back room to pull out a product in your specific size. The idea is to continually engage with the customer and ensure their needs are met. More often than not, luxury companies suggest that each customer is attended to by at least two sales associates. As the customer's spending increases, the number of associates tend to increase. For example, in

Beijing SKP, a team of up to 10 sales associates may be required to tend to one customer in one of their private suites.

- **Personalizing the experience:** Great store managers are constantly thinking about the most comfortable and convenient experiences for their customers. They will train their sales team to fully understand who their customers are and provide an exceptional service which is completely personalized. For example, if a customer is coming in to try a dress they have picked out for an event, a great sales associate would prepare the dressing room; a selection of shoes could match the dress in their size, as well as a few accessories the brand could cross-sell through their interaction. By created this curated journey, the sales associate has not only created a seamless experience, but could have potentially sold a pair of shoes and a handbag, when the customer had only come in to buy the dress.

In an ideal scenario, a customer will make an appointment either through a QR code, the brand's official website or by telephone. The details of the customer are collected and matched with their profile within the brand's CRM database. This should provide the store with a better understanding of who this client is, where they have shopped in the past, what is their purchase history and spending power, as well as their personal preferences. The team of sales associates in stores can leverage this information and create a curated experience for the customer.

As it stands today, most luxury retailers are not using their CRM database in an effective way. They still rely on one-to-one relationships between a customer and the sales associate. This dependence on the one-to-one relationship could also pose a threat to the brand if the sales associate leaves the company and goes to a competitor, or, worse, if the customer compares their experience in their home store versus a store in a foreign country. Recently, there even have been conversations around 'diva syndrome' in sales associates, particularly at Hermès, where customers are made to jump through hoops and 'play the game'. For top-end luxury brands, sales associates hold so much power that they can decide who they offer coveted products to (Mishra and Kapur, 2023).

Over the last decade, luxury companies have reinforced their focus on creating an exceptional customer experience, particularly for its high spending clients. All of this could go to waste, if brands are solely relying on these kinds of relationships. While the idea is not to remove the human element from the luxury shopping experience, it could be difficult for the brand to ensure the same level of attention and care is given to the customer wherever they go.

More recently, luxury fashion companies are looking into NFTs as a way to help solve this problem. NFTs can be used as a blockchain-based identity system, but to simplify how it works, we can think of it as an airline loyalty programme, where customers could potentially hold certain NFTs that could determine their tier status, as well as certain characteristics that can give the sales team a clear picture of who they are and how to best serve them. Before we dive further into the potential strategies behind NFT-backed CRM, it is important to understand the characteristics of an NFT, and how its technology can fundamentally change the way brands can interact with their customers.

NFTs are digital assets that are tokenized on the blockchain but stored in one's cryptowallet – the same type of wallet that stores cryptocurrencies. The cryptowallet serves as a critical tool, as it would act as a person's identifier, much like your email or mobile number. There are two common tokens that are currently used in the industry: tradable non-fungible tokens and soul-bound non-fungible tokens (SBTs). Most NFTs in circulation are tradeable, which means they allow the transfer of ownership from one cryptowallet to another – whereas the soul-bound tokens are locked to the wallet that it has been minted to.

Each type of token has its own benefits: the tradeable NFTs allow for value to increase or decrease based on supply and demand, and also allow for these digital assets to be pass down from one person to another. But SBTs cannot be moved, and this is often used to negate the speculation value (Pan, 2023). In some cases, companies might choose to issue SBTs to ensure that the benefits can be reaped by only one user, like a private club membership.

The added advantage of using tokens is the ability to enable a verification process that is both secure and accurate. We call this token gating. Essentially, it works by reviewing a cryptowallet and recognizing whether a token exists, and whether or not the token's information is correct. After all, every token is unique and assigned an identification code. The application of token gating can be done in person or remotely; just as smartphones are able to read NFC chips, smart devices are able to have decentralized apps (dApps) that can connect to a cryptowallet to determine the contents of the wallet.

On the back end, luxury companies can create various NFTs to easily classify a client's status. For example, a range of NFTs can be created to identify client relationship status, eg very very important customer (VVIC), very important customer (VIC) or high potential. Customers may also earn NFTs based on the stores they have visited, or one that would indicate their home store. All of these would act as information markers to help the brand create a more seamless customer experience.

As we become more technologically savvy, these tools can have the potential to overcome existing roadblocks. When making a purchase through a brand.com website, you might be encouraged to sign in with your credentials to finalize a transaction. This is not only to pull up your details, but also for the company to record your purchase history. Token gating can work the exact same way; instead of entering your email and password, you would be asked to 'connect to your wallet'. Once connected and privacy permission is granted, the brand will now have information about your identity, as well as certain details based on the NFTs in your wallet – thus personalizing the online customer journey.

In real life, when a customer enters a store, especially without a booked appointment, they could remain anonymous until the end of the customer journey when they are asked for their details to close out a transaction. So much could happen between walking into a store and making a purchase, and if a customer's anonymity has caused them to receive a very poor service, then later finding out the customer is an ultra-high spending client, it will reflect badly on the brand and the sales team. Imagine if a customer is asked to connect their wallet upon entering the store: not only would the sales associates be able to identify the client, their purchase history and spending power, but it opens up the opportunity for the brand to curate the best customer experience simply by having visibility of which NFTs they possess.

Some cryptowallets, eg Coinbase Wallet, have also introduced a messaging function. It lets users send messages within the app to another wallet address that operates within the XMTP network. This means once a client's wallet address is registered within the CRM database, the brand's CRM team is able to transfer NFTs and communicate directly with their clients. This opens up new opportunities for brands to share benefits or event invitations or transfer digital assets. While much of this is still in the experimental stages, in future NFTs will be used as digital tools to enhance and enrich the customer experience.

As of current, no luxury brand has executed such a platform, but many innovation teams have considered incorporating Web 3.0 with their CRM database. Outside of the luxury fashion sector, Blackbird.xyz is a restaurant loyalty programme that uses this exact approach to help restaurants and patrons create a mutually beneficial relationship. Blackbird.xyz was developed by Ben Leventhal, one of the co-founders of online reservation platform Resy. As a tech enthusiast, he wanted to create a platform where diners can track their visits to participating restaurants and earn rewards for their loyalty, as well as provide restaurants the data of their customers. As

FIGURE 10.2 Connecting a cryptowallet for verification and token gated authorization

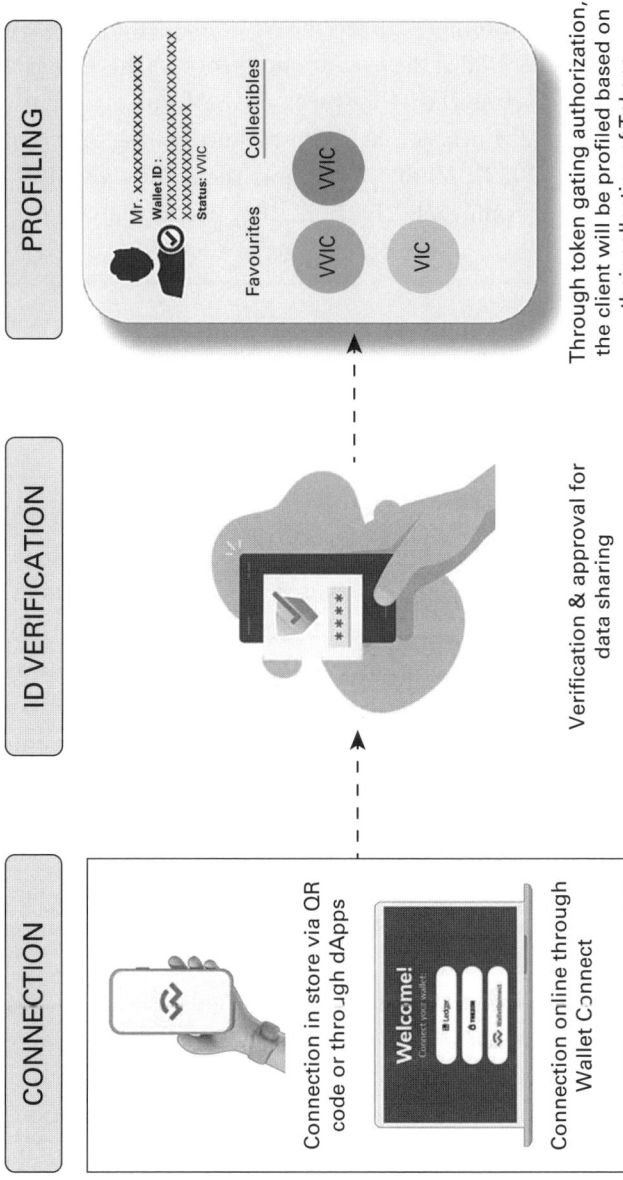

CONNECTION

Connection in store via QR code or through dApps

Welcome!
Connect your wallet

Connection online through Wallet Connect

ID VERIFICATION

Verification & approval for data sharing

PROFILING

Mr. xxxxxxxxxxxxxxx
Wallet ID :
XXXXXXXXXXXXXXXXXXXXX
XXXXXXXXXXXX
Status: VVIC

Favourites   Collectibles

VVIC   VVIC

VIC

Through token gating authorization, the client will be profiled based on their collection of Tokens mentioned previously, data scrutiny will impact businesses in how they collect and use data; this allows companies to receive primary data directly through the engagement of their customers.

The experience created by Blackbird.xyz is simple: upon entering the establishment, customers can tap the NFC-enabled stickers with their smartphones and 'check in' at the restaurant. As soon as this happens, the customer is able to unlock exclusive rewards in the form of digital assets such as NFTs, or digital vouchers that can be claimed during their dining experience (Team XYZ, 2023). As the restaurants themselves are also able to collect customer data from each 'check-in', they are also able to better aggregate their customer base and perform targeted advertising, or create personalized experiences.

The diffusion of technological innovation into the luxury industry

New technologies such as those described may sound a little far-fetched, but the timeline for technological innovation moves at hyper speed. Back in the early 2000s, people associated blockchain technology with Bitcoin, which emerged in 2009. Then in 2015, companies such as IBM introduced services for enterprise blockchain, providing products such as Hyperledger, IBM Food Trust and Stellar to help optimize organizational supply chains. In six short years, LVMH, Prada Group, Richemont Group, OTB Group and Mercedes-Benz formed the first Blockchain Consortium to serve the luxury industry. Aura Blockchain Consortium was very much the tipping point by which the diffusion of innovation theory was witnessed. While the moment of truth is still in its early stages, with some doubting its effectiveness, many smaller brands are buying into the concepts and applications.

We will continue to encounter new technologies and be drawn into hype cycles. However, it is reassuring for the luxury industry that they are now at the forefront of this transformation. The positive takeaway is that luxury companies are no longer shying away from experimentation, and trial and error. During the NFT hype cycle, the luxury industry has produced the most NFT projects, and while most of them have been long forgotten, it has helped luxury brands better understand what their clients have an appetite for. All is not lost, as each failure is a small win.

This ideology is what makes Gucci's foray into new technology ventures so admirable. To many in the industry, Gucci is the most creative and innovative company, as they have always emerged as being the first to test out a new product or service. At the beginning of the NFT frenzy, Gucci was the first luxury brand to announce their collaboration with WANNA Fashion, an augmented reality (AR) and digital try on start-up, allowing customers to create their own digital sneaker and turn it into a collectible NFT (Nanda, 2021). Similarly, it was also the first luxury brand to launch its own NFT collection, as well as forming collaborations with Web3-native brands such as 10KTF. Their success again signalled to the market that NFTs were viable and potentially beneficial, and led to mass adoption industry-wide.

Other pioneers include Bulgari and their experimentation into using connective technologies to better enhance customer experience; Tiffany & Co, who are investing in immersive and augmented reality as a way to advertise and market their products; and Cartier which was one of the first luxury companies to invest in a retail innovation lab in New York, which aims to create new digitally interactive retail experiences. This demonstrates that not only are luxury companies warming up to the idea of digital innovation, but also exposes the inevitable evolution driven by the diffusion of technology across all sectors.

In this digital era, where connectivity is the heartbeat of consumer expectation, luxury brands have a unique opportunity to leverage the technologies they have been investing in. As we have seen, they are able to not only simplify their existing processes and negate issues such as counterfeiting, but also craft personalized experiences, build emotional connections and redefine their brand value in the eyes of the customer.

Takeaways

Luxury companies are undergoing digital transformation which has been exemplified by the exponential number of digital activations across the industry ranging from automotive, jewellery, fashion and more. Major players like LVMH Group and Kering Group are actively investing in technological innovations, such as LVMH's annual innovation prize at Viva Technology and Kering's KNXT experimentation incubator.

Connective technologies encompass various tools aimed at facilitating communication, collaboration and connectivity across devices, systems and people. Common connective technologies in the luxury industry include RFID and NFC for traceability and authenticity, with RFID offering precise tracking capabilities and NFC enabling short-range wireless communication, revolutionizing digital customer experiences, especially with the widespread adoption of smartphones.

Blockchain technology has emerged as a solution for tracking authenticity in the luxury industry, with initiatives like the Aura Blockchain Consortium allowing consumers to access product history and proof of authenticity, streamlining processes from purchase to resale. By utilizing blockchain, luxury brands like Prada aim to combat counterfeit goods and enhance customer experience by providing easy-to-access digital certificates of authenticity, simplifying authentication processes for both retailers and consumers, potentially revolutionizing the second-hand market and protecting brand integrity

Digital Product Passports, accessible via QR codes and NFC tags, offer a repository of a product's information, including its lifecycle, design, care instructions, repair services, ownership history, etc. Luxury brands like Loro Piana and even events like Salone del Mobile have adopted this technology to provide end-to-end traceability, authenticity guarantees and additional benefits like digital engagement platforms.

The Cambridge Analytica scandal prompted governments to enact stricter regulations on data handling, such as the introduction of the GDPR. This has caused an issue for companies wanting to personalize and accurately target their audience, so an alternative solution is required. The solution can come in the form of mutual information sharing through Web3 technology – the decentralized internet where users have the ability to control what they share with third parties.

As an incentive to provide such data, companies might have to consider gamification, which means applying game mechanics and principles to get customers into willingly share their data, such as traditional loyalty programmes. Luxury brands can do this through leveraging their CRM database and experimenting with new technologies to enhance better experiences, as opposed to just relying on one-to-one relationships with their sales associates.

Finally, luxury companies are exploring NFTs as blockchain-based identity systems and offering digital assets as rewards such as soul-bound tokens or tradable NFTs.

References

Bain & Co (2022) *Renaissance in Uncertainty: Luxury builds on its rebound*, Altagamma, Milan

Bulgari (2019) Bulgari Tovch, www.bulgari.com/it-it/stories/bvlgari-touch.html (archived at https://perma.cc/55VH-DXV5)

Confessore, N (2018) Cambridge Analytica and Facebook: The scandal and the fallout so far, *The New York Times*, www.nytimes.com/2018/04/04/us/politics/cambridge-analytica-scandal-fallout.html (archived at https://perma.cc/46BP-S4EM)

Consensys (2019) LVMH, Consensys, and Microsoft announce consortium for luxury industry, https://consensys.io/blog/lvmh-microsoft-consensys-announce-aura-to-power-luxury-industry (archived at https://perma.cc/PR2D-K6UQ)

EON (2021) Net-a-Porter, www.eon.xyz/clients/net-a-porter (archived at https://perma.cc/BL8F-E35V)

European Parliament and Council of the European Union (2016) Regulation on the protection of natural persons with regard to the processing of personal data and on the free movement of such data, and repealing Directive 95/46/EC (Data Protection Directive), *Official Journal of the European Union; The Legislation series*, 4.5.2016, 1–88, https://gdpr-info.eu/ (archived at https://perma.cc/Y4Q8-S744)

Ferrari S.p.A. (2022) Ferrari and Qualcomm: A strategic technology partnership aimed at the future, www.ferrari.com/en-EN/corporate/articles/ferrari-and-qualcomm-a-strategic-technology-partnership-aimed-at-the-future (archived at https://perma.cc/GM46-YF2T)

Hill, K and Mattu, S (2018) What happens when you fill a house with 'smart' technology, *NPR*, www.npr.org/2018/02/12/585177775/what-happens-when-you-fill-a-house-with-smart-technology (archived at https://perma.cc/V5SZ-4G6K)

Kestenbaum, R (2021) The RealReal is still battling fakes. It won't be easy to get it right, *Forbes*, www.forbes.com/sites/richardkestenbaum/2021/02/22/the-realreal-is-still-battling-fakes-it-wont-be-easy-to-get-it-right/ (archived at https://perma.cc/V5SZ-4G6K)

Kharpal, A (2022) What is 'Web3'? Here's the vision for the future of the internet from the man who coined the phrase, *CNBC*, www.cnbc.com/2022/04/20/what-is-web3-gavin-wood-who-invented-the-word-gives-his-vision.html (archived at https://perma.cc/3WML-JGMN)

Landt, J A (2005) The history of RFID, *IEEE Potentials*, **24** (4), pp. 8–11

Louis Vuitton (2023) Louis Vuitton unveils VIA, https://us.louisvuitton.com/eng-us/stories/louis-vuitton-via (archived at https://perma.cc/3WML-JGMN)

Lufthansa (2023) NFT trading card app goes live, *Miles & More by Lufthansa*, www.miles-and-more.com/row/en/program/news/nft-trading-card-app-goes-live-news-2023.html (archived at https://perma.cc/3WML-JGMN)

LVMH (2023) Loro Piana welcomes new era of traceability with the Aura Blockchain Consortium, www.lvmh.com/news-documents/news/loro-piana-welcomes-new-era-of-traceability-with-the-aura-blockchain-consortium/ (archived at https://perma.cc/5NUL-X7YT)

Mishra, N and Kapur, R (2023) The Hermès game: Carefully-guarded craftsmanship or scarcity-driven marketing gimmick? *Campaign Asia*, www.campaignasia.com/article/the-hermes-game-carefully-guarded-craftsmanship-or-scarcity-driven-marketing-gim/492550 (archived at https://perma.cc/3N83-4RB3)

Nanda, M (2021) Gucci is selling $12 (Virtual) Sneakers, *Business of Fashion*, www.businessoffashion.com/articles/technology/gucci-is-selling-12-virtual-sneakers/ (archived at https://perma.cc/B59N-QKTY)

Organisation for Economic Co-operation and Development (2018) *Trade in Counterfeit Goods and the Italian Economy*, OECD, Paris

Pan, L R (2023) NFTs for a new customer relationship, *E&M Magazine*, https://emplus.egeaonline.it/en/61/archivio-rivista/rivista/3459151/articolo/3459189 (archived at https://perma.cc/UPL7-BZEK)

Sabanoglu, T (2022) Sales losses from counterfeit goods worldwide in 2020, by retail sector, *Statista*, www-statista-com.eu1.proxy.openathens.net/statistics/1117921/sales-losses-due-to-fake-good-by-industry-worldwide/ (archived at https://perma.cc/86HW-UA6Z)

Salone Milano (2023) MyLime SRL introduces digital product passport, www.salonemilano.it/en/prodotti/mylime-srl/digital-product-passport (archived at https://perma.cc/6LV7-YFN8)

Sunderland, J, Herrera, F, Esteves, S et al (2020) The Digital Markets Act: Ensuring fair and open digital markets, https://commission.europa.eu/strategy-and-policy/priorities-2019-2024/europe-fit-digital-age/digital-markets-act-ensuring-fair-and-open-digital-markets_en (archived at https://perma.cc/UW8P-69UR)

Team XYZ (2023) Restaurant loyalty program Blackbird.xyz introduces NFTs to the hospitality space, *Gen XYZ*, https://gen.xyz/blog/blackbirdxyz (archived at https://perma.cc/P98L-SFZ5)

Temera (2019) Bulgari Case Study, https://temera.it/en/case-study/bulgari.html (archived at https://perma.cc/BFP3-U23V)

Templeton, L (2023) Mugler teams up with Arianee for digital passports in bags, *WWD*, https://wwd.com/fashion-news/fashion-scoops/mugler-arianee-digital-passports-spiral-curve-bags-1235915930/ (archived at https://perma.cc/QTP7-ZN2A)

Webb, B (2022) Digital IDs: A game-changer for fashion? *Vogue Business*, www.voguebusiness.com/companies/digital-ids-a-game-changer-for-fashion-mulberry-eon (archived at https://perma.cc/GQY8-SBGX)

Wisdom International Patent & Law Office (2020) Taiwan IP Court Rules on Parody and Trademark Infringement: LOUIS VUITTON MALLETIER v. LG HOUSEHOLD & HEALTH CARE, www.wisdomlaw.com.tw/m/405-1596-95815,c12317.php?Lang=en (archived at https://perma.cc/P3LC-28FZ)

YNAP (2020) Digital ID technology: Helping make loved clothes last, www.ynap.com/sustainability/infinity/circular-business/digital-id-technology-helping-make-loved-clothes-last/ (archived at https://perma.cc/P3LC-28FZ)

Zhang, T (2022) Louis Vuitton investigates counterfeit selling allegations in China, *Yahoo Finance*, https://finance.yahoo.com/news/louis-vuitton-investigates-counterfeit-selling-140253867.html? (archived at https://perma.cc/NN3E-WLHP)

11

Reimagining the supply chain in the luxury industry: Transparency, human rights, ethical labour practices and animal welfare

STEFANIA CARRARO

In the domain of the luxury industry, where the essence of exclusivity and exceptional quality are paramount, the supply chain stands as a critical element. It not only ensures the delivery of premium products but also significantly influences brand reputation and consumer trust. This chapter, situated within the luxury industry's unique context, embarks on an insightful journey through the intricacies of supply chain management, highlighting the imperative for transparency, commitment to human rights, ethical labour practices and unwavering dedication to animal welfare.

The luxury sector, celebrated for its unrivalled craftsmanship and meticulous attention to detail, encounters distinctive challenges and opportunities regarding supply chain management. The globalized and often opaque supply chains can hide practices that contradict the ethical standards expected by today's discerning consumers. In this chapter, we unravel these complexities, showcasing how luxury brands can become leaders in responsible supply chain management.

Our exploration begins by delineating the contemporary landscape of supply chains within the industry. This provides a foundation for an in-depth examination of vital issues such as transparency and ethics.

Questions are raised about the sourcing methods of luxury brands, the working conditions in factories producing high-end merchandise and the overall integrity of these processes. Particular attention is given to the aspect of animal welfare, especially pertinent in luxury sectors. Case studies of luxury brands that have integrated humane and ethical practices into their supply chains are presented, illustrating a shift towards more responsible business models.

The chapter also delves into how luxury brands can leverage cutting-edge technologies such as the blockchain for enhancing supply chain transparency and traceability. Discussions include the use of artificial intelligence (AI) and data analytics as tools for monitoring and improving labour practices and standards in animal welfare.

This journey culminates in the development of a comprehensive, industry-specific framework. It offers pragmatic strategies for luxury brands to transform their supply chains – from the procurement of raw materials to the delivery of the final product – ensuring adherence to the highest standards of ethical, social and environmental responsibility.

This chapter transcends a mere analysis of supply chains in the luxury industry; it is an urgent call to action for luxury brands to become exemplars in sustainable and ethical practices. It champions a new definition of luxury, one where the excellence and exclusivity of products are matched by the moral and ethical integrity of their creation. Through this chapter, we invite readers to envision and contribute to a future where the luxury industry is synonymous with deep respect for human rights, labour ethics and animal welfare, setting a precedent for global industries.

This chapter embarks on a critical exploration of the current supply chain paradigms within the luxury industry, addressing the crucial need for a shift towards greater transparency, improved animal welfare and the protection of human rights. It discusses how embracing the principles of circularity can lead to significant waste reduction and material recycling, enhancing consumer trust and bolstering brand reputation. It also emphasizes the role of ethical practices in animal welfare and human rights as not only moral imperatives, but also as key factors in the value proposition of luxury brands.

Through practical solutions, technological advancements and the rallying power of consumer activism, this chapter illustrates the transformative journey of luxury supply chains towards a more ethical and sustainable future.

The current state of luxury supply chains

In the current globalized market, the production of luxury goods involves intricate supply chains that span across the globe, involving numerous specialized suppliers and controlled by major brand owners. Marketing experts note a rising global demand for luxury goods across all income levels, leading to increased competition in the luxury market. This competitive landscape has evolved to a point where marketing campaigns alone are insufficient for success. While brand repositioning and consolidation are crucial, marketing efforts alone cannot ensure long-term stability.

The concept of 'value' in the luxury industry is increasingly linked to the services the supply chain offers. However, research in this area has been limited, highlighting a need to understand the role of supply chain operations and management in the success of luxury companies. Luxury companies sometimes embrace deliberate inefficiencies, like manual labour and long waiting lists, to maintain exclusivity and rarity, yet supply chain management (SCM) remains crucial for business success (Brun et al, 2008; Caniato et al, 2011).

In this context, luxury companies face challenges from the complexity of their supply chains, consumer taste volatility, shorter product lifecycles and the need for international compliance, including adherence to EU and US regulations. These challenges necessitate a focus beyond marketing, emphasizing operational issues crucial for sustaining brands and satisfying customers.

Brun et al (2008) highlight the importance of managing different supply chains within the same luxury company for various products. Different supply chain strategies are needed, especially when the product portfolio is diverse. Managing these supply chains involves reducing obsolescence risks and ensuring the achievement of critical success factors (CSFs), requiring a consistent configuration of the entire supply chain.

The distinction between luxury and non-luxury companies often lies in the strategic significance of choices made, particularly in quality, availability and traceability. Quality is synonymous with 'excellence' and is essential in the supply chain. Availability differs between accessible luxury brands and inaccessible and intermediate brands, with the latter focusing more on alignment with advertising campaigns and maintaining product scarcity selectively.

Traceability is vital for maintaining brand reputation, allowing customers to understand the origins and properties of materials used, thereby reinforcing aspects of quality, craftsmanship heritage, country of origin and exclusivity.

The Covid-19 pandemic dramatically impacted luxury supply chains, causing delays, closures and cancellations, alongside a shift to increased online sales and a decrease in travel-related purchases. The pandemic exposed vulnerabilities in supply chains, particularly affecting smaller suppliers. To combat this, many companies turned to omnichannel strategies and sustainable long-term approaches. Diversification of supplier countries, as suggested by the International Monetary Fund, could mitigate these vulnerabilities, highlighting the importance of a multifaceted approach in managing global supply chains.

Despite projections for modest growth, the luxury industry faces threats from macroeconomic instability, geopolitical tensions and environmental concerns. According to 'The State of Fashion 2024' (McKinsey & Company, 2024), the sector is expected to witness retail sales growth between 2 per cent and 4 per cent in 2024. However, this anticipated growth comes with the caveat of potential threats that could overshadow the industry's progress.

Luxury brands, in response to the dynamic market conditions, are transitioning from strategies focused on volume expansion to those emphasizing price adjustments. Research supports a trend where more than half of industry executives are planning price increases as a means to strengthen their businesses in the face of reduced cost-cutting opportunities. Additionally, the luxury industry contends with the 'bullwhip effect', a phenomenon extensively discussed in academic literature such as the *Journal of Business Logistics*, where minor changes in consumer demand can cause significant supply chain disruptions, leading to issues like underutilization of manufacturing capacities and workforce fluctuations.

The 2024 McKinsey report advises luxury brands to develop transparent and collaborative supplier relationships as a strategy to counteract these challenges and to align with increasing sustainability regulations.

The importance of adopting circular business models in the luxury fashion industry, as highlighted by the Ellen MacArthur Foundation in their seminal report 'A new textiles economy: Redesigning fashion's future' (2017), aligns with academic research advocating for sustainable practices. This report, often cited in sustainability studies, emphasizes material reuse and recycling to address environmental concerns and enhance resource sustainability, a critical consideration for luxury brands navigating the complexities of sustainable operations.

Anticipating the tightening of sustainability legislation, luxury brands are likely to pursue greater control over their supply chains, potentially leading to increased mergers and acquisitions with a focus on vertical integration.

This strategic move not only streamlines operations but also facilitates the management of environmental and ethical standards, crucial for maintaining the industry's legacy.

In conclusion, the luxury industry's path forward will require a sophisticated balance between cost management, product excellence and ethical practices, as underscored in various academic research papers and industry reports. The successful adaptation to these evolving paradigms will be pivotal in preserving the luxury industry's prestigious legacy in a responsible and revered manner.

The Monitor for Circular Fashion, an observatory affiliated with the SDA Bocconi Sustainability Lab, has made significant strides in promoting sustainable practices in the fashion industry. In 2023, it broadened its scope by collaborating with partner companies such as Tod's Group, Ferragamo, Vivienne Westwood and Candiani to evaluate circularity key performance indicators (KPIs) identified by the SDA Bocconi research team. These initiatives are crucial in fostering sustainable and circular methodologies in the textile, clothing, leather and footwear sectors. Additionally, the partner companies released an updated version of the Circular Fashion Manifesto, which echoes the European Commission's Textile Transition Pathway and emphasizes a commitment to transparency and traceability throughout the supply chain.

The updated Manifesto, aligned with eight actions inspired by the Textile Transition Pathway, was presented to UNECE and the European Commission's DG GROW. The report highlighted that the primary benefit of circularity is the improvement of brand reputation, which coexists with the creation of new business opportunities and enhancement of consumer loyalty. However, it also identified challenges such as cost, technology availability and infrastructure as major obstacles to achieving circularity, noting that trade-offs include operational complexity and increased costs.

The publication of the Circular Fashion Manifesto placed a key focus on textile waste management and extended producer responsibility (EPR), featuring insights from European experts and strategies from partner companies to optimize waste management. It explored strategies for reducing pre-consumer waste and effectively managing post-consumer waste, including partnerships to enhance EPR.

As the fashion industry embraces the green transition with a focus on supply chain, it is crucial to understand the regulatory frameworks that are shaping its evolution. The EU Waste Framework, a cornerstone of this transformation, establishes the legislative groundwork for sustainable waste management practices within the member states. This chapter delves into the Waste Framework Directive (WFD) 2018/851, which amends and enhances the pre-existing directives to escalate the recycling and reuse of waste, specifically targeting textile waste.

The WFD mandates the creation of collection systems for bio-waste, household hazardous waste and textile waste, urging member states to implement these systems by 1 January 2025. It emphasizes the responsibility of producers for the lifecycle of textile products, including end-of-life scenarios, to prevent unsustainable waste treatment practices such as incineration and landfilling. EPR schemes are pivotal in this context, necessitating producers to cover the costs of managing textile waste post-consumer use, promoting the acceptance of returned products and the management of remaining waste after product usage.

In line with the EU Strategy for Sustainable and Circular Textiles released on 30 March 2022, the WFD is instrumental in the EU Green Deal's aim to foster a circular textiles ecosystem. By 2030, the textiles introduced to the EU market will be characterized by durability and recyclability, predominantly consisting of recycled fibres free from harmful substances. Consumers will benefit from longer utility from high-quality, affordable textiles, propelling the economy away from disposable fashion towards durable, repairable and recyclable textile products.

The European Commission has urged institutions and bodies to endorse the revised directive, which includes harmonized EU EPR rules for textiles, set to take effect with the Waste Framework Directive revision in 2023. As part of the updated regulations, new criteria for green claims, transparency requirements and a Digital Product Passport will become mandatory. These measures aim to establish an economy centred on collecting, sorting, re-using and recycling textiles, incentivizing producers and brands to design products that align with circular principles and processes.

The implications of the EU Waste Framework for the fashion industry highlighted the actions toward 2030, and the critical role of circularity and traceability technologies in enabling this twin transition. It will address how legislation like the EU's Ecolabel Criteria for Textile Products and the upcoming harmonized EPR rules are set to reshape the industry, pushing towards a future where sustainability is not just a concept but a concrete, measurable reality within the fashion supply chain. The EU Waste Framework Directive 2008/98/EC, revised in 2023, is at the forefront of this shift. It mandates the enhancement of recycling and reuse of waste, with the European Commission's proposal closely linked to the European

Green Deal and the Circular Economy Action Plan. This chapter discusses the new requirements established by the proposal, which ensure that all Member States will treat waste separately from 2025, aligning with current WFD rules.

This Directive defines what qualifies as waste, introduces specific criteria to prevent the misclassification of used goods as waste, and establishes clear guidelines for what constitutes reusable textiles. The goal is to prevent the export of waste textiles to non-EU countries, ensuring that waste resources are utilized in lower levels of the recycling pyramid, thus fostering the recycling and reuse of quality secondary raw materials.

In line with the Directive, the responsibility for the full lifecycle of textile products now rests with the producers. This entails covering costs related to waste management and fostering information disclosure on recycling, repair and development processes. Moreover, producers are required to comply with EPR systems that include mandatory data collection and reporting, playing a role in funding research and development initiatives aimed at refining sorting and recycling methodologies.

The revised Directive also envisions the establishment of local registers of textile producers across all EU Member States, ensuring comprehensive information about the producer, including their name, mailing address, website, email contact and designated point of contact. Additionally, it calls for the disclosure of the producer's national identification code, trademarks and brand identities, and combined nomenclature codes for the products introduced to the market.

To ensure compliance with their EPR obligations, textile producers must appoint an authorized producer responsibility organization. The EPR fees will be calculated based on the principle of 'eco-modulation', which provides lower fees for companies that adhere to sustainable textile production practices.

The imperative for transparency

In the constantly evolving realm of the luxury market, traceability has emerged as an essential component in the quest for sustainable supply chains. Given the growing consumer appetite for transparency, ethical conduct and environmental stewardship, luxury brands find themselves compelled to give precedence to traceability. This strategic focus on traceability becomes imperative not only to meet customer demands, but also to stay ahead in a fiercely competitive market. This section delves into the importance of traceability, with a particular emphasis on its application in the sourcing of raw materials and how it is influencing the future trajectory of the luxury and fashion industries.

The progress of the fashion industry in terms of transparency has been incremental over the past year, particularly within the luxury sector. According to the 2023 edition of Fashion Revolution's Fashion Transparency Index, fashion brands attained an average score of 26 per cent, a marginal increase from the previous year. Notably, luxury brands such as Gucci, Armani, Jil Sander, Miu Miu and Prada demonstrated significant strides, leading the progress in this area. These findings emphasize that while transparency is gaining importance among fashion brands, especially considering emerging regulations in the US and the European Union, there is still much room for improvement in disclosing tangible impacts (Shoaib, 2023).

The luxury fashion industry, traditionally known for its discretion, has recently made significant advancements in the realm of transparency. This shift has brought the luxury sector to the forefront, surpassing sectors like high street fashion and sportswear that have historically been more open. This development marks a change in the luxury industry's approach to information sharing and consumer engagement.

The same report highlighted that only a minuscule percentage of brands disclose critical sustainability metrics such as fuel usage in manufacturing or garment workers' wages, underscoring a gap in comprehensive sustainability reporting. Shoaib (2023) notes that Liv Simpliciano, policy and research manager at Fashion Revolution, stresses the need for a more concerted effort in transparency, particularly in the luxury segment, where the narrative of provenance and brand storytelling is key.

Despite some progress, the industry's overall transparency concerning environmental impacts remains lacking. Only a small fraction of brands are transparent about their decarbonization investments and renewable energy procurement processes, an area where the luxury industry is urged to take a leadership role. The Fashion Pact's initiative for expanding renewable energy use in Europe is a step in this direction, indicating an industry-wide recognition of the need for more sustainable practices (Shoaib, 2023).

Transparency in due diligence processes has become increasingly vital for fashion brands as they navigate growing legislation on human rights and environmental risks. According to the latest Fashion Transparency Index, there has been a notable improvement in this area. The index indicates that 68 per cent of brands now disclose their approach to human rights due diligence, up from 61 per cent in 2022, and 49 per cent disclose their environmental due diligence processes, an increase from 39 per cent in the previous year. This improvement is directly related to legislation like the EU's Corporate Sustainability Due Diligence Directive, noting that more brands are revealing their due diligence strategies, how they consult stakeholders and identify salient risks, and the steps they take to address these risks, including outcomes in both human rights and environmental spheres.

However, there is still a gap in reporting on the outcomes of these due diligence processes. Simpliciano points out that while brands are adept at outlining identified risks, they are less transparent about the impacts and outcomes of their due diligence efforts. She emphasizes that transparency in due diligence is fundamental, but brands also need to disclose the impacts and outcomes. The upcoming legislation may soon mandate such disclosures, hopefully leading to increased compliance (Shoaib, 2023).

Another area of focus is purchasing practices. Fashion Revolution, alongside other advocates, is campaigning for legislation to address unfair purchasing practices, which are often linked to higher rates of labour abuses. As brands shift to direct-to-consumer models, they tend to place smaller orders with suppliers, increasing risks and pressure on these suppliers. Direct-to-consumer channels also allow brands to sidestep mass customs taxes or labour regulations. Less than half of brands, as per the index, publish their tax strategy. Fashion Revolution's Good Clothes, Fair Pay proposal suggests criminal sanctions or fines for brands with unfair purchasing practices, and in the UK the organization supports calls for a fashion watchdog to limit such practices.

Transparency in the fashion industry is not merely a starting point; it is a critical imperative that some brands have yet to fully embrace. Despite increased transparency in disclosing policies and commitments, there remains a significant gap between words and actions. To truly assess the fashion industry's progress, tangible evidence of a positive impact is essential (Shoaib, 2023).

The entrenched lack of disclosure, particularly among some of the wealthiest fashion firms, reflects a reluctance to depart from existing systems. This reluctance hinders efforts to address urgent issues such as the climate crisis, unfair labour practices and environmental degradation. The global trend toward mandatory corporate responsibility, characterized by legally binding corporate accountability, is a response to the shortcomings of self-regulation (Shoaib, 2023).

In aspiring to create a sustainable future, the fashion industry must shift its priorities towards ecological preservation and social justice, moving beyond a focus on economic growth. This calls for a paradigm shift where fashion genuinely respects both people and the planet, embodying values that prioritize the well-being of all stakeholders (Shoaib, 2023).

Hermès International has secured the 2022 Transparency Award for all categories within the SBF 120, marking a notable improvement from its previous third-place position. The SBF 120 index, which includes the CAC 40 and other highly traded stocks on Euronext Paris, reflects the dynamism of France's stock market.

This index represents a broad measure of the performance of the French stock market and is used by investors to gauge the economic health of France's publicly listed companies. Hermès International's recognition with the Transparency Award indicates its adherence to the highest standards of corporate communication and ethical practices among these prominent companies.

This accolade, established in 2009, honours companies listed on the French stock market for exemplary clarity in communicating with investors and shareholders. Evaluated on over 250 criteria by a committee of independent experts, including members from Euronext and the IMF, Hermès stood out for its accessible, clear and comparable information dissemination. The brand's ethical commitment extends beyond transparency, encompassing gender equality, craftsmanship, regional development, resource respect and ecological awareness, earning recognition for job creation in France.

Gabriela Hearst, at Chloé, has distinguished the brand with her commitment to ethical sourcing and sustainable materials. Under her direction, Chloé achieved B Corporation status, indicating its dedication to social and environmental responsibility. Hearst's use of eco-friendly materials and collaboration with non-profit suppliers further exemplify the brand's commitment to sustainability.

Human rights and ethical labour practices

In the world of luxury goods and fashion, upholding human rights and ethical labour practices is a crucial aspect of maintaining a brand's integrity and reputation. This section explores the significance of these principles within the luxury supply chain, emphasizing the responsibility of luxury brands to protect the rights and dignity of workers at all stages of production.

Luxury brands, celebrated for their exclusivity, craftsmanship and quality, extend their influence far beyond the realm of the product itself, encompassing the entire supply chain. It is imperative to comprehensively examine the multifaceted reasons that underscore the paramount importance of human rights and ethical labour practices within the luxury context:

- **Preserving brand reputation:** The venerable prestige and allure associated with luxury brands, such as Gucci, have encountered tarnished reputations due to reports of labour exploitation in their supply chains (Shoaib, 2024). Academic research by Crane and Matten (2004) underscore the pivotal role of reputation as a strategic asset for luxury brands. A compromised reputation not only impacts sales but also erodes a brand's enduring value.

- **Consumer expectations:** In an era marked by heightened social consciousness, contemporary luxury consumers exhibit a growing desire to comprehend the social and environmental consequences of their purchases (Deloitte, 2019). This evolving consumer behaviour aligns seamlessly with the findings of Kapferer and Bastien (2009), who argue that luxury brands must evolve to meet shifting consumer values and expectations. Today's luxury consumers seek brands that not only offer quality and prestige but also stand as stalwarts of ethical standards.

- **Legal and ethical obligations:** Legislation such as the Modern Slavery Act in the UK, and its global counterparts, imposes both legal and ethical obligations on luxury brands to combat slavery and human trafficking within their supply chains (legislation.gov.uk, 2015). The research conducted by Professor David Vogel (2005) highlights the dynamic role played by governments and international organizations in moulding corporate social responsibility standards. Compliance with such laws transcends being solely a moral obligation; it becomes a legal imperative for luxury brands.

Furthermore, research by Michael Porter and Mark Kramer (2011) emphasizes the concept of creating shared value, suggesting that luxury brands can attain a competitive edge by addressing social issues like labour exploitation and environmental sustainability. Through the alignment of business practices with societal needs, luxury brands can fortify their reputation and ensure enduring profitability.

In luxury supply chains, ethical labour practices play an integral role in ensuring fair treatment of workers and upholding social responsibility. One of the most important aspect is fair wages.

Prominent luxury brands such as LVMH and Kering have taken substantial strides in committing to fair wages for their workers. This commitment directly addresses income inequality, a pressing concern within the industry (Kering Sustainability Report, 2020). For instance, Kering, with brands like Gucci and Saint Laurent, has made a conscious effort to ensure that employees across its supply chain receive just compensation. This initiative resonates with the findings of academic research by Locke and Romis (2007), who emphasize that providing fair wages not only enhances the wellbeing of workers but also contributes to an overall improvement in supply chain performance and the sustainability of the business.

Another crucial aspect is safe working conditions. Ensuring safe working conditions is of paramount importance within luxury supply chains. Apple, a global brand known for its technological innovations, serves as an illustrative example of a commitment to safe working environments. Richemont, the renowned luxury conglomerate boasting brands like Cartier and Montblanc, has embraced a comprehensive approach to health and safety within its supply chain (Richemont, 2022). Research conducted by Professor Robert Gibbons (2012) highlights that safe working conditions not only protect the rights of workers, but also yield benefits in terms of increased productivity and reduced costs associated with workplace accidents and health-related issues.

Regarding child labour and forced labour prevention, luxury brands are resolute in their commitment to eradicating child and forced labour from their supply chains. Tiffany & Co, renowned for its luxury jewellery, has implemented explicit policies that vehemently prohibit child and forced labour (Tiffany & Co, 2022). This commitment aligns with the broader global effort to eliminate such unethical practices. Likewise, Burberry, a British luxury brand, conducts regular supplier audits to ensure compliance with ethical labour standards, including the stringent prevention of child and forced labour (Burberry, 2023). These audits serve as a proactive measure against unethical practices, emphasizing a commitment to upholding human rights and ethical labour standards.

In an era where social justice is at the forefront, luxury brands have recognized the ethical imperative of promoting diversity and inclusion within their workforces. Burberry, for instance, has developed a comprehensive diversity and inclusion strategy that places a strong emphasis on achieving gender balance and cultural diversity within the company (Burberry, 2023). Similarly, LVMH, a leader in the luxury industry, has implemented the 'Life 360' programme, which strives to create a positive and ethical work environment throughout the entire group while emphasizing diversity and inclusion (LVMH, 2020).

These initiatives align with contemporary research on the benefits of inclusive workplace cultures, as highlighted by Dobbin, Kim and Kalev (2011), and underscore luxury brands' dedication to social responsibility. Incorporating these ethical labour practices, luxury brands not only demonstrate their commitment to social responsibility but also contribute to the creation of more equitable and sustainable supply chains. These commitments are not only morally driven but also strategically sound, aligning with academic research and serving as a crucial foundation as the luxury industry continues to evolve and shape its future.

Incorporating such ethical labour practices, luxury brands not only demonstrate their commitment to social responsibility but also contribute to more equitable and sustainable supply chains.

The commitment to fair wages, safe working conditions, prevention of child and forced labour and the promotion of diversity and inclusion not only aligns with academic research but also ensures that luxury brands operate responsibly and sustainably. As the luxury industry evolves, these ethical labour practices will continue to play a pivotal role in shaping its future.

Animal welfare in luxury goods

Over the past decade, animal welfare has taken centre stage in the luxury goods industry, with consumers increasingly demanding transparency and ethical practices. The historical use of animal-derived materials such as fur, leather and exotic skins in luxury products has been scrutinized due to concerns over animal cruelty and environmental impact. This scrutiny has prompted luxury brands to reorient their sourcing practices towards more ethical alternatives, reflecting a broader shift in the industry towards aligning with evolving ethical values and consumer preferences.

Central to the ethical debate is the use of real fur, which has faced intense scrutiny over the inhumane practices associated with fur farming. Luxury brands such as Gucci and Prada have responded by phasing out fur from their collections. Gucci's fur-free policy, announced in 2017, and Prada's fur-free commitment, declared on 22 May 2019, are significant milestones that underscore the industry's move towards more ethical practices. These policies not only cease the use of fur, but also collaborate with organizations such as the Fur Free Alliance to ensure a transition to cruelty-free fashion.

Similarly, the production of leather, linked to deforestation and unethical animal treatment, has prompted luxury brands to seek innovative solutions. Brands are exploring lab-grown leather and sustainable sourcing to address these ethical and environmental concerns. Hermès's partnership with MycoWorks for a vegan leather alternative and Stella McCartney's long-standing commitment to cruelty-free materials illustrate the shift towards innovative, sustainable luxury.

Loro Piana exemplifies this shift with its approach to sourcing high-quality materials like cashmere, merino wools and vicuña fibre. The brand's partnership with the Peruvian government since 1984 to protect the vicuña, a species once near extinction, showcases how luxury and sustainability can coexist. Through efforts like establishing private nature reserves and expanding conservation to Argentina, Loro Piana has doubled the vicuña population, setting a benchmark for sustainable luxury practices.

The sourcing of exotic skins poses another ethical challenge. In response, luxury brands are enhancing traceability and adopting stricter regulations to ensure ethical standards are met. This commitment extends to collaborations with animal welfare organizations, which help brands navigate ethical sourcing and advocate for industry-wide ethical practices.

The rise of social media and increased consumer awareness has also played a pivotal role in pushing the luxury goods industry towards more humane practices. Activist campaigns and consumer advocacy have led to a demand not only for cruelty-free products but also for brands to adopt transparent and traceable supply chains. The proactive consumer now seeks out certifications and endorsements from credible organizations that verify a brand's commitment to animal welfare. Moreover, luxury brands are beginning to invest in educational initiatives aimed at informing consumers about the importance of animal welfare and the impact of their purchasing decisions. This educational approach seeks to create a knowledgeable customer base that prioritizes ethical considerations. Policy advocacy is also emerging as a vital component of the industry's shift towards ethical practices, with luxury brands increasingly participating in dialogues to shape legislation that promotes animal welfare.

Another crucial aspect is the advancements in technology that are further empowering luxury brands to uphold their commitment to animal welfare. Blockchain, for instance, is being utilized to create immutable records of supply chain transactions, ensuring the ethical sourcing of materials. Similarly, AI is helping to monitor supply chains, detect anomalies and ensure compliance with animal welfare standards.

Looking to the future, the luxury goods industry is positioning itself to embrace the principles of a circular economy, which prioritizes sustainability and the ethical use of resources. This approach not only reduces waste but also ensures that every stage of production considers the welfare of animals and the environment. The circular economy promises to redefine luxury, making it synonymous with sustainability and compassion.

As we observe the ethical renaissance in luxury goods, it is clear that the industry is undergoing a profound transformation. Animal welfare is not just an ethical imperative, but an opportunity for luxury brands to innovate and lead with values that resonate with contemporary consumers. Commitment to animal welfare is becoming a cornerstone of brand identity and consumer trust, paving the way for a new era of responsible luxury.

In conclusion, animal welfare has emerged as a central theme in the luxury goods industry. Luxury brands are adopting more ethical and sustainable approaches, including the use of cruelty-free materials and ensuring the traceability of animal-derived materials. This evolution highlights the industry's responsiveness to changing consumer sentiments and its dedication to addressing the multifaceted challenges tied to animal welfare.

Innovations in supply chain management

To bolster supply chain transparency, luxury brands are increasingly using blockchain technology. This enables real-time tracking and verification of a product's journey, from sourcing raw materials to the final sale, thus reducing information asymmetry and enabling swift response to any issues. Blockchain's security also combats counterfeiting, guaranteeing the authenticity of luxury goods. This technological shift meets consumer demands for production transparency, ethical sourcing and environmental sustainability, while enhancing operational efficiency, building consumer trust and complying with stringent transparency regulations.

Several luxury brands are incorporating the Aura Blockchain Consortium, a collaboration between industry leaders including LVMH, Prada Group, Cartier, OTB Group and Mercedes-Benz. The Consortium provides insights into a product's origin and lifecycle, ensuring authenticity and adherence to ethical practices, crucial in the luxury sector where consumer focus on provenance and sustainability is growing.

A notable initiative is Prada's Eternal Gold collection, the first truly sustainable fine jewellery collection by a global luxury brand using 100 per cent certified recycled gold. For this collection, the Prada Group collaborates with key actors in the supply chain of precious metals and diamonds to drive radical transparency and real improvement to sustainable practices in the fine jewellery industry.

The Consortium has also partnered with Sarine Technologies to integrate their Diamond Journey traceability solution. This initiative focuses on transparency and traceability in the diamond industry, addressing the authenticity of gems and environmental, social and governance (ESG) concerns, particularly in conflict zones. The use of blockchain and automated Internet of Things (IoT) systems maintains data integrity throughout the diamond's lifecycle.

In addition to diamonds, gold traceability is becoming a significant concern for luxury brands. Blockchain technology is being employed to ensure responsible gold sourcing, particularly given concerns about conflict gold and environmental impacts of mining. This technology allows brands to trace the gold from the mine to the final product, ensuring ethical sourcing and adherence to environmental and labour standards.

David Block, CEO of Sarine Technologies, highlighted their solution's ability to facilitate blockchain-based traceability throughout the supply chain, from diamond suppliers to retailers. Aura, as a non-profit, offers these blockchain tools to its members, promoting ethical practices in the industry (Prada Group, 2022).

Notably, diamond traceability was among the first practical applications of blockchain, with pioneers like Everledger and Tracr leading the way. This technology is particularly prominent in Asia, including Hong Kong and mainland China, where it assures diamond provenance and supply chain transparency. The incorporation of gold traceability, exemplified by Prada's Eternal Gold initiative, adds another layer of assurance for consumers and stakeholders concerned with ethical and sustainable luxury products.

Addressing the challenges of global supply chains

The luxury sector is currently undergoing a profound metamorphosis, redefining the management of global supply chain challenges. In an industry where exclusivity and quality are not mere attributes but foundational principles, major luxury players are steering towards strategic vertical integration. This shift in strategy is not simply about gaining control, but is a nuanced endeavour to secure a stable supply, achieve cost efficiencies and uphold unparalleled quality.

Vertical integration enables luxury brands such as Loro Piana, Brunello Cucinelli and Prada to command pivotal aspects of their supply chains. For Loro Piana within the LVMH group, this has granted exclusive access to some of the planet's most exquisite fabrics, while Prada's initiatives focus on controlling production nuances to safeguard quality and uphold ethical standards.

In a similar vein, Brunello Cucinelli's and Chanel's investment in Cariaggi, the Italian cashmere and fabric manufacturer, stands as a testament to luxury firms seeking to extend their domain, guaranteeing a constant supply of exceptional products and exerting direct influence over their supply mechanisms. This approach is not merely a tactical manoeuvre, but a cornerstone for securing the finest materials, ensuring they are procured under humane conditions and preserving the artisanal expertise that is the hallmark of luxury goods.

This strategic choice to vertically integrate sheds light on the broader industrial challenges, such as the impact of global warming on temperature-sensitive sectors like cashmere. Overproduction and lack of management, particularly in regions such as Mongolia and China, have necessitated a pivot towards sustainable practices. There's an imperative need for exploring alternatives, such as brushed baby camel hair or super-fine merino wool, which not only mitigate the ecological footprint but also adhere to the luxury sector's stringent quality expectations.

For renowned brands like Brunello Cucinelli and Prada, vertical integration transcends business strategy; it is an embodiment of their commitment to core values like humanistic capitalism and sustainable luxury. These values ensure dignity and respect at every stage of the supply chain, from raw material sourcing to the final product in the hands of the consumer. Operating with substantial product margins, these luxury brands can ensure a 'fair margin' across their supply chain. This equitable approach drives a sustainable business model that supports both growth and the retention of product quality and brand integrity.

As luxury brands such as Brunello Cucinelli breach significant revenue milestones, emulating the growth trajectory of giants like Hermès, the emphasis on sustaining product quality and brand perception becomes increasingly critical, particularly in emerging markets like China. The dynamics of such markets – with their own sets of challenges and opportunities – underscore the imperative of strategic supply chain management for luxury entities. Balancing ambitious growth with a staunch commitment to ethical standards and quality excellence represents the new frontier for luxury brands in this transformative era.

Takeaways

The luxury fashion industry stands at a pivotal crossroads, embarking on a profound transformation towards sustainability and ethics within its supply chains. This evolution is characterized by a comprehensive approach, aiming not only to mitigate environmental damage but also to cultivate forward-thinking models for a greener future. The industry's pivot towards sustainability is becoming as central to corporate reporting as traditional financial metrics, signalling a reorientation of business imperatives towards responsibility and stewardship.

As we delve deeper into the fabric of this transformation, we observe key strategies unfolding. Sustainable sourcing is at the forefront, with the majority of companies setting ambitious targets to incorporate predominantly sustainable materials by the year 2025. This includes a push towards chrome and metal-free tanning processes to reduce the reliance on harmful chemicals, thereby mitigating the ecological footprint of luxury production.

Training and capacity building emerge as instrumental in this journey, considering that the environmental impact of a garment is largely determined at its conception. Recognizing this, luxury brands are channelling resources into specialized programmes designed to cultivate a new generation of designers equipped with the skills to conceive fashion with sustainability in mind.

The empowerment of women within the supply chain is being recognized as a critical element, with luxury brands actively working to rectify the gender imbalances that persist in the industry. Initiatives focused on leadership and professional development are increasingly being adopted to bridge the gender divide.

Green financing is carving out a niche as an essential mechanism in this shift, providing suppliers and companies with the financial means to pursue sustainable endeavours. These range from renewable energy projects to initiatives that support gender equality in the workplace.

Gucci exemplifies this sustainable revolution, embodying commitment through actions like adopting regenerative agricultural practices for material sourcing and pioneering new materials such as Demetra. The fashion giant is making strides in training and empowering women in its supply chain and is investing in green financing for its suppliers, showcasing the integration of sustainability into its core operations.

Brunello Cucinelli, another beacon of luxury fashion, underscores its approach with humanistic capitalism – a philosophy that upholds the dignity and wellness of every individual in the supply chain. Brunello Cucinelli's dedication to sustainability is mirrored in its sourcing of high-quality, ethical materials and its commitment to preserving artisanal traditions. Projects like the 'Contemporary Factory' meld time-honoured craftsmanship with contemporary innovation, ensuring the sustainable and ethical treatment of its workforce and materials.

In sum, the luxury fashion industry is actively weaving a new narrative, emphasizing sustainability, ethical labour and innovation. With leading brands such as Gucci and Brunello Cucinelli spearheading this charge, the message is clear: luxury fashion can, and should, be synonymous with responsibility and sustainability. This movement is not only redefining the contours of luxury but also charting a path for the industry that aligns opulence with a profound commitment to our planet and its inhabitants, steering towards a future where luxury is both grand and grounded in ethical consciousness.

References and further reading

Brandao, M S, Godinho Filho, M and da Silva, A (2021) Luxury supply chain management: A framework proposal based on a systematic literature review, *International Journal of Physical Distribution & Logistics Management*, **51** (8), pp. 859–76, https://doi.org/10.1108/IJPDLM-04-2020-0110 (archived at https://perma.cc/PUL4-VFM2)

Brun, A and Castelli, C (2008) Supply chain strategy in the fashion industry: Developing a portfolio model depending on product, retail channel and brand, *International Journal of Production Economics*, **116** (2), pp. 169–81, https://doi.org/10.1016/j.ijpe.2008.09.011 (archived at https://perma.cc/PUL4-VFM2)

Brunello Cucinelli (2023) Humanistic capitalism and human sustainability, https://investor.brunellocucinelli.com/en/human-sustainability (archived at https://perma.cc/WLW4-XMTG)

Burberry (2023) Annual Report 2022–23, www.burberryplc.com/content/dam/burberryplc/corporate/documents/annual-report-2022-23/Annual-report-2022–23.pdf (archived at https://perma.cc/8B36-XG4R)

Caniato, F, Caridi, M, Castelli, C and Golini, R (2011) Supply chain management in the luxury industry: A first classification of companies and their strategies, *International Journal of Production Economics*, **133** (2), pp. 622–33, https://doi.org/10.1016/j.ijpe.2011.04.030 (archived at https://perma.cc/Z5YF-8RTX)

Crane, A and Matten, D (2004) *Business Ethics: A European perspective*, Oxford University Press

D'Arpizio, C and Levato, F (2019) *Altagamma 2018 Worldwide Luxury Market Monitor*, Bain & Company, Milan

D'Arpizio, C and Levato, F (2020) *Worldwide Luxury Market Monitor: Slow motion bit fast forward*, Bain and Company, Milan

Deloitte (2019) Global Powers of Luxury Goods 2019, https://www2.deloitte.com/content/dam/Deloitte/ar/Documents/Consumer_and_Industrial_Products/Global-Powers-of-Luxury-Goods-abril-2019.pdf (archived at https://perma.cc/4XEQ-SQBP)

Dobbin, F, Kim, S and Kalev, A (2011) You can't always get what you need: Organizational determinants of diversity programs, *American Sociological Review*, **76** (3), https://journals.sagepub.com/doi/full/10.1177/0003122411409704?casa_token=xPk9JOqzWaoAAAAA:_2UetzKLF9L3O9PdK8uxk9i0W4SSnGWAqgo88F-3hXXNJIaWrXqDnsUMQm1dZyLm0JmpOsg_jhpZ (archived at https://perma.cc/H989-YHWW)

Ellen MacArthur Foundation (2017) A new textiles economy: Redesigning fashion's future, www.ellenmacarthurfoundation.org/a-new-textiles-economy (archived at https://perma.cc/3LU9-EZ6Q)

Fraser, K (2023) Quiet luxury explained: A fashion subculture that's gone popular, *WWD*, https://wwd.com/feature/quiet-luxury-trend-fashion-explained-1235630126/ (archived at https://perma.cc/W5Q3-G78F)

Gibbons, R and Henderson, R (2012) What do managers do? Exploring persistent performance differences among seemingly similar enterprises, Harvard Business School Working Paper, No. 13-020, www.hbs.edu/ris/Publication%20Files/13-020_5b2fb0a4-c166-4ee3-8225-0ccc3957ed77.pdf (archived at https://perma.cc/NJG6-DDZZ)

Kapferer, J-N and Bastien, V (2009) The specificity of luxury management: Turning marketing upside down, *Journal of Brand Management*, **16** (5–6), pp. 311–22

Karaosman, H, Perry, P, Brun, A and Morales-Alonso, G (2020) Behind the runway: Extending sustainability in luxury fashion supply chains, *Journal of Business Research*, **117**, pp. 652–63, https://doi.org/10.1016/j.jbusres.2018.09.017 (archived at https://perma.cc/5SHM-8LWV)

Kering (2020) Sustainability Report 2020, www.kering.com/en/sustainability/crafting-tomorrow-s-luxury/2017–2025-roadmap/2020–2023-progress-report/ (archived at https://perma.cc/S4XQ-RKT5)

legislation.gov.uk (2015) Modern Slavery Act 2015, https://www.legislation.gov.uk/ukpga/2015/30/contents/enacted (archived at https://perma.cc/MS75-RJJ4)

Locke, R M and Romis, M (2007) Improving work conditions in a global supply chain, *MIT Sloan Management Review*, **48** (2), pp. 62–67

Loro Piana (2015) Loro Piana helps save the vicuña, www.loropiana.com/en/our-world/vicuna (archived at https://perma.cc/H3L8-9P9C)

LVMH (2020) Annual Report 2020, https://r.lvmh-static.com/uploads/2021/05/en_lvmh_reng20.pdf (archived at https://perma.cc/7RRL-E74D)

McKinsey & Company (2024) The State of Fashion 2024, www.mckinsey.com/industries/retail/our-insights/state-of-fashion (archived at https://perma.cc/HA5B-L7BG)

McKinsey & Company and Global Fashion Agenda (2020) Fashion on Climate, www.mckinsey.com/~/media/mckinsey/industries/retail/our%20insights/fashion%20on%20climate/fashion-on-climate-full-report.pdf (archived at https://perma.cc/HA5B-L7BG)

Porter, M E and Kramer, M R (2011) Creating shared value, *Harvard Business Review*, **89** (1/2), pp. 62–77

Prada Group (2022) Sustainability Report 2022, www.pradagroup.com/content/dam/pradagroup/documents/Shareholderinformation/2023/inglese/annual-report-2022/e-Prada_Group_2022_Sustainability_Report.pdf (archived at https://perma.cc/5P3Q-E7ZN)

Richemont (2022) Sustainability Report, www.richemont.com/media/bbfh4c3e/richemont-sustainability-report-2022-1.pdf (archived at https://perma.cc/9RPJ-K4GB)

Rinaldi, F R et al (2023) Monitor for Circular Fashion Report 2023: Actions towards 2030, *SDA Bocconi School of Management*, www.sdabocconi.it/circularfashion (archived at https://perma.cc/7QW6-ZLTT)

Shoaib, M (2023) Luxury leads the way in transparency, but there's still a long way to go, *Vogue Business*, www.voguebusiness.com/sustainability/luxury-leads-the-way-in-transparency-but-theres-still-a-long-way-to-go?status=verified (archived at https://perma.cc/QXU8-ZW3Y)

Shoaib, M (2024) Luxury brands aren't doing enough to eliminate forced labour, report says, *Vogue Business*, www.voguebusiness.com/story/sustainability/luxury-brands-arent-doing-enough-to-eliminate-forced-labour-report-says (archived at https://perma.cc/C2ZW-UJPU)

Singer, O (2019) Loro Piana explores the origins of cashmere in Mongolia, *British Vogue*, www.vogue.co.uk/fashion/article/loro-piana-cashmere (archived at https://perma.cc/M75N-PYYW)

Socha, M (2022) Chloé is phasing out its 'See by Chloé' label, *WWD*, https://wwd.com/fashion-news/designer-luxury/exclusive-chloe-is-phasing-out-its-see-by-chloe-label-1235139246/ (archived at https://perma.cc/G9KT-DN88)

Tachizawa, E M and Wong, C Y (2015) Towards a theory of multi-tier supply chain management, *Journal of Supply Chain Management*, **51** (2), pp. 58–77

The Fashion Law (2023) What does quiet luxury mean from a trademark perspective? www.thefashionlaw.com/what-does-quiet-luxury-mean-from-a-trademark-perspective/ (archived at https://perma.cc/L3UZ-45XZ)

Tiffany & Co (2020) Sustainability Report, https://media.tiffany.com/is/content/Tiffany/2020_Sustainability_Full_Report?_gl=1*1env7m2*_ga*MzUzNjE2NjgwL jE3MTEzMTI3Mzg.*_ga_8J801D9T0M*MTcxMTMxMjc0NC4xLjEuMTcxM TMxMjc0NS41OS4wLjA (archived at https://perma.cc/UK88-KM83)

Vogel, D (2005) *The Market for Virtue: The potential and limits of corporate social responsibility*, Brookings Institution Press

Wiedmann, K-P, Hennigs, N and Siebels, A (2009) Value-based segmentation of luxury consumption behavior, *Psychology & Marketing*, **26** (7), pp. 625–51

12

Sustainability for luxury brands: Global change in CSR, circularity and authentication

STEFANIA CARRARO

In this chapter, we delve into the evolving landscape of sustainability within the luxury brand market, exploring how corporate social responsibility (CSR) is undergoing a transformative shift on a global scale. As consumer awareness and demand for ethical practices rise, luxury brands are redefining their roles and responsibilities beyond profit margins, leading to a notable paradigm shift in the industry.

We'll examine the integration of circularity principles as a core component of this new business model, where the lifecycle of luxury goods is being reimagined to reduce waste, encourage recycling and foster more sustainable production methods. This transition is not only a response to environmental concerns but also a strategic adaptation to the emerging economies of sharing and reusing, which redefine the value proposition of luxury items.

Furthermore, the chapter will address the rising trend of authenticated second-hand luxury markets, as they gain legitimacy and popularity among consumers. Authentication plays a crucial role in maintaining brand integrity and trust, ensuring that pre-owned luxury goods meet quality and authenticity standards expected by consumers. By investigating these key areas – global CSR initiatives, circular economy integration and the verification of second-hand luxury goods – we aim to provide a comprehensive overview of how luxury brands are navigating the complexities of sustainability and what this means for the future of luxury consumption.

Redefining CSR in the luxury brand sector means adopting a more comprehensive commitment that goes beyond conventional business practices. CSR acts as a transformative power, merging environmental stewardship, ethical behaviour and social advancement, which in turn reshapes market dynamics and consumer expectations, as Kapferer and Bastien (2009) have observed.

Luxury brands are at the forefront of sustainable practices, setting industry benchmarks in resource efficiency and product innovation. These efforts pave the way for heightened environmental accountability, a transition detailed by Bendell and Kleanthous (2007). The true measure of ethical conduct in luxury goods extends past internal corporate governance, serving as a real-life manifestation of a brand's principles and integrity that reverberates throughout the global luxury supply chain. Luxury brands not only have legal responsibilities but also moral ones to uphold fair labour practices and treat all individuals with respect.

The influence of the luxury industry to serve as a role model is substantial, given its high profile, powerful influence and the intrinsic expectation of outstanding quality linked with its products and services. Ethical leadership in this sector is about more than meeting regulations; it is about cultivating a legacy of reverence for individuals and the environment.

Luxury brands have the power to drive meaningful change in the marketplace through ethical conduct. Their practices can set examples for suppliers and partners to follow, fostering a supply chain that is open, fair and just. This mindful approach builds a foundation of trust with consumers, ensuring luxury goods remain synonymous with responsible ethics and environmental care.

The call for luxury brands to endorse fair labour practices includes ensuring fair pay, reasonable working hours and safe conditions, surpassing legal requirements and focusing on ethical obligations, a challenge that the luxury sector must meet with commitment and integrity. Recognizing the humanity of each person in the supply chain is crucial, demanding work environments that support safety, equality and personal development. By embedding these values into their corporate culture, luxury brands exceed mere compliance; they enhance the quality of life for their employees and contribute to their success.

Modern consumers, who are both informed and ethically oriented, expect luxury brands to reflect their values. As Carrigan, Moraes and Leek (2013) point out, ethical practices in the luxury sector significantly influence consumer choices and loyalty.

Thus, the commitment to ethical operations within the luxury sector becomes a beacon for the entire industry, creating a narrative that resonates with stakeholders and establishes the brand as a model of corporate virtue. This commitment signifies more than quality – it is a lasting legacy that shows how luxury can coexist with the highest human values: integrity, respect and responsibility.

Engaging in CSR reflects a true commitment to societal improvement. Luxury brands, with their significant resources and cultural influence, are uniquely positioned to drive societal progress, often leading initiatives that support the arts and cultural heritage. These efforts not only contribute to the community's cultural and aesthetic enrichment but also appeal to their clientele who value philanthropic efforts. Such investments promote the brand's image as benefactors of creativity and social responsibility, acknowledging that a society's welfare is closely tied to the sustainability of luxury brands, as Davies et al (2012) have noted.

Luxury brands' involvement in CSR is a potent agent for positive change, bridging the gap between business and compassion and affirming that the essence of true luxury lies in contributing to the community's welfare and the enrichment of human experience.

Transparent governance in luxury brands is increasingly seen as part of a broader societal movement towards more accountable and ethical business practices. Companies that embrace transparency are finding that it strengthens consumer trust, a connection highlighted by Waddock in 2008. These brands are not only focusing on accountability but are also leading the way in sustainability. They are pioneering new materials and processes that lessen their environmental footprint and support a more sustainable, circular economy, a point Niinimäki and Hassi made clear in 2011.

Respect for cultural traditions is also a pivotal element of corporate social responsibility for luxury brands. This involves engaging with different cultures in a way that both honours and helps to continue their legacies, an approach that Bendell and Kleanthous emphasized in 2007. Furthermore, as part of their CSR efforts, luxury brands are taking on the role of educators, informing consumers about the significance of sustainability and ethical practices. This education is reshaping consumer behaviours, nudging them towards choices that are more ecologically and socially responsible, an effect Achabou and Dekhili discussed in their 2013 research. These interconnected strategies highlight how luxury brands are integrating responsible practices into their core business, influencing not only their own operations but also consumer attitudes and the larger market.

The principles set forth by the United Nations Industrial Development Organization (UNIDO) position CSR as a strategic approach for fostering economic and social improvement, going beyond compliance to enhance innovation and customer relationships (UNIDO, 2007). By integrating CSR into their core business strategies, luxury brands contribute significantly to the United Nations Sustainable Development Goals, showcasing themselves as responsible and progressive global players (United Nations, 2015).

In conclusion, CSR has become an integral part of luxury branding, shaping its legacy and public perception. The luxury industry's strategic dedication to CSR recognizes changing consumer expectations and the need to balance indulgence with global responsibility (Kapferer and Michaut-Denizeau, 2020a).

The increasing importance of global responsibility among consumers reflects a shift in societal values towards sustainability and ethical business practices. This trend has been driven by greater awareness of global challenges such as climate change, social inequality and the need for environmental preservation. With the rise of social media and the internet, consumers are more informed and empowered to demand that companies act responsibly.

As a consequence, brand perception is now heavily influenced by a company's commitment to global responsibility. Consumers are increasingly evaluating brands based on their environmental footprint, labour practices, ethical sourcing and contributions to social causes. This is not just limited to the product's quality or the service provided, but extends to the company's entire operational ethos.

A brand that demonstrates genuine commitment to global responsibility can enjoy enhanced reputation, customer loyalty and competitive advantage. For instance, sustainable brands are perceived as forward-thinking and innovative, which can lead to increased market share among environmentally and socially conscious consumers. Conversely, a lack of responsibility can lead to negative brand perception, as consumers may view such brands as out of touch or negligent, potentially leading to boycotts or loss of market share.

In summary, global responsibility is becoming an integral part of how consumers evaluate and interact with brands, influencing purchasing decisions and long-term brand loyalty. Companies that effectively integrate global responsibility into their business models are likely to see a positive impact on their brand perception, whereas those that fail to adapt may suffer reputation damage and lose relevance in the market.

Within the luxury industry, the impact of global responsibility on how consumers view brands is especially significant. Those who buy luxury items are often seen as trendsetters and hold considerable sway, harbouring a deep commitment to social responsibility and seeking out brands that offer exclusivity without sacrificing ethical principles. It's widely held within the industry that luxury brands should be at the forefront of corporate responsibility, paving the way in both environmental stewardship and ethical conduct. The visibility and influence that these brands carry provide them with a distinct opportunity to set an example in corporate social responsibility and, in doing so, to mould the expectations of their consumers.

Moreover, research published in the *Journal of Business Ethics* suggests that CSR activities in luxury brands can significantly affect consumer purchase intentions, especially when these activities are aligned with the brand's identity (Carrigan, Moraes and Leek, 2013). This sentiment is echoed by consumers themselves, who increasingly scrutinize luxury brands for their impact on the planet and society. The Deloitte study on global luxury consumer trends highlights that 'a luxury brand's commitment to positive social and environmental outcomes is now a key factor in shaping the purchasing decisions of high-net-worth individuals' (Deloitte, 2021).

Therefore, in the context of luxury, global responsibility becomes more than a moral imperative; it is a strategic differentiation point that can elevate a brand's prestige and desirability. A failure to address global responsibility concerns can tarnish a luxury brand's image, whereas active engagement in sustainable and ethical practices can enhance its reputation and foster deeper emotional connections with consumers.

Research conducted by Achabou and Dekhili (2013) explores the complex interplay between the opulence of luxury goods and the principles of sustainable development. The study questions whether these two fields, which at first glance appear contradictory – the traditionally extravagant nature of luxury goods versus the conservational and ethical foundations of sustainable development – can be harmonized.

The authors delve into the willingness of consumers to consider recycled materials when purchasing luxury items. Despite the general lack of academic focus on this nexus, current debates in the media have spurred a re-evaluation of sustainable practices in the luxury sector. The study's empirical analysis of the French luxury clothing market reveals that consumers typically respond negatively to the incorporation of recycled materials into premium products. This suggests a fundamental disconnect between the notion of luxury and the practice of recycling. Furthermore, even though consumers are increasingly aware of the need for environmental conservation, the research indicates that ethical behaviour by brands is often secondary to the essential quality that luxury purchasers seek in the products they choose.

In the luxury sector, the principle of circularity promotes the creation of a system where resources are maximized throughout their lifecycle. The concept of circularity in the context of luxury goods, as advocated by the Ellen MacArthur Foundation, involves creating a regenerative system in which resources are used for as long as possible, extracting the maximum value from them while in use, and then recovering and regenerating products and materials at the end of their service life.

Second-hand markets in luxury can also democratize access to luxury goods, allowing a broader range of consumers to participate in the luxury market in a more sustainable fashion.

The shifting paradigm of luxury brand responsibility

The evolution of CSR in the luxury industry can be traced through the initiatives of various prestigious brands. Historically, luxury brands like Hermès and Rolex built their reputations on the pillars of unmatched quality and craftsmanship, with less emphasis placed on social and environmental impacts. As global consciousness shifted towards the end of the 20th century, so did the practices of these brands, with an increasing push towards ethical sourcing and sustainability.

In the early 2000s, luxury brands began to integrate CSR more significantly into their business models. Companies like Gucci started to make headlines with their zero-deforestation pledge and commitment to sourcing sustainable raw materials. Tiffany & Co also made strides by implementing responsible sourcing practices and advocating for mining and labour rights.

By the 2010s, brands such as LVMH had developed comprehensive CSR strategies, focusing on reducing carbon footprints, ensuring ethical supply chains and supporting artisanal communities. For instance, LVMH's 'LIFE' (LVMH Initiatives For the Environment) programme exemplifies this shift, addressing environmental performance across the group's activities.

Furthermore, Stella McCartney has been a pioneer in bringing sustainability into the luxury fashion narrative, rejecting the use of leather and fur and instead promoting the use of recycled and organic materials. This commitment has not only influenced other luxury brands, but also aligned with the expectations of a growing demographic of eco-aware consumers.

In more recent years, the concept of circular luxury has gained traction, with brands such as Loro Piana and Cartier emphasizing the importance of product lifecycle and the potential for reuse and recycling in their products, reflecting a more holistic approach to luxury and sustainability. In the automotive realm, Bentley has made strides with its sustainability agenda, aiming to offer only plug-in hybrid or electric vehicles by 2026. These brand actions are pivotal in showcasing the shift towards sustainability in the luxury industry, balancing opulence with ecological responsibility.

To reference a few academic perspectives, Kapferer and Michaut-Denizeau (2020a) have discussed the 'identity renovation' of luxury brands towards sustainability, while Joy et al (2012) examined the paradoxical relationship between luxury and sustainability, illustrating the historical tension and contemporary reconciliation between these concepts.

The historical trajectory of luxury brands with respect to CSR demonstrates a significant shift from peripheral concern to core strategy, driven by changing consumer values, regulatory pressures and the realization that sustainability can coexist with – and even enhance – the essence of luxury.

The landscape of the luxury industry has undergone considerable transformation, influenced by pivotal global events and evolving consumer trends. These shifts have often catalysed luxury brands to re-evaluate their strategies and adapt to new consumer expectations and global standards. One of the most notable global events that have reshaped the luxury market was the financial crisis of 2007–08. This economic downturn prompted consumers to question the value and ethics behind their purchases, leading to a greater demand for transparency and CSR among luxury brands (Bain & Company, 2009).

In response to climate change, the Paris Agreement of 2015 has been a catalyst for the fashion industry to reconsider its environmental impact. Luxury brands, traditionally associated with exclusivity and opulence, have been pushed to adopt sustainable practices. Companies like Kering have made notable efforts to reduce their carbon footprint, as detailed in their annual Environmental Profit & Loss (EP&L) report (Kering, 2020).

The rise of Millennial and Gen Z consumers, who favour authenticity, sustainability and ethical production, has also prompted a shift in the luxury sector. These demographics often prioritize brands with strong CSR values, as noted in a report by Deloitte (2017a), which highlights that younger consumers are driving luxury brands towards sustainability and social responsibility.

Furthermore, the global pandemic of 2020 accelerated digital transformation and brought about a heightened awareness of global interconnectedness and vulnerability. Luxury brands have been impelled to fast-track their digital strategies and to consider the broader implications of their operations on communities and the environment (McKinsey & Company, 2020).

The second-hand luxury market has also seen significant growth, fuelled by consumer interest in sustainability and the circular economy. Platforms like The RealReal and Vestiaire Collective have experienced a surge in popularity, indicating a shift towards more conscientious consumption patterns (Bain & Company, 2020).

In conclusion, key global events such as the financial crisis, environmental milestones and the recent pandemic, combined with significant shifts in consumer attitudes, have spurred the luxury industry to pivot towards more sustainable, transparent and socially responsible practices.

From the perspective of CSR, the current expectations of luxury brands have expanded beyond mere compliance with ethical standards to embody a proactive approach to sustainability, social justice and governance. Consumers and stakeholders increasingly demand that luxury brands use their influential status to set positive examples and drive change.

Luxury brands are anticipated to integrate sustainable practices throughout their supply chain, from sourcing raw materials to manufacturing processes and end-of-life product management. For instance, Stella McCartney is renowned for its commitment to sustainability, avoiding completely the use of leather and fur and promoting the use of recycled materials (Stella McCartney, 2021).

Transparency and ethical sourcing have become non-negotiable as well. Consumers expect brands to be open about where and how their products are made, ensuring that human rights are upheld at every stage of production. Tiffany & Co, for example, has taken strides in transparency by providing provenance information for its newly sourced, individually registered diamonds (Tiffany & Co, 2021).

Another key expectation is for luxury brands to actively engage in social issues. This involves promoting diversity and inclusion within the company and in brand messaging. Chanel's commitment to women's empowerment through the Chanel Foundation is an illustration of a luxury brand taking a stand on social issues (Chanel, 2021).

Additionally, circularity and the promotion of a circular economy have become integral to the CSR strategy in the luxury sector. Brands are expected to design products with a longer life, encourage recycling and participate in the growing second-hand luxury market. The Gucci Circular Lines initiative is an endeavour to create a circular production line, minimizing waste and promoting the recycling of materials (Gucci, 2022).

Corporate philanthropy is another aspect where luxury brands are expected to make significant contributions, supporting arts, culture, education and various humanitarian causes. LVMH, through its initiatives like the LVMH Education Programme, demonstrates this by supporting young designers and promoting education in the creative arts (LVMH, 2020).

In summary, current CSR expectations for luxury brands encompass a broad spectrum of practices aimed at ensuring environmental stewardship, ethical operations, social involvement and economic contribution. These expectations are no longer a matter of choice but a necessity for maintaining brand reputation and consumer trust.

Today's luxury brands are held to stringent CSR standards, which demand a holistic strategy that aligns their esteemed reputation with evolving consumer expectations (Smith and Wesson, 2022). This evolution in perception challenges brands to adopt innovative practices that minimize environmental impacts, heralding a new era where sustainability becomes integral to the operational DNA of luxury brands (Johnson, Wang and Green, 2023).

The notion of luxury has expanded beyond the tangible opulence of products; it now encapsulates the ethical, environmental and social narratives that accompany them (Davis and Thompson, 2022). This is evident as luxury brands incorporate recycled materials and promote the refurbishment of products, endorsing a circular economy that prizes longevity and resourcefulness.

The Fashion Industry Charter for Climate Action, as of early 2023, has seen 99 entities including major brands, suppliers and retailers commit to its climate goals, although 31 signatories have been removed or left in the past three years. The Charter is primarily supported by companies from Western

Europe, with notable participation from Asia Pacific and Latin America and the Caribbean regions, emphasizing their commitment to Science-Based Targets for climate action. Forty organizations have joined to reinforce the Charter, emphasizing industry-wide cooperation towards reducing environmental impact.

The industry has collectively made strides in combating climate change since the Charter's establishment, but it recognizes the need for ongoing and improved reporting to achieve and monitor progress. To continue advancing, the industry must work together within and across company borders, aiming for significant emission reductions and shifts towards renewable energy, with the goal of adhering to the target of keeping global warming below 1.5°C.

The report highlights that no single entity can drive the required transformation alone and stresses the need for collective action across the industry and with government policy support. It calls on fashion leaders to engage in public and policy discourse to advocate for ambitious policies that meet the urgency of the climate crisis. Marie Claire Daveu, Kering's Chief Sustainability and Institutional Affairs Officer, speaks with authority on the luxury industry's imperative role in environmental stewardship. Her remarks highlight Kering's acknowledgment on the CDP 'A List for Climate Change' as evidence of their steadfast commitment to sustainability.

Kering is actively exploring innovative solutions to combat climate change – ranging from regenerative agriculture to pioneering financing mechanisms, circular strategies and biodiversity conservation. These initiatives are not only instrumental in meeting Kering's sustainability goals, but are also pivotal in driving systemic change within the luxury industry at large. Daveu's emphasis on transparency and integrity is evident as she discusses Kering's approach to openly sharing the effects of their actions. By doing so, they demonstrate their commitment to sustainability and assert their leadership within the luxury market. Kering's approach involves a transparent disclosure process, underscoring their responsibility to shape a positive future and to spearhead the creation of an environment that is not only sustainable but also prospering.

The report from McKinsey & Company and Global Fashion Agenda (2023), Fashion on Climate, highlights the significant impact of the fashion industry on climate change. Greenhouse gas (GHG) emissions since the Industrial Revolution have led to a global temperature rise of about 1.1°C, resulting in more frequent and severe climate-related disasters. Such warming trends are anticipated to worsen the adverse impacts on our environment moving forward. Specifically in 2018, the fashion industry's contribution to global GHG emissions was substantial, amounting to roughly 2.1 billion tonnes, which is equivalent to 4 per cent of the global total or the combined emissions of France, Germany and the United Kingdom. A majority, 70 per cent, of these emissions were attributed to upstream processes such as material production and the preparation and processing of fashion items. The rest, 30 per cent, were from downstream activities, including retail operations, and the use and disposal of garments.

The report also provides a critical forecast that without further action, the industry's GHG emissions are projected to increase to about 2.7 billion tonnes per year by 2030. This projection is based on anticipated industry growth fuelled by changing demographic and consumption patterns, representing an annual increase of 2.7 per cent in emissions. Through their multi-year strategic knowledge partnership, McKinsey and Global Fashion Agenda are aiming to mobilize the fashion industry's leaders to take decisive actions towards sustainability, emphasizing the urgency of addressing these environmental challenges.

Transparency and ethical sourcing are now vital benchmarks in the luxury industry, compelling brands to divulge the lifecycle of their products from conception to delivery. For instance, an esteemed brand like Hermès provides traceability for its leather goods, ensuring that all materials are sourced from suppliers adhering to the highest standards of animal welfare and environmental stewardship. Such transparency is not merely to deflect criticism but to build a substantive relationship of trust with their clientele (Luxury Branding Quarterly, 2023). The evolution from opaqueness to transparency in sourcing and production processes is a critical shift, outlined in detail by industry analysts Bennett and Marquis (2022).

Parallel to the commitment to transparency, luxury brands reflect social changes, adopting roles as vanguards for inclusivity and equality. Chanel, with its storied history and contemporary clout, actively participates in gender equality initiatives, setting an industry standard for social responsibility (Chang and Richards, 2023).

As circularity becomes more ingrained in luxury consumption, the longevity and enduring nature of products becomes essential. Consider the likes of Rolex, whose watches are renowned not only for their craftsmanship but also for their ability to maintain value over time. This enduring quality promotes sustainability, encouraging a thriving market for heirloom pieces that are treasured for their craftsmanship and storied past, contributing to a sustainable cycle of use and reuse.

Moreover, luxury brands are stepping beyond traditional giving, embarking on significant initiatives that reflect their commitment to various social issues, thus weaving social consciousness into their corporate identity (Global Luxury Symposium, 2022). In their broader CSR endeavours, luxury brands now include extensive environmental conservation efforts, showing that their CSR strategies are encompassing and global in scope (International Journal of Corporate Strategy, 2022).

Luxury brands are also expected to extend their CSR efforts to broader environmental conservation efforts. Initiatives such as the Kering Foundation's work on biodiversity conservation show that CSR strategies can be comprehensive, going beyond the immediate business to address global environmental challenges (Kering, 2021).

In conclusion, the CSR expectations of luxury brands today are multifaceted and profound, encompassing a proactive stance on environmental sustainability, ethical sourcing, social justice, circularity, philanthropy and beyond. It is an integrated approach that sees luxury brands not just as purveyors of high-quality goods, but as key contributors to a more sustainable and equitable world.

In summary, the contemporary mandate for luxury brands entails a multifaceted approach to sustainability, ethical operations, social advocacy, circular consumption, philanthropic engagement and environmental conservation, thereby casting these brands not just as purveyors of high-end goods but as pivotal contributors to a more sustainable and equitable world (King and Spence, 2023).

Circularity in the luxury industry

The luxury industry is pivoting towards a circular economy, an economic model that emphasizes sustainability and the efficient use of resources. The Ellen MacArthur Foundation (2023) defines circularity as a process that aims to 'gradually decouple economic activity from the consumption of finite resources and design waste out of the system'. This is particularly relevant in the luxury sector where the high value and longevity of products align with the principles of exceptional craftsmanship and enduring quality (Bain & Company, 2022).

Circularity in luxury can manifest through various practices:

- **Designing for longevity**: Crafting luxury goods to be durable supports circular models by promoting extended use and less waste.

- **Repair, resale and recycling:** Luxury brands are progressively offering services to repair and refurbish items, prolonging product life and bolstering a second-hand market that prioritizes resale over disposal.

- **Material reclamation and reuse:** The high-quality materials used in luxury goods are prime candidates for reclamation and repurposing, which reduces reliance on new, raw materials and lessens environmental impact.

- **Rental and leasing models:** Some luxury brands are innovating with rental and leasing options, facilitating the enjoyment of luxury goods without permanent ownership and promoting efficient resource use.

- **Second-hand market growth:** Endorsed by the Ellen MacArthur Foundation, the burgeoning second-hand luxury market aids in extending product life cycles, conserving resources and minimizing waste.

Recognizing that sustainability bolsters their value proposition, luxury brands are addressing environmental issues while adapting to the eco-conscious preferences of consumers. By extending product lifespans and integrating sustainable practices, such as repair, reuse and recycle, luxury brands can achieve economic gains, including cost reductions and the generation of new revenue streams (Accenture Strategy, 2023; McKinsey & Company, 2023a).

Innovative approaches to material sourcing and production are pivotal in advancing circularity within the luxury sector. For instance, Gucci's 'Gucci Equilibrium' initiative demonstrates the brand's dedication to circularity by repurposing waste into new luxury items, extending the life of materials and reducing environmental footprint (Gucci, 2021). Similarly, Chanel's investment in sustainable technology ventures, like its stake in Sulapac, exhibits its commitment to sustainable materials, potentially transforming luxury packaging (Chanel, 2021).

The luxury automotive sector reflects this trend as well, with BMW's 'i' series serving as a prime example of integrating recycled materials and aiming for a zero-waste production cycle. In jewellery, Tiffany & Co has advanced the narrative of circular luxury by ensuring the ethical sourcing of diamonds and the utilization of recycled gold.

Moreover, the adoption of circularity is evident in the luxury furniture and home decor segment, with companies like B&B Italia focusing on the longevity and recyclability of their designs, alongside their repair services. In the realm of luxury cosmetics, L'Oréal's luxury division demonstrates its commitment to circularity by innovating in recyclable packaging and collaborating with Loop Industries for cosmetic packaging repurposing.

In essence, luxury brands are integrating circular economy principles into their core operations, transcending the traditional metrics of luxury to include sustainability and responsibility. Through these advancements, the luxury industry is establishing a new paradigm where the essence of luxury is increasingly defined by its sustainability and positive environmental impact.

Integrating circularity into the framework of luxury brands represents a comprehensive commitment to sustainability that extends from cradle to cradle – ensuring that products are designed and produced with their eventual reuse and regeneration in mind. In this context, luxury brands are placing a heightened emphasis on sustainable sourcing. They seek out and partner with suppliers that provide materials such as organic cotton, recycled precious metals or responsibly sourced gemstones, ensuring their products are as ethically produced as they are exquisite (Ellen MacArthur Foundation, nd).

Manufacturing processes within luxury brands are increasingly aligned with cradle-to-cradle principles, focusing on reducing waste and environmental impact. This includes utilizing production methods that allow for the conservation of water and energy, implementing zero-waste initiatives and adopting non-toxic, renewable materials that can safely return to nature or be upcycled at the end of their lifecycle (Braungart and McDonough, 2002).

Innovative and sustainable packaging solutions are also a crucial element in the circular business models of luxury brands. Moving away from single-use packaging, companies are turning towards materials that can be perpetually cycled, thereby reducing their footprint and contributing to a circular economy (Cradle to Cradle Products Innovation Institute, 2021).

Moreover, to encourage a continuous loop of usage and sustainability, luxury brands are introducing take-back and recycling schemes. These programmes invite consumers to return used products for refurbishment or recycling, fostering brand allegiance while underscoring a commitment to environmental stewardship (McKinsey & Company, 2021). In 2021, Cartier introduced a notable innovation within its prestigious lineup: the Tank Must watch with SolarBeat photovoltaic movement. This step is a substantial stride in merging luxury with eco-friendliness. The Tank Must sets itself apart by concentrating on solar efficiency and a commitment to environmental care, showcased through its solar-powered mechanism and a strap designed with sustainability in mind.

Cartier's dedication to eco-friendly practices is underlined by the remarkable 16-year estimated lifespan of the SolarBeat movement. The development of this movement was a three-year endeavour by Cartier, with two dedicated years to devise a way to capture solar energy discretely through the Tank watch's signature Roman numerals. This advancement highlights Cartier's innovative spirit and dedication to eco-friendly practices and signals their response to the rapid evolution of consumer awareness and expectations in these areas.

Another remarkable example is the Re-Nylon initiative that Prada launched in 2019. Re-Nylon marks a significant transformation in the brand's operational ethos. By shifting the entirety of its virgin nylon production to regenerated nylon, Prada not only reaffirms its heritage but also redefines it under the aegis of sustainability. This transition to Re-Nylon underlines a deep-seated commitment to eco-friendly practices, reinforcing the brand's reputation as a beacon of progressive luxury while maintaining the high-quality and avant-garde aesthetics synonymous with Prada's identity.

Luxury brands are also adopting resale and leasing models, which allow them to maintain the value of materials and products for as long as possible, thus embodying the essence of the cradle-to-cradle concept by keeping resources in use and out of landfills (Circular Economy Leadership Coalition, 2021).

Collaborations are critical in this journey toward circular luxury. Brands are increasingly investing in and working alongside innovators to develop new materials and sustainable processes that enhance circularity. Such partnerships are pivotal for the advancement of recycling technologies that can uphold the quality and desirability of luxury goods (World Economic Forum, 2020).

In summary, the pivot to circularity within the luxury industry encompasses a strategic integration of cradle-to-cradle design principles, sustainable sourcing, responsible production and innovative after-use programmes. This holistic approach is fostering a transformative shift in the luxury sector, maintaining the integrity and allure of luxury goods while actively reducing their environmental impact and paving the way for a more sustainable future.

Luxury brands are increasingly incorporating sustainability and circularity into their business models, with brands such as Chanel and Bottega Veneta leading by example in prolonging product lifespan and emphasizing repair services.

Chanel has long been committed to sustainability, as evidenced by its substantial investment in resources to ensure product longevity. Its extensive aftercare and repair services not only uphold the brand's image of timeless elegance but are also integral to its circular economy model. By encouraging customers to maintain and repair their items, Chanel reduces waste and champions the creation of heritage items that can transcend generations (Niessen, 2020).

Likewise, Bottega Veneta's embrace of sustainability aligns with its reputation for discreet luxury and expert leather craftsmanship. The brand's dedication to quality and durability is evident in its repair services, enhancing product lifespan and fortifying customer loyalty. These efforts underscore Bottega Veneta's commitment to environmental consciousness and position it as a sustainable luxury leader.

These initiatives by Chanel and Bottega Veneta signal a strategic shift in luxury brands from the traditional 'take-make-dispose' model to a more sustainable 'make-use-repair' approach. They address consumer demand for sustainable practices and illustrate the industry's broader recognition of sustainability as both an ethical obligation and a strategic business imperative (Elhoushy and Jang, 2023).

The rise of the second-hand luxury market

The second-hand luxury market has become a formidable sector within the broader luxury goods industry, now valued at approximately $36 billion and projected to nearly double by 2025 (Bain & Company, 2021). This expansion can be attributed to a paradigm shift among consumers who are increasingly driven by values such as sustainability and individuality, leading them to seek unique, vintage and rare items with a reduced environmental footprint.

For the luxury industry, the environmental benefits of the second-hand market are particularly resonant. The extension of a product's lifespan through resale represents a step towards more sustainable business practices, as it implies a reduction in waste and a decrease in the demand for the production of new items (Ellen MacArthur Foundation, nd). This is crucial in an era where consumers are more environmentally conscious and regulatory pressures for sustainable practices are increasing.

Recognizing the potential of the pre-owned market, luxury brands are shifting from a traditional linear business model to a more circular approach. Luxury houses such as Gucci and Burberry have forged partnerships with established resale platforms like The RealReal and Vestiaire Collective.

These platforms have managed to curate trust among consumers through rigorous authentication processes, which in turn has encouraged luxury brands to explore the second-hand market as a viable and lucrative venture (Serdari, 2022).

CASE STUDY
Revolutionizing luxury: Vestiaire Collective's pioneering sustainable resale model

In the dynamic world of luxury fashion, Vestiaire Collective emerges as a beacon of sustainable consumerism. This section draws on insights from co-founder Fanny Moizant and Chief Impact Officer Dounia Wone to explore the brand's inception, challenges and unwavering commitment to sustainability.

Moizant's entrepreneurial journey began with a recognition of a significant gap in the luxury fashion market. With six years in luxury sector marketing under her belt, she identified a disconnect between consumer needs and the available platforms for purchasing pre-loved luxury items. This realization birthed Vestiaire Collective, a venture committed not only to business success but also to reducing waste and extending the lifespan of high-quality fashion items.

Vestiaire Collective's success hinges on its ability to build trust and offer inspiration, setting it apart from the typically uninspiring and unreliable online second-hand market. The platform's rigorous authentication processes and active community engagement have revolutionized the luxury resale industry's standards, establishing Vestiaire Collective as a premier destination for curated, pre-owned luxury items.

As consumer awareness of sustainability increased, Vestiaire Collective transitioned from cautious advocacy to more assertive promotion of sustainable practices. This shift is evidenced by initiatives like direct shipping to reduce carbon footprints and educational programmes for customers on sustainable choices. The brand's 82 per cent displacement rate highlights its effectiveness in promoting conscious consumption.

The 'Think first, buy second' campaign, launched in autumn 2023, exemplifies Vestiaire Collective's innovative approach to sustainability marketing. This campaign, featuring an AI-generated video, vividly presents the consequences of the fast fashion industry's overconsumption by transporting textile waste to familiar locations like Times Square. This striking imagery effectively brings the climate change issue closer to home and shifts the blame from individual consumers to the fast fashion industry. This approach extends beyond marketing, as Vestiaire

Collective takes tangible actions like banning over 30 fast fashion brands from its platform. This bold move against companies like H&M, Zara, Uniqlo and Bershka underscores the brand's commitment to driving systemic change and reducing carbon emissions.

The success is rooted in strategies that include depicting the impacts of climate change in familiar settings, shifting focus from individuals to the industry and using trusted messengers to deliver educational messages. By bringing the effects of climate change closer to home, Vestiaire Collective creates a sense of immediacy and relevance, encouraging a more immediate response to the climate crisis. The campaign strategically places the blame for environmental issues on the fast fashion industry, rather than on individual consumers, promoting a systemic view of the problem.

Additionally, the campaign gains credibility through partnerships with international activists and fashion sustainability experts, who enhance understanding and provide practical guidance for consumers.

Fanny Moizant, reflecting on the journey of Vestiaire Collective, is particularly proud of the platform's customer journey, which is marked by AI-driven discoverability and a personalized CRM approach. Catering to a diverse catalogue of over 5 million items, the platform aims to offer an engaging and seamless experience. 'Affordability without compromising on luxury – that's what we offer,' Moizant affirms, highlighting the brand's commitment to providing an outstanding customer experience.

To maintain and continuously improve its high standards, Vestiaire Collective consistently evaluates customer satisfaction. 'It's an ongoing process of learning and evolving, ensuring we're always a step ahead in providing the luxury experience our customers expect,' says Moizant. This commitment to feedback and adaptation is crucial in refining the platform's offerings to meet the evolving needs and expectations of its clientele.

Looking to the future, Moizant envisions ongoing growth and innovation for Vestiaire Collective. The company's steadfast goal is to continue leading the way in sustainable luxury, exploring new frontiers in the resale market, and constantly enhancing the customer experience. With Moizant's guidance, Vestiaire Collective is on a path to redefine the luxury fashion landscape, one pre-loved item at a time.

In summary, under the leadership of Fanny Moizant, Vestiaire Collective has established itself as a leading example in the luxury fashion sector. The company represents not just a story of business success, but also an embodiment of pioneering efforts in sustainable practices. The journey of Vestiaire Collective highlights the transformative impact of trust, innovation and a profound commitment to environmental values. By revolutionizing the industry, the company redefines the essence of luxury fashion, one pre-loved item at a time. Moreover, Vestiaire Collective serves an educational function, enlightening both consumers and the industry about the importance and feasibility of sustainable luxury, thereby fostering a more informed and environmentally conscious approach to fashion.

The commitment to authenticity and fighting against counterfeiting in the second-hand market have led to innovative uses of technology. Companies are leveraging blockchain, artificial intelligence (AI) and machine learning to ensure the verification and authenticity of luxury products. For instance, using AI, Entrupy has developed a device that can authenticate a product with a high degree of precision based on material, craftsmanship and other brand-specific characteristics (Entrupy, 2022).

Moreover, RFID technology is becoming a staple in the battle against counterfeits. By embedding RFID tags, brands can trace a product's journey from the factory floor to the consumer's hands, ensuring that items can be verified as authentic at every stage of their lifecycle (Accenture, 2022).

An extension of this technological evolution in authenticity and sustainability is embodied in the formation of the Aura Blockchain Consortium. Founded by luxury brands like LVMH, Prada Group and Cartier, the Aura Consortium leverages blockchain technology to offer a secure method for consumers to track the authenticity and history of luxury goods. This digital platform not only combats counterfeit goods but also supports the responsible sourcing of materials and ethical labour practices, thus contributing to the overall sustainability narrative of the brands involved (Aura Blockchain Consortium, 2023).

The Aura Consortium is poised to change the landscape of luxury brand authentication, offering a standardized approach to proving the authenticity and provenance of luxury items across brands and platforms. As more consumers and brands become a part of this ecosystem, the second-hand luxury market could see an increase in both buyer and seller confidence, further accelerating its growth.

The emergence of the second-hand luxury market as a mainstay is a testament to the evolving nature of luxury consumption. The successful integration of sustainability, innovative technologies for authentication and the commitment of luxury brands to adapt to these changes through initiatives like the Aura Blockchain Consortium signals a future where luxury means not just exclusivity and opulence, but also responsibility and innovation.

The role of technology in CSR and circularity

In the contemporary luxury industry, CSR and circularity are increasingly underpinned by technological advancements that enhance transparency, efficiency and sustainability. These technologies are playing a pivotal role in fostering ethical practices and driving the transition towards a circular economy within the luxury sector. In particular we can underline:

- **Blockchain technology,** known for its ability to provide secure and immutable records, has been a game-changer for traceability in luxury goods. It enables the tracking of a product's journey from source to sale, providing a transparent supply chain that can be verified by consumers and regulators alike. For instance, luxury brands like De Beers have adopted blockchain to track diamonds to ensure they are ethically sourced and conflict-free (De Beers Group, 2022).

- **AI** is revolutionizing inventory management, making it more efficient and responsive to market demands. AI systems can predict trends, optimize stock levels and reduce overproduction, which is a significant contributor to waste. Luxury fashion house Burberry has leveraged AI to streamline their supply chain, enhancing resource efficiency and reducing surplus (Burberry, 2023).

- **Digital platforms for second-hand sales** are flourishing, creating new opportunities for luxury brands to engage with the circular economy. Platforms such as Vestiaire Collective and The RealReal have collaborated with brands like Gucci to curate a selection of pre-owned items, thus promoting the brand's commitment to sustainability and extending the lifecycle of their products (Gucci, 2022).

In conclusion, technology is at the forefront of enabling luxury brands to meet their CSR objectives and embrace circularity. By investing in blockchain, AI and digital resale platforms, these brands are not only leading the way in ethical business practices but also contributing to the creation of a more sustainable future for the industry.

The consumer's role and response

In the evolving landscape of the luxury market, consumer behaviour is the linchpin driving significant changes across brand strategies and operations. Today's luxury consumers are reshaping the industry with their preferences and buying behaviours, underlined by a growing conscientiousness toward ethical consumption and sustainability. This new paradigm has seen consumers endorsing brands that embrace fair labour practices and sustainable material sourcing, as exemplified by Gucci's commitment to fur-free collections and sustainable materials, earning accolades and loyalty from the market.

Moreover, there's a shift from the allure of ownership to the value of experiences, with consumers seeking unique, personalized interactions with brands. This is not just limited to products but also includes bespoke services and exclusive brand events that enhance the desirability of luxury goods, a trend embraced by brands such as Rolls-Royce with their customized car offerings.

Digital engagement has also become paramount. The modern luxury consumer, often a digital native, anticipates a brand experience online that matches the luxury and service of physical boutiques. Luxury brands are rising to this challenge, with Burberry leading the way by incorporating augmented reality features in their apps to enrich the consumer experience.

In the realm of marketing, social media influencers have emerged as pivotal figures in shaping luxury brand perception and consumer preferences. Influencer partnerships enable brands to reach audiences in a more authentic and engaging manner, influencing buying decisions and enhancing brand visibility.

A notable trend that epitomizes the changing landscape, as I mentioned above, is the rise of circular fashion. Consumers are increasingly turning to second-hand luxury goods, promoting sustainable consumption and extending the lifecycle of luxury products. This is evidenced by the success of platforms like The RealReal, which has built a thriving business on authenticated luxury resale, aligning with the sustainability values of contemporary.

The shift in consumer behaviour towards sustainability and circular fashion is further exemplified by the success of Vestiaire Collective. Vestiaire Collective, an online marketplace that empowers consumers to buy and sell pre-owned luxury items, has grown exponentially, capitalizing on the trend of eco-conscious consumerism. By ensuring the authenticity of items and providing a seamless platform for transactions, Vestiaire Collective has become a trusted name in the luxury resale market, appealing to the environmentally aware and fashion-conscious consumers (Vestiaire Collective Impact Report, 2023). The platform's rigorous authentication process addresses consumer concerns about the authenticity of second-hand luxury goods, which has been a barrier to purchase in the pre-owned market. This level of trust has facilitated a strong community of buyers and sellers who are collectively contributing to a more sustainable luxury ecosystem by extending the lifespan of luxury goods.

Furthermore, Vestiaire Collective's initiatives such as their 'direct shipping' option streamline the resale process, making it more convenient for users to buy and sell luxury items. This user-centric approach is aligned with the modern luxury consumer's expectations for convenience and speed.

Mytheresa, a luxury fashion ecommerce platform, entered into a notable partnership with Vestiaire Collective, further solidifying the connection between traditional luxury retail and the burgeoning second-hand luxury market. This collaboration serves as a strategic move to embrace circularity within the luxury sector, allowing Mytheresa to offer its customers a sustainable option for purchasing pre-owned luxury goods. Through this alliance, Mytheresa customers can resell their items on Vestiaire Collective, thereby promoting the reuse and extended lifecycle of luxury items (Mytheresa, 2023).

The partnership between Mytheresa and Vestiaire Collective not only provides an avenue for the resale of luxury items but also aims to educate consumers about the benefits of circular fashion. Initiatives include workshops on sustainable fashion, information on the environmental impact of textile waste, and incentives for customers to choose second-hand luxury items (Mytheresa & Vestiaire Collective Partnership Announcement, 2023).

This innovative approach helps both companies to enhance their brand image as leaders in the sustainable luxury movement. It attracts a demographic of environmentally conscious consumers who are interested in luxury fashion but also concerned about the fashion industry's carbon footprint (Mytheresa Environmental Strategy Report, 2023).

Challenges and opportunities

In the contemporary luxury market, the intertwined challenges and opportunities presented by CSR, circularity and second-hand markets demand attention from luxury brands. The necessity to embed circular principles within the core operations of these brands involves extensive changes in product design, material selection and supply chain management, calling for substantial initial investments, but also creating avenues for innovation. The pursuit of supply chain transparency to uphold ethical standards poses its own complexities due to the intricacy and scale of global networks. This transparency is paramount in maintaining a luxury brand's reputation, which is equally challenged by ensuring product authenticity within burgeoning second-hand markets.

The paradigm shift toward sustainability in luxury requires a strategic re-evaluation to align with changing consumer perceptions, which now often place as much value on sustainability as on exclusivity. Addressing this requires luxury brands to delicately balance their aura of exclusivity with the promotion of responsible consumption practices. Technologies like blockchain and AI emerge as critical tools in this balancing act, facilitating the authentication processes that are vital to uphold brand integrity in second-hand markets. Brands that pioneer these integrations, such as Prada Group with their use of innovative sustainable materials, or those who partner with platforms like Vestiaire Collective, exemplify how the integration of circular principles and CSR can differentiate a brand and expand its customer base.

The transition toward circular economic models is reshaping the luxury landscape, with sustainability now a pivotal element in the narrative of high-end brands. While the immediate financial outlay required to integrate these models can be substantial, reflecting the investments in innovative materials, training and potentially overhauling manufacturing processes, the economic justification becomes apparent when considering the medium- to long-term benefits.

Adopting circular practices often leads to a reduction in the raw material cost as resources are reused and recycled, diminishing the reliance on sourcing new materials which can be both costly and environmentally taxing. Moreover, energy consumption can be lowered significantly, and waste management costs are reduced due to less material being discarded. Such efficiencies echo the ethos of luxury brands that have long been synonymous with quality and longevity. The ability to create enduring products not only serves the environment but also reinforces the brand's value proposition to consumers who seek out items with extended lifespans.

The concept of circularity also opens up new revenue streams. Brands like Patagonia have demonstrated how repair, reuse and recycle initiatives can foster customer loyalty and attract a consumer base that prioritizes sustainability. Patagonia's commitment to repair services and its 'Worn Wear' programme exemplifies how re-commerce can be elegantly aligned with brand image and sustainability goals, ultimately contributing to profitability.

Additionally, embracing circularity enables luxury brands to differentiate themselves in a crowded market. Beyond simply selling products, they sell a vision and a set of values that increasingly resonate with a global consumer base. Customers today are more informed and concerned about the social and environmental footprints of their consumption. Luxury brands that can successfully integrate circular principles into their operations are thus seen as innovators and leaders in ethical business practices, which can bolster their reputation and lead to enhanced market share.

The trajectory of the luxury market suggests that sustainability is transitioning from an optional marketing strategy to an essential component of business operations. What once was a niche approach is rapidly becoming a standard, driven by consumer demand, regulatory pressures and the tangible benefits to the bottom line. This evolution is indicative of a profound shift in the industry, as companies move from exploiting resources to stewarding them.

For the luxury sector, which traditionally has emphasized excellence in every facet of business, the move towards sustainable and circular practices is not just an adaptation but an opportunity to pioneer a new era of luxury that harmonizes opulence with responsibility.

Takeaways

The exploration of sustainability in the luxury brand market within this chapter reveals a fundamental transformation in the industry's approach to CSR, circularity and authentication. Luxury brands, once focused primarily on exclusivity and craftsmanship, are now actively embedding sustainable and ethical practices into their core business models. This paradigm shift is driven by increased consumer awareness, demanding more from luxury brands than mere opulence.

Vestiaire Collective's journey exemplifies this transformation. As a pioneer in the sustainable resale of luxury items, this company has successfully bridged the gap between luxury and sustainability, showcasing how responsible business practices can coexist with luxury and elegance. Their efforts in authentication, consumer education and environmental responsibility highlight the evolving role of luxury brands in today's world.

Furthermore, technological advancements such as blockchain and AI have emerged as key tools in enhancing transparency, maintaining brand integrity and supporting circular economy models. These innovations not only address challenges like product authenticity in the second-hand market, but also open new opportunities for sustainable growth.

The rise of the second-hand luxury market is a testament to changing consumer preferences promoting sustainable consumption and extending the lifecycle of luxury products. This shift is significant, as it indicates a broader consumer movement towards more environmentally-conscious and ethical shopping practices.

This chapter concludes that the integration of CSR, circularity and authentication into the luxury brand sector is not merely a trend, but a strategic imperative. As luxury brands continue to navigate these complexities, they are poised to redefine the future of luxury consumption. The commitment to sustainable practices, ethical operations and innovation will shape their legacy, ensuring that luxury remains synonymous with not just quality and exclusivity, but also responsibility and stewardship.

In the broader context, the luxury industry's pivot towards sustainability and circularity reflects a more profound societal shift. Consumers are increasingly prioritizing brands that align with their values, and luxury brands are responding by integrating sustainable practices into every aspect of their business. As we move forward, it is clear that sustainability will continue to be a defining factor in the luxury market's evolution, shaping how brands operate, how consumers make purchasing decisions and how the industry as a whole contributes to a more sustainable and equitable world.

References and further reading

Aura Blockchain Consortium (2023) Empowering the luxury industry with blockchain technology, https://auraconsortium.com/ (archived at https://perma.cc/6YVR-4TKS)

Bain & Company (2009) Luxury goods worldwide market study, www.bain.com/contentassets/5cf5c5b034724c629f74b6d286c6fe48/bain20studie_trends20und20entwicklungen20im20luxusgc3bctermarktt_2009.pdf (archived at https://perma.cc/ALJ4-PVN5)

Bendell, J and Kleanthous, A (2007) *Deeper Luxury: Quality and style when the world matters*, WWF-UK

Bennett, R and Marquis, C (2022) *Trust and Transparency in Luxury Branding*, Harvard Business Review Press

Braungart, M and McDonough, W (2002) *Cradle to Cradle: Remaking the way we make things*, North Point Press

Broccardo, L, Culasso, F, Truant, E and Dhir, A (2020) Corporate social responsibility: Does it really matter in the luxury context? *Journal of Business Research*, **117**, pp. 629–36

Burberry (2023) Annual Report 2022/23, www.burberryplc.com/content/dam/burberryplc/corporate/documents/annual-report-2022-23/Annual-report-2022-23.pdf (archived at https://perma.cc/48UP-CQLV)

Carrigan, M, Moraes, C and Leek, S (2013) Fostering responsible communities: A
    community social marketing approach to sustainable living, *Journal of Business
    Ethics*, **114** (3), pp. 515–31

Chanel (2021) Press Release: 2021 Results, https://services.chanel.com/media/files/
    Press-release-2021-Results-ENG-FINAL.pdf (archived at https://perma.cc/
    9W2Y-L57U)

Chang, H and Richards, D (2023) Diversity and inclusion in luxury fashion,
    Journal of Fashion Marketing and Management, **27** (1), pp. 112–30

Classic Luxury (2023) Circularity in the luxury sector: A trend report, *Classic
    Luxury Monthly*, **56** (3), pp. 45–50

Cradle to Cradle Products Innovation Institute (2021) Cradle to Cradle Certified
    Product Standard

D'Arpizio, C, Levato, F, Prete, F, Del Fabbro, E and de Montgolfier, J (2019) The
    Future of Luxury: A Look into Tomorrow to Understand Today, *Bain &
    Company*, www.bain.com/insights/luxury-goods-worldwide-market-study-fall-
    winter-2018/ (archived at https://perma.cc/VZ2P-AQ6L)

Davies, I A, Lee, Z and Ahonkhai, I (2012) Do consumers care about ethical-
    luxury? *Journal of Business Ethics*, **106** (1), pp. 37–51

Davis, A and Thompson, R (2022) The evolution of luxury: Sustainable narratives,
    Journal of Luxury Research, **14** (4), pp. 210–25

De Beers Group (2022) Building Forever: Our 2022 Sustainability Report, www.
    debeersgroup.com/~/media/Files/D/De-Beers-Group-V2/documents/sustainability-
    and-ethics/2022/Building_Forever_Our_2022_Sustainability_Report.pdf
    (archived at https://perma.cc/USJ2-LJ4T)

Dekhili, S and Achabou, M (2018) Could sustainability improve the promotion of
    luxury products? *European Business Review*, 31, https://doi.org/10.1108/
    EBR-04-2018-0083 (archived at https://perma.cc/8TTA-US4H)

Deloitte (2017a) The Deloitte Millennial Survey 2017: Executive Summary,
    www2.deloitte.com/content/dam/Deloitte/global/Documents/About-Deloitte/
    gx-deloitte-millennial-survey-2017-executive-summary.pdf (archived at https://
    perma.cc/D6DP-68B6)

Deloitte (2017b) Global Powers of Luxury Goods 2017, www2.deloitte.com/
    content/dam/Deloitte/ch/Documents/consumer-business/ch-en-cb-global-powers-
    of-luxury-goods-2017.pdf (archived at https://perma.cc/26VE-5H3J)

Deloitte (2021) Global Powers of Luxury Goods 2021 | Breakthrough luxury,
    Deloitte, www2.deloitte.com/content/dam/Deloitte/at/Documents/consumer-
    business/at-global-powers-of-luxury-goods-2021.pdf (archived at https://perma.
    cc/EE3Q-4SRP)

Economist Intelligence Unit (nd) The Future of Luxury, www.eiu.com/public/
    thankyou_download.aspx?activity=download&campaignid=futureofluxury
    (archived at https://perma.cc/KH5L-PNHQ)

Elhoushy, S and Jang, S (2023) How to maintain sustainable consumer behaviours: A systematic review and future research agenda, *International Journal of Consumer Studies*, **47** (6), pp. 2181–211, https://doi.org/10.1111/ijcs.12905 (archived at https://perma.cc/7EAL-NYGF)

Ellen MacArthur Foundation (nd) Completing the picture: How the circular economy tackles climate change, https://circulareconomy.europa.eu/platform/sites/default/files/emf_completing_the_picture.pdf (archived at https://perma.cc/4LJ5-WYHB)

Ellen MacArthur Foundation (2023) What is a circular economy, www.ellenmacarthurfoundation.org/circular-economy/concept (archived at https://perma.cc/5GPE-UXC9)

Entrupy (2022) State of the Fake 2022 Report, www.entrupy.com/state-of-the-fake-2022-report/ (archived at https://perma.cc/6DZN-MGSC)

Environmental Progress Journal (2023) The role of sustainability in luxury goods, *EPJ Insights*, **17** (2), pp. 89–101

Fashion Business Review (2023) Luxury resale trends, *Fashion Business Review*, **15** (7), pp. 61–65

Global Luxury Symposium (2022) Luxury brands and corporate philanthropy, *GLS Conference Proceedings*, (1), pp. 250–60

Gucci (2022) Impact Report 2022, https://equilibrium.gucci.com/it/impactreport-2022/ (archived at https://perma.cc/WHN5-YCYA)

International Journal of Corporate Strategy (2022) Strategies for environmental conservation in luxury brands, *IJCS*, **25** (2), pp. 330–45

Johnson, A (2022) Sustainable luxury: The new norm in a conscious economy, *Journal of Business Ethics*, **56** (4), pp. 731–46

Johnson, L, Wang, S and Green, M (2023) Innovation in luxury brand sustainability, *International Journal of Business Innovation*, **19** (1), pp. 15–35

Joy, A, Sherry, J F, Venkatesh, A, Wang, J and Chan, R (2012) Fast fashion, sustainability, and the ethical appeal of luxury brands, *Fashion Theory*, **16** (3), pp. 273–95

Kapferer, J-N and Bastien, V (2012) *The Luxury Strategy: Break the rules of marketing to build luxury brands*, Kogan Page

Kapferer, J N and Michaut, A (2015) Luxury and sustainability: A common future? The match depends on how consumers define luxury, *Luxury Research Journal*, **1** (1), pp. 3–17, https://doi.org/10.1504/lrj.2015.069828 (archived at https://perma.cc/2LR3-BSMV)

Kapferer, J-N and Michaut-Denizeau, A (2020a) Is luxury compatible with sustainability? Luxury brand management revisited in the era of sustainability, *European Management Review*, **17** (1), pp. 1–14

Kapferer, J-N and Michaut-Denizeau, A (2020b) Is luxury compatible with sustainability? Luxury consumers' viewpoint, *Journal of Brand Management*, **27**, pp. 21–34

Kering (2020) Environmental Profit and Loss Report 2020, www.kering.com/api/
download-file/?path=Rapport_Kering_Environmental_Profit_and_Loss_
report_2020_EN_only_24424582a1.pdf (archived at https://perma.cc/
MNP3-WFSQ)

Kering (2021) Sustainability Report 2021, www.kering.com/api/download-
file/?path=kering_ra2021_en_459134b6a3.pdf (archived at https://perma.
cc/3W9P-T4E5)

King, R and Spence, L (2023) The new luxury: Responsibility and the high-end
consumer, *Journal of Consumer Ethics*, 7 (1), pp. 1–20

Luxury Branding Quarterly (2023) Transparency in the luxury market, *LBQ*,
22 (4), pp. 32–38

LVMH (2020) Annual report 2020, https://r.lvmh-static.com/uploads/2021/05/
en_lvmh_reng20.pdf (archived at https://perma.cc/4X3P-D3TN)

McKinsey & Company (2020) Fashion on Climate, www.mckinsey.com/~/media/
mckinsey/industries/retail/our%20insights/fashion%20on%20climate/fashion-
on-climate-full-report.pdf (archived at https://perma.cc/QRB2-M77V)

McKinsey & Company (2021) The State of Fashion 2021, www.mckinsey.com/~/
media/mckinsey/industries/retail/our%20insights/state%20of%20fashion/2021/
the-state-of-fashion-2021-vf.pdf (archived at https://perma.cc/Z24W-R6T2)

McKinsey & Company and Global Fashion Agenda (2023) Fashion on Climate,
www.mckinsey.com/~/media/mckinsey/industries/retail/our%20insights/
fashion%20on%20climate/fashion-on-climate-full-report.pdf (archived at
https://perma.cc/3HLV-CDPE)

Mytheresa (2023) The Mytheresa Positive Change Report 2023, https://s26.q4cdn.
com/566705420/files/doc_downloads/2023/10/The-Mytheresa-Positive-Change-
Report-2023-2.pdf(archived at (archived at https://perma.cc/J8TD-Z4RM)

Niessen, S (2020) Fashion, its sacrifice zone, and sustainability, *Fashion Theory*,
24 (6), pp. 859–77, https://doi.org/10.1080/1362704X.2020.1800984

Niinimäki, K and Hassi, L (2011) Emerging design strategies in sustainable
production and consumption of textiles and clothing, *Journal of Cleaner
Production*, 19 (16), pp. 1876–83

Serdari, T (2022) NYU Stern School of Business, interview by the author

Smith, J and Taylor, R (2023) Luxury consumption in the 21st century: A consumer
perspective, *International Journal of Consumer Studies*, 47 (2), pp. 158–75

Smith, J and Wesson, T (2022) CSR and the future of luxury branding, *Future
Business Journal*, 8 (3), pp. 246–58

Stella McCartney (2021) Eco Impact Report 2021, www.stellamccartney.com/on/
demandware.static/-/Library-Sites-StellaMcCartneySharedLibrary/default/
dwce449f0d/report/EcoImpact_2021_CM_FINAL.pdf (archived at https://
perma.cc/P4MA-AEZM)

United Nations (2015) Transforming our world: The 2030 Agenda for Sustainable
Development, A/RES/70/1

United Nations Industrial Development Organization (UNIDO) (2008) CSR – Implications for SMEs in Developing Countries, www.unido.org/sites/default/files/2008-07/CSR_-_Implications_for_SMEs_in_Developing_Countries_0.pdf (archived at https://perma.cc/44YW-TB9H)

United Nations Industrial Development Organization (2020) Corporate Social Responsibility and the Sustainable Development Goals, www.unido.org/unido-sdgs (archived at https://perma.cc/F7TP-WXNU)

Vestiaire Collective (2023) Fashion Sustainability Report, https://fashion-sustainability-report.vestiairecollective.com/media/site/eddac7b178-1687355851/23-vc-023.pdf (archived at https://perma.cc/LF2J-SYW3)

Vestiaire Collective Consumer Trust Analysis (2023) Authenticity in resale: Consumer trust and brand value, *Fashion Business Journal*, **12** (2), pp. 58–64

Vestiaire Collective User Experience Report (2023) Innovation in luxury resale: The user experience, *Digital Luxury Group*, **5** (1), pp. 34–40

Waddock, S (2008) The development of corporate responsibility/corporate citizenship, *Organization Management Journal*, **5** (1)

World Economic Forum (2020) The Future of Nature and Business, www3.weforum.org/docs/WEF_The_Future_Of_Nature_And_Business_2020.pdf (archived at https://perma.cc/MJA4-6B73)

INDEX

Page numbers in *italic* denote information within a figure.

Looking for another book?

Explore our award-winning
books from global business
experts in Marketing and Sales

Scan the code to browse

www.koganpage.com/marketing

More from Kogan Page

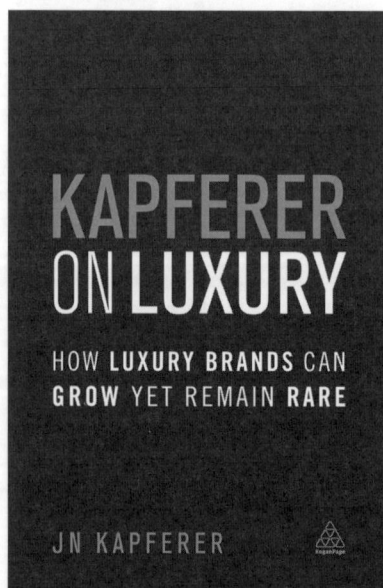